ICONS OF BLACK AMERICA

ICONS OF BLACK AMERICA

Breaking Barriers and Crossing Boundaries

VOLUME 3

Matthew C. Whitaker, Editor

GREENWOOD ICONS

GREENWOOD

AN IMPRINT OF ABC-CLIO, LLC
Santa Barbara, California • Denver, Colorado • Oxford, England

Copyright 2011 by Matthew C. Whitaker

Library of Congress Cataloging-in-Publication Data

Icons of Black America : breaking barriers and crossing boundaries / Matthew C. Whitaker, editor.
 p. cm. — (Greenwood icons)
 Includes bibliographical references and index.
 ISBN 978–0–313–37642–9 (hard copy : acid-free paper) — ISBN 978–0–313–37643–6 (ebook)
1. African Americans—Biography. I. Whitaker, Matthew C.
E185.96.I26   2011
920.009296073—dc22   2010030784

ISBN: 978–0–313–37642–9
EISBN: 978–0–313–37643–6

15 14 13 12 11   1 2 3 4 5

This book is also available on the World Wide Web as an eBook.
Visit www.abc-clio.com for details.

Greenwood
An Imprint of ABC-CLIO, LLC

ABC-CLIO, LLC
130 Cremona Drive, P.O. Box 1911
Santa Barbara, California 93116-1911

This book is printed on acid-free paper ⊗

Manufactured in the United States of America

For Jackson Asanté Whitaker and Anastacia Ami Whitaker,
and the future of Black America.

Contents

List of Photos

Muhammad Ali (page 1). Muhammad Ali, who was born Cassius Marcellus Clay, Jr., is regarded by millions as "The Greatest" boxer of all time, and one of the most distinguished proponents of peace in the modern era. (Getty Images)

Maya Angelou (page 13). Maya Angelou is one of the premier U.S. poets of the twentieth century. (National Archives)

Apollo Theater (page 23). The Apollo Theater, located in Harlem, a neighborhood in New York City. (Getty Images)

Louis Armstrong (page 33). Louis Armstrong is one of the towering figures in the history of jazz. (Library of Congress)

Arthur Ashe (page 43). Tennis legend Arthur Ashe. (Courtesy ProServ, Arlington, VA)

Ella Baker (page 53). Ella Jo Baker was a founder of the Student Nonviolent Coordinating Committee during the civil rights movement of the 1960s. (Library of Congress)

Joséphine Baker (page 63). Josephine Baker, a young dancer from New York City's Harlem neighborhood, was the star attraction in the 1920s at the Folies Bergères in Paris. (Library of Congress)

James Baldwin (page 73). James Baldwin, author of the novel *Go Tell It on the Mountain* (1953), wrote about the effects of race, religion, and sexuality on personal identity. (Library of Congress)

Charles Barkley (page 83). Phoenix Suns forward Charles Barkley shoots over Houston Rockets forward Robert Horry during the first quarter in their playoff game on Thursday, May 11, 1995 in Phoenix. (AP/Wide World Photos)

Angela Davis (page 209). A militant communist and fervent civil rights activist, Angela Davis is most recognized for causing a nationwide uproar in the 1970s when she was charged with several crimes in connection with a gunfight at a California courthouse. She was acquitted and in 1980 she ran unsuccessfully for vice president on the Communist Party ticket. In 1991, Davis became a professor at the University of California at Santa Cruz. (AP/ Wide World Photos)

Miles Davis (page 219). Miles Davis was always at the cutting edge of modern jazz. His extraordinary trumpet improvisations and fine ensemble work pushed boundaries of rhythm, harmony, and melody and continuously posed musical challenges that suggested future paths for jazz. (AP/Wide World Photos)

Sammy Davis, Jr. (page 229). Entertainer Sammy Davis, Jr. (Popperfoto/ Archive Photos)

Frederick Douglass (page 239). Frederick Douglass, leader in the abolition movement, author, speaker, ambassador to Haiti, and one of the most famous and influential Americans during the nineteenth century. (Library of Congress)

W. E. B. Du Bois (page 249). W. E. B. Du Bois, called the father of pan-Africanism for his work on behalf of the emerging African nations, devoted his life to the struggle for equality for African Americans and all people of color. (Library of Congress)

Duke Ellington (page 259). Jazz musician and band leader Duke Ellington. (Library of Congress)

Ralph Ellison (page 271). Ralph Ellison, whose novel *Invisible Man* has become a classic of modern American fiction, wrote compellingly of the experience of African Americans in a society that has tended to ignore their problems. (National Archives)

Louis Farrakhan (page 281). Nation of Islam leader Louis Farrakhan addresses the National Press Club in Washington, D.C. on May 3, 2004. The charismatic African American leader has been criticized as a racist for his extreme separatist views, but has also been praised for his role in calling for a renewed community commitment to assisting others in need. (Photo by Mark Wilson/Getty Images)

54th Massachusetts Infantry (page 291). The assault on Fort Wagner at Charleston Harbor on July 18, 1863. The Confederacy delivered a crushing defeat to the Union forces lead by Brig. Gen. Quincy A. Gillmore and the mostly African American 54th Massachusetts Volunteer Infantry Regiment. Although the loss was embarrassing to the Northern states, the battle proved the worth of African American soldiers and helped to raise Union Army recruitment. (The Illustrated London News Picture Library)

Ella Fitzgerald (page 301). Jazz vocalist Ella Fitzgerald in 1940. (Library of Congress)

Aretha Franklin (page 311). Aretha Franklin performs at New York's Radio City Music Hall, July 6, 1989. (AP/Wide World Photos)

Marcus Garvey (page 319). Marcus Garvey launched the first mass movement of African Americans in the United States that was based on racial pride, self-help, and separatism. (Library of Congress)

Marvin Gaye (page 329). Soul singer Marvin Gaye was Motown's top-selling solo artist during the 1960s. (AP/Wide World Photos)

Nikki Giovanni (page 337). Poet Nikki Giovanni (left), Kay Mazzo, ballet dancer with the New York City Ballet, and fashion designer Betsey Johnson receive the first Sun Shower Award in New York City in January 1971. The award is given to outstanding women who have achieved new heights in their careers. (AP/Wide World Photos)

Alex Haley (page 345). Alex Haley won the Pulitzer Prize for his best-selling book *Roots: The Saga of an American Family*. His book, which was made into a popular television miniseries, marked the first time an African American descended from enslaved people had traced his family's history back to its origins in Africa. (Hulton Archive/Getty Images)

Fannie Lou Hamer (page 355). Fannie Lou Hamer, a Mississippi field hand for most of her life, became a prominent advocate of civil rights. As Mississippi's Democratic Party refused African American members, Hamer helped form the Mississippi Freedom Democratic Party (MFDP) whose members attempted to unseat the regular party delegation at the Democratic National Convention in 1964. (Library of Congress)

Harlem Globetrotters (page 365). Basketball acrobatics are displayed by Michael Wilson of The Harlem Globetrotters in 2002. (AP/Wide World Photos)

Jimi Hendrix (page 377). Jimi Hendrix discovered an unknown world of expression within the electric guitar. Though his superb, highly amplified guitar playing was often upstaged by galvanizing theatrics, his brief, explosive career was a relentless quest to expand the horizons of music and sound. (Hulton Archive/Getty Images)

Billie Holiday (page 387). Billie Holiday performs in 1947 in New York. (William P. Gottlieb/Library of Congress)

Lena Horne (page 395). One of the United States's best and most enduring performers, Lena Horne worked tirelessly to promote equal rights for African Americans. Unlike most of her fellow entertainers, Horne's career hit its apex in her later years when she starred in the one-woman Broadway show *Lena Horne: The Lady and Her Music* in 1981. (Hulton Archive/Getty Images)

Langston Hughes (page 405). For more than five decades, Langston Hughes wrote poetry, fiction, and plays that were meant to capture the essence of the black experience in the United States. A prolific writer of rare versatility, he wrote for the men and women he saw struggling first for survival and then for equality from the 1920s through the 1960s. (Library of Congress)

Zora Neale Hurston (page 415). Zora Neale Hurston was an American novelist, folklorist, anthropologist, and prominent member of the circle of writers associated with the Harlem Renaissance of the 1920s. (Library of Congress)

Michael Jackson (page 425). Michael Jackson, the number-one selling pop vocal artist in history, performs at opening night of his Victory Tour at Dodger Stadium in Los Angeles, California, December 1, 1984. (AP/Wide World Photos)

Jay-Z (page 435). Rapper and current president and CEO of Def Jam and Roc-A-Fella Records, Jay-Z, 2001. (Photofest)

Earvin "Magic" Johnson (page 445). Earvin "Magic" Johnson, is a five-time National Basketball Association (NBA) Champion, a highly successful businessman, and a distinguished humanitarian. (UPI/Bettmann/Corbis)

Jack Johnson (page 455). Jack Johnson was the first African American heavyweight boxing champion of the world. (Library of Congress)

James Weldon Johnson (page 471). Portrait of author and civil rights activist during the Harlem Renaissance, James Weldon Johnson. (National Archives)

Robert L. Johnson (page 481). Robert L. Johnson, founder of the Black Entertainment Television (BET) cable network, and Lifetime Achievement Award winner, comments at the fourth annual CNBC Executive Leadership Awards at the New York Public Library in New York on March 31, 2008. (AP/Wide World Photos)

Quincy Jones (page 491). Composer and record producer Quincy Jones poses onstage of the Auditorium Stravinski at the 42nd Montreux Jazz Festival in Montreux, Switzerland in 2008. (AP/Wide World Photos)

Barbara Jordan (page 499). Sen. Barbara Jordan sworn in as governor of Texas in 1972. Jordan became the first black woman to serve as governor of any state, became governor for a day when the Texas governor and lieutenant governor were out of the state. (AP/Wide World Photos)

Michael Jordan (page 509). Widely regarded as the best basketball player in history, Michael Jordan is an NCAA basketball champion, six-time NBA champion, two-time Olympic gold medalist, and current majority owner of the NBA's Charlotte Bobcats. (Photofest)

Florence Griffith Joyner (page 519). Sprinter Florence Griffith Joyner wins the women's 100-meters final at the Seoul Olympics on September 25, 1988. Joyner gained worldwide fame for her performance in the 1988 Summer Olympics in Seoul, South Korea and for the style and glamour she brought to the sport.

Martin Luther King, Jr. (page 531). Theologian, civil rights activist, and proponent of peace, Martin Luther King, Jr. answers questions at a press conference in March 1964. King was a strong opponent of the Vietnam War. (Library of Congress)

Spike Lee (page 541). U.S. filmmaker Spike Lee, looks at the camera as he arrives at the Bellas Artes Museum in Caracas in 2009. (AP/Wide World Photos)

Joe Louis (page 551). Heavyweight boxer Joe Louis served as a symbol of the power of the American dream in the 1930s, promoting racial unity, national strength, and opportunity. (Hulton Archive/Getty Images)

Malcolm X (page 561). Portrait of Malcolm X, spokesman for the Nation of Islam who later converted to Sunni Muslim. He was assassinated on February 21, 1965. (Library of Congress)

Thurgood Marshall (page 571). Thurgood Marshall, the first African American appointed to the U.S. Supreme Court, built a remarkable legal career on the premise that all forms of racial segregation were unconstitutional. (Joseph Lavenburg, National Geographic Society, Collection of the Supreme Court of the United States)

Hattie McDaniel (page 583). Hattie McDaniel, the first African American to win an Academy Award, plays a tune as she portrays the title role of "Beulah" in the CBS Radio Network's comedy series in New York City in 1951. (AP/Wide World Photos)

Morehouse College (page 593). Students walk on the campus of historical Morehouse College in Atlanta, Georgia, in 2009. (AP/Wide World Photos)

Toni Morrison (page 603). Toni Morrison is one of the most significant American authors of the twentieth century. She was awarded both the Pulitzer Prize and the Nobel Prize for literature. (Olga Besnard)

Motown Records (page 613). Stevie Wonder and Marvin Gaye around a microphone at the Motown recording studio in Detroit in 1965. (Redferns/ Getty Images)

Elijah Muhammad (page 623). Elijah Muhammad, as spiritual leader of the Nation of Islam in the United States, established a religious organization that gave poor urban African Americans a sense of racial pride and economic and political self-sufficiency. (Library of Congress)

Negro Baseball Leagues (page 635). Negro Leagues baseball star Buck O'Neil stands with a statue of himself at the Negro League Baseball Museum in Kansas City in 2005. Since 1990, he's been a tireless fundraiser and goodwill ambassador for the Negro Leagues Baseball Museum in Kansas City's historic jazz district, traveling the country to keep the legacy of black baseball alive. (AP/Wide World Photos)

Huey P. Newton and Bobby Seale (page 645). Huey Newton (right), founder of the Black Panther Party, sits with Bobby Seale at party headquarters in San Francisco, July 1967. (Ted Streshinsky/Corbis)

Barack Obama (page 657). Democrat Barack Obama became president of the United States in 2009. The first African American to hold that position, his election promised to usher the United States into a new era of opportunity, diversity, and multinationalism. (U.S. Department of Defense)

Michelle Obama (page 667). Michelle Obama, first African American first lady of the United States (2009–). (Department of Defense)

Jesse Owens (page 677). American sprinter, Jesse Owens, is pictured with the four gold medals he won at the 1936 Olympic Games in Berlin. (The Illustrated London News Picture Library)

Rosa Parks (page 687). Rosa Parks is fingerprinted in Montgomery, Alabama. Parks's arrest for refusing to give up her seat on a bus to a white man on December 1, 1955, inspired the Montgomery Bus Boycott, a prolonged action against the segregated Montgomery, Alabama, bus system by African American riders and their white supporters. (Library of Congress)

Sidney Poitier (page 697). In 1958, Sidney Poitier became the first African American to be nominated as Best Actor by the Academy of Motion Pictures Arts and Sciences for his costarring role in the Hollywood film *The Defiant Ones*. In 1963, he became only the second African American actor to win an Oscar, and the first to win the Academy Award for Best Actor, for his performance in the film *Lilies of the Field*. He is credited with paving the way for public acceptance of African American men in U.S. films, and such contemporary film figures as Eddie Murphy and Spike Lee have him partially to thank for their huge success. (AP/Wide World Photos)

Colin Powell (page 707). The first African American man to serve as chairman of the Joint Chiefs of Staff of the U.S. military, and as U.S. Secretary of State,

Colin Powell is one of the most highly regarded military authorities and political leaders in U.S. history. (AP/Wide World Photos)

Richard Pryor (page 717). Trailblazing comedian-actor Richard Pryor, performing in 1977. (AP/Wide World Photos)

A. Philip Randolph (page 727). A. Philip Randolph won respect for his quiet dignity and his firmness in a lifelong commitment to racial justice. A union organizer and socialist early in life, he became the country's best-known African American trade unionist and a nationally prominent leader in the struggle for civil rights during the early to mid-twentieth century. (Library of Congress)

Ishmael Reed (page 741). Novelist, essayist, and poet Ishmael Reed. AP/Wide World Photos.

Condoleezza Rice (page 751). Secretary of State Condoleezza Rice speaks at a news conference near President George W. Bush's Crawford, Texas ranch on August 6, 2006. During the news conference, Rice discussed the Iraq War and the conflict between Israel and Lebanon. (AP/Wide World Photos)

Paul Robeson (page 761). Paul Robeson, world famous stage and film performer, leads workers in singing "The Star-Spangled Banner" at the Moore shipyard in Oakland, California in September 1942. Robeson entertained Allied forces during World War II. (National Archives)

Jackie Robinson (page 771). Jackie Robinson was the first African American to play Major League Baseball, playing for the Brooklyn Dodgers from 1947 until 1956. Robinson won the first Rookie of the Year award in 1947 and the Most Valuable Player award in 1949. He was inducted into the Baseball Hall of Fame in 1962. (Bettmann/Corbis)

Bayard Rustin (page 783). Bayard Rustin was one of the most skillful organizers among the leaders of the civil rights movement. He was also influential in a range of other causes: pacifism, refugees, nuclear disarmament, Japanese-American rights, and gay rights. (Library of Congress)

Dred Scott (page 793). Dred Scott, plaintiff in one of the most important cases of constitutional law in U.S. history. (Library of Congress)

Tupac Shakur (page 803). Tupac Shakur as Ezekiel "Spoon" Whitmore in the 1997 movie *Gridlock'd*. (Photofest)

Russell Simmons (page 813). Russell Simmons arrives at the 2008 MTV Video Music Awards held at Paramount Pictures Studio. (AP/Wide World Photos)

Tommie Smith and John Carlos (page 819). At the Summer Olympic games in Mexico City, Mexico in October 1968, runners Tommie Smith and John

Carlos outraged the U.S. Olympic Committee by giving a black power salute during the medal ceremony. (Bettmann/Corbis)

Will Smith (page 829). Actor Will Smith poses at the *Hitch* photocall during the 55th annual Berlinale International Film Festival on February 18, 2005 in Berlin, Germany. (Dreamstime)

Spelman College (page 837). Spelman College in Atlanta, Georgia. (Spelman College)

Mary Church Terrell (page 847). Activist, Philanthropist, first African American Woman to earn a college degree, and co-founder of the National Association of Colored Women. (Library of Congress)

Sojourner Truth (page 857). A poster celebrating Sojourner Truth's fight for suffrage, and commemorating her famous " 'Ain't I a Woman?' " speech from the 1851 Women's Rights Convention. Not until the 1960s did African Americans truly receive the right to vote throughout the United States, with the help of additional federal legislation and sometimes military force. Women of all races received the right to vote through the Nineteenth Amendment, ratified in 1920, but due to poll taxes and confusing ballots many African American women's votes were never counted. (Library of Congress)

Harriet Tubman (page 867). Portrait of Harriet Tubman, leader of the Underground Railroad. (Library of Congress)

Nat Turner (page 877). A newspaper cartoon depicts the violent slave uprising led by Nat Turner that began on August 22, 1831 when Turner killed his master and his master's family. The revolt only lasted about a week but Turner eluded capture until October of that year. He was later tried and hanged for the crime. (Library of Congress)

Tuskegee Airmen (page 887). Tuskegee Airmen, including Benjamin O. Davis, Jr. (third from left), in Alabama, 1942. The Tuskegee Airmen were the first African American pilots in the U.S. Army Air Corps. (Library of Congress)

Alice Walker (page 897). One of the best and most influential writers of her generation, Alice Walker (shown here in 1990) has affected modern American life not only through her brilliant poetry and novels, but through her actions as a black feminist ("womanist") and social activist. Her novel *The Color Purple* is perhaps her most popular work so far. It was made into a movie starring Oprah Winfrey in 1985. (AP/Wide World Photos)

Madam C. J. Walker (page 905). Madam C. J. Walker founded a successful cosmetics business, actively spoke out on African American political issues, and sponsored philanthropic organizations. She was the wealthiest African American woman of the early twentieth century and an influential voice for the economic self-empowerment of African American women. (Madam C. J. Walker Collection, Indiana Historical Society)

Booker T. Washington (page 919). As the head of Tuskegee Institute (a leading center of African American education), Booker T. Washington was a major spokesperson for African Americans during the late nineteenth and early twentieth centuries. (Library of Congress)

Denzel Washington (page 931). Actor Denzel Washington won an academy award for Best Supporting Actor in 1990 and another for Best Actor in 2001. (AP/Wide World Photos)

Ida B. Wells-Barnett (page 943). As an anti-lynching crusader and the founder of the African American women's club movement and other civil rights organizations, Ida Wells-Barnett was one of the most influential African American women of the late nineteenth and early twentieth centuries. (Department of Special Collections, University of Chicago)

Cornel West (page 957). Dr. Cornel West speaks at the Conference on the State of the African-American Professoriate hosted at Ramapo College of New Jersey April 20, 2002. (AP/Wide World Photos)

Venus Williams and Serena Williams (page 967). Williams sisters Venus and Serena pose with trophy following the US Open in 2009. (Dreamstime)

Oprah Winfrey (page 979). Oprah Winfrey on the cover of her O magazine. (PRNewsFoto/Oxmoor House)

Stevie Wonder (page 989). Singer-songwriter Stevie Wonder at the 39th NAACP Image Awards in Los Angeles. (Shutterstock)

Tiger Woods (page 999). Professional golfer Tiger Woods. (Shutterstock)

Carter G. Woodson (page 1009). Carter G. Woodson established a model for African American history through the Association for the Study of Negro Life and History, which helped to correct the prejudice with which historians and the general public viewed African American abilities. (AP/Wide World Photos)

Richard Wright (page 1019). Richard Wright (photographed in 1939) is best known for his first published novel, *Native Son*, which introduced a new realism to literary treatments of the United States's racial problems, rendering sympathetically the always fearful, sometimes violent psychology of the oppressed. (Library of Congress)

A. Philip Randolph
(1889–1979)

From 1925 to 1965, A. Philip Randolph was a force in both the American labor movement and the Civil Rights Movement. During this period, he was a major transitional figure in successfully leading African Americans in their quest for politico-economic freedom from legal discrimination in the mid-twentieth century. Randolph is one of the first leaders to successfully embrace socialism and infuse it with black activism. In 1925, as a trade union advocate, he successfully organized the Brotherhood of Sleeping Car Porters (BSCP). By 1929, it became the first African American union to be incorporated into the American labor movement with a semi-autonomous charter within the American Federation of Labor (AFL). Eight years later, the BSCP broke precedent to become a completely autonomous black union within the AFL and the Pullman Company—complete with collective bargaining power.

In addition, as a civil rights leader, Randolph was very effective in pioneering direct-action politics and applying Gandhian tactics of nonviolent civil disobedience to protests and mass demonstrations that flourished in the 1950s–1960s. His most notable achievements in this field include being the chief organizer of the March on Washington Movement during World War II and during the Civil Rights Movement, and pressuring President Harry S. Truman into desegregating the U.S. Armed Forces in 1948.

Asa Philip Randolph was born on April 15, 1889, in Crescent City, Florida, the second son of James and Elizabeth Randolph. James was a struggling AME minister, and Elizabeth was a housewife raising her sons. Despite their hardships, Randolph and his brother William were raised to respect themselves, respect others, and respect learning. They were also raised to fight social injustice and inequality whenever it was encountered. In 1891, the Randolphs moved to Jacksonville, Florida. Randolph received his primary and secondary education at local public schools, including graduation from high school at the Cookman Institute.

During the spring of 1911, Randolph moved to New York City. Here, he became a City College of New York student at night, and worked as an elevator operator, porter, and waiter during the day—a routine similar to when he went to the Cookman Institute in his teens. At CCNY, Randolph took a wide range of general education courses, including economics, history, literature, philosophy, political science, and oratory. In particular, young Randolph became fascinated with *The Communist Manifesto* of Karl Marx and Friedrich Engels, and the history of European working class movements. At the same time, he took up stage acting, and became very familiar with the expanding American socialist movement through close contact with student-activist groups. By 1917, Randolph was a member of the Socialist Party (SP)—a commitment that his wife of three years, beautician Lucille Campbell Green, supported until her passing in 1963.

From 1917 to 1925, Randolph was intellectually more committed to socialism and American reform than he was to black liberation. For young Randolph, the root problem with the United States and its race problem was capitalism.

It promoted economic greed, individualism, and perpetual social division that worked to the advantage of industrial owners because it pitted working-class people in a fierce competition against one another for jobs and other scarce resources. Moreover, Randolph believed that racial segregation, lynching, poverty, and other racial oppressions impacting African Americans would come to an end if "workers of the world" took over the government and the industrial means of production. Prior to the Great Depression, the path of black leadership that Randolph represented broke sharply with the accommodationist, Talented Tenth gradualist, and black nationalist strategies of **Booker T. Washington, W. E. B. Du Bois**, and **Marcus Garvey**, respectively. These leaders used politico-economic strategies that dominated the scope of black political thought from 1890 to the 1940s.

Randolph's initial goal was to be a radical reformer whose leadership transcended the color line. His approach addressed class as the collective quest for racial integration and equality, a daring approach during the Nadir that was arguably the worst period in U.S. race relations—roughly from 1880 to 1920. His far-reaching objective was unfathomable to most Americans. Nevertheless, in the early-twentieth century, Randolph was driven to make this happen by fusing politico-economic thought with action. This was most evident in his organizing unions, protest movements, and in publications such as the black newspaper, *The Messenger*.

From 1917 to 1923, Randolph and fellow black socialist, Chandler Owen, co-published *The Messenger*. This arrangement ended in 1923, when Owen left Harlem for Chicago to distance himself from socialism, becoming instead the managing editor of the black newspaper, the *Chicago Bee*. During *The Messenger*'s socialist heyday, it boldly provided news and commentary for working people on politics, trade unions, and leading radicals and literature. In black America, *The Messenger* provided the most outspoken criticism of the United States entering World War I. It also advised blacks and working people to resist the military draft and Jim Crow discrimination. This led to Randolph and Owen being imprisoned in August 1918 on charges of violating the Espionage Act. When the judge presiding over Randolph's and Owen's case saw their relatively young black faces, he was shocked. He was expecting older, more worldly looking white men before him. Going through *The Messenger*, the judge refused to believe that Randolph and Owen wrote the paper, and suggested that white socialists wrote it and were using them:

> Then he turned to [them]: "You really wrote this magazine?" We assured him that we had. "What do you know about socialism?" he said. We told him we were students of Marx and fervent believers in the socialization of social property. "Don't you know," he said, "that you are opposing your own government and that you are subject to imprisonment for treason?" We told him we believed in the principle of human justice and that our right to express our conscience was above the law. (Anderson, 107)

Within the partnership of Randolph and Owen, the former was the bolder and more dominant voice. Randolph's compassionate analytical approach to U.S. race and class relations made the pair the first African Americans to be infamously labeled by U.S. intelligence as the "most dangerous Negroes in America." This distinction includes them in the legacy attributed to icons such as Marcus Garvey, Dr. **Martin Luther King, Jr., Malcolm X** (a.k.a. El-Hajj Malik El-Shabazz), **Huey P. Newton**, and **Angela Davis**, to name a few. In addressing world politics, Randolph fearlessly denounced President Woodrow Wilson for segregating federal agencies and buildings. In 1919, Randolph supported the establishment of Communist Russia. This happened during a period when anti-communism sentiment was fierce in the United States (a.k.a. the first "Red Scare"). This resulted in both Randolph and Owen being censored for sedition in 1919 by the New York State Legislature. They were placed under close surveillance by J. Edgar Hoover, head of the new General Intelligence Division of the Department of Justice (now the F.B.I.) and assistant to the U.S. Attorney General.

Seemingly undaunted by these turns-of-events, which included his being falsely labeled a Bolshevik (or communist) by critics, Randolph attempted to apply his political-economy philosophy to labor relations and electoral campaigns as an organizer. From 1919 to 1923, he attempted to organize black workers in Harlem with the intent to persuade voters to denounce the Republican Party and become Socialist Party members. Randolph was staunchly opposed to the two-party electoral system in the United States. To him it was a system perpetuating racism, capitalism, complacency, and extremes in wealth and poverty. To Randolph, blacks had nothing in common with the post-Reconstruction Republican Party, which abandoned its civil rights agenda to give legislative support to corporate dominance over key U.S. industries and public policy. As for the Democratic Party, prior to the New Deal era, most Americans viewed it as solely the party of white supremacy. For Randolph, there were more political constituencies not being represented in the U.S. political process; in particular socialism, which best represented the collective will of working people and was the answer to U.S. race and class relations.

In the attempt to connect political thought to action, Randolph organized the United Brotherhood of Elevator and Switchboard Operators in 1919. This was a union representing black hotel and apartment workers that lasted only several months. Between 1919 and 1923, Randolph organized other unions that suffered similar fates—such as the National Brotherhood Workers of America, Friends of Negro Freedom, National Association for the Promotion of Labor Unionism, and United Negro Trades. The first two unions were interracially oriented; whereas, the latter two represented black workers, many of whom were members in the Friends of Negro Freedom.

Politically, Randolph campaigned for the Socialist Party in New York. His first foray into electoral politics occurred in 1917, as he promoted SP's candidate for mayor, Morris Hillquit, in black Harlem. Three years later, in 1920, the SP nominated Randolph to run for state comptroller of New York. Randolph's last attempt at public office occurred in 1922, as he represented the Socialist Party in his run for the Office of Secretary of New York. In 1944, Randolph turned down the SP's nomination of him as Vice President of the United States.

In the mid-1920s, Randolph became a major race and labor relations leader as the organizer of the Brotherhood of Sleeping Car Porters (BSCP). In this period, he noticeably altered his political thought from revolution to reform, no longer looking to transcend the color line, but to engage it fully. Randolph did this by addressing class and paying more attention to black institutions, black issues, and the African American quest for freedom based on their own terms: he stopped framing black liberation within the ideological bounds of the European working class as his socialist white counterparts did. By 1925, this was evident in Randolph's writing in *The Messenger*, and in his public addresses. He became less doctrinaire in socialist rhetoric, which was often his taking-off point in criticizing black businesses, black churches, and black leaders such as Du Bois and Garvey—the institutions and people crucial to black survival whose efforts were aimed at inspiring racial self-determination, pride and unity, but who had different approaches toward achieving black liberation.

By the mid-1920s, Randolph was openly acknowledging that socialism had its limits for African Americans ideologically, economically, and sociopolitically. Ideologically, many white socialists considered race and skin-complexion to be incidental to the American socioeconomic problem, which for them was centered on persons of European descent, class, and labor relations. Economically, white supremacy triumphed in labor relations by racially excluding most African Americans from industrial labor opportunities, trade unionism, and economic opportunities for achieving a quality standard of living. Sociopolitically, most white socialists accommodated America's color line by not addressing racist practices that contributed to their privilege, such as black political disenfranchisement and lynching.

In addition, Randolph rejected the emerging left of the Socialist Party, which aggressively splintered off and became the core of the Communist Party of the United States of America (CP), consolidating in 1921. Before they broke with the SP, their initial intent was to take over the party and transfer control to the Communist International (a.k.a. Comintern) in Moscow, Russia. Fewer than 10 percent of the original CP members were native English speakers. Moreover, most members were immigrants from Central and Eastern European countries directly involved in the Bolshevik Revolution of 1917. Similar to SP members, their rhetoric sounded revolutionary; however, unlike most people remaining with the SP, many first-generation CP members attempted to fuse such rhetoric with seemingly revolutionary deeds, which went beyond reforming the United States' political economy from within established positions of power. To Randolph, the communists' radical stance jeopardized coalition efforts between workers and progressive reformers, because they often used very aggressive tactics to accomplish a goal, and they wanted the power to control the American Left through the Comintern in far-away Moscow. This was especially true for blacks organizing the American Negro Labor Congress and the National Negro Congress, groups that Randolph summarily denounced in 1925 and again in 1940, because to him they were effectively pawns of the CP and had no domestic base of power, nor did they have a plan that directly addressed black freedom. Furthermore, Randolph distanced himself from the CP to minimize attracting further state and corporate attempts to end his civil rights and labor movement agendas. These experiences and revelations pushed Randolph politically and economically to the left of center as a reformer, taking on practical, less idealistic projects such as promoting black trade unionism and organizing the BSCP.

Most historians trace Randolph's shift toward pragmatic-radical reform to August 25, 1925. On this date, he accepted the role of chief organizer of the BSCP at Harlem's Elk Auditorium. What made Randolph an ideal recruit for this position was that he was intelligent, attractive, and well spoken. He was also an experienced organizer and a dignified person, and was not a Pullman Company employee—the last item placing Randolph beyond Pullman's reprisals; and being dignified made it hard for the Pullman Company to defame his character and thus discredit the Brotherhood with him at the helm. In turn, Randolph saw this as a great opportunity to become a leader of the black working class, dealing with real issues and performing beyond abstract theories. The immediate issues confronting Pullman porters were low wages, bad work conditions, and not being allowed to bargain collectively for better hours, wages, and work conditions.

Pullman porters have provided quality service on luxurious rail accommodations for long-distance travelers since the Pullman Palace Car Company's founding in 1867. "By the late nineteenth century, the Pullman Company had become the single largest employer of African American labor in the United States, with some 12,000 black porters on its payroll by World War I" (Arnesen, 288). The advantages of being a porter were that they were perceived to be well-paid, well-groomed, and the travel from city to city often endowed them with a middle-class urban sophistication which ran counter to stereotypical rural simplicity.

The disadvantages of being a Pullman porter were much more complex. In 1925, more than 10,000 Pullman porters pejoratively named "George" (after the company's founder) worked an average of 400 hours a month, versus 240 hours for white men in other positions such as conductor. They were also expected to act in a servile manner, and perform menial and sometimes degrading tasks for white managers and passengers. In addition, few porters advanced to the position of conductor. Conductors were stereotypically white men who made twice as much as black porters, and were in a constant state of anxiety over the prospect of competing with black porters for conductor positions.

Moreover, the porter constantly faced institutional discrimination, such as "running in charge, doubling out . . . PM time," and a tipping system in which most porters depended on tips for the majority of their pay (Henderson, 23). Running in charge meant that a porter could be assigned the duties of the conductor, along with his own work, and receive only a tenth of the conductor's pay, and 20 percent of what he would normally earn. Doubling out was a process that was closely connected to PM time, in which former BSCP President C.L. Dellums explained:

> If they ordered the porter to do work at 12:01 P.M. his pay wouldn't start until midnight. They never started a porter's pay on PM time. [The same happened in reverse for the porter working on the A.M. shift.] Later on, when the company was forced to make some changes, they set up "a mileage Month," which was eleven thousand miles that he worked. When they did that, they didn't start his pay until the train moved. The porter could go to work—in the yards in West Oakland at five o'clock in the afternoon and start receiving passengers at 7:30 or 8 o'clock. But the trains might not leave until 11:30, midnight, or maybe one o'clock in the morning. His pay didn't start until the train moved because then the time book showed only the departure of the train and [its] arrival. (Henderson, 14)

For Randolph, organization and Pullman porter conduct were crucial to BSCP success in combating Pullman Company threats and deep resources that were geared toward busting the union. From 1925 to 1928, *The Messenger* was given a new life as the newspaper of the Brotherhood. Its new creed was "independence without insolence; courtesy without fawning; servicing without servility." Moreover, BSCP success depended on Randolph's honest recognition of his strengths as an organizer and public figure, as well as his weaknesses. He was a sub-par administrator because of his indifference to day-to-day operations, and he was not a Pullman porter. To this end, he leaned heavily on the administrative talents, independent thought, and grassroots presence of senior Pullman porters such as Milton P. Webster and C. L. Dellums. They formed the core of a national network of Pullman porter administrators/ advisors whose strongholds were in Chicago, Detroit, Pittsburgh, St. Louis, New York, and Oakland.

In 1929, the BSCP as a collective pressured the AFL into granting their small union "federal" charters for 13 Brotherhood locals. These were firsts for black unions. However, in being granted a federal charter and not an international one, the BSCP was not given independent status to bargain collectively or to influence national work policies and procedures as their white counterparts could. Instead, their charter fell under the control of AFL president William Green and its Executive Council. This in turn undermined Randolph's power as the first BSCP President, a position to which he had been elected during the Brotherhood's first annual convention in 1929.

Within AFL's leadership, Randolph was marginalized until the 1950s. From 1929 to the 1960s, he used the AFL conventions to promote black worker issues which included addressing customary racism, racial exclusion, and institutional racism. The AFL in turn seldom took black labor issues seriously. According to historian Benjamin Quarles, black labor concerns were looked over by committees that stereotyped the BSCP, and "recommended non-concurrence, counseled patience, or expressed hopes for a more friendly spirit in the house of labor" (Quarles, 151).

The BSCP became fully recognized by the AFL and Pullman Company in 1936 and 1937. They accomplished this by taking full advantage of President Franklin D. Roosevelt's labor policies during the Great Depression. Success for the Brotherhood began when the Railway Labor Act of 1934 gave railroad employees the right to organize independently and bargain collectively. This policy also outlawed company unions, which were notorious for undermining worker-led labor unions like the BSCP. In 1935, the BSCP won an election contest in a landslide against the Pullman Porters and Maids Protective Association, in a campaign to determine who would be the collective bargaining agent representing porters and maids. The Brotherhood's victory over this Pullman-sponsored union further legitimized political-economic struggle as a political tactic among African Americans. More important, it forced the AFL to retract from releasing the BSCP, because the AFL now had to take them seriously as a powerful labor union that influenced national labor policy. To this end, the BSCP was granted an international charter with the AFL, and autonomous status in 1936. The Pullman Company followed suit in 1937. This victory resulted in Randolph becoming the preeminent leader for mass direct-action politics in black America. Nowhere was his dominance in this field more apparent than during the March on Washington Movement (MOWM) of the 1940s.

The MOWM was Randolph's response to black poverty rooted in pre-Great Depression racial inequities and industrial exclusion at the start of World War II. At the beginning of the war, black unemployment was approximately 25 percent. In particular, red-lined areas located in older urban neighborhoods, where most blacks lived, were the most impoverished communities, whereas many exclusively white communities in suburbs, on hills, or near beaches and universities began recovering from the Depression immediately after manufacturing industries converted their assembly lines to producing arms in the late 1930s. Essentially, blacks were locked out of this unprecedented economic activity that revolved around America's Lend-Lease policy, which primarily produced arms for the Allies of World War II in the European and Asian theaters. To combat this exclusion, Randolph advised blacks to be smart consumers and long-range economic planners, and to form consumer co-operatives—strategies that he pioneered in the late 1920s to stave off further despair, while his inner circle urgently searched for resolutions that would guarantee African Americans total access to federal war industries.

The MOWM began on September 27, 1940, during a meeting with the President at the White House attended by Randolph, Walter White of the National Association for the Advancement of Colored People (NAACP), and T. Arnold Hill of the National Urban League (NUL). The focus of the meeting was industrial inclusion and desegregating the armed forces. On both issues, the "Big Three" of the top civil rights representatives (at the time) made little impact on Roosevelt's political convictions, which called for patriotism and personal sacrifice, and was staunchly opposed to a march on the National Mall at Washington, DC. Determined not to repeat Du Bois's World War I blunder, which called for blacks to drop their anti-Jim Crow grievances and "Close Ranks" as U.S. patriots, around January 25, 1941, Randolph placed ads in black newspapers requesting that 10,000 blacks march on Washington. Their slogan was, "We Loyal Negro American Citizens Demand the Right to Work and Fight for Our Country." This request sparked wide enthusiasm from black workers, leaders, and media. It also pressured the politically moderate NAACP and NUL to get involved in the then Left-leaning, direct-action nonviolent tactics of Randolph, or risk being upstaged by his prompt political-economy response and be called "Uncle Toms." On July 1, 1941, this coalition formed the nucleus of the March on Washington Committee. Its core organizers were Randolph and seven other black leaders. To reciprocate, Randolph assisted the NAACP and NUL in fighting lynching and assisting black emigrants' transition into the urban North and West, respectively. Moreover, white communists and white liberals were excluded from the MOWM as core participants. Their exclusion was an unprecedented move for Randolph, because he steered the movement away from his cherished liberal coalition-building toward developing a movement centered on black self-determination and black unity, to demonstrate to white Americans that African Americans could unify and win political concessions on their own.

In early June, President Roosevelt responded to the MOWM by sending emissaries who were in good standing with the black community. Their mission was to persuade the March on Washington Committee to call off the march. First Lady Eleanor Roosevelt, and New York Mayor Fiorello H. La Guardia, both failed to end the march. A 30-minute White House meeting on June 18 also failed to cancel the march. Ending this march was very important to President Roosevelt because such an event in the nation's capital by the largest population of oppressed U.S. citizens, African Americans, would have been catastrophic for America's war rhetoric as a Democracy whose citizens were supposedly remote from Italian fascism, German totalitarianism, Japanese imperialism, and Russian communism. With knowledge that the MOWM participants were growing far beyond the expectations of its Committee (100,000 estimated marchers), on June 25, President Roosevelt issued Executive Order 8802, outlawing segregation in defense industries that received federal government contracts. It was enforced by the Fair Employment Practices Commission (FEPC) and War Manpower Commission. These agencies were in turn unofficially overseen and investigated by the MOWM, which cancelled its march and reconstituted itself to fighting for civil rights and integration in the labor market and military.

The unprecedented success of the MOWM opened industrial jobs to a critical mass of African Americans. Crucial was the FEPC, which handled more than 10,000 cases of discrimination in court, setting a precedent for the federal government to combat legal segregation. In addition, some industries and unions did not want the hassle of federal government oversight, and opened their factories and shipyards to women and people of color. The end result was that many blacks were proletarianized—in other words, they acquired an industrial worker consciousness. This included many becoming fully unionized after auxiliary unions were banned following *James v. Marinship* (1943). This turn of events also sparked the Second Great Migration and the Double-Victory movement against racism at home and fascism abroad.

Despite the successes of Executive Order 8802, it did not desegregate the armed forces. Nor was it a permanent policy. It was an emergency war policy that quietly ended soon after the war, during the spring of 1946. The ramifications of this left most blacks stranded in the ghettoes in the urban North and urban West, and laid off from living-wage jobs that quickly left central cities for suburbia. To Randolph's credit, he attempted to form a national council for a permanent FEPC in 1943; however, by 1946, this group was financially broke and had too much internal dissent to pressure the federal government into passing a permanent FEPC into law. Randolph, a pragmatist, temporarily halted this pursuit to revive his quest toward desegregating the armed forces.

The passing of the Universal Military Training bill (1947) triggered Randolph and New York State Commissioner of Corrections, Grant Reynolds, into organizing the short-lived Committee against Jim Crow in Military Service and Training. This occurred in November 1947. Randolph began his assault on Congress to prevent the passage of a draft law that did not include a ban on Jim Crow practices in the armed forces by using a tactic he pioneered in 1928 against the Pullman Company called "the big bluff." Using public opinion as a weapon against a much larger opponent was central to this tactic's effectiveness. With this said, the ramifications for Congress failing to comply with Randolph's demand would be for him to counsel potential black and white conscripts against enlisting and to organize a mass civil disobedience movement similar to Gandhi combating "the British in India" (Quarles, 159). Not heeding Randolph's warning, the Senate Armed Services Committee passed the Selective Service Act of 1947 without banning legal segregation in the armed forces. Randolph in turn formed the League for Non-Violent Civil Disobedience against Military Segregation. This organization was designed to pressure President Harry S. Truman into passing an Executive Order to undermine the Southern-dominated Democratic Congress and Armed Forces officials, who fiercely opposed desegregating the military. On August 16, Randolph threatened to organize a march on Washington, cognizant of the new

Cold War politic and Truman's dependence on the black vote in the urban North and urban West. Not willing to test Randolph's "bluff," on July 26, 1948, Truman issued Executive Order 9981. Randolph was nearly 60 years old.

Randolph continued to be a dynamic race and labor leader well into the 1970s, despite his advancing age. As a labor leader, he was appointed as the co-vice president of the American Federation of Labor and Congress of Industrial Organizations (AFL-CIO) in 1955. This arrangement lasted until 1959. He resigned after having far too many irreconcilable disagreements with AFL-CIO President, George Meany, on the federation's record on race relations and its reluctance to expel AFL-CIO trade unions that were still discriminating. This inspired Randolph to organize and to preside over the Negro American Labor Council (NALC) from 1960 to 1966. The NALC was a black trade union made up of workers from the auto, rubber, and steel industries, whose aim was to pressure the AFL-CIO into addressing their concerns and grievances on race relations in the workplace. To this end, NALC started making notable headway after 1962.

As a civil rights leader, Randolph continued to play a central role as an organizer and spokesperson. To civil rights icons such as Dr. Martin Luther King, Jr., Randolph was a luminary figure in the modern black freedom movement. It was his pioneering tactics that convinced civil rights activists in the 1950s and 1960s "that nonviolent protests and mass demonstrations were the best way to mobilize public pressure" (AFL-CIO). On May 17, 1957, these tactics were central to the Prayer Pilgrimage for Freedom at Washington, DC. Randolph co-sponsored the event at the request of King and the Southern Christian Leadership Conference. At the Lincoln Memorial, Randolph gave an inspirational speech to a crowd of between 20,000 and 30,000 people, around the event's theme of hope for better race relations and pressuring the federal government into taking further action on civil rights public policy. Several months later, on September 9, 1957, the pressures of the incipient Southern Civil Rights Movement and the Leadership Conference on Civil Rights (LCCR) forced President Dwight D. Eisenhower and Congress to issue the Civil Rights Act of 1957.

The LCCR was co-founded in 1950 by Randolph, Roy Wilkins of the NAACP, and Arnold Aronson of the National Jewish Community Relations Advisory Council. It was a civil and human rights coalition that most notably lobbied Congress for successful passage of civil rights bills in 1957, 1964, 1965, and 1968.

Moreover, Randolph worked closely with **Bayard Rustin**, James Farmer, and the Congress of Racial Equality, as the group's advisor. In 1942, they pioneered the use of direct-action tactics to civil rights activism in urban America. In the 1960s, they applied these tactics to freedom rides and sit-in demonstrations geared toward integration in employment, education, and housing. Randolph made arguably his greatest contribution to American society as the chief organizer of the 1963 March on Washington.

This event originally was called the March on Washington for Jobs and Freedom. This was the brainchild of Randolph and his former assistant Rustin (who was to become Dr. King's advisor in the 1950s and 1960s). The original goal of the second MOWM was to pressure the House and Rules Committee in Congress into passing civil rights and economic equality legislation on the 100th anniversary of the Emancipation Proclamation. The Jobs and Freedom connection was based on Randolph's long-held conviction that "freedom requires a material foundation" (Quarles, 160). In February 1963, with the backing of the civil rights establishment, Randolph announced the march to the global public from his office in Harlem. Between 200,000 and 300,000 people responded to the civil rights establishment call of "Freedom Now" and participated enthusiastically in the march. This was the zenith of the Civil Rights Movement and the use of direct-action tactics for black freedom and civil rights legislation. During the event, Randolph gave a stirring keynote speech that was overshadowed only by King's legendary speech, "I Have a Dream." Ultimately, the March on Washington played a major role in inspiring the passage of the 1964 Civil Rights Act and the 1965 Voting Rights Act.

Despite the March's success, participants glossed over economic inequities and poverty impacting millions of African Americans, especially young people who were losing hope in U.S. democracy. The event sacrificed the "Jobs" component to pressure President John F. Kennedy into passing his modest, yet unprecedented civil rights bill on public accommodations (signed by President Lyndon Baines Johnson and Congress posthumously on July 2, 1964). Ironically, Randolph was the person who perhaps saved the civil rights bill and the "dignity" of the march for moderate civil rights activists, mainstream reporters, and spectators. He compromised his cherished economic agenda by persuading John Lewis of the Student Nonviolent Coordinating Committee (SNCC) to mollify his speech, which boldly criticized the Kennedy bill and the state of U.S. race and economic relations. The lack of an economic empowerment plan arguably had terrible ramifications for most black communities, through the continuation of the ghetto, poverty, de facto segregation, police brutality, and the creation of two black Americas in the post-civil rights era: one middle class, and the other poor. Lewis originally wanted to address many of these issues at the Lincoln Memorial. After 1965, this largely unaddressed situation created an impasse in the black freedom struggle among older and younger activists that led to the rise of the Black Power Movement (1966–ca. 1974).

With the emergence of Black Power, Randolph noticeably fell out of step with its practitioners who also subscribed to "Freedom Now." This included his underestimating the tenacity of white supremacy, and objecting to Black Power's deliberate move away from liberal coalition politics toward black separatism and gestures such as Black Power that to him lacked long-term sustainability in positively changing America and the world.

On May 16, 1979, Randolph passed away in New York City. In his dynamic life, he outlived, complemented, and arguably outperformed iconic contemporaries such as W. E. B. Du Bois, Marcus Garvey, and Dr. Martin Luther King, Jr. This history lacks greater acknowledgement and assessment because African Americans and the working class are marginalized in the consciousness of the American mainstream. With that said, Randolph's legacy deserves much greater study, because his contributions and measured impact as a labor and civil rights organizer are unmatched in the American experience. What would the African American economic experience be without Randolph's contributions? Would blacks have organized a Double Victory movement of hope to become first-class citizens and migrate by the millions from the South during World War II without a MOWM? Without a spark of hope that black industrialization, emigration, and the Double Victory movement provided, would there have been a successful Civil Rights Movement in the 1960s? Without a Civil Rights Movement and the Second MOWM, would Congress have passed civil rights legislation without being pressured by people progressive on issues of race? What would the United States and world be without A. Philip Randolph's contributions?

Herbert G. Ruffin II
Syracuse University

FURTHER READING

A. Philip Randolph Pullman Porter Museum. *A. Philip Randolph: Pullman Porter Museum*. http://www.aphiliprandolphmuseum.com/index.html.

Anderson, Jervis. *A. Philip Randolph: A Biographical Portrait*. Berkeley: University of California Press, 1986.

Arnesen, Eric. *Brotherhoods of Color: Black Railroad Workers and the Struggle for Equality*. Cambridge, MA: Harvard University Press, 2002.

Bates, Beth Tompkins. *Pullman Porters and the Rise of Protest Politics in Black America, 1925–1945*. Chapel Hill: The University of North Carolina Press, 2001.

George Meany Memorial Archives of the National Labor College. *A. Philip Randolph Exhibit*. http://www.nlc.edu/archives/apr.html.

Henderson, Joyce. *C. L. Dellums: International President of the Brotherhood of the Sleeping Car Porters and Civil Rights Leader*. Berkeley: The Regents of the University of California, 1973.

Kersten, Andrew E. *A. Philip Randolph: A Life in the Vanguard*. Lanham, MD: Rowan and Littlefield, 2006.

Pfeffer, Paula F. *A. Philip Randolph, Pioneer of the Civil Rights Movement*. Baton Rouge: Louisiana State University Press, 1996.

Quarles, Benjamin. "A Philip Randolph: Labor Leader at Large." In *Black Leaders of the Twentieth Century*, edited by John Hope Franklin and August Meier. Urbana: University of Illinois Press, 1982.

Ishmael Reed (1938–)

Ishmael Reed, writer, educator, cultural activist, and publisher, was born Ishmael Scott in Chattanooga, Tennessee, in 1938 during the Depression. His father, Henry Lenoir, worked as a fundraiser for the Young Men's Christian Association (YMCA), and his mother, Thelma Coleman, worked as a department store sales person. Thelma Coleman later married Benie Reed, an automobile factory worker, and the family moved to Buffalo, New York, in 1942. As a child, Ishmael Reed immediately began his lifelong passion for reading and writing. Reed begun composing stories in the second grade, and by age 14 he had started contributing a regular jazz column to a local black newspaper, the *Empire Star Weekly*. He attended Buffalo Technical High School from 1952 to 1954, and graduated from East High School in 1956. Reed studied briefly at Millard Fillmore College in Buffalo, and then transferred to the State University of New York at Buffalo. He selected American Studies as his major, but withdrew for financial reasons.

During his time in Buffalo, Reed met, courted, and married Pricilla Rose. The couple had a daughter, and in 1962 the Reeds moved to New York City. Reed pursued a career as a writer, finishing his first play, *Ethan Booker*, and editing the *Newark Advance*. Reed also participated in the Umbra Workshop, a Black Arts Movement writers guild, and in the first American Festival of Negro Art in 1965. Four years later, he served as the chief organizer of the festival. Reed also co-founded the *East Village Other*, an underground newspaper. In each of these various venues, Reed developed a unique writing style and philosophy of the arts.

Reed's efforts in the 1960s demonstrate the crystallization of his personal theory of arts and literature, what he has termed "neo-hoodoo" aesthetics. Reed's aesthetics incorporate the language, history, mythologies, rituals, folklore, and knowledge of African, Caribbean, and African American cultures. The terms "voodoo," "hoodoo," and "neo-hoodoo" occur throughout his fiction, poetry, and critical essays. Reed's novels cross genre boundaries as he has employed the literary elements of westerns, science fiction, and detective novels. He also incorporated history, journalism, satire, mysticism, mass media, and African literary traditions to create his narratives. Reed credits Vodun for its strong influence on his ideology, particularly its multiculturalism and its conceptions of time and syncretism.

By the late 1960s, college campuses across the United States, especially on the West Coast, erupted in student protests and demonstrations. Black students demanded that colleges and universities employ black professors who taught African- and African-American-centered curriculum in separate departments with administrative control. In 1967, Reed published his first novel, *The Free-Lance Pallbearers*, and moved across the country to begin teaching at the University of California in Berkeley. Reed would go on to publish eight additional novels over the next 25 years, including *Yellow Back Radio Broke-Down* (1969), *Mumbo Jumbo* (1972; nominated for the National Book Award), *The Last Days of Louisiana Red* (1974; winner of the National

Institute of Arts and Letters Awards), *Flight to Canada* (1976), *The Terrible Twos* (1982), *Reckless Eyeballing* (1986), *The Terrible Threes* (1989), and *Japanese by Spring* (1993).

Reed also published collections of poetry and essays that articulated his politics and promoted his neo-hoodoo aesthetics. His poetry includes *Catechism of D Neoamerican Hoodoo Church* (1970), *Conjure: Selected Poems, 1963–1970* (1972, nominated for the National Book Award and the Pulitzer Prize for poetry), *Chattanooga; poems* (1973), *A Secretary to the Spirits* (1978), and *New and Collected Poems* (1988). Among his collection of essays are *Shrovetide in old New Orleans* (1978), *God Made Alaska for the Indians: Selected Essays* (1982), *Writin' Is Fightin': Thirty-Seven Years of Boxing on Paper* (1988), *Airing Dirty Laundry* (1993), *Multi-America: Essays on the Cultural Wars and Cultural Peace* (1997), *The Reed Reader* (2000), *Another Day at the Front: Dispatches from the Race War* (2003), and *Blues City: A Walk in Oakland* (2003).

Among his novels, *Mumbo Jumbo* represents Reed's most influential and critically acclaimed work. The text truly reflects the spirit of Hoodoo, and best articulates Reed's cultural aesthetic and politics. The novel seeks to discover the origin and composition of the "true Afro-American aesthetic." *Mumbo Jumbo*'s plot is given as bits of a widely scattered concept. The reader must work to piece together the component parts so that by the end of the narrative, the reader comes to his/her own conclusions concerning the novel's meaning and significance.

The first chapter of *Mumbo Jumbo* lays out the details of the complicated plot in synopsis or news-flash form. Reed wrote the book in part to respond to white literary critics' remarks that black Americans lacked a literary tradition, and that this was why their work was often "raving" or "unfocused" (Martin, 180). Thus, Reed has a Hoodoo detective, a houngan named Papa LaBas (the Hoodoo god, Legba), search out and reconstruct a black aesthetic from various remnants of literary and cultural history. To lend the narrative authenticity, he adds favored scholarly components: facts from nonfictional, published works; photographs and historical drawings as evidence, and a bibliography. There is an unstated sub-text throughout the book that can be crudely paraphrased as, "My aesthetic is just as good as yours—maybe better—and certainly is founded on no more ridiculous a set of premises than yours."

At the opening of the novel, set in the 1920s, white municipal officials in New Orleans are trying to respond to "Jes Grew," an outbreak, as it seems, of people acting outside of socially conditioned roles; white people are "acting black" as they dance half-dressed in the streets to an intoxicating new loa (spiritual essence of a fetish) called jazz. People give up racist and oppressive endeavors because it is more fun to "shake that thing." They speak in tongues. Jes Grew is described as the "germ" that helps its host, relieving the host of stress. One of the doctors assigned to treat the pandemic of Jes Grew comments, "There are no isolated cases in this thing. It knows no class, no race, no consciousness.

It is self-propagating and you can never tell when it will hit" (Reed, *Mumbo Jumbo*, 8). No one knows where the germ has come from; it "Jes Grew." The omniscient narrator states that Jes Grew is actually:

> an anti-plague. Some plagues caused the body to waste away, Jes Grew enlivened the host. Other plagues were accompanied by bad air (malaria). Jes Grew victims said the air was as clear as they had ever seen it and that there was the aroma of roses and perfumes which had never before enticed their nostrils. Some plagues arise from decomposing animals, but Jes Grew is electric as life and is characterized by ebullience and ecstasy. Terrible plagues were due to the wrath of God; but Jes Grew is the delight of the gods. (Reed, *Mumbo Jumbo*, 9)

In Reed's method, Jes Grew represents the spiritual part of his writing style. His positivism may take on any number of stylistic guises, but its intent is to illuminate and enliven the reader.

In addition to its response to white literary critics, Reed also critiques religion in *Mumbo Jumbo*. Reed challenges both Islam and Christianity for their failings and their infringements on the ego and individual expression. Again, Reed responds to his critics under the guise of Papa LaBas. Christianity is called "Atomism," a word with its origin in the worship of the one, true sun-god, Aton of ancient Egypt. Atonists are forever at war to stamp out Jes Grew, as it threatens their way of doing things and their base of power. Variations of Atomism in the United States, including Mormons and the Nation of Islam, are attacked vigorously.

In addition to his critique of Christianity, Reed also challenges the Nation of Islam. Abdul Hamid, the Muslim character, is trying to convince others that the way to black solidarity and prosperity is through the promotion of one religious platform; in this case, a platform composed of the belief in Allah and Islam. In the course of his diatribe, Reed demonstrates the precarious nature of a religion based upon increasing the number of its followers, and the shallowness of a religion determined to generate wealth, to accumulate land, and to strengthen the power of its leaders. Hamid says:

> This is the country where something is successful in direct proportion to how it's put over; how it's gamed. Look at the Mormons. Did they recruit 1000s of whites to their cause by conjuring the Druids? No, they used material the people were familiar with and added their own. The most fundamental book of the Mormon Church, the Book of Mormon, is a fraud. If we Blacks came up with something as corny as the Angel of Moroni, something as trite and phony as their story that the book is the record of ancient Americans who came here in 600 BC and perished by AD 400, they would deride us with pejorative adjectival phrases like "so-called" and "would-be." They would refuse to exempt our priests from the draft, a privilege extended to every white hayseed's fruit stand which calls itself a Church. But regardless of the put-on, the hype, the Mormons got Utah, didn't they? (Reed, *Mumbo Jumbo*, 42)

Ironically, it is later Hamid's own mono-theistic religious views that prompt him to burn the ancient Scroll of Thoth, the text Jes Grew had been searching for since it became lost after being placed in a tabernacle by Moses.

In his critique of shallow religious organizations, Reed employs a stylistic trope: the use of facts to further fictional ends. The Atonist order does not simply war against non-whites and non-Christians. It is equally intolerant of whites who will not follow the Atonist path. Reed asserts that the Knights Templar, one of the militaristic Christian orders during the Crusades, were slaughtered by the Teutonic Knights because the Templars had attained too much power and were threatening the Atonist hierarchy. Reed uses the historical existence of the Teutonics and the Templars in his fictional account of the demise of the Templars.

Reed employs historically accurate newsflashes in other novels in addition to *Mumbo Jumbo; however, the stories become* complicated by the "false" newsflashes incorporated throughout many of the texts. Thor Wintergreen, a white member of the Mu'tafikah, a multi-ethnic gang which "liberates" Third World countries' art from Western museums, is killed by another white, Biff Musclewhite, head of the Center for Art Detention in New York. Wintergreen was audacious enough to side with those of different ethnic backgrounds. Biff Musclewhite's escape and murder of Berbelang is given in a newsflash from a New York newspaper. Reuter's informs the reader that the Wall-flower Order, the para-military branch of the Teutonic Knights, has induced "Its Running Dog Medical Societies and its Jackanape Punk Freudians to issue a report which 'Scientifically' proves that Jes Grew is hard on the appendix..." the shimmy, that descendant of the Nigerian Shika Dance, is outlawed ... doctors in Yakima Washington announce that "the source of man's wickedness is a 'Torrid Zone' in the brain, an inch and a half thick from the ears up" (Reed, *Mumbo Jumbo*, 131). Here, Reed is further trying to confuse fact with fiction for rhetorical ends: the actual news insert seems as ridiculous and/or believable as the contrived ones. Are the pelvic and feet controls instituted in 1914 to keep white dancers from the hypnotic and "trance-like" effects of black movements "real" or fictional?

> Do not wriggle the shoulders.
> Do not shake the hips.
> Do not twist the body.
> Do not flounce the elbows.
> Do not pump the arms.
> Do not hop—glide instead.
> Drop the Turkey Trot, the Grizzly Bear,
> the Bunny Hug, etc. These dances are ugly, ungraceful, and out of fashion.
> (Reed, *Mumbo Jumbo*, 160)

Reed filled the novel with historical facts and fictions so that the reader can no longer disseminate truth from lie. Is the biographical material about the "Five

Negro Presidents" from historian J. A. Rogers true or untrue? Is the book *Warren Harding, President of the United States*, from the Rare Book Room of the New York Public Library, worth $2 million per copy? In this case, these "truths" are facts. Reed's point is that "facts" from history are often either fabricated or too biased or incredible to be believed. Fact overlaps with fiction, and only when the two are juxtaposed can one see the similarities. Similar to Reed's stance on religion, he demonstrated to his reader that one can simply believe what one wants to believe, and to the individual, those beliefs become fact whether grounded in truth or lies. One man's fiction is another man's fact, and who is to say which is which and whose fact or fiction is more valid?

Another major trope in *Mumbo Jumbo* is the concept of Hoodoo time. Reed used present-tense verbs at the beginning of the narratives of selected consequential chapters. The synchronic effect is achieved at the beginning of a new chapter, in which actions have built upon the preceding chapter and sequentially, with new actions, or cardinal functions, in a new chapter that has verbs and situations set in the present tense. This effect introduces the reader to the simultaneity of the text, and elicits the reader-response ambience which mirrors the Hoodoo/oral culture feeling in the text. The reader "feels," responding emotionally to the structure of the text, that all of the catalytic actions in the individual cardinal units are thematically and rhetorically related because they all seem to have significance to each other. All of the events seem to be happening in the same narrative time frame.

In addition to using Hoodoo time, Reed also creates characters in many of his novels that are meant to be symbolic of, or emanations of, Hoodoo fetishes. The symbolic characters possess certain ascribed qualities of a fetish; emanations of the fetish are characters possessed by a god or said to be a loa, the spiritual part of a god physically manifested in a character. The gods of Hoodoo number in the thousands, but Reed employs three primary fetishes in his novels: the female fetish Erzulie, and the male fetishes Legba and Ogun. Erzulie is known as a love/romance/sexual fetish in Hoodoo. In the United States, W. C. Handy's "woman with the red dress on" and Josephine Baker exemplify Erzulie. Earline in *Mumbo Jumbo* originally symbolizes, and later represents an emanation of, Erzulie, and she is always molded with a large, protruding penis. LaBas, and certainly Benoit Battraville, the Haitian houngan who dispatches Von Vampton, symbolizes Legba. They maintain the Hoodoo order, and their potency as leaders is often exemplified by acts of physical prowess. Reed employed Ogun, the fetish of iron and war, in two other novels. In *The Last Days of Louisiana Red* (1947), Blue Coal, who dispenses punishment to the Moochers, and Black Peter, who disrupts and attempts to take over the Nicolaites (followers of Santa Claus) in the *Terrible Twos* (1982), represent emanations of Ogun.

Reed also drew from a body of peculiar North American additions to the Hoodoo pantheon, which does not take human form at all. These fetishes are usually represented by emanations of creative, artistic, and original natures.

Jazz, be-bop, rock and roll, super-realistic painting, and scat poetry are all North American fetishes. Sometimes the North American fetish does not take human form, such as Marie Laveau (knowledge of rites and dogma), Voodoo Queen of New Orleans, Charlie Parker (originality), or Julius Erving (beauty and grace). These qualities are purposely used in characters to make them more representative of Hoodoo fetishes. As Reed wrote in the article, "I Hear You Doc [Duvalier]," describing his visit to Haiti in 1977:

> In Haitian art, based on Vodoun principles, the artist uses certain universal forms, to which he brings his own individual aesthetic sense. This approach is what I have attempted to use in my novels. Though my characters are often called "stereotypes," their forms fall solidly within Vodoun tradition. (Reed, *Mumbo Jumbo*, 312)

At the end of *Mumbo Jumbo*, Jes Grew withers away with the burning of its text, the Book of Thoth, which listed the sacred spells and dances of Osiris. LaBas says Jes Grew will appear some day to make its own text. "A future generation of young artists will accomplish this," says LaBas, referring to the writers, painters, politicians, and musicians of the 1960s, "the decade that screamed," according to Reed. In the course of the narrative, Reed constructs the history of the "true Afro-American aesthetic," which includes his generation's contributions to African American history, art, and culture.

Reed has demonstrated through the course of his text that the cultural productions of the 1960s have their roots in a very long history. The Atonist Order is traced to Set, brother of Osiris. Set was the evil force and wanted everything his way. He became, according to LaBas, "the first man to shut nature out of himself. He called it discipline" (Reed, 185). The dances Osiris performed were learned from the Elders of Nysa, Ethiopia, where Osiris received his education. The dances were dances of fertility, and under the spell of Osiris, the country's agriculture blossomed. Eventually, the jealous Set murders Osiris, and Thoth flees from Egypt with the Text. Subsequently, Dionysus (which can be read as "God from Nysa") appropriates the dances and carries them back to Greece. As the Osirian cults die out under persecution in Greece, Moses (1350–1250 BC) appropriates a bad version of Thoth's Text from the spirit of Isis. After a disastrous experiment with the spells in the book, Moses, fearful of the Text's power, hides it. It is not discovered again until the librarian for the Knights Templar, Hinckle Von Vampton, stumbles upon it while doing his shelving in 1187. Von Vampton dispelled the Text's power by sending it around the United States to various repositories that did not know what they possessed. In this way, the Text would not be in one place where Jes Grew could find it and unite with it.

Reed explained that through paid mailing, Hamid first encounters the Text. Hamid practices his own form of censorship and burns the Text. Thus, Jes Grew, the spirit of the Afro-American aesthetic, must wait again to be united with his corporeal emanation, the Text. If the two again united, they would be too powerful to refute. Reed's underlying message concerns the uniting of Afro-American tradition, folklore, art, and history, with a written code, a text, a literate recapitulation of history and practice. Symbolically, having a black man burn the Text challenges the new black aesthetic critics. These critics, like Addison Gayle, Houston Baker, and Amiri Baraka, had the chance to codify Afro-American tradition. In Reed's eyes, however, they failed because their perceptions were too narrow and because their standards were at least partly set by training in white universities, which caused them to ignore important parts of Afro-American tradition. By calling for a unification of a text and tradition, Reed equates the Text (the Afro-American aesthetic) with the *Vedas*, the *Pentateuch*, the *Koran*, the *Latin Vulgate*, the *Book of Mormon* and all the "Holy" codifications of faith. *Mumbo Jumbo* is itself the Text, and it appears in 1972 as a direct, written response to the assertion that there is no "black" way of doing things; that black contributions to world culture have been insignificant at best.

Reed's construction of this "aesthetic" represents a double insult to his critics. First, the strained relationship of past history and present conditions in *Mumbo Jumbo* is, on the face of its construction, ridiculous, and yet, by juxtaposition on paper, no more ridiculous than skies filled with gods representing different aspects of human personality, burning bushes which speak and yet are not consumed by flame, virgin birth, resurrection, or ancient North Americans appearing from nowhere in 600 BC. Reed equates his aesthetic—based on different myths—with other aesthetics based on other myths.

Secondly, Reed heightened the insult by insisting that his notion of an aesthetic is better than others in key humanistic aspects. He especially insisted that his aesthetic was superior to those based on Americanized, European, Christian dogma. *Mumbo Jumbo* contains a different notion of a black aesthetic than the new black aesthetic critics had outlined, all of whom were trained in the Western tradition "to be English professors" according to Reed. As was true of the kids in *Yellow Back Radio Broke-Down*, Reed had "decided to create [his] own fiction" in response to ridicule and mono-cultural arrogance. His method had found its spiritual corollary in Hoodoo, and now had a physical manifestation, a manual of codification, in *Mumbo Jumbo*. After outlining his method in *Mumbo Jumbo*, Reed employed the aesthetic extensively in his next two novels, *The Last Days of Louisiana Red* (1974) and *Flight to Canada* (1976). These works demonstrated Reed's belief that Hoodoo, now understood as a spiritual part of the Afro-American aesthetic, can be used as a base of literary response.

Syncretic and synchronic in form, Reed's most successful novel focused most often on social circumstances which inhibit the development of black people in American society. As satire is usually based on real types, Reed draws from history and the news as nonfictional events to satirize America's mono-cultural arrogance and the price paid in the face of that arrogance by those who are not "vital people," that is, members of the dominant culture or the moneyed class.

His assertion that Hoodoo is "solidly in the American tradition" is supported by his collation of myth, fact, and apocryphal data into a history. From that history, which began with Osiris and continued through *Mumbo Jumbo*, a method or aesthetic is drawn not only for formulating art and multi-cultural standards, but also for formulating a different and more humane way of experiencing and influencing the world.

In addition to novels, poetry, and essays, Reed has written a number of plays: *Mother Hubbard* (1982), *The Lost State of Franklin* (with his second wife, Carla Blank, and Suzushi Hanayagi, 1976), *The Ace Boons* (1980, performed at the Julia Morgan Theatre in Berkeley), *Hubba City* (premiered later that same year in Missouri), and *The Preacher and the Rapper* (1994, premiered at the Nuyorican Poets Café in New York).

In addition to publishing his own works, Reed has created institutions to help other writers publish their works. He co-founded two independent publishing houses: Yardbird Publishing Company in 1971, which published an annual Yardbird Reader, and Reed, Cannon, and Johnson Communications in 1973. Reed formed the Before Columbus Foundation in 1976 to promote the works of ethnic writers and to publish anthologies. In 1990, Reed, along with Al Young, founded a literary magazine, *Quilt*, which was also devoted to minority student writings.

Reed has enjoyed much public success. He has lectured at many prestigious universities, including Harvard, Yale, Columbia, and Dartmouth. He has also earned many awards and literary grants, including a Guggenheim Award for fiction, the American Civil Liberties Award, the Pushcart Prize, the George Kent Award, the Hanayagi Award from the Osaka Community Foundation, and an honorary doctorate in letters from the State University of New York at Buffalo in 1995. Reed's work has established him as one of the most provocative, influential and distinguished black writers in American history.

Reginald Martin
University of Memphis

FURTHER READING

Martin, Reginald. "An Interview with Ishmael Reed." *Review of Contemporary Fiction*. 4, no. 2 (Summer 1984): 176–87.
Martin, Reginald. *Ishmael Reed and the New Black Aesthetic Critics*. New York: St. Martin's Press, 1988.
Reed, Ishmael. *Chattanooga*. New York: Avon, 1972.
Reed, Ishmael. *Conjure*. New York: Avon, 1972.
Reed, Ishmael. *Flight to Canada*. New York: Avon, 1976.
Reed, Ishmael. *The FreeLance Pallbearers*. New York: Bantam, 1967.
Reed, Ishmael. *God Made Alaska for the Indians*. New York: Atheneum, 1982.
Reed, Ishmael. *Japanese by Spring*. New York: Atheneum, 1993.

Reed, Ishmael. *The Last Days of Louisiana Red*. New York: Avon, 1976.

Reed, Ishmael. *Mumbo Jumbo*. New York: Avon, 1972.

Reed, Ishmael. *Reckless Eyeballing*. New York: Atheneum, 1988.

Reed, Ishmael. *The Savage Wilds*. New York: Atheneum, 1990.

Reed, Ishmael. *Shrovetide in Old New Orleans*. New York: Avon, 1978.

Reed, Ishmael. *The Terrible Twos*. New York: Atheneum, 1982.

Reed, Ishmael. *The Terrible Threes*. New York: Atheneum, 1990.

Reed, Ishmael. "When State Magicians Fail." *Journal of Black Poetry* (Summer/Fall 1969): 17.

Reed, Ishmael. *Yellow Back Radio Broke Down*. New York: Bantam, 1969.

Condoleezza Rice
(1954–)

Condoleezza Rice became the public face of national security in the wake of the terrorist attack on September 11, 2001. Unlike other national security advisors, Rice's unflappable demeanor and ability to put complex problems into simple terms made her a perfect spokeswoman for President George W. Bush's plans to attack the Islamic group behind the attacks, al Qaeda, and then Iraq. Her very public support for the Iraq war and her close personal friendship with Bush has made her a very controversial figure in U.S. politics, particularly after support for the war soured.

Rice grew up in the most violently segregated city in the South—Birmingham, Alabama—in the midst of the Civil Rights Movement. All of her extended family emphasized education and told her that she had to be twice as good as whites just to seem equal, and three times as good to excel. Her father, John Wesley Rice, was the second Presbyterian minister in his family. Her mother's family, the Rays, had been attracted to the industrial jobs available in Birmingham. Albert Robinson Ray worked as a miner, and made enough money to enter the small middle class. In the 1920s, hers was one of few black families to own its own car. They dealt with Jim Crow by avoiding segregation in any way that they could. With their own car, they were able to avoid the divided busses. Ray often asked his children to not drink from segregated fountains or use segregated toilets, but to wait until they got home.

Rice was born November 14, 1954. She grew up immersed in her father's Presbyterian church. Her parents, John and Angelena Rice, filled her life with Western culture—orchestral music, ballet, foreign languages, and books.

Angelena loved music; all the women in her family played piano, and she wanted Rice to learn to play too. She gave her daughter a name taken from an Italian music term, *con dolcezza*, which means to play sweetly. When Rice was three years old, she would sit and listen to her grandmother teaching piano lessons. Rice asked her grandmother to teach her how to play, and learned how to read music before words. Even while a little girl, she was intensely focused, and would practice without anyone reminding her. Throughout her entire childhood and adolescence, piano always came first. At 10, she was the first black student admitted to the Birmingham Conservatory of Music, where she studied piano, violin, ballet, and French. She was determined to become a professional pianist.

John Rice, in addition to being a minister, was also a teacher and coach. He had hoped for a son, but when blessed with a daughter, he decided to teach her all he knew about sports. They sat together on Sunday afternoons and watched football, while he explained all the rules. Rice took that love, too, into her adulthood. When George W. Bush asked her if she would like to join his campaign as foreign policy expert, she agreed only if her dream job—NFL commissioner—was taken.

Education was paramount for the Rices, and they focused much energy on their only child's education. After Rice learned to read, her parents gave her a speed reading machine to teach her how to move quickly through books.

Rice was so advanced that she skipped the first and seventh grades. Her mother wanted to expose her to many different environments, so she enrolled Rice in several different public schools throughout her elementary years.

As both John and Angelena Rice were teachers, the family was able to take long summer vacations. Rice remembered that where other families would visit national parks such as Yellowstone, her family visited universities. Her parents kept close tabs on all the different aspects of American colleges. Some summers, they took graduate classes at the University of Denver. They had to travel 1,300 miles to that university, in part, because the nearby University of Alabama did not accept black students. To keep herself busy while her parents were in school, Rice took ice skating lessons. She loved flowing across the ice. She had already learned grace from ballet; ice skating added speed.

When the police commissioner of Birmingham, Bull Connor, began to threaten civil rights demonstrators with extensive jail time and violence, national leaders such as Martin Luther King, Jr. descended on the city to lead the campaign. When King was thrown into jail, local leaders decided to lead a children's march in protest. Elementary, junior high, and high school students went downtown on May 2, 1963, to march in the streets. Connor turned fire hoses and dogs on the marchers. The images of German shepherds attacking children and teenagers flew around the national press, raising intense awareness of the state of relations in the South. They caused President John F. Kennedy to start drafting the Civil Rights Act, which passed in 1964, after he was assassinated.

Rice was not among the young marchers that day. Her father did not believe in putting children in harm's way. The family stood at a distance, watching the demonstration. Rice missed many days of school because of the frequent bomb threats. A few months later, when the 16th Street Baptist Church was bombed, she could feel the ground shaking from two miles away. Denise McNair, a friend from kindergarten, was one of the four black girls killed.

During the upheaval, whites bombed the home of attorney Arthur Shores, a Rice family friend. To protect their families, John Rice and several other black men patrolled the neighborhoods with guns. Rice always explained her opposition to gun control laws with this image of her father. If he had had to register those guns, Bull Connor could have taken them away and left the Rice family open to greater harm.

The summer before Rice entered high school, her father graduated with an MA from the University of Denver. The university hired John Rice as director of admissions, and the family moved to Denver. Rice was excited for the move because she would be able to ice skate all year long.

Talking to other professors and deans at the University of Denver, John Rice discovered that the best girls school around was St. Mary's Academy, a private Catholic school. When she was 13, John enrolled his daughter in her first integrated school. Though not the first black student to attend the academy, she was still among the minority.

After initial testing, a counselor told Rice that she was not college material, despite her straight-A record and numerous athletic triumphs. In Birmingham, all her friends had assumed that they would go to college. Her parents rallied around her, and reminded her that she was a Rice and a Ray. She had three generations of college graduates behind her. With such support, she was able to shrug off the counselor's words.

Rice was busy from morning until night in Denver. She got up at 4:30 a.m. to skate, attended school all day, and then practiced piano for several hours each night. The practice paid off; at 15, she won a competition and played with the Denver Symphony Orchestra.

In Denver, the Rice family attended Montview Presbyterian Church, where John Rice became an associate pastor. This church was unique in the nation because it actively strove to maintain an integrated congregation. In an attempt to manage white flight, they asked their congregants to take a pledge that they would practice nondiscrimination in any and all housing sales. When a group of leaders met with Mr. Rice, he asked if they were all committed to integration, and they assured him that they were. Then he asked where the nearest black Presbyterian Church was; it was just a few blocks away. He then encouraged some of them to join that church. They realized that they had expected African Americans to take all the steps toward integration, when they themselves needed to be proactive.

Before her senior year in high school, Rice had acquired enough credits to graduate. She continued at St. Mary's in the mornings, and took classes at the University of Denver's Music School in the afternoons. Soon, she was so caught up in college that she wished she was going there full time. She took a college hockey player to prom, surprising her friends and embarrassing him. At 16, she graduated from St. Mary's and enrolled in the University of Denver full time on an honors scholarship.

For two years, Rice poured herself into her piano performance major. The summer after her sophomore year, she and other majors attended the Aspen Music Festival. There she encountered 11-year-olds who could sight-read music that it had taken her the entire year to learn. She decided that while she was technically proficient, she would never achieve the emotional intensity needed for a really great career. She could become a piano teacher or church music director, but she wanted to perform at Carnegie Hall. So she decided to switch her major. Her entire life to that point had been geared toward becoming a pianist. With what could she replace that intense focus?

Rice spent the fall semester of her junior year trying to decide what to major in. She did not find English literature analytical enough. The speed reading machine she had used as a child ruined her ability to read for pleasure. Government was not challenging enough for her. In the spring semester, she finally found her new passion.

She took an introductory class in international politics taught by Josef Korbel, a Central European diplomat who had fled first the Nazis and then the communists. His daughter, Madeleine Albright, became the first female Secretary of State under President Clinton. The topic on that first day of class was Stalin, which instantly fascinated Rice. From that day forward, she studied the Soviet Union. She became Korbel's prize student and began studying Russian intensely. Though a difficult language, Rice found that her previous language studies helped her master it.

After graduating from the University of Denver at the age of 19, in 1974 Rice went to the University of Notre Dame for a master's degree in Soviet Studies and International Politics. After being told at 13 that she was not college material, she graduated from DU as the most honored female undergraduate, cum laude, and as a member of Phi Beta Kappa (the country's oldest honor society). Both Rice and her father were excited by the combination of intellectual rigor and spirituality that Notre Dame offered. Though she had only been studying international affairs for two years, she went in as a strong master's student because she had done extensive reading on her own. She graduated from Notre Dame in 1975 with a master's, and returned to her parents' home in Denver. With Korbel's encouragement, she entered the University of Denver's Graduate School of International Studies to study for her PhD.

Rice is a realist. After studying the struggle between the United States and the Soviet Union at the heart of the Cold War, she decided it was not so much a struggle over ideology—communist or capitalist—but rather a power contest between two mighty players with differing national interests.

Rice registered as a Democrat, and voted for Jimmy Carter in 1976. However, she became increasingly uncomfortable with the way he handled foreign affairs, particularly his response to the Soviet invasion of Afghanistan, which she thought was too weak. International relations was her passion; it also became her testing rod for all politics. She realized by the next election that the Republicans were more aligned with her idea of how to interact with foreign countries. She was attracted to their rhetoric of a small government because she thought the government could not solve all social problems. In 1980, she voted for Ronald Reagan.

Very few African Americans have belonged—now or then—to the Republican Party. Rice liked to tell the story of the best Republican she knew—her father. In 1950s Alabama, when John Rice had gone to register to vote, the Dixiecrat Democrats plunked down a jar full of beans in front of him. They said, if you can guess how many beans are in this jar, you can vote. When he heard that the Republicans did not require such outlandish games, he joined their party. This story said nothing about the Republicans' contemporary commitment to civil rights, while making it seem like they supported it.

African Americans had begun to turn toward the party of Franklin Delano Roosevelt during the Great Depression, and away from the party of Lincoln. For the most part, it was after President Lyndon B. Johnson signed the Civil Rights Act and the Voting Rights Act that the Democrats began to be the party that recognized the needs of minorities. Similarly, there were those who used to be Southern Democrats, but as a sign of the solidarity of the white race switched to the Republican Party (Senator Strom Thurmond, for instance). After spending time in Russia and writing a dissertation on the Czech military called "The Politics of Client Command: The Case of Czechoslovakia 1948–1975," Rice graduated with her PhD at age 26.

After graduation, Rice had a one-year, post-doc position lined up at Stanford University's Centre for International Security and Arms Control. During her first presentation at the center, she impressed the other members with her knowledge and professional bearing. They decided to offer her a job right then. Even though they did not need another Soviet specialist, they wanted to snatch up such a talented black woman while they had the chance. The center was overwhelmingly white and male at that point. Later, when Rice attacked Affirmative Action, she would acknowledge that she had been a recipient of it, but only to the extent that it got her in the door. The other professors informed her that she would receive no leeway when it came to renewal or the tenure process, which she thought was fair.

Rice spent the next eight years, from 1981 to 1989, establishing herself at Stanford. She moved swiftly through the tenure process (after professors publish enough and earn good teaching recommendations they can achieve "tenure," which means they cannot be fired without a major problem). She also became known as one of the best teachers on campus, earning two major university teaching awards, the Walter J. Gores Award for Excellence in Teaching in 1984, and the School of Humanities and Sciences Dean's Award for Distinguished Teaching in 1993.

Rice treated students with respect. In one of her senior seminars, all of the students felt as though they were her favorites. One student remembered that she embodied what they wanted to see in an academic: she was well versed in the complexities of her subject, but did not close off other opinions. She frequently used football metaphors and role-playing to help her students immerse themselves in the issues at hand. Role-playing helped students understand how individual personalities and emotions could influence political decisions. Students were often surprised at the way they acted during the heat of the assignment.

In 1989, President George H. W. Bush tapped Rice for a position as advisor on Soviet affairs. She served under the national security advisor, Brent Scowcroft, during a tumultuous two years. In 1989, the Soviet-controlled Eastern bloc began to fall apart. Mikhail Gorbachev, general secretary of the Soviet Union, decided that he needed to open up politics and economics to stimulate the economies of the Eastern bloc. He did not expect the speed with which Eastern European countries would begin to declare independence.

First, Poland had a bloodless revolution led by Lech Walesa, a leader of industrial workers. Then Hungary opened its borders to Austria, allowing transportation to the West for the first time in decades. And then in November 1989, the Berlin Wall—that greatest symbol of East-West conflict—fell, torn down by

East and West Berliners. Rice convinced Bush to aggressively protect the burgeoning capitalist countries in the East through extensive aid packages.

In 1991, Rice decided to return to Stanford University. She did not want to give up her professorial position to become a full-time government worker. Two years later, the president of Stanford asked her to become the provost, or second in command. Most people rose to that rank after serving as chair of a department and dean of a school, neither of which Rice had done. The greatest controversy of her assuming the position arose not over her race, gender, or inexperience, but rather over her political affiliations. Most of Stanford's professors were Democrats and they feared that Rice's allegiance to the Republican Party would affect the way she conducted her job. She assured them it would not. She remained provost for six years; her primary success was in balancing the university's budget.

After returning to Stanford, Rice did not confine herself only to academics. She and her father (who had moved out from Denver to be near her after her mother died of breast cancer in 1985) started a children's center, The Center for a New Generation, to help low-income students in Palo Alto go to college. Rice also played piano at a church and with an on-campus quartet, and pursued her passion for football. In Denver she had dated a Bronco; in California, she dated a 49er. She never found anyone she wanted to marry.

During the 1990s, Rice joined several corporate boards, including Chevron, Transamerica Insurance, and Hewlett-Packard. At Chevron, she oversaw their plan to build an oil pipeline through Kazakhstan, one of the countries that had previously been a part of the Soviet Union. The company named a tanker after Rice for all of her aid.

When George W. Bush became governor of Texas, Bush Sr. encouraged Rice to meet with him. Rice and Bush Sr. had become friends during the two years she worked for him. Rice and George W. Bush almost immediately hit it off. When he began to plan for a presidential campaign, he requested that Rice join him as a foreign affairs advisor and she agreed, ready to get back into international politics after so many years as a university administrator. Bush was not one to sit and chat, so they would talk strategy while running side by side on the treadmill, while fishing at his Crawford, Texas Ranch, and while watching football. They also bonded over their strong Christian faith. During the campaign, Rice only left Bush's side to travel with his mother and wife on the "W is for Women" tour. It was the job of these women to stress Bush's "compassionate conservatism," which they hoped would attract more women to the party.

Bush won the 2000 presidential election after the Supreme Court got involved. The election was so close that it came down to a few votes in Florida, including several that had been mismarked (the infamous "hanging chad"). The Supreme Court had to decide whether to allow a recount or not. They decided not, making Bush the winner. When he took up residence in the Oval Office, Bush installed Rice in an office just down the hall.

As his national security officer, Rice was in charge of the National Security Council (Vice President; Secretaries of Defense, Treasury, and State; Chairman of the Joint Chiefs of Staff; Director of National Intelligence; Chief of Staff for the President; and others). It was her job not to create policy, but to harmonize the different opinions on the council so that the government would put forth a united front.

Also, she needed to synthesize the information put forth by these different individuals and explain it to the President in plain terms. One of the reasons that Bush liked her so much was that she was able to take complex ideas and facts, and explain them to him simply and clearly. Her mentor at the University of Denver 20 years before had insisted that all his students learn how to explain foreign affairs in language that anyone could understand. She had learned that lesson well. Because Bush did not like to read updates, one of the ways that she explained foreign affairs to him was by using the role-playing technique that had proved so successful with undergraduates.

Rice kept a fairly low profile for her first few months in office. The administration asked Chevron to rename the *Condoleezza Rice* oil tanker, as it boldly declared the connection between the Bushes and big oil. The Security Council met every two weeks.

The morning of September 11, 2001, everything changed for Rice. First, she was handed a memo from one of her aids saying that a passenger plane had flown into one of the towers of the World Trade Center. Both she and the president (who was then visiting school children in Florida) thought, "what a weird accident." Then, 18 minutes later, an aide told Rice that the second tower—on live television—had been hit by a plane. They knew then that it was a terrorist attack. Rice tried to convene the Security Council to decide what to do, but they were spread out over the country. The Secretary of Defense was in the Pentagon when it was hit. Bush did not return to the White House until later that evening, when they could be assured that it was safe for him to do so.

Over the next several months, Rice worked closely with the President to establish plans to hunt down the al Qaeda operatives involved in the attack. They went to war in Afghanistan because the Taliban, the ruling powers in Afghanistan, were linked to al Qaeda. Before the attack, Rice had not condoned using the U.S. military as an international police force or involving themselves in complicated conflicts internationally. After the attack, however, she fully condoned Bush's plan to invade Iraq, though the connections between Saddam Hussein, the Iraqi dictator, and al Qaeda were tenuous at best. Her horror over the attack and her support for President Bush had changed her mind.

Rice justified the attack on Iraq, which began in the spring of 2003, in a way that directly contradicted her earlier arguments against U.S. involvement overseas. She said that Hussein was an evil man who was dangerous to his own people and to the rest of the world. She warned that history proved the danger of inaction, when powerful countries did not confront dictators. Brent

Scowcroft, the national security advisor she served under during Bush Sr.'s administration, publicly condemned this line of thinking.

After Bush's re-election in 2004, several cabinet and administration members left or were reassigned, including Secretary of State **Colin Powell**. Bush nominated Rice in his place. She was the first black woman (the second black person and second female) to become Secretary of State. *Forbes* named her the most powerful woman in the world. Ta-Nehesi Coates, a writer for the *Atlantic Monthly*, described his fascination with her, even though he found her political positions reprehensible. It was her smile that caught him:

> You see it often when she's jousting with, say, Tim Russert [host of NBC's *Meet the Press*]. She'll flash it just as he's cornered her with a pointed query. Her eyes light up and her lips part as she reveals an answer that shows Russert has her exactly where she wants him. That smile is written in Ebonics. A loose translation: "I'm here sparring with the best thing white folks have to offer, and I'm creaming him."
>
> That smile is the reason Rice can work for a president who got the lowest percentage of the black vote since Barry Goldwater, and yet still pick up a President's Award from the NAACP. Think Clarence Thomas could do that? It's also why Democrats—who are utterly tied to the black vote—should pray she never runs for office. (Coates, "Rice Rice Baby")

Rice's power was based in two primary facets of her person: her ability to be cool and collected in front of the press and her close personal relationship to George W. Bush. That relationship came under scrutiny when Rice made a slip of the tongue at a dinner party in 2004, saying "As I was telling my husb . . ., as I was telling President Bush . . .," an odd slip since she has never been married (Felix, 225).

As Secretary of State, Rice supported Bush's attempt to foster democracy in the rest of the world, and attempted to broker peace between Israel and Palestine. During her tenure, Israeli-Palestine peace talks reached a new low when Israel and Lebanon started bombing each other. Also, Israel refused to talk to Hamas, the new political power in Gaza, because the Palestinian group did not believe in Israel's right to exist. After eight years of being in the limelight, Rice returned to her Stanford professorship when **Barack Obama** took his oath of office. Hillary Clinton replaced her as the Secretary of State.

Condoleezza Rice chose her political party based upon foreign relations policies. She would suggest that her choice illustrates a victory of the Civil Rights Movement because she was able to create her political and academic roles outside of race. At the same time, she earned much criticism for ignoring the continued influence of racism on national politics. In her chosen field, Rice's role in global politics during the 2000s will be viewed as contentious for many years to come.

Lauren L. Kientz
Michigan State University

FURTHER READING

Bumiller, Elisabeth. *Condoleezza Rice: An American Life: A Biography*. New York: Random House, 2009.

Coates, Ta-Nehisi. "Rice, Rice, Baby! My Big Fat Crush on Condoleezza." *Village Voice*. July 22, 2003. http://www.villagevoice.com/2003-07-22/news/rice-rice-baby/.

Felix, Antonia. *Condi: The Condoleezza Rice Story*. New York: Newmarket Press, 2005.

Mabry, Marcus. *Twice as Good: Condoleezza Rice and Her Path to Power*. Emmaus, PA: Modern Times, 2008.

U.S. State Department Web site. "Secretary of State Condoleezza Rice." http://2001-2009.state.gov/secretary/.

Paul Robeson
(1898–1976)

Paul Leroy Robeson dominated stage and screen during the 1920s and 1930s in Europe and America, before having his passport revoked in the 1940s by the U.S. government for having praised the Soviet Union. At 6'2" and with a deep bass voice, Robeson was a commanding presence on Broadway, in London's West End, and in several movies. His most famous song was "Ol' Man River" from the musical *Show Boat*. In the 1930s, Robeson began to feel an affinity for the working class, which he expressed by learning many languages (several from Africa) and gathering folk music wherever he traveled. In 1936, he and Max Yergan founded the Council on African Affairs to lobby for the political freedom of African colonies.

Robeson's childhood was dominated by his extreme regard and respect for his father and brothers. He liked to say that "The glory of my boyhood years was my father. I loved him like no one in all the world" (Robeson, 14). He was the youngest of five living siblings. His father, William Drew Robeson, had been born a slave in North Carolina and was old enough to be Paul's grandfather. As a teenager, William ran away and later attended Lincoln University in Pennsylvania for a bachelor's degree and a theology degree. He pastored Witherspoon Street Presbyterian Church in Princeton, New Jersey for 30 years. He pushed his children to academic success, sending the two closest in age to Robeson to boarding school and all three sons to Lincoln University (one daughter attended a teachers college).

When Paul was six years old, his mother Maria Louisa Robeson, by then an almost-blind invalid but who had been a schoolteacher of black abolitionist heritage, was killed when a coal stove in their house turned over and caught her dress on fire. With his mother gone and siblings at boarding school and college, Robeson spent a lot of one-on-one time with his father. A large extended family and close black community in Princeton rallied around the motherless boy and provided support and discipline.

Robeson enjoyed a warm mentoring relationship with his brothers; one taught him how to play baseball, another taught him how to stand up for himself, and a third taught him how to study. One brother, Ben, played baseball well enough to make the major league (in Robeson's estimation) if it had not been closed to black players at that point. He tutored Robeson in proper technique. Robeson was always a quick study in school, so after he dashed off his homework, he had long afternoons to play all the games the neighborhood boys devised.

Another brother, Reeve, refused to accommodate himself to the racial hierarchies of Princeton. After dropping out of Lincoln University, he obtained a hack and horses to drive a taxi around Princeton. But whenever white students (especially those from the South) used their driver as the butt of racial slurs and jokes, he would take them out and pound into them a lesson in racial etiquette by the side of the road. If there was a group, he would swing a sack of rocks around that he kept under his chair. Finally, his father had gotten him out of jail one too many times and asked him to leave town, fearing his influence on the young Robeson. But Robeson always remembered the advice that Reeve gave him not to give in to bullies, but to hit back harder than he'd been hit.

Robeson's oldest brother, Bill (17 when the younger brother was born), taught him how to study. He remembered that Bill would quiz him on his homework. Bill was never content with the right answer, but would pester Robeson until he had explained why it was the right answer. No matter the subject, Bill mastered it quickly. Unfortunately, he never found a job that could utilize his demanding mind (he became a doctor when he wanted to be a researcher), and he died young, an embittered man.

In 1901, a factional dispute within the church dismissed Reverend Robeson from his pulpit in Princeton. He worked for several years hauling ash before he switched denominations to the African Methodist Episcopal Zion, whose bishops assigned him first to a church in Westfield, New Jersey, then to one in Somerville, New Jersey. In Westfield, Robeson attended a white elementary school, but in Somerville there was a large enough black community to support a segregated school (then the norm in New Jersey). He graduated from eighth grade in 1912 with two others. One of his classmates still remembered his stirring oration of Patrick Henry's speech on Liberty almost 60 years later.

In addition to a reverence for religion, sports, and education, Robeson's family also taught him to love oratory and song. His household was filled with the sound of the human voice, and every Sunday, Robeson listened to his father's rolling bass expounding the light of the scriptures. All of his siblings, save his sister, were on debating teams and often practiced their speeches in front of the family. They also had special family performances, with most of the brothers giving speeches and reading essays. When his brothers discovered that Robeson could sing, his role in these family times was to raise his voice in song. He also joined the church choir. In his integrated high school, all these interests came together. He played on four teams—football, basketball, baseball, and track and field—joined the debating and glee clubs, excelled academically, and performed Othello in a theatrical medley. In his role as Othello, he was struck stiff by stage fright. His teacher's direction and his father's insistence on good diction played in his mind on endless repeat. He was determined never to try acting again.

Robeson won a four-year scholarship to Rutgers College, located only 15 miles from his house, and in 1915 became one of only three blacks to attend that institution since its founding in 1766. At the school, he continued his rigorous academic and extra-curricular schedule. When he tried out for the football team, the whites also trying out were determined not to play with a black man, so they did all they could to injure him. On the first day, during a scrimmage, one man smashed his nose (something which he struggled with throughout his singing career) and others jumped on him hard enough to dislodge his collar bone.

Robeson felt like quitting, but his family ethics came out in full force. He remembered how his father had patiently worked as an ash man for several years before resuming his pulpit. He also remembered his father telling him that he represented all the black boys who wanted to play and go to college, but couldn't. His brother, Ben, told him he could quit, but that he did not think they had quitters in their family. Robeson went back to practice, and at one point a player with cleats stepped with full force on his hand, barely missing breaking his bones, but scrapping off all the fingernails on that hand. Furor swept through Robeson, and during the next tackle, he grabbed the ball holder up over his head, ready to body-slam him into the ground. Seeing him, the coach shouted out that he was on varsity. The shout lessened his anger, and he set the player down.

Eventually, Robeson won over his teammates and they became friends. By his junior year, Robeson dominated the team. When another team balked at having to play a black man, the Rutgers coach complained to the opposing coach, the famous "Greasy" Neale—"What do you want me to do, Greasy—give you the game? I can't play without Robeson. He's the team!" After playing the first half against Robeson, Greasy told his players "See here, boys, any player who can take the beating that Robeson has taken from you, without squealing, is not black. He's a white man! Now go out there and play like hell—and give him a break!" (Stewart, 40). Greasy's statement illustrates how tied many Americans were to the idea that "white" was a positive word that encompassed all forms of good attributes, whereas "black" was its very opposite. They tied the game at 7–7.

Robeson was named to the All-American team in his junior and senior years, especially after Rutgers soundly defeated that team in a huge upset match. During his junior year, he did not actually play with them because World War I intervened. Throughout this phenomenal career on the football team, Robeson still played his three other sports—baseball, basketball, and track and field—and maintained a rigorous academic level. He was one of three students to be named to Phi Beta Kappa, a national honors society, in their junior year. He also joined a literary society and won awards for his speeches. He participated in the oratorical contests as one of the last wishes of his father, who died in 1918 at age 73. His death devastated Robeson and cemented his powerful presence in Robeson's memory.

Following graduation in 1919, Robeson went to Columbia University in New York City for law school. To put himself through school, he coached football at Lincoln University and on the weekends he played for the National Football League (which did not ban black players until 1934). During this time, he also appeared in several plays off-Broadway, and discovered a love for the stage that his high school self could not have dreamed of.

At the same time, his sparkling personality attracted many friends and admiring women. He did not focus on any one woman until, recuperating from a football injury at New York's Presbyterian Hospital, he met and started dating Eslanda "Essie" Goode, who was a pathology technician there. They married on August 17, 1921.

Before graduating from Columbia in 1923, he made his professional acting debut, quit professional football, and took his first trip to London. After graduating, Robeson worked briefly for a law firm, until he confronted the barriers between him and a full law practice. When a white stenographer-secretary was assigned to him, she announced loudly that she wouldn't take dictation from a "nigger." The head of the law firm also made it clear to Robeson how narrow his future opportunities in law would be; he could open a branch of the firm in Harlem eventually, but that was about it. Robeson decided that he need not stand for such treatment, especially when his acting career had begun to show promise.

Quitting law practice allowed him to focus even more on acting. In 1924, he received the lead role in two of Eugene O'Neill's plays, *All God's Chillun Got Wings*, and *Emperor Jones*. O'Neill was one of the most prominent white playwrights in American history. Both scripts had stereotypical portrayals of black men—primitive, passionate brutes. It was very rare at that point in time for African Americans to have lead roles in any play on Broadway. Robeson felt that taking the roles, and bringing all the sophistication and dignity that he could to them, was somehow advancing the race. It also, certainly, advanced his career.

Despite the stereotypical parts, his performance still raised the rancor of racist journalists who set up a huge cry of protest that the white actress in the play kissed Robeson's hand. The Ku Klux Klan threatened Robeson for that kiss.

While appearing in plays, Robeson also began to explore his singing potential. Ollie Harrington, a cartoonist and Harlem friend, remembered that Robeson sang songs which awakened some part of him that had long been asleep. Robeson collaborated with Lawrence Brown, a talented black composer. Brown taught Robeson that the songs of his childhood could become significant pieces of a concert repertoire. With Brown's help, Robeson developed a concert repertoire of African American music that became very popular. His fame soared after he appeared in a small part in the Kern and Hammerstein musical *Show Boat*. Despite his few lines, he dominated the stage with every appearance, particularly when he sang "Ol' Man River." When that song first became central to his concert repertoire, he left the words evoking a stereotypical lazy black man the same, including in 1936, when he played the role of Joe in the movie version of *Show Boat*. In later years, however, he changed the words to be about fighting prejudice.

Paul and Essie Robeson made several trips across the Atlantic for Paul to play in different shows on the West End in London and on Broadway in New York. Finally though, they decided to stay in London permanently. Robeson justified leaving the United States for the same reason that so many black people migrated north in the same period, during and after World War I. He recognized that London was much better to him than Chicago or New York had been to these migrants. In London, Robeson was acclaimed as a great actor and the Robesons were invited by rich socialites, nobility, and leftist activists (such as

Emma Goldman) to dine at their tables. In 1927, early in their London sojourn, Paul Jr. joined their family.

They continued to mingle only with the wealthy until something occurred that awakened Robeson to race relations in Britain. He and his wife were treated so well because they were anomalies. Most people of African and Indian descent in Britain did not fare similarly. Late one evening, the Robesons received an invitation to tea from Lady Colefax, asking them to join her at the Savoy Grill in the famous Savoy Hotel, a popular spot for British gentry. They had attended such dinners before, including at that hotel. But when they walked through the door this time, a hotel staff person rushed to them and refused to let them come in. He explained that the hotel now barred all black people. The reason for this change in policy is unclear, though some speculate that white American guests had begun to demand it. In shock, Robeson began seeking out other people in Britain to commune with. He found workers and immigrants with rich cultures, and began to formulate his theory of the universal brotherhood of the working class. He thought that all members of the working class shared the same fight and also the same culture. Everywhere he went he gathered the songs of the local area and added them to his concerts, attempting to connect folk music to different groups far and wide.

Robeson's greatest stage triumph came in 1930 when he appeared as Othello. This Shakespeare tragedy, which has a black man (a Moor) as the titled lead, was usually played by a white man in black face, which included dark makeup and large white circles around the mouth and eyes. Robeson's performance made Shakespeare's words for one of the first times into a play about the black condition in the Western World.

Robeson traveled all over the world, performing in plays and singing. In 1934, he felt called to visit the Soviet Union, spurred by the stories told by friends including **W. E. B. Du Bois** and Claude McKay about its openness to people of color. He and Essie traveled to Moscow by train, stopping first in Berlin. He had not been to the German capital since Hitler had taken over and was shocked at the changes. The art scene had been dismantled and strangers in the street glared at him with hatred for walking with his light-skinned wife.

When they finally arrived in the Soviet Union, they viewed the multicultural welcoming committee with great relief. Children came up to them, eager to touch the big man's coat. Robeson concluded that they had not been taught to fear black men. His warm acceptance was like nothing he had before experienced; in the Soviet Union he was a full human being who could walk the streets with dignity. His initial impressions were confirmed when he learned about the liberal nationalism policy, which encouraged protection of national cultures within the Soviet Union. Like many visitors to the Soviet Union, Robeson was only shown the most positive aspects of the country. He was unaware of the millions of people—political enemies, Jews, and others—that leader Josef Stalin was ordering killed during the time of his visit.

Robeson met Africa first in Britain. At that time, the British Empire controlled a swath of Africa from the Cape of Good Hope almost to Cairo, Egypt. Many African elites came to Britain for an education at Oxford, Cambridge, or the London School of Economics. The Robesons and other black Americans socialized with Kwame Nkrumah (first black president of Ghana, 1952–1966), Jomo Kenyatta (first black president of Kenya, 1963–1978), and others. Robeson also went down to the docks to hang out with African sailors and longshoremen. These associations, coupled with Essie's study in African cultures, raised Robeson's interest in the political state of Africa.

He began to realize that African peoples held under British colonialism suffered many of the same fates as blacks in America. Thus, he added the study of African languages, including Yoruba, Efik, Twi, and Swahili, to his already full schedule (he had already studied several European languages, in part to sing folk songs in the original tongues). He thought he could bring the beauty and flexibility of these African languages back to Americans, including blacks, who were overwhelmingly ignorant of their existence.

In the 1930s, Robeson began focusing more and more on a screen career to complement his stage and singing careers. He performed in several very different movies, with different types of black characters. At first, he was just excited to be given a major part in a movie, and did not focus too strongly on the way the character portrayed black people. For example, in 1935, in his first British movie *Sanders of the River*, Robeson played an African chief in a movie that ended up glorifying British Imperialism for bringing order and justice to wild Africa. Many black critics lambasted Robeson for playing the part. In response, he began to research African cultures even more, traveling with Essie throughout the continent, and more carefully defining his roles, like that of the strong, moral black man he played in *Jericho* in 1937.

In addition to parts with more positive portrayals of black men, Robeson also sought out films that could express the working-class ethos he was beginning to embrace more and more since his trip to Russia and since spending more time with people in the working class. He particularly enjoyed Welsh miners, who had a rich choral tradition that he added to his repertoire. He explored their culture and economic struggles in the 1940 movie *Proud Valley*.

Where many artists would have been content to leave their interest in working class and African cultures at the cerebral and aesthetic level, Robeson turned his concern into action. In 1937, he spoke with Max Yergan about creating the Council on African Affairs to work for the end of colonialism in Africa. Yergan was a black American who had served as a YMCA missionary for almost two decades in South Africa, but was then turning from religion to the more secular salvation found in communism. Over the next 18 years of the Council's existence, Robeson often said that though he was involved with many organizations, he loved the Council the most.

The Council focused on two main areas of work: information and organization. The first was dissemination of information about the political situation in Africa. Robeson's worldwide fame and booming voice proved perfect for promoting their message. They created a research department that provided accurate press releases and background information to American newspapers, kept a library of African books, movies, and exhibit materials that could be loaned out wherever needed, and circulated their own monthly bulletin, pamphlets, and reports. To organize, they held assemblies at many different venues, from small communities to a Madison Square Garden rally. They paid for the legal defense of Jomo Kenyatta when he was charged with conspiracy, and provided for the families of jailed protesters in South Africa.

In 1948, the Council came under the McCarthyite gloom of suspicion, as did Robeson himself. The Council struggled to continue their work under this haze until it dissolved in 1955. Robeson's passport, which he had had since 1922, was revoked in 1950, effectively ending a major portion of his income derived from international performances. The State Department excused this act by pointing out Robeson's friendly attitude toward the Soviet Union and his work for African liberation from colonialism for more than a decade.

The United States was in the beginning stages of the Cold War; the federal government had begun positioning itself in opposition to the communist Soviet Union at the end of the Second World War. As each country developed nuclear weapons, the rivalry became fiercer, and Senator McCarthy began prosecuting everyone he could find with communist ties or supposed communist ties. Robeson believed that his passport was revoked also because of his frequent efforts to fight for African American rights. White and African Americans who fought for justice for blacks were usually suspected of radical politics and followed by the FBI. Robeson's friend and major black intellectual, Du Bois, had also had his passport revoked for speaking positively about communism.

Robeson pressed his case in court, trying to get the government to return his passport. In one 1955 hearing on the case in a Federal Court, U.S. Attorney Leo A. Rover blamed Robeson for criticizing black Americans' situations in the United States while on concert tours. In response, Robeson wrote that he was only being true to his convictions. He criticized the United States during concerts in the United States; he would not suddenly change his opinions when he stepped off U.S. soil.

While closed off from his international audience, Robeson made many attempts to remain an international performer. In 1952, he traveled to Seattle, Washington, and sang on the border between the United States and Canada (though a passport was not required to travel to Canada, he was also banned from that neighboring country). Robeson sang in Peace Arch Park, and his voice was piped across to 30,000 spectators on the Canadian side of the border. Another time, he sang a concert over the phone for an audience first of English supporters, including several Members of Parliament, and then for 5,000 Welsh miners. The president of a mining union in Wales wrote Robeson after the recording that the transmission was a great success. All the people listening clung to every note, hoping that Robeson would soon be released from his immobility.

Robeson fought diligently to have his passport reinstated, which it finally was in 1958. He took an international trip to celebrate, but in many ways his long fight had broken his spirit and his mind. When he returned, he suffered from severe depression and went into isolation, living with his sister in Philadelphia for the rest of his life. He died on January 23, 1976.

Paul Robeson, Jr., protected the memory of his father for the many years that Americans showed little interest in the great singer and actor. After the fall of the Soviet Union, the fear of communism lessened in this country, and people began to reinvestigate Robeson's legacy. His son was there to tell the researchers many stories about his father. In 1995, he was finally admitted to the College Football Hall of Fame. After many books and retrospectives had been published, the Criterion Collection, which collects and distributes great films in the highest quality possible, and with significant text and film supplements, released the entire collection of Robeson's movies in 2008, as well as a documentary about his life. Robeson is again appreciated for being one of the finest American singers and actors of the twentieth century.

Lauren L. Kientz
Michigan State University

FURTHER READING

Balaji, Murali. *The Professor and the Pupil: The Politics of W. E. B. Du Bois and Paul Robeson.* New York: Nation Books, 2007.

The Criterion Collection, 2008. "Paul Robeson: Portraits of the Artist." http://www.criterion.com/boxsets/443.

Robeson, Paul. *Here I Stand.* London: D. Dobson, 1958.

Stewart, Jeffrey C., ed. *Paul Robeson: Artist and Citizen.* New Brunswick, NJ: Rutgers University Press and the Paul Robeson Cultural Center, 1998.

Bettmann/Corbis

Jackie Robinson
(1919–1972)

Jackie Robinson was one of baseball's greatest athletes—a deadly accurate hitter and an electrifying and unnerving base runner. But to the Brooklyn Dodgers, Robinson's character mattered as much as his batting average, for he was chosen by General Manager Branch Rickey to break the color barrier in America's national pastime. In the process, Robinson became a national icon and a true American hero, a political activist and a leading advocate for civil rights, whose legacy off the diamond is as enduring as his life on it.

Jack Roosevelt Robinson, the youngest of five children, was born January 31, 1919, on a plantation near Cairo, Georgia, near the Florida state border. His parents, Jerry Robinson and Mallie McGriff Washington, were separated by the time Robinson was born, and his mother was left to care for young Jackie and his four siblings while working on a sharecropping farm. Mallie was a religious woman and the daughter of relatively affluent parents, who were determined to see that she was educated through the sixth grade, no small feat for a Southern black woman in the early twentieth century.

At the time of Robinson's birth, Georgia was—statistically at least—the most virulently anti-black state in the Union, based on the number of lynchings that occurred each year. Mallie understood that Cairo was not a safe place to raise a family, so a year after Robinson's birth, she took her five children and moved to Pasadena, California, which at the time was the richest city, per capita, in the nation.

Despite the affluence of the city, or perhaps because of it, Jim Crow was pervasive throughout Pasadena and much of the rest of Southern California. Unemployment among blacks was very high, and poverty and hunger were prevalent in the minority population. When later asked about growing up in Pasadena, Robinson said, "Sometimes there were only two meals a day, and some days we wouldn't have eaten at all if it hadn't been for the leftovers my mother was able to bring home from her job . . . other times . . . we subsisted on bread and sweet water."

Race relations were tense in Pasadena, and only through Mallie Robinson's persistent efforts were the Robinsons accepted in their neighborhood. She turned her home into a safe haven where everyone was welcome and food was always provided when needed. In these early years in Pasadena, Mallie inculcated in her children a strong sense of family, an attitude of good will toward people generally, and a strong faith in God. Robinson's childhood was also shaped by the excellent local schools and, particularly, their sports programs. Despite many of Robinson's opponents and teachers being white, they respected Robinson for what he was capable of doing and accepted him as an equal. The experience of this type of acceptance and respect between the races on a personal level convinced Robinson that Jim Crow was an unnatural creature.

Robinson understood at an early age that his athletic abilities could open doors and break down walls. He liked the competition because he was aggressive and most importantly, he was good. Robinson knew that as long as he succeeded against any type of competition, white or not, he would gain the respect of his peers. Despite all his success on the field, Robinson experienced the usual growing pains and difficulties relating to adolescence. His grades began slumping and, outside of his close group of friends, he became reclusive and shy. He began to overcompensate for his lack of social skills with women and others by acting out and developing what many perceived as a "cocky" attitude.

As much as he was shaped by sports, Robinson was equally influenced by his family relationships. Having no father at home, and a mother who was forced to work much of the time, Robinson quickly attached himself to his older brothers, Frank and Mack. Frank always watched out for Robinson and encouraged him in his efforts both on and off the field, much as a surrogate father. Robinson truly admired Mack for his athletic ability. Mack won the silver medal in the 1936 Berlin Olympics, coming in second to Jesse Owens. The Robinsons were thrilled with the news, but Mack was not greeted as a hero at home. A newspaper of the time wrote, "In many places [Robinson and Mack] would be given the key to the city. Here we take them in stride, for granted. Never have they received their just due, from their own home citizens." Robinson was strongly affected by this lack of respect and due recognition, and would use it as motivation throughout his life.

As Robinson grew older and began to approach his high school graduation, he grew more and more frustrated with the policies of Jim Crow. He loved to swim, but blacks were denied access to pools in Pasadena; he also wanted to use the high-quality sports facilities at the local YMCA, but his requests for membership were repeatedly denied. Robinson took out his frustrations on the sports field, and in 1937 enrolled in Pasadena Junior College. Robinson chose Pasadena JC for a myriad of reasons: free tuition, a chance to display his sports skills on a bigger stage (with the hopes of attracting scholarship offers to larger universities), and a liberal campus climate that afforded black students unlimited access to all school facilities.

Robinson enrolled at the University of California, Los Angeles, on February 15, 1939. Shortly thereafter, his older brother Frank died in a motorcycle crash, an event that profoundly affected Robinson and redoubled his focus on sports. He excelled at everything he tried, and became the first player in UCLA history to letter in four different sports in the same year: basketball, track, baseball, and football. Robinson's time at UCLA was brief but it was where he met his future wife, Rachel Isum.

Also during this period, Robinson's eldest brother Edgar was beaten and robbed by two Pasadena police officers and subsequently denied treatment at a local hospital. Edgar later explained that the policemen were angered to see a black man at the Tournament of Roses Parade and when he refused to leave they charged him with resisting arrest. After beating Edgar, they robbed him of the $60 they found in his pockets, saying, "We don't allow Negroes in Los Angeles to make this kind of money."

Robinson and Edgar took the case to the local offices of the NAACP and convinced them to file an official complaint with the City of Pasadena. The complaint was simply ignored. This incident was one in a string of frustrating events that caused Robinson to hate Pasadena and to move on from college. After two years he decided to leave UCLA because he was convinced that no amount of education would help a black man get a job. Despite UCLA offering Robinson and Rachel extra support, he decided to leave.

Jackie Robinson became an athletic director for a short time for the National Youth Association, a New Deal governmental agency set up to provide jobs for young Americans from 18 to 25 years of age. After the Association folded following enactment of the Selective Training and Service Act of 1940, Robinson moved to Hawaii to play for a semi-professional football team. He had a mediocre season, however, and decided to return to Los Angeles on December 5, 1941, two days before the Japanese attack on Pearl Harbor. The signing of Executive Order 8802 (also known as the Fair Employment Act) in 1941, the first federal law to promote equal opportunity and end racial discrimination in the defense industry, enabled Robinson to secure a job with Lockheed Aircraft. Upon returning to California, Robinson proposed to Rachel Isum, his college sweetheart, and they were married shortly after.

On March 23, 1942, Robinson received his "Order to Report for Induction" to the U.S. military. As the war raged on, Robinson and his battalion continued their training and became a skilled fighting unit. They came to realize, however, that the military was not interested in rushing an all-black unit into combat. Robinson became increasingly discouraged as his role turned from fighting commander to morale booster or cheerleader. It was an uphill struggle, as Jim Crow persisted throughout his tenure in the Army.

In April 1944, Robinson had a falling out with Rachel over her decision to join the Nursing Corps. Robinson was jealous over her contact with other men and gave her the ultimatum to either quit the Nursing Corps or end their engagement. Rachel chose to end it, and by the next week Robinson had transferred to Camp Hood, Texas, to prepare for overseas military duty. His unit was the 761st Tank Battalion, and he was named a platoon leader. Robinson won over his troops with his candor and humility, and was respected throughout the camp.

Immediately prior to Robinson's journey overseas, however, he was involved in a racial dispute aboard a bus that was traveling from the military hospital to Camp Hood. The Army had outlawed segregation throughout the military, including on busses, so Robinson sat in the front. The white bus driver, a man named Milton N. Renegar, demanded that Robinson move to the back of the bus. Robinson refused, Renegar threatened Robinson, but Robinson steadfastly stayed put.

The Army met with Robinson and raised the possibility of a court martial for the incident, based on a charge of "insubordination." Robinson was given leave while the Army decided what to do. In the interim, he traveled to San Francisco and was able to rekindle his romance with Rachel. Soon after, he had to return and face his court-martial hearing. The *Pittsburg Courier* had been giving Robinson's case a lot of publicity, and Robinson was able to obtain a skilled defense attorney from Michigan. He was acquitted of all charges and given an honorable discharge from the Army in November 1944.

Robinson's time with the Army was disappointing for many reasons. He was an able commander and leader of men who could have successfully aided the U.S. war effort. The blindness of Jim Crow kept him and his battalion out of duty just because of their race. This frustration weighed heavily on Robinson. During his time in the military he met a man named Alexander who played for the Kansas City Monarchs of the Negro American League. Alexander told Robinson that it was a fun way to "make a buck" and invited him for a tryout during spring training. Robinson did not enjoy the experience, and later marveled at how that many players stuck it out for so long because the conditions were terrible—no hotels, no eating facilities. Notwithstanding these difficulties and challenges, Robinson believed that God, through baseball, was helping him reach a higher purpose. This is one reason that Robinson felt compelled to break the ban on blacks in baseball; he came to believe that it was his mission in life.

During the war, W. Branch Rickey, club president of the Brooklyn Dodgers, began scouting the Negro Leagues for "superior negro talent." Rickey had been fighting for civil rights ever since an incident occurred when he was the manager of the Ohio Wesleyan baseball team. The only black player on Rickey's team, Charles Thomas, was denied entrance to the hotel where the team was staying. Rickey protested, and the manager agreed to let the student stay in Rickey's room. Rickey returned to his room and found Thomas trying to pull his skin off. "That scene haunted me for many years . . . and I vowed that I would always do whatever I could to see that other Americans did not have to face the bitter humiliation that was heaped upon Charles Thomas."

Rickey sent his top three scouts out to independently scour the country for black ball players, and their consensus pick was Jackie Robinson, not only for his evident skills, but for the fact that he was known to oppose Jim Crow. Rickey called it his "noble experiment" and the player he wanted had to be thick skinned, able to take verbal abuse, play baseball, and still have a spirit. Rickey picked Jackie Robinson as that player.

Rickey invited Robinson to his office and offered him a contract. After Robinson accepted, Rickey assaulted his new hire with virulent racial epithets to test his resolve. Robinson remained calm, and listened as Rickey told him that he must always adhere to a philosophy of nonviolent or passive resistance. Rickey read Robinson a passage from the Bible and, unwittingly, referenced the same peaceful teachings that so influenced **Martin Luther King, Jr.**—those of Mohandas K. Gandhi. "I had to do it for several reasons," Robinson later recalled, "For black youth, for my mother, for Rachel, for myself. I had already begun to feel I had to do it for Branch Rickey."

On October 23, 1945, Jackie Robinson became the first black American to sign a contract with the Major League Baseball Association and the effects were immediate. The President of the New York Baseball Giants, Horace Stoneham, made a public statement promising to scout black players the following season and issued strong verbal support for Rickey's move. The best and most famous black ball player of the day, Satchel Page, who was passed over for the man to end Jim Crow, responded by saying, "They didn't make a mistake by signing Robinson. They couldn't have picked a better man."

The **Negro Baseball League**, after some initial resistance, also bowed to popular opinion and supported Robinson's signing. "I feel that I speak the sentiments of 15 million Negroes in America who are with you 100 percent, and will always remember the day and date of this great event," stated J. B. Martin, president of the Negro American League. The following spring, preceding Robinson's first foray into the big leagues, he and Rachel were wed on February 10, 1946. Rachel later described the feelings she felt at the time: "It suddenly felt so right to be there, with Robinson in that room, knowing we would now be together all the time, forever and ever. Really, when the door closed, I felt that all my troubles had melted away, and that a wonderful new life was beginning for Robinson and for me."

Throughout the entire signing process, Robinson heard the same word used over and over to describe what he would need to succeed: guts. Did he have the "guts" to fight against Jim Crow, to fight for integration and against racism and to meet the challenges of playing at the highest level of baseball? Robinson knew he did and proved it during his first season playing for the Montreal Royals, the Dodgers minor league affiliate. During his first year in the minors, Robinson led the league in batting average, and his team won the minor league World Series against a rigidly segregated Louisville team. This victory was important because it demonstrated that allowing black Americans the right to play led to victory and to profit: the Montreal Royals had their highest attendance in history with more than 800,000 people attending games during the 1946 season.

Throughout the season Robinson encountered much adversity: Jim Crow establishments, racism from the stands, and hate mail. At the same time, however, there were also signs of encouragement for Robinson: "black fans were beginning to turn out in unprecedented numbers, despite extremely adverse conditions . . . Their presence, their cheers, their pride, all came through to me and I knew they were counting on me to make it. It put a heavy burden of responsibility on me, but it was a glorious challenge." Robinson's experience in Baltimore during the season was emblematic. Early on, Baltimore had been one of the worst cities for Robinson to play in, due to the repeated and vicious racial slurs being tossed at him from the stands and from the other players. When the Royals returned to Baltimore at the end of the season, Robinson was met with a standing ovation.

Following the minor league World Series championship game, the fans in Montreal waited for Robinson so that they could congratulate him. "They grabbed me, they slapped my back. They hugged me. Women kissed me. Kids grinned and crowded around me. Men took me . . . on their shoulders and went around the field, singing and shouting." Sam Martin, a local sportswriter would later quip, "It was probably the only day in history that a black man ran from a white mob with love instead of lynching on its mind."

Following the 1946 season, Robinson prepared himself for his promotion to the Major League Brooklyn Dodgers. On November 18, 1946, Jackie Robinson, Jr. became the first child of Jack and Rachel Robinson. This event brought the young married couple even closer, an important milestone after such a grueling season where the couple leaned on each other heavily for support and encouragement.

Spring training with the Dodgers was tumultuous. Robinson and management were second-guessed by Dodger teammates, by sportswriters, and by fans. Rickey had to quell some player dissent by informing disgruntled players they were welcome to find employment elsewhere. Notwithstanding the tumult, Robinson formally joined the Dodgers as their opening day first baseman on April 10, 1947. The *Boston Chronicle* headline spoke volumes on what this meant to black Americans when it trumpeted, "Triumph of Whole Race Seen in Robinson's Debut in Major League Ball."

Robinson's rookie season was a roller coaster. Throughout the season he faced such torrents of venomous racism that he nearly gave up on numerous occasions. He faced discrimination in nearly every city he visited; he was barred from restaurants and hotels; death threats were commonplace; and he faced opposing teams who threatened to organize strikes or boycotts merely to avoid stepping onto the same playing field.

Fortunately, his family and teammates had become his twin anchors. His wife Rachel had always been his rock, but Robinson found an unexpected ally in his teammates, who increasingly spoke out in his defense for "one who could not defend himself." Robinson also had an enormous amount of support from fan letters, and the Dodgers experienced a tremendous surge in home attendance. The result is that despite the assault of negativity and harassment, Robinson never broke and he never gave in.

Robinson knew he was acting not only for himself, but for his entire race. Others knew this as well. Roger Wilkins, who was 15 when Robinson broke into the majors, and who later would head up the NAACP, wrote that Robinson was as important to him and other blacks as a parent would have been. Wilkins said that he instilled pride in everyone, he was honest, spiritual, and knew that if he failed, blacks failed. The 1947 season culminated in a loss to the Yankees in the World Series, but for Jackie Robinson, the year on the field was a success. He played in 151 games, hit .297, led the National League in stolen bases, and won the Rookie of the Year Award. He had solidified himself as a starter for the Dodgers and went on a speaking tour across the South, which was wildly successful and Robinson's first foray into the public arena of civil rights. During the 1948 season, Robinson was moved from first to second base, where he spent most of his career. He ended the season hitting .298 with 12 home runs and 85 runs batted in.

In 1949, Jackie Robinson got what he wanted from Rickey—free reign to stick up for himself. Rickey issued his "Emancipation Proclamation" for Robinson and told him that he was free to be himself for the first time in his professional career. Enough black Americans had become involved in Major League Baseball that Robinson was under less scrutiny. Robinson later said the year 1949 defined his life and who he was as a person. Robinson said 1949 taught him that even after proving himself, a black man will still be denied his rights and that despite this, young blacks were not willing to tolerate this any longer.

It was during this period, when he was allowed to speak his mind, that Robinson's thoughts on race relations in the United States began to crystallize. While always an advocate of nonviolent or passive resistance, Robinson never allowed himself to be rigid in his thinking. For example, commenting on **Malcolm X**'s statements regarding the "progress" of black Americans, Robinson said, "I disagreed with Malcolm vigorously in many areas during his earlier days, but I certainly agreed with him when he said, 'Don't tell me about progress the black man has made. You don't stick a knife 10 inches in my back, pull it out three or four times, then tell me I'm making progress.' "

Robinson argued that anytime a black man would stand up and protest his current situation, he would be patronizingly answered with ". . . but you've come a long way." He noted that Americans failed to recognize the unjust head start that whites were given, a situation that seemed to permanently handicap black Americans' efforts to achieve equality, and he encouraged black people to never become complacent. In his arguments, Robinson inadvertently echoed Marx's critique of capitalism by illustrating how whites helped maintain the status quo by pointing to a handful of blacks, such as Robinson, who had "made it." "I want to be an inspiration to our young, but I don't want them lied to . . . For each example of a black who has 'made it' . . . I can give you a sordid piece of factual information on how they have been mistreated, humiliated."

In July 1949, Robinson testified in front of the House Un-American Activities Committee. The Committee was attempting to build a case against the famous singer, **Paul Robeson**, who was accused of association with the Communist Party. Robinson felt that black Americans were fighting a war at home against racism and a war against foreign enemies, and that blacks must not give up. "As my friend the Reverend Jesse Jackson says, 'It ain't our government, but it's our country.' " Robinson, despite some letters of protest, gave his speech to the Committee, and told them that while he was not an expert in the field of communism, he was an expert when it came to his race. He noted that, while some progress had been made, there was still a long way to go. He emphasized that the government could not simply write off black Americans as communist agitators and that one man does not speak for the entire race.

The press wrong-headedly praised Robinson for "handing it" to the communist Robeson. Robinson felt he did not do that; that he merely spoke his mind about the truth as he saw it, which was helping clarify that one man's opinion was not indicative of the entire race. He felt he was a religious man and so he cherished the freedoms the United States gave, and that the United States would probably never be finished fighting race discrimination. Jackie Robinson was always proud of the words he spoke in front of the Congressional Committee because it was a chance most people never get—especially black Americans—to speak up to some of the most powerful men in the country. This was a tipping point for Robinson because he thereafter became more and more focused on championing civil rights.

From 1949 through 1954, Jackie Robinson was on top of his game at all levels. He won an MVP award and three pennants. In 1950, a movie, *The Jackie Robinson Story*, was made about his life, with Robinson playing himself. His family expanded as two more children, Sharon and David, entered the fray. The racism expressed toward Robinson, although ever present, began to fade somewhat. Robinson had become liberated once he was able to stand up for what he believed, and baseball had flourished because of him. Many players gave their thanks for helping to empower black people throughout the nation. Jackie Robinson fought segregation in baseball because he did not believe in separatism. However, Robinson believed in blacks having a unique identity, and said, "I believe there is a valid necessity for blacks to stand apart and develop themselves independently, however. We must have a sense of our own identity and we must develop an economic unity so we can build an independent power base from which to deal with whites on a more equal basis." Later in his life, Robinson would help fund the "Freedom Bank Venture," a bank that gave much-needed loans to black families. In 1955, Robinson won his only championship ring, when the Dodgers beat the New York Yankees in the 1955 World Series. After the 1956 season, Robinson was traded by the Dodgers to the New York Giants. Rather than accept the trade, he chose to retire at the age of 37.

Robinson retired on January 5, 1957. He then joined the Chock Full 'O Nuts Corporation as an executive of the company. His new position of corporate power attracted the attention of Roy Wilkins of the NAACP, who invited Robinson to become the national chairman of the Freedom Fund Drive, a project to help raise money for the NAACP's many activities. Along with Franklin Williams, Robinson's charisma helped raise millions of dollars for the NAACP until his retirement in 1967. Robinson later regretted his retirement and said that his reasons were due to growing doubts about the NAACP's leadership and his concern that they were no longer in touch with many of the current problems afflicting many black Americans.

In 1960, Robinson threw his popularity and fame behind Richard Nixon in the presidential election against John F. Kennedy. He did so reluctantly, saying at the time that he felt it was "a last-ditch battle to keep the Republicans from becoming completely white." Robinson realized his mistake when Nixon failed to act after Martin Luther King, Jr. was jailed during a civil rights protest. Kennedy quickly reached out to the King family with his support, and King responded by backing Kennedy's presidential candidacy.

In 1962, Robinson received two very special awards: The first was his induction into the Major League Baseball Hall of Fame, in his first year of eligibility. He was the first black man to be inducted. Shortly thereafter, Dr. Martin Luther King's Southern Christian Leadership Conference (SCLC) created a unique Hall of Fame award to recognize and congratulate Robinson on the hard work he had done for civil rights and for the SCLC. The rest of Robinson's life was devoted to politics and civil rights. From 1962 to 1964, Robinson helped convince New York Governor Nelson Rockefeller to issue a series of sweeping reforms that established blacks in many of the state's highest governmental positions, which brought millions of dollars to impoverished minorities through needed social service reforms and programs. In these efforts, Robinson took a lesson from Malcolm X's demand, "[I] want not only the cup of coffee but also the cup and saucer, the counter, the store, and the land on which the restaurant stands." Robinson said, "I believed blacks ought to become producers, manufacturers, developers, and creators of businesses, providers of jobs."

Nelson Rockefeller agreed with Robinson, and invited him to become one of the six deputy national directors of his campaign to run for President against Senator Barry Goldwater. "I was not as sold on the Republican Party as I was on the governor. Every chance I got, while I was campaigning, I said plainly what I thought of the right-wing Republicans and the harm they were doing . . . I admit freely that I think, live, and breath black first and foremost. That is one of the reasons I was so committed to the governor and so opposed to Senator Barry Goldwater."

Following Rockefeller's defeat in the GOP primary, Robinson and Rockefeller both turned their energies to the "Republicans for Johnson" campaign, and took satisfaction in seeing Lyndon B. Johnson emerge victorious as President of the United States. Johnson would later help usher in an era of sweeping reforms that came to be known as the "Great Society." Robinson's activities during the civil rights era were heavily influenced by Martin Luther King. Robinson drew heavily upon King's teachings, and used them as a source of strength and companionship. King and Robinson worked together in many fund raising and speaking opportunities throughout the 1960s.

Robinson also had contact with Malcolm X, although theirs was a more confrontational relationship. Robinson and Malcolm X disagreed vehemently about the way the Civil Rights Movement should proceed, but they respected each other's views. The two shared a well publicized "duel of words" in Robinson's nationally syndicated newspaper column. Robinson was deeply saddened by the assassinations of King and Malcolm X, and realized that his time in politics was drawing to a close.

During Robinson's remaining years, he continued to publish articles and write letters to politicians urging them to continue to fight for his people. His last few campaigns were to establish the first "black bank," the Freedom Bank, an enormous venture that helped blacks across the nation. The stress of this effort took a great toll on Robinson's health, and he subsequently was diagnosed with diabetes. In his waning years he campaigned for baseball to hire its first black manager, a position he believed should have been filled years earlier. Shortly after Robinson's death, Frank Robinson would be the first black manager in Major League Baseball, appointed by the Cleveland Indians in 1974.

Jackie Robinson died on October 24, 1972, in Stamford, Connecticut. Along with **Joe Louis** and **Muhammad Ali**, Robinson was one of three pioneer black Americans who used the "religion" of sports to pry open the door of racial segregation and advance the cause of civil rights and of all black people. But Robinson's life and career were special—while Louis and Ali competed *against* white men, Robinson competed *with* them. And this sense of shared and common struggle of white and black players together, an integration of effort on the field against a common foe, touched all Americans and made Robinson's life and legacy off the diamond particularly profound and consequential. Despite all the adversity, pain and struggle that Jackie Robinson faced throughout his life, from persistent racism to the death of his son in an automobile accident, he remained hopeful. He knew that black Americans had come a long way, but that they had a long way to go, and any and all progress would require continual struggle and effort. Basically, however, Robinson loved his country and believed that progress could be made as long as people continued to work together and strive for a better future. Robinson had a profound impact on shaping America through civil rights and through the national game of baseball, and will always be remembered as a national hero.

Adam P. Boyd
University of California, Los Angeles

FURTHER READING

Rampersad, Arnold. *Jackie Robinson: A Biography*. New York: Ballantine Books, 1998.

Robinson, Jacki, and Alfred Duckett. *I Never Had It Made: An Autobiography of Jackie Robinson*. New York: Harper Perennial, 2003.

Bayard Rustin
(1912–1987)

Bayard Taylor Rustin was one of the first Americans to introduce Gandhian nonviolent resistance to the Civil Rights Movement. Many of the choices he made early in his life led some civil rights leaders to reject his role in the movement. He was a Quaker and a pacifist who went to jail in the 1940s for objecting to World War II. After briefly flirting with the Communist Party in the 1930s, he rejected the Party's choices without rejecting his communist friends. And he was an out-of-the-closet homosexual who was at one time jailed for having gay sex. When civil rights leaders accepted Rustin despite the harm he could do to their reputation, like **A. Philip Randolph** did while planning the 1964 March on Washington, Rustin excelled. **Martin Luther King, Jr.** could never have given his "I Have a Dream" speech without Rustin's careful administration.

Rustin's grandmother, Julia Davis Rustin, grew up in a family of black Quakers. Her parents had been purchased and set free by a Virginia Quaker family (Quakers were often abolitionists). With their freedom, they moved north and settled in a Quaker area of Pennsylvania, in the town of West Chester. Most African Americans did not become or remain Quakers, because despite their excellent abolitionist record, Quakers segregated their worship meetings. The Davises, however, did stay in the church and raised their children in their beliefs, including a strong belief in pacifism. Julia left the church when she met her husband, Janifer Rustin, but never left their teachings.

Janifer was a caterer, and would often bring leftovers home. It was at those feasts that the younger Rustin learned what good food tasted like. In his later life, he became a gourmet in preference, though he never let it stand in the way of enjoying meals with all types of people.

Janifer and Julia had seven children. The oldest, Florence, became pregnant at 17, and was abandoned by her father. At first, Julia was so upset that she wanted nothing to do with her daughter or her grandson. But after watching the child sleep one day, she decided that her daughter was too immature to raise the boy, so she and Janifer adopted him as their own.

That boy, born March 17, 1912, was Bayard Taylor Rustin. He was named after a famous nineteenth-century Quaker, Bayard Taylor. He did not find out that Julia and Janifer were in fact his grandparents—not his parents, and Florence his mother—until he was 11. Rustin was steeped in the traditions of both the Quakers and the AME church. Julia supported, even indulged, Rustin in whatever he wanted to do. His aunts (who were more like siblings) thought he would be a minister because of how voluminously and eloquently he spoke, even as a small child. He even preached sometimes in their AME church as a teenager.

In elementary school, Rustin had a favorite teacher who focused on clear diction and precise language. From her, Rustin adopted a British accent that he perfected throughout his childhood. For the rest of his life, he spoke with a British accent that surprised those he met. As a young man, he would often correct the language of his friends, so intent was he upon speaking properly.

The teenaged Rustin realized that he was attracted to boys, not girls. When he discussed this with his grandmother, she asked if that was really the case, and he said yes. She said, "Well, I guess that's the way it will be then." Rustin, then, was never really in the closet, nor did he have a traumatic coming out story like others he knew. However, the society in general was not so accepting. Gay sex was illegal, and charges of homosexuality were often enough to ruin a career and a reputation.

Rustin graduated from high school with honors. He had been an outstanding member of the choir and the drama club. The entire local black community was excited for him, because it was rare for black students to graduate from high school. There were so few jobs for blacks greater than menial labor, that most students felt it made more sense to begin their labors rather than complete school. Rustin, however, was determined to finish. Most of the students who graduated with honors received scholarships to college, but not Rustin. Julia was furious and demanded that the school officials give him a scholarship, but they would not. She then began asking around, and the minister of an AME church in Philadelphia, Dr. R. R. Wright, Jr., gave Rustin a scholarship to Wilberforce University in Ohio, an AME sponsored school. He left home not sure yet whether he wanted to be a singer, a teacher, or a social activist.

Rustin only spent three semesters at Wilberforce, from 1932 to 1933, majoring in music. While he was there, he was the lead soloist and first tenor in a quartet that traveled around the country raising money for the school. During the touring, he came to love and appreciate black spirituals. He had dismissed them before, influenced by a high school teacher who discounted their worth.

He was kicked out of Wilberforce after one year, either because he had fallen in love with the son of the college president or because he had staged several protests over the condition of the food at the school. After Wilberforce, Rustin returned home to his grandparents and attended a local teachers college. He only lasted a semester there before he was kicked out for doing something "bad" (as he later admitted, without explaining).

He worked near his home until he was 25, when he took a peace training seminar. The Quakers sent him to Auburn, New York, to preach pacifism for a summer. He was by this time committed to Gandhi's ideas about nonviolent resistance, and taught them to the others with him. He was also firmly against war in all its forms, including the Spanish Civil War then being fought between fascists and republicans. Those traveling with him realized that nonviolence and pacifism were not just political tactics for Rustin, but enveloped his entire way of life.

On the way home that summer, he stopped in New York City with some of the other pacifists who lived there. He fell in love with the city and, after working with communists in Philadelphia, moved there. He lived in New York City for the rest of his life, between frequent travels and speaking tours. Rustin attended his third college in New York, this time at the behest of the communists. He took just enough classes at the City College of New York (CCNY) to make him look like a student. In reality, though, he was the leader of the Young Communists, and tried to organize students on campus. He had finally committed himself wholly to being an activist.

Rustin worked with the communists until he felt they betrayed African Americans and his belief in pacifism. The communists were one of the few groups of whites who made African American's rights a priority. This attracted a lot of black intellectuals and writers to them during the thirties, including Richard Wright and Ralph Ellison. At the beginning of World War II, the communists campaigned against the war, in part because Josef Stalin and Adolph Hitler had made a non-aggression pact. But when Hitler attacked the Soviet Union in 1941, the American Communists immediately changed their plans. They began to campaign for the war, encouraging everyone to join up. They also told Rustin to stop agitating for the end of discrimination in the military because he was causing dissension when everyone should be focused on winning the war.

Rustin dropped his allegiance to the Communist Party and worked for A. Philip Randolph briefly. Randolph was the leader of a major black union, the Brotherhood of Sleeping Car Porters, and an influential national voice. Randolph was planning a March on Washington for the summer of 1941 to force President Franklin Roosevelt to stop discrimination in the military. Rustin was eager to continue his campaign and was excited by the idea of a crowd of black people descending on Washington, nonviolently demanding their rights. He was disappointed when Randolph accepted Roosevelt's offer to end discrimination in factories producing military supplies. This ended Randolph's and Rustin's relationship for a time, though they later became close.

After leaving Randolph, Rustin became a peace activist full time. He joined the Fellowship of Reconciliation (FOR), led by A. J. Muste. FOR advocated absolute pacifism and total nonviolence. Like Rustin, they were deeply influenced by Gandhi and by Christ's statement that we should "turn the other cheek" when hit. Rustin became a member of the national staff and was put in charge of the youth campaign. He became so close to Muste that others in the office called them "Muste and Rusty." They often espoused the same opinions without even consulting each other. Muste taught Rustin even more about nonviolent resistance, lessons he later took to Martin Luther King, Jr.

During his first year with the Fellowship, he traveled more than 10,000 miles encouraging people to choose pacifism and setting up member organizations. He was a brilliant speaker who captivated his audiences by singing and through his vibrant words. He loved to tell dramatic stories to such an extent that his friends and coworkers often wondered whether he was telling the truth. If someone pointed out a flaw in his story, he would flash them a smile and admit his exaggeration.

During all of his tours for the Fellowship, Rustin practiced civil disobedience. He never accommodated segregation practices when he traveled. Instead, he would calmly and quietly ask "why," always keeping his dignity intact. When a waitress in Indiana told him that they did not serve black people, he asked "why." She told him it was because they would scare off white customers. So he suggested that he sit in the front window for 10 minutes with a hamburger in front of him and if he scared away any white customers, he would leave. During the 10 minutes, several white customers entered, oblivious to Rustin's presence. The waitress then served him a fresh hamburger. Other incidents did not end so peacefully, and he was often beaten and jailed.

At the beginning of World War II, Rustin had signed up for conscientious objector status based upon his affiliation with the Quakers, a historically pacifist denomination. At that time, conscientious objector status was only available to religious people. When, in 1944, Rustin was called up by the military to join a Civilian Public Service Camp—the service available to conscientious objectors—Rustin refused to join. On the one hand, he felt like that was still aiding the war effort. On the other, he did not agree that conscientious objector status should be only available to religious people. For his refusal, he was sent to jail in Kentucky for more than two years. He used his time in jail to continue his protests, especially against the segregated facilities and dining areas. He also taught classes in prison; it was a success in that the white Kentuckians learned from a black teacher.

After he got out of jail, Rustin joined the Journey of Reconciliation in 1947. The Supreme Court had recently declared segregation on interstate transportation illegal, but most of the South did not head the declaration. FOR sponsored James Farmer's new organization, the Congress of Racial Equality (CORE), and CORE decided to take an interracial group on a bus ride through the South. The National Association for the Advancement of Colored People (NAACP) promised legal protection for the riders. The bus riders divided up into small groups that would sit with whites in the back and blacks in the front on each bus. Throughout the journey they were thrown off the bus, attacked, and jailed.

Rustin ended up with one jail sentence that he could not shake because the black lawyer had "lost" the ticket stubs that proved his journey was across state lines. He had to serve 22 days on a chain gang. Later, he documented the range of abuses on that chain gang, including prisoners hung by their wrists on the bars of jail cells with their feet dangling. Rustin's exposé, "Twenty-Two Days on a Chain Gang" was published in the *New York Post* and caused prison reform.

After the conclusion of the Journey of Reconciliation, which did not have many immediate affects, and before his time on the chain gang, Rustin visited London and India. He thoroughly enjoyed his brief time in London when he was frequently in demand as a speaker, and returned there many times during his life. He wanted to go to India to meet with Gandhi, but the great man was assassinated only days before Rustin set sail in January 1949. Rustin met with Gandhi's son and with other Gandhi followers in the country. They wanted him to stay and try to talk sense into the nationalists who wanted to devote

50 percent of the Indian budget to defense, even while espousing Gandhi's way of life. Muste, though, said that no matter where Rustin went, he would always be in great demand and at that moment, the United States and FOR needed him more.

A few years later, the same thing happened when Rustin visited Africa. This time, though, Rustin decided to raise money to stay in Africa for a while to help defeat colonialism. During his fund-raising tour of the states in 1953, Rustin was caught having sex with two men in California. He was jailed for the act. He was no stranger to a jail cell, but this was the first time it was for something he did, rather than a protest he made. More heart rending, Muste immediately called for his resignation from FOR because of the way Rustin's actions would damage the religious organization's reputation. Muste suggested that Rustin go into therapy to be "cured" of homosexuality (it was still standard at that time for the psychological community to believe that homosexuality could be cured). Rustin, who had always felt and acted like Muste's son, went into a deep depression.

After emerging from the depression, Rustin joined the national board of the War Resister's League as executive secretary. The WRL was a secular pacifist organization, which had long wanted to lure him away from FOR. He worked for the WRL for 12 years, in part continuing his civil rights work and in part fighting nuclear proliferation.

In 1955, the black community of Montgomery, Alabama came together to protest segregated bus lines. Blacks overwhelmingly used the buses to get to work and travel around town, but were routinely treated badly and thrown off the bus to make room for whites. The civil rights leadership in town decided to start a bus boycott after Rosa Parks was jailed for refusing to give up her seat for a white man. Parks was following the rules of civil disobedience that Rustin also advocated. However, the leadership—including the inspiring young pastor who rallied the boycotters each night, Dr. Martin Luther King, Jr.—did not fully understand nonviolent resistance. King had read some things by Gandhi, but had never seen them acted upon.

Up in New York, Rustin and his friends heard about the bus boycott. The WRL decided to send Rustin south to advise King. The first day that King, 26, and Rustin, 44, met, Rustin explained all the possible ways that he could tarnish King's reputation—from his anti-war stance to his connections to the communists to his homosexuality. King replied that he needed all the help he could get. So Rustin spent the next few months helping Montgomery African Americans plan the boycott and teaching them the parameters of nonviolent resistance. For instance, he suggested that King get rid of the gun he kept in his house after it had been bombed. If King's followers knew he had a gun, and were attacked, then they would attack back. But if he had no gun, they would stand solid and nonviolent, keeping the moral high ground.

After more than a year walking many miles and car pooling, the black people of Montgomery prevailed. The bus company desegregated its buses.

For a few years, Rustin became one of King's closest aids. The older man had a depth of experience and breadth of creativity than King valued. Ministers across the South joined together into the Southern Christian Leadership Conference (SCLC) and invited Rustin to lead them. Together, they planned more protests and nonviolent demonstrations. The Civil Rights Movement was in full swing.

In 1959, Randolph and King began planning protests for the Republican and Democratic conferences, and again turned to Rustin to oversee the details. Adam Clayton Powell, Democratic Representative from Harlem, feared what a protest at the Democratic convention would do to his place in Congressional Leadership. He was then trying to be nominated to an important committee in the House. He also feared that such a demonstration would damage John F. Kennedy's campaign. Powell threatened King that if he did not cancel the protest, he would leak a rumor that King and Rustin were involved in an affair. King was definitely not homosexual; his extra marital affairs were all with women. Nevertheless, such a rumor could harm his reputation. Randolph urged King to go on with the protest, but sacrificed Rustin to the rumor.

Rustin returned to his work with the War Resisters League, traveling extensively and campaigning for human rights and nuclear nonproliferation. He traveled often to Africa. But the American Civil Rights Movement did not benefit from his sagacity or creativity for the next three years. In the winter of 1962, Randolph proposed another March on Washington (for Jobs and Freedom), this one to mark the centenary of Lincoln's Emancipation Proclamation and to urge Kennedy and Congress to pass the Civil Rights Act. The first person he turned to with the idea was Rustin, whom he asked to write up a blueprint for the march. Randolph then took the blueprint to all the different civil rights organizations. He wanted the march to have as wide a coalition of support as possible, bringing together direct action people from CORE and Student Nonviolent Coordinating Commission (SNCC) and the older, more cautious people from the NAACP and the Urban League.

The latter only agreed to participate if Randolph called off any plans for civil disobedience. Randolph knew he needed the support of these large organizations, so he agreed. The students were frustrated by this turn. Part of Randolph's agreement included nominating Rustin to plan the march. With much debate, Rustin was finally nominated to the position.

After all the arguments had subsided, Rustin had only seven weeks to plan for 100,000 people to march from the Capitol down the National Mall to the Lincoln memorial. He knew that if any disruptions occurred, they would be blown up by the press and by opponents, obscuring any positive message from the march. So he decided to take care of any and all needs that the marchers might have. He first publicized the march far and wide, then sent those interested information about chartering buses and planes. Everyone had to arrive in the morning of August 28 to begin marching by 10:00 a.m., and begin leaving the city by 5:30 so that they would be gone by nightfall.

Rustin also arranged for enough mobile toilets and large water tankers for drinking water. He urged marchers to bring a box lunch with nonperishable foods, like peanut butter sandwiches and apples, but also arranged to sell 50,000 ham and cheese sandwiches, hamburgers, and hot dogs. He arranged for 2,000 police officers to patrol the crowd and asked a respected black New York policeman to train civilian marshals. Some people teased Rustin that this was the most comfortable protest march they had ever heard of.

During his preparation, Senator Strom Thurmond and others called Rustin all the names that the NAACP officials (particularly executive secretary Roy Wilkins) had feared. This time, however, Randolph, Wilkins, and others stood up for Rustin. The rumors soon died out. The morning of August 28 dawned hot, sticky, and still. Most of the white residents of DC had fled the city, fearing a riot. Kennedy had national troops marshaled across the river, waiting for trouble. At first only a handful of marchers showed up. Rustin tried not to appear worried and when asked about the low attendance by a journalist, said it was all part of the plan. Coretta Scott King could see from her hotel room window the long stream of cars and busses. By 10 in the morning, the 100,000 they had hoped for had long since been surpassed. The official estimate by the police was 250,000. Some of the platform speakers thought it was more like 400,000. A quarter of that number was white.

After all those gathered marched to the Lincoln memorial, there were hours of speeches. Everyone got to have a turn at the microphone. Well, not quite everyone. There were almost no black women represented among the leadership, not even **Ella Baker**, who had founded and guided SNCC. Some of the more radical speakers were asked to tone down their speeches. SNCC's John Lewis obliged and removed some of his more militant rhetoric, though his speech was still the most hard-hitting of the day. Author **James Baldwin** refused to give the speech prepared for him, so actor Burt Lancaster delivered it instead.

Rustin planned for Martin Luther King, Jr. to speak last. He did not want the marchers to disperse early and knew that the promise of King speaking to them would keep them under the hot sun. Several speakers had petitioned Rustin not to put them after King, knowing as soon as he spoke, the march would be over. Indeed, there could have been no better conclusion than King's famous "I Have a Dream" speech.

After King was done, the marchers began to quietly disperse. There had been no disruptions. There was none of the violence that so many whites had feared. Rustin saw Randolph standing at the corner of the stage and went up to him. The 74-year-old man was quietly weeping. After so many years, he had finally seen his dream come true.

A week later, Rustin and Randolph appeared together on the front cover of *Life* magazine. Without Randolph's vision and Rustin's careful planning, King's speech would never have been possible. Less than a month later, the march was overshadowed by the church bombing in Birmingham that killed four girls. The nonviolent impulse that had held marchers and activists together began to weaken.

Rustin continued to advise King for the next few years. He adopted a new kind of political strategy—coalition building. Rustin no longer advocated absolute pacifism, because he believed that it was the moral stance of an individual, not a politically realistic solution. After the passage of the civil rights and voting rights bills in 1964 and 1965, respectably, Rustin turned his attention away from race problems to economic ones. And economic problems, he believed, needed coalitions for their solutions. Congress would not support a plan meant for the economic well being of only 10 percent of the population, but might pass something that also had the support of the liberals and the unions.

Rustin had always had many admirers among the younger activists. They admired his long record of civil disobedience. This new adherence to coalition building, however, put them off. A final rift occurred at the 1964 Democratic convention. A group from Mississippi called the Mississippi Freedom Democratic Party (MFDP) came to the convention. They declared themselves the true representatives of Mississippi because the Democrats did not allow blacks to vote in the primaries. SNCC had spent the previous summer registering voters throughout the South. One woman particularly influenced by the campaign was **Fannie Lou Hamer**, a Mississippi sharecropper. She and the rest of the MFDP demanded that they be seated instead of the Mississippi delegation. Lyndon B. Johnson was then campaigning for re-election. He organized a compromise where two of the MFDP's representatives would be seated with the white Democrats. Rustin urged the MFDP to accept the compromise, believing it was as good as they would get. The MFDP did not want to compromise with the white Democrats, however; they wanted to replace them. SNCC and all the students aligned with them rejected Rustin.

The relationship continued to deteriorate as many African Americans turned to Black Power instead of nonviolent resistance. Rustin rejected Black Power because he wanted an interracial working class alliance to fight for the end of poverty. He also criticized Black Studies programs, one of the greatest successes of the Black Power movement, because he did not think they could address the problem of jobs or poverty.

After the March on Washington, several civil rights leaders set up the A. Philip Randolph Institute with Rustin at its head, so that Rustin would finally have an official leadership role in the movement. The organization encouraged a school boycott in New York City to support the teacher's union (which was primarily white). Rustin's support for their strike undermined his hope for black and white worker alliances. Throughout the strike, white protesters and black counter protesters clashed. Rustin also worked to re-establish Black-Jewish alliances and fought Anti-Semitism. With each choice, criticism from other black leaders fell upon his head.

Regardless of the vehement criticism flying his way, Rustin did not ever give up protesting. After the Civil Rights Movement, he moved many of his struggles to Africa and the Caribbean. In 1977, he met Walter Naegle, who became his romantic companion for the rest of his life. Naegle, his only long-term boyfriend, encouraged Rustin to fight for gay rights during the 1980s. Only days before he died on August 24, 1987, of a ruptured appendix, he and Naegle had visited Haiti to support the election process. Bayard Rustin acted on his convictions throughout his life, even when he earned the rancor of all around him. When his ideas were popular, he led. When his ideas were unpopular, he served.

Lauren L. Kientz
Michigan State University

FURTHER READING

Anderson, Jervis. *Bayard Rustin: Troubles I've Seen: A Biography*. New York: HarperCollins, 1997.

Podair, Jerald E. *Bayard Rustin: American Dreamer*. Lanham, MD: Rowman & Littlefield Pub, 2009.

Rustin, Bayard. *Time on Two Crosses: The Collected Writings of Bayard Rustin*. San Francisco: Cleis Press, 2003.

Dred Scott
(1795/1805–1858)

Born into slavery, and freed only months before his death, Dred Scott is known for his petition to sue for his freedom and the freedom of his family. Eventually, Scott's lawsuit resulted in the U.S. Supreme Court ruling that black persons were not citizens, and that the Missouri Compromise was unconstitutional because the U.S. Congress could not prohibit slavery in American territories. Scott was not the only individual to sue for freedom in the decades before the Civil War. In fact, many successful cases predated Scott's petition. Scott's significance lies, however, in the Supreme Court's rulings for the *Scott v. Sandford* case, as well as in the public and political reactions to those decisions. Scott's fight for freedom correlated with the country's increased sectionalism, heated emotions over slavery, and, in some ways, the political rise of the Republican Party and Abraham Lincoln, ultimately bringing the country closer to a civil war. Timing and political influences, therefore, made and continue to hold Dred Scott as a historical icon. He became someone who not only represented the increased tensions that slavery had inflicted upon the nation, but also the individuals and communities who desired freedom.

Unfortunately, other than the mark of the letter "X" that Scott made on his petition for freedom, he did not leave behind—in his own words—records of his life. Moreover, what we do know about his life, family, and personal characteristics stems from information found in court files surrounding the *Dred Scott v. Sandford* case. Regardless of this fact, the life of Scott, an enslaved husband and father who lived in multiple locations, states and territories, is the only reason the famous court case ever existed.

Although the exact date of Scott's birth remains a speculation, ownership records suggest that Scott was born sometime between 1795 and 1805, most likely in the state of Virginia, and enslaved to the Peter Blow family. In 1818, the first movement in a series of life travels for Scott occurred with the Blow family's relocation to Alabama to become cotton growers. The fact that Scott moved to and from areas as dictated by his owners was common for enslaved individuals, but where he specifically went became a key factor in his argument for freedom. Some research suggests that Scott was married while under Blow family ownership, although his wife's name and reasons to why the marriage ended remains unknown. In 1830, Scott moved west with the Blow family to St. Louis, Missouri, where Peter Blow opened a boarding house called the Jefferson Hotel. Not long after the opening of the boardinghouse, the family faced financial complications and both Blow and his wife Elizabeth became seriously ill, resulting in the death of Blow on June 23, 1832. Documentation of Blow's estate inventory demonstrates that the family sold a slave before his death, and then sold an additional slave following his death to cover creditor claims; making it probable that the sale of Scott to Dr. John Emerson for $500 occurred between 1832 and 1833.

At the time of the sale, Emerson was serving as a replacement doctor at the Jefferson Barracks of the U.S. Army. Estimated to have stood at just over five feet tall, some believe Dred served as Emerson's personal valet. Through the assistance of friends in public office, Emerson secured a position in December of 1833 as assistant surgeon and moved with Scott to Fort Armstrong in Illinois. Given the numerous attempts Emerson had made for a transfer back to the Jefferson Barracks through claims of health concerns, Emerson's construction of a log cabin on a section of land across the Mississippi River most likely depended on Scott's labor. When the Army vacated Fort Armstrong in 1836, Emerson then transferred, accompanied by Scott, to Fort Snelling, a part of the Wisconsin Territory. This particular move became significant to Scott's future, as Fort Snelling resided within lands acquired by the Louisiana Purchase, and prohibited slavery under the Missouri Compromise. According to the Missouri Compromise, all territory acquired by the United States above the 36° 30′ north latitude would remain free from slavery. Congress made this decision in an effort to ease tensions between slave and free states, which each feared that the other would gain a majority within the Legislative branch. The compromise, therefore, was that the Southern territories could allow slavery, and that the Northern territories could restrict slavery. Slaver owners like Emerson, however, did occasionally bring enslaved persons into free territories or states. The question of whether or not Scott personally became a free person upon living in the free territory would later arise during his court trials.

It was also at Fort Snelling where Scott met Harriet Robinson. Scott, about 40 years of age at the time, met his future wife, estimated at 17 years old, at the Army fort shortly after he and Emerson had arrived. Under the ownership of Indian Agent Major Lawrence Taliaferro, Robinson had technically lived in a territory free from slavery since the early 1830s, possibly as a chambermaid or housekeeper, and assisted Taliaferro's wife Elizabeth. Although the exact date of Scott and Robinson's marriage is uncertain, occurring sometime between May of 1836 and September of 1837, records prove that the two had an official wedding ceremony conducted by Taliaferro, a Justice of the Peace within the Wisconsin Territory. Contrary to many unions formed between slaves, Dred and Harriet Scott wed under legal authority, symbolic not only of the couple's desire for family security in their future, but also of the complexity that existed for black individuals' legal rights. For in their future fight for freedom, courts would decide that they were not citizens, and therefore, could not claim rights reserved for citizens, yet their wedding in a free territory possessed the same legal markers evident in white marriages.

After the two married, records indicated that ownership of Harriet Scott transferred to Emerson. Emerson's request to leave Fort Snelling came in the spring of 1837, at which time Emerson moved back to the Jefferson Barracks in St. Louis, but left the Scotts, due to weather complications, at Fort Snelling. During this time, Emerson possibly rented out the Scotts to other occupants of the fort for miscellaneous services. Upon Emerson's arrival in St. Louis, he received new orders that transferred him to Fort Jessup in Louisiana. Emerson sent for the Scotts to join him in the spring of 1838, shortly after Emerson's marriage to Elizabeth Irene Sanford. Only a few months later, the Emersons and the Scotts moved back to Fort Snelling. During this journey, Harriet Scott gave birth to the couple's first daughter, Eliza, north of the Missouri border in territory free of slavery. During this time, however, a child's freedom was dependent on the status of their mother; thus when the Scotts later petitioned for their freedom they also petitioned for the freedom of their children.

The two families remained at Fort Snelling for less than two years before the army transferred John Emerson to Florida in May of 1840. At this time, however, Elizabeth Emerson and the Scotts moved to St. Louis. In 1842, the Emersons reunited in Davenport, Iowa, where John attempted to keep a private medical practice. During this time, the Scotts stayed in St. Louis with Elizabeth Emerson's brother-in-law, Captain Henry Bainbridge, most likely at the Jefferson Barracks. In December of 1843, John Emerson died of consumption, and the ownership of the Scott family passed to his wife. The executor of Emerson's will was the widow's brother, John F. Sanford. The local court then appointed Elizabeth Emerson's father, Alexander Sanford, as the estate's administrator.

With the granted permission of the surviving Emerson, Bainbridge then took Scott to Florida in 1843, followed by Fort Jessup in 1844, and possibly to Texas in 1845. By 1846, Scott was back in St. Louis at the Jefferson Barracks. It was at this time and location when Scott proposed to buy his family's freedom from Emerson. Emerson, however, refused Scott's offer and promptly hired the Scotts out to Samuel Russell while she moved to Massachusetts to stay with family. Remaining thereafter in St. Louis, Dred and Harriet most likely assisted Russell at his wholesale grocery store.

It is uncertain why the Scotts waited until this moment or what other parties may have been involved, but on April 6, 1846, both Dred and Harriet Scott filed separate petitions for their freedom with the St. Louis Circuit Court, claiming trespass for assault and false imprisonment against Elizabeth Irene Emerson. As had been established in previous freedom suits, the Scotts' had a strong case according to Missouri law. Previous rulings, such as *Winny v. Whitesides*, had stated that it was unlawful to bring a person emancipated by their residence in a free state or territory back into Missouri and claim or treat said person as a slave. The first *Scott v. Emerson* trial, however, was in favor of Emerson, as the Scotts' lawyer, Francis B. Murdoch, could not prove that Mr. Emerson claimed or held Scott as a slave when Scott returned to Missouri. If one recalls, the Scotts were not directly working for Emerson, and therefore, Scott's attorney was unable to provide examples of their enslavement to her specifically.

A year after the first trial, Scott's second attorney, Charles Drake, pushed for a retrial, and this time listed Alexander Sanford and Samuel Russell as defendants in addition to Emerson. The Missouri circuit judge, Alexander Hamilton, granted a retrial for the case against Emerson on December 2, 1847, and after two postponements, as well as a failed appeal by Emerson's attorney for *writ of error*, the second trial began on January 12, 1850. Presented with examples of enslavement from all three defendants, the jury for this second trial found Scott, now under the council of Samuel Mansfield Bay, to be a free man.

During the *Scott v. Emerson* processes, according to some researchers, Dred and Harriet had their second daughter, Lizzie Scott, while others maintain Lizzie was nearly seven by the time the trials began. Nevertheless, the freedom of both Eliza and Lizzie still depended on the status of their parents, and shortly following the verdict of the retrial, Emerson's attorney filed for the case's appeal to the Missouri Supreme Court. It was at this time that Emerson granted the sheriff of St. Louis County charge of the Scott family. Shortly thereafter, the Missouri sheriff hired Dred and Harriet out to Charles Edmund La Beaume of St. Louis. The Scotts remained hired out to La Beaume for the next seven years while arguments for freedom continued in the courts. This was because the freedom granted to them in the last trial was not official upon the defendants appeal.

By the time the defense's appeal reached the higher court, Missouri's Democratic Party was dividing over issues surrounding the annexation of Texas, with two of the three Supreme Court judges being pro-slavery and encouraging the annexation. Some supporters of the Texas annexation became very critical of previous decisions by Congress toward acquired territories, as they wanted the new western lands open to slavery and they did not want Congress to eliminate that option. As mentioned earlier, the state of Missouri had ruled in favor of petitions to freedom before Scott's case because the individuals had at one time lived in a free state or territory. If state officials believed, however, that Congress had overstepped its powers to declare those lands free, then judicial decisions might reflect these new opinions. At a national level, issues of sectionalism had become more intense with the proposal of the Wilmot Proviso, which moved to prohibit slavery in lands taken from Mexico following the Mexican-American War. Although neither of these events affected Scott's case directly, the opinions and attitudes influenced the countries judicial system and altered the state of Missouri's interpretation of freedom cases.

The verdict of Scott's third trial, decided upon by John F. Ryland, William Napton, and James Birch, found that although Scott's owner took him into a free territory and state, the status of enslavement reattached to him after returning to Missouri, which was a slave state. Thus, the judges declared that Scott was still a slave. The Missouri courts, therefore, ruled uncharacteristically for the state, but they did not voice an opinion on Congressional powers, which came later in the U.S. Supreme Court's decision.

The natural progression for Scott's attorney to take would have been to appeal the case to the U.S. Supreme Court. The Missouri Supreme Court judges, however, failed to produce an official opinion of the *Scott v. Emerson* case before the elected replacement of judges Napton and Birch in 1851. Without an official opinion, the case could not proceed on the appeal circuit. The court, therefore, scheduled the case for re-argument. On March 22, 1852, judges Ryland and William Scott stated that Dred Scott was still a slave under Missouri law, with Judge Harry Gamble in opposition. Following their decision, the judges ordered the case back down to the lower courts for a new trial to take place bearing the influence of Supreme Court's verdict.

Meanwhile, Emerson remarried to Calvin C. Chafee in 1851, with her brother John F. Sanford, who lived in New York, acting on her behalf at the trials as she stayed in Massachusetts. Although not unusual changes, the residency of Irene and her brother John became an added complexity to Scott's fight for freedom, as Scott's new and fourth attorney, Roswell M. Field, pushed for a federal lawsuit under the diverse citizenship clause, which allowed Scott to bring cases against residents of different states. Field noted the defendant as John F. Sanford, but due to misspelling during the suit's processing, *Scott v. Sandford* became the title of this historical case. Speculations exist as to why Sanford did not deny ownership of the Scotts, as his sister had never legally transferred the Scotts to him. Nevertheless, from this point, Sanford became the main defendant.

Sanford's attorney questioned Scott's ability to claim citizenship in Missouri given the legal uncertainty of his general citizenship as a black man of African decent, and argued non-citizens cannot invoke diversity jurisdiction. By the 1850s, there were states that acknowledged the citizenship of free black males to various extents, but regardless of one's citizenship status, certain Constitutional articles could be available to them. Judge Robert W. Wells, therefore, declared that one did not need to qualify as a citizen under Article IV of the Constitution to qualify for diversity jurisdiction under Article III, thus muting Field's argument. Nevertheless, the U.S. Circuit Court declared on May 15, 1854 that Sanford was not guilty and that the Scott family remained enslaved. That December, Scott's attorney filed an appeal to the U.S. Supreme Court, and public anticipation for the court's rulings began to grow.

Cases involving claims for freedom had reached the U.S. Supreme Court before Scott's suit arrived, but within Scott's claim for freedom were three questions: what was the limit of Congressional power, was the Missouri Compromise constitutional, and what was the U.S. Government position on black persons' citizenship. The opinions of Supreme Court Justices have the power to set legal precedence for the rest of the country. Their decision, therefore, would affect sectional and racial issues confronting the nation at that very moment. With more Justices supporting slavery than not, the public was anxious to see if the court would use its powers to determine the country's next course of action. Would they allow for the expansion of slavery into new territories and states? Would they uphold Congress's decision on the Missouri Compromise, or would slave states take the majority? Furthermore, would the Justices clearly decide, for the first time in the nation's history, that the law viewed black individuals as legal citizens? The determination of Scott's freedom became a stage for answers to volatile questions that involved the entire country.

The U.S. Supreme Court trial for *Scott v. Sandford* began on February 11, 1856. Scott's attorney, now Montgomery Blair, focused on defending the lower court's consideration that Scott was a freed man for the purpose of diversity jurisdiction. The argument for Scott's emancipation due to his residence in a free location emphasized the time Scott spent in the free state of Illinois, as well as the previous claims by the Missouri courts that slavery could not reattach to an individual upon their re-entry into the state. Blair added that the Missouri court's recent change that slave status could reattach was the result of partisan influences, and therefore, the court should consider the earlier decision.

Sanford's attorney argued that Congress lacked authority to prohibit slavery in territories acquired in the Louisiana Purchase, thus charging that the Missouri Compromise, which determined a territory's slave status, was unconstitutional. Rather than addressing the issue of reattachment, they questioned whether Scott was ever legally a free man even if he resided in a free state or territory. A decision could not be made, however, as the chief justices disagreed over the jurisdiction of the case, and therefore, ordered a new trial for that coming December.

On March 6, 1857, after the re-argument of the case, which closely resembled the previous trial, seven of the nine Supreme Court Justices, including Chief Justice Roger Brooke Taney, declared that Scott was still a slave. All of the seven Justices recorded their opinion to the case, but as the official majority opinion, Judge Taney's has remained the most significant and influential to the history of judicial decisions. Taney stated that black persons were not citizens of the United States, which not only marked the first official opinion on the matter, but also contradicted multiple Northern states' constitutions that said free black men were citizens. This statement alone not only prevented Scott from obtaining freedom, it affected the rights and legal standings of every slave and free black person in the entire country. Taney also declared that the Missouri Compromise was unconstitutional, as Congress did not have authority to prohibit slavery in federal territories. This decree demonstrated the power of the judicial branch, and opened the expansion of slavery into all territories and new states.

Several if not all of the justices who found Scott to be a slave were recognized as Democrats and supporters of slavery, resulting in the immediate backlash to the court's decisions by antislavery groups, Northern politicians, and the rising Republican Party. Outcry ensued that Taney's opinion was disgraceful, immoral, and possessed the intentions of granting slave states control of the country. The Democratic Party became very defensive of the decision, and backed Taney's argument that Congress did not posses the power to prohibit slavery. The controversy of the trial spread into national and local newspapers, influencing political elections as well as altering politicians'. discussion of sectional and race issues. This was possible because candidates would use their opinion of the Scott decision to connect with voters of the same beliefs, or tried to discredit other candidates by declaring they had an opposing view.

A year after the verdict against Scott's freedom, a young candidate for senator of Illinois, Abraham Lincoln, rejected the *Scott v. Sandford* decision in debates against Senator Stephen A. Douglas. Although Lincoln lost, he gained support by the Republican Party and antislavery groups in the years to come. The Supreme Court decision also led to political harassment toward Massachusetts Congressman Calvin Chafee and his wife Irene Emerson Chafee. Calvin Chafee had been known as an antislavery politician, and claimed to have been unaware of his wife's famous slave until the federal trial. The Chafees quickly transferred ownership of the Scotts to Taylor Blow, the son of Scott's late owner Peter Blow. The Blow family had financially assisted the Scotts throughout the trial processes, although it is uncertain why the family did so since they had previously owned Scott as a slave. Speculation exists that similar to the generational differences seen in other antebellum families, the Blow children had grown to dislike the institution of slavery, unlike their parents who had owned slaves.

On May 26, 1857, in the St. Louis Circuit Court where the legal journey had begun, Taylor Blow emancipated Dred and Harriet Scott. Regardless of the courts' decisions, the Scott family was finally free. The Scotts remained in St. Louis, where Dred worked as a hotel porter and Harriet as a laundress. Although *Scott v. Sandford* remained a popular topic, as it still is today, the Scott family quickly fell off the political radar. Scott, however, did become somewhat of a local celebrity following the trial, as people wanted to meet the man behind the controversial case.

Unfortunately, for the Scott family, those who were able to know him, and the thousands his story influenced, Scott died on September 17, 1858, of consumption or, as others later recorded, from tuberculosis. They originally buried Scott, who only lived as a free man for little over a year, in the St. Louis Wesleyan Cemetery. After the abandonment of that cemetery, Taylor Blow moved Scott's remains to the Calvary Cemetery in 1867, which is where Blow's granddaughter eventually marked the grave with a granite headstone. Allegedly, Scott's wife Harriet and daughter Eliza only survived him a few years. His daughter Lizzie went on to marry and have her own family, of whose descendants appeared at Scott's centennial observance in 1957.

Rumors continued long after Scott's death about his life and the now historical trial. One story circulated that Scott actually lived to be a very old man who conversed with famous people from all areas, and that he had once served dinner to the Prince of Whales, or later King Edward VII of England. Other not as favorable accounts of Scott's personal characteristics emerged nearly a half a century later from members of the Blow family, now in their later years of life. Interestingly enough, these reports from Blow's descendants coincided with the public's improved perspectives of late Chief Justice Taney. The old judge had received critical reviews immediately following the *Scott v. Sandford* decision, and his opinion for that trial lost most of its credible influence with the onset of the Civil War and the adoption of the Constitution's Thirteenth Amendment in 1865, which abolished slavery. Three years later, the Fourteenth Amendment distinguished that black men were legal citizens, followed by the Fifteenth Amendment in 1870, which specified that the right to vote cannot be denied to someone due to their race, color, or because they were previously enslaved. Taney may not have been forgotten, but his opinions on black persons had been reversed.

Jim Crow laws at the end of the nineteenth century applied Taney's opinion to argue the inferiority of black persons, but the Civil Rights Movement in the middle of the twentieth century help strengthen the Constitutional Amendments brought to the country from the Civil War and Reconstruction eras. Various cases have also cited the Scott decision when questioning the powers of the legislative branch. The *Scott v. Sandford* case lived on through all of the people who could identify with some element of Taney's decision. Overall, the verdict against Scott's freedom has been regarded as one of the most influential decisions in judicial history because Scott's struggle became a symbol of half the country's fight to abolish slavery, and that in losing his case, the sectional issues addressed drove the country to the brink of war.

Jacki Hedlund Tyler
Arizona State University

FURTHER READING

Fehrenbacher, Don E. *The Dred Scott Case: Its Significance in American Law and Politics*. New York: Oxford University Press, 1978.

Finkelman, Paul. *Dred Scott v. Sandford: A Brief History with Documents*. Boston: Bedford Books, 1997.

Maltz, Earl. *Dred Scott and the Politics of Slavery*. Lawrence: University Press of Kansas, 2007.

Public Broadcasting Service. "People and Events: Dred Scott's Fight for Freedom, 1846–1857." 1999. http://www.pbs.org/wgbh/aia/part4/4p2932.html.

VanderVelde, Lea, and Sandhys Subramanian. "Mrs. Dred Scott." *Yale Law Journal* 106 (1997): 1033–1122.

Seale, Bobby. *See* Huey P. Newton and Bobby Seale

Photofest

Tupac Shakur
(1971–1996)

Tupac Amaru Shakur was an extraordinary actor, writer, dancer, and rapper. While his premature death at the age of 25 enhanced his iconic status, Shakur demanded universal recognition as a social outlaw in his own lifetime. He took great pride in his defiant nature, and was willing to use violence to secure respect or fear from those he encountered. Furthermore, he urged others to fight, be it for self-respect or out of respect for our loved ones. Yet Shakur also rebelled against society's expectations of young African American men by sharing his unique worldview and his many talents with society. Overall, he possessed the uncommon ability to express collective righteous anger while providing hope to those who were most desperate.

At the time of Tupac Shakur's birth, his mother, Afeni Shakur (Alice Faye Williams) had recently gained release from jail. She was an affiliate of the New York Panther 21, a group of Black Panther Party members who were falsely accused of arson, possession of explosives, and conspiracy to commit armed robbery and murder in the spring of 1969. While she was free on bail, Afeni had a relationship with her comrade Billy Garland, and became pregnant. However, when several of her alleged accomplices fled New York, authorities revoked Afeni's bail, placing the expectant mother in the Women's House of Detention in Greenwich Village. Ultimately, after deliberating for only two hours, a jury acquitted Afeni Shakur and her codefendants of all charges in May 1971.

Tupac Amaru Shakur (Lesane Parish Crooks) was born shortly thereafter on June 16, 1971, in Brooklyn, New York. His mother ultimately named him in memory of Túpac Amaru, an eighteenth century revolutionary leader among Indigenous peoples in Peru and Bolivia who claimed descent from Inca rulers. Afeni later took the name Shakur, Arabic for "thankful to God," when she formed a family with Mutulu Shakur (Jeral Williams), their daughter Sekyiwa, and Mutulu's son Maurice Harding, also known as Mopreme.

During his adolescence, Tupac Shakur's mother worked as a paralegal in the Bronx while continuing her work with the Black Panther Party. Yet the Shakurs' nuclear family began to collapse shortly after Mutulu's sister, Assata Shakur, escaped from a New Jersey penitentiary in 1979. The Federal Bureau of Investigations suspected Mutulu of having helped his sister break out of prison, and wanted him for the robbery of a Brinks armored truck in 1981 as well. Shakur's mother was then forced to raise her two children alone, and relied on friends and family in Harlem and the Bronx for assistance.

As Afeni struggled to keep her family together, she recognized the value of artistic expression, and enrolled her son in the 127th Street Repertory Ensemble. In 1983, Shakur portrayed Travis in the company's production of Lorraine Hansberry's *A Raisin in the Sun*, which they performed at the Apollo Theater in Harlem. Acting provided Shakur with a necessary escape from reality, and he savored his experiences on stage. As Shakur sought comfort in his new creative outlet, his mother was developing an addiction to crack cocaine. Gradually, it became impossible for Shakur's mother to support her habit and her children. The family could no longer rely on friends in Harlem for shelter and necessities, and made their way into the homeless system in White Plains, New York.

Lured by the promise of a job, Shakur's mother later moved the family from White Plains to Baltimore, Maryland, in 1986. However, they were unable to leave behind the interrelated challenges of poverty, neighborhood violence, and drug abuse of New York, as these were symptoms of a much deeper and broader hopelessness among America's underclass. Shakur was fortunate to have the opportunity to express himself in creative ways as a student at a prestigious charter school, the Baltimore School for the Arts. Although he initially felt like an outcast at his new school, Shakur developed a close, long-lasting friendship with fellow student Jada Pinkett Smith. However, by the age of 17, Shakur grew overwhelmed by his mother's addiction and ongoing violence in his neighborhood, which had claimed the lives of several of his friends.

In 1988, Shakur moved to Marin City, California, located to the north of the San Francisco Bay Area. Shortly thereafter, Shakur's mother and sister joined him. The family lived with Linda Pratt, the wife of Shakur's godfather, Elmer "Geronimo" Pratt. During the late 1980s, Geronimo Pratt was serving a 27-year prison term for a robbery-murder, and therefore could only mentor Shakur from a distance. A judge finally overturned Pratt's conviction in 1997.

Frustrated by his mother's drug habit and the desire to be independent, Shakur moved into an apartment with several friends and got a job at a pizza parlor. He and his roommates formed a hip-hop group, One Nation Emcees, in which Shakur performed under the name MC New York. Shakur also began selling drugs to make extra cash to help his mother.

Although initially enrolled at Tamalpais High School in Marin County, Shakur stopped attending classes. In interviews, Shakur explained that his frustration was with the high school curriculum, which he felt could not prepare him to cope with real-life situations related to poverty, violence, and racism. Through reading, Shakur secured the knowledge that local high schools were incapable and unwilling to provide. He read broadly in American literature, philosophy, sociology, and political theory. Shakur drew inspiration from Niccolò Machiavelli, Sun Tzu, as well as **Maya Angelou**, and infused many of his socially conscious songs with literary references.

During this chaotic period in his life, Shakur met Leila Steinberg, a dancer and promoter who brought diverse musical performers to Marin, Nevada, and Sonoma county schools. Steinberg also held writing and performance workshops for students. Although Shakur had given up on high school, he attended Steinberg's workshops and shared her love for literature. Steinberg and her husband, a local deejay, mentored Shakur and introduced him to Atron Gregory, manager for the local hip-hop group Digital Underground.

Shakur auditioned for Digital Underground in 1990, and earned a spot as a dancer and roadie on their impending tour. The group featured members Shock-G, MC Humpty Hump, Money-B, and DJ Fuze, who earned success in 1989 with their Grammy nominated album *Sex Packets*. Shakur's tour with Digital Underground introduced him to the music industry, and he was determined to succeed in his work. Performing under the name 2Pac, Shakur joined Digital Underground on "Same Song," the first track of their 1991 album *This is an EP Release*. "Same Song" also appeared on the soundtrack for the film *Nothing but Trouble*, starring Dan Aykroyd, Chevy Chase, and John Candy.

Next, Shakur performed on Digital Underground's subsequent album *Sons of the P*, yet he devoted most of his time and energy to his solo project. Shakur's manager, Atron Gregory, first attempted to negotiate a contract on Shakur's behalf with Tommy Boy Records. However, the company did not believe Shakur was bankable as a solo artist. Interscope Records recognized his talent, and signed a contract that allowed Shakur to begin his first album, *2Pacalypse Now*. His album debuted in fall 1991; one month after the release of *Sons of the P*, and his partners from Digital Underground joined him on several tracks. The album included the socially relevant track, "Brenda's Got a Baby," which addressed the increasing number of single, teenage mothers.

While several songs on the album were praiseworthy for their critique of social injustices and celebration of urban culture, the song "Soulja's Story" secured negative national attention. In 1992, a young man in Texas shot a state trooper to death and later claimed his action was motivated by "Soulja's Story," which he was listening to shortly before the violent incident. Consequently, the state trooper's widow named Shakur in a civil suit.

Yet the most formidable attack came from Vice President Dan Quayle, who often cited Shakur's work and the Texas shooting in his public criticisms of gansta rap. Quayle and other critics argued that Shakur's work glorified violence toward law enforcement, particularly in the phrases, "Cops on my tail, so I bail til' I dodge 'em/They finally pull me over and I laugh/'Remember Rodney King?' and I blast on his punk ass/Now I got a murder case." (2Pac 1991). Quayle's assault on Shakur's music was a major talking point during the 1992 re-election campaign, and he recommended that record stores remove *2Pacalypse Now* from their shelves. This incident initiated ongoing criticism of the rapper from various sectors of the population.

As evidenced in Shakur's lyrics, and later his film roles, he took pride in being a thug. He espoused a philosophy of Thug Life, which attempted to account for violent behavior in the context of a war against systems of oppression and hatred. Shakur's distinctive sense of responsibility was evident in his acronym for Thug Life, "the hate u give little infants fucks everyone" (Dyson, 115). Like many other hip-hop artists, Shakur also attempted to invest the term "nigga" with a positive, essentialist meaning to generate solidarity among African Americans across lines of class.

Hence, while Shakur did not hide his lack of respect for the Establishment, particularly for police officers, mainstream critics often misinterpreted his attempts to convey authenticity as simply promoting indiscriminate violence. Although the song "Soulja's Story" referenced violence and drug abuse, it also noted the causes of such behaviors, particularly lack of paternal influence and negative social expectations of poor African American men. In keeping with Shakur's general philosophy of life, the song concluded that the consequences of violent behavior (i.e., going to jail or death, both negatively influence the next generation).

Thus, Shakur's solo career began with controversy. Rather than being deterred by his critics, Shakur expanded his aspirations. In 1992, he appeared in Ernest Dickerson's film *Juice*, costarring Omar Epps, and featuring fellow hip-hop artist Queen Latifah. Shakur adopted the persona of Bishop, a young man gradually consumed by paranoia and the power derived from wielding a gun. Shakur later secured a small role as Sharif in the film *Menace II Society*, directed by Allen and Albert Hughes. However, the filmmakers fired the rapper in fall 1992 for allegedly causing trouble on the film set. The following year, Shakur released his second album *Strictly 4 My N.I.G.G.A.Z.* (1993), which was an immediate success with songs such as "Holler If Ya Hear Me," "I Get Around," "Keep Ya Head Up."

Meanwhile, Shakur devoted even more time to his acting pursuits. He guest starred in an episode of the television series *A Different World* in the unsurprising role of Piccolo, a young man visiting his high school friend from Baltimore, Lena James, portrayed by Jada Pinkett Smith. Shakur showed flexibility as an actor in his portrayal of the character "Lucky" in John Singleton's *Poetic Justice* (1993) costarring Janet Jackson. After the film's release, Shakur began work on *Above the Rim* in New York alongside actors Duane Martin, Leon Robinson, Marlon Wayans, and Bernie Mac.

By the time the film premiered in 1994, Shakur had recorded an album with his stepbrother Mopreme along with Big Syke, Macadoshis, and The Rated R as the group Thug Life. *Thug life: Thug Life Vol. 1* hit stores in 1994, released by Shakur's own record label with Interscope, Out Da Gutta Records. The album achieved moderate praise for the tracks "Cradle to the Grave" and "Pour out a Little Liquor," the latter of which also appeared on the soundtrack for *Above the Rim*.

While Shakur reached new heights in his career throughout 1993 and 1994, he also found himself overwhelmed by a succession of legal disputes. Shakur allegedly assaulted a limousine driver after the taping of the sketch comedy series *In Living Color*. Ultimately, he settled the case in June 1996. Later, authorities in Atlanta, Georgia accused Shakur of shooting two off-duty police officers. Many witnesses to the shooting indicated that one of the off duty officers drew and fired his weapon first. A court later dismissed charges against Shakur. Then, in March 1993, six months after the Hughes brothers fired Shakur from the film *Menace II Society*, Shakur and several friends retaliated by attacking Allen Hughes. Shakur later bragged about the assault in an interview with the MTV cable network. In spring 1994, a judge convicted Shakur of assault and battery, and sentenced him to 15 days in jail, 30 months of probation, and 45 days of community service, including 15 days on freeway cleanup.

Shakur also struggled to defend himself outside of court. In the aftermath of Vice President Quayle's attack on Shakur, other critics began to dissect the rapper's lyrics for "offensive" content. C. Delores Tucker, founder of the National Political Congress of Black Women, now known as the National Congress of Black Women, initiated a campaign against sexism in hip-hop, with Shakur serving as her primary target. Tucker initiated a boycott against the NAACP's Image Awards ceremony in early 1994 because Shakur's portrayal of "Lucky" in the film *Poetic Justice* earned him a nomination for Outstanding Actor in a Motion Picture. Later that year, Tucker testified against gansta rap at congressional hearings and called for a boycott against major record stores that continued to sell Shakur's music. Overall, Tucker was critical of the misogyny promoted by many hip-hop artists.

Shakur was unable to develop a good counterargument to Tucker's accusations in early 1994, as he was busy defending himself against charges of sexual abuse in court. In November 1993, Shakur had met Ayanna Jackson at a nightclub New York City, and the two reportedly had consensual sex. On a subsequent evening, Jackson willingly visited Shakur's hotel room. There, she engaged in a sexual encounter with members of Shakur's entourage, during which Jackson claimed she was a victim of sexual abuse. In December 1993, the state filed charges of sexual abuse, sodomy, and illegal possession of weapons against Shakur and three members of his entourage. Shakur accepted blame for not being more attentive of the situation as it developed, but maintained his innocence of any sexual assault.

Shakur's trial for sexual abuse was well underway in November 1994 when he was shot and robbed at Quad Recording Studios in New York. Three unidentified men attacked Shakur and two friends, shooting Shakur at least four times and stealing $40,000 worth of jewelry. He was extremely fearful for his safety in the days following the attack. Shakur publicly speculated that artists with the Bad Boy music label were involved in the shooting, particularly rapper Notorious B.I.G., (Christopher Wallace) also known as Biggie, and Sean "P. Diddy" Combs. This incident proved to be the spark that ignited a battle between Shakur and his West Coast associates against his former friend, Biggie, and other East Coast rappers.

Although doctors objected to Shakur's appearance in court after the shooting, he arrived for sentencing in the sexual abuse case in a wheelchair. While the judge acquitted Shakur on the sodomy and weapons charges, he sentenced Shakur to eighteen months to four and a half years in prison on two counts of sexual abuse. Shakur then spent Christmas of 1994 incarcerated in New York's Bellevue Hospital, as he was still recuperating from his gunshot wound. In February 1995, Shakur moved to the Clinton Correctional Facility in Dannemora, New York. While there, he spent two months confined to his cell after guards reportedly smelled marijuana in his cell; Shakur subsequently failed a drug test.

Meanwhile, Interscope Records released one of Shakur's most celebrated albums while the rapper himself was in prison. Shakur had recorded *Me*

Against the World prior to his confinement, and it hit record stores in 1995. One of the more popular tracks on the album was "Dear Mama," Shakur's "thank you letter" to Afeni. Ultimately, the album secured double platinum certification and earned two Grammy nominations, including Best Rap Album.

While Shakur continued in his professional success behind bars, he also took a new direction in his private life. In April 1995, while serving his sentence at Clinton Correctional Facility, Shakur married Keisha Morris. Despite this presumably joyful occasion, Shakur's friends noticed his optimism began to fade while he was in prison, as if he no longer possessed a sense of purpose in his career or life in general. Therefore, there was little surprise when Shakur had his marriage to Morris annulled shortly after his release from prison.

Shakur secured his release on bail in mid-October 1995, after eight months in prison, pending the appeal on his conviction. Shakur obtained the necessary $1,400,000 in bail through an arrangement with Marion "Suge" Knight of Death Row Records. Shakur agreed to a recording contract with Death Row in exchange for the bail bond. Death Row Records also resolved an unsettled lawsuit against Shakur stemming from the death of nine-year-old Qà id Walker Teal in Marin City, California. A stray bullet had killed the young boy during a shooting involving several members of Shakur's entourage. A court ordered Shakur and Death Row Records to settle the suit for $300,000.

Shakur wasted little time in fulfilling his contractual obligation. His 1996 album, *All Eyez on Me*, was the first double album by a hip-hop artist and featured rappers Snoop Doggy Dog and Dr. Dre. Due to the number of hit singles from the album, including "California Love," "How Do U Want It," and "I Ain't Mad at Cha," the album was certified platinum nine times. While *All Eyez on Me* gained in popularity, Shakur continued recording new music. Yet his legal battles and conflicts with other rap artists continued to warrant media attention.

In April 1996, a court found Shakur guilty of violating his probation from his 1994 assault and battery conviction, as he had failed to complete the 15-day freeway cleanup portion of his community service. The judge sentenced Shakur to 120 days in jail and a $1,000 fine. Shakur appealed the decision and remained free on bail pending further proceedings. The following month, Shakur plead guilty to a felony weapons charge in Los Angeles. Subsequently, Shakur's antagonism toward artists at Bad Boy Records created tension at the *Soul Train* Music Awards and later at the MTV Music Video Awards in fall 1996. Shakur also severed ties with Death Row founder Dr. Dre, stemming from personal disagreements.

This mounting tension in Shakur's life ultimately shaped the various ways in which Americans have accounted for his violent death. On September 7, 1996, Shakur and Suge Knight were visiting Las Vegas to attend a boxing match between Mike Tyson and Bruce Seldon. While riding in the passenger's seat of a BMW en route to Knight's nightclub, Shakur was shot four times. Las Vegas police advised the press that Shakur's wounds "were not life threatening." Emergency crews rushed him to Las Vegas's University Medical Center where he underwent surgery and remained in critical condition until he suffered respiratory failure on September 13. His co-passenger, Suge Knight, suffered minor injuries.

While national news media debated whether life imitated art and the future of hip-hop, Shakur's fans simultaneously mourned and challenged reports of his death. While many of Shakur's friends and fans commemorated his legacy in poetry, murals, and song, others became amateur detectives relying on mainstream news reports and conspiracy theories. The notion that Shakur staged his death gradually developed in his absence with his posthumous release of six albums, three films, and a book of poetry.

Shakur's professional success did not end with his death in September 1996. The following month, fans saw him as Tank in the film *Bullet*, costarring Mickey Rourke, which Shakur had filmed prior to his 1994 conviction for sexual abuse. In his next film, *Gridlock'd*, Shakur worked with actors Tim Roth and Thandie Newton in his portrayal of Ezekiel "Spoon" Whitmore. Shakur shattered expectations in portraying Detective Rodríguez in his last film, *Gang Related*, costarring James Belushi and rapper Kool Moe Dee. Meanwhile, in 1999 Shakur's former mentor Leila Steinberg organized samplings of his poetry under the title *The Rose That Grew from Concrete*.

The posthumous project that contributed the most to conspiracy theories proved to be Death Row's production of *The Don Killuminati: The 7 Day Theory*. Released in November 1996 under the name of Makaveli, based on Niccolò Machiavelli, author of *The Prince*, the album featured songs "Hail Mary," "To Live and Die in L.A.," and "Me and My Girlfriend." *The Don Killuminati* was simply the first of a growing list of posthumous albums from Shakur. Afeni Shakur assumed the responsibility of sharing her son's music through the founding of Amaru Entertainment. As a testament to his enduring relevance, the song "Thug Mansion" ranked 19th on *Billboard* magazine's Hot 100 almost six years after the rapper's death. Furthermore, *Forbes* Magazine listed Shakur among its top-earning celebrities in 2003.

As his professional success continued, so too did the conflict that seemed to surround him. Approximately one year after Shakur's murder, C. Delores Tucker filed a 10 million dollar lawsuit against Shakur's estate for emotional distress and slander related to the songs "How Do U Want It?" and "Wonda Why They Call U Bitch" on the album *All Eyez on Me*. While Shakur's lyrics retaliated against Tucker for her criticism, a U.S. district judge ultimately dismissed the lawsuit. Several years later Amaru Entertainment went to court against Morgan Creek Production Company regarding the rights to produce a film based on Tupac Shakur's life. Through Amaru Entertainment, Afeni Shakur is fighting to maintain the rights to her son's story.

More importantly, Afeni Shakur has upheld her son's memory through the Shakur Family Foundation, which she founded in 1997 and later renamed the

Tupac Amaru Shakur Foundation (TASF). Through the TASF, Shakur has provided workshop training to young people who possess a passion for the arts. The Foundation has hosted annual Performing Arts Day Camp at the Tupac Amaru Shakur Center for the Arts (TASCA) in Stone Mountain, Georgia. Overall, the TASCA has attempted to develop young artists' skills in set design, entertainment management, acting, dance, spoken word, creative writing, and vocal performance.

Throughout his professional career, critics condemned Shakur for debasing African American culture in general. They pointed to his lyrical glorification of violence, promotion of drug culture and misogyny, as well as his own reckless behavior. Conversely, those who analyzed Shakur's body of work respectfully acknowledged his attempts to engage the social and historical contexts of ongoing classism, racism, and sexism in America. He tried to account for the disproportionate number of people of color, particularly single mothers, living in poverty in one of the wealthiest nations in the world. Meanwhile, Shakur only rarely stepped outside of the Thug Life mentality in films, and his lifestyle generated the drama, violence, and death that followed him in his brief adulthood.

Ultimately, Shakur is a symbol of the diversity that exists in black America, as he refused to conform neatly to labels imposed on him. Despite his Black Panther lineage and keen understanding of capitalist greed, he celebrated money and material possessions. While he held his mother and other black women in the highest regard, he often described women in demeaning, sexist terms. Although he glorified the street hustler's lifestyle, his lyrics also drew on his knowledge of **W. E. B. Du Bois**, Derrick Bell, and George Orwell. In this sense, Shakur not only attempted to function outside the law, but also outside of American society. He has remained an iconic figure in death because his work continues to inspire individuals to fight against hopelessness.

Monica L. Butler
Seminole State College

FURTHER READING

Dyson, Michael Eric. *Holler if You Hear Me: Searching for Tupac Shakur*. New York: Basic Civitas, 2001.

Guy, Jasmine. *Afeni Shakur: Evolution of a Revolutionary*. New York: Atria, 2004.

Hampton, Dream. "Hellraiser," *Source* 62 (1994): 80–82, 84–85, 88–89.

Hoye, Jacob, and Karolyn Ali, eds. *Tupac: Resurrection 1971–1996*. New York: Atria, 2003.

Sandy, Candace, and Dawn Marie Daniels. *How Long Will They Mourn Me?: The Life and Legacy of Tupac Shakur*. New York: Random House, Inc., 2006.

Shakur, Tupac A. *The Rose That Grew from Concrete*. New York: Pocket Books, 1999.

White, Armond. *Rebel for the Hell of It: The Life of Tupac Shakur*. New York: Thunder's Mouth Press, 1997.

Russell Simmons (1957–)

Russell Simmons is an entrepreneur who is often credited with bringing hip-hop culture and style into the mainstream. Simmons has been recognized for launching the careers of many famous hip-hop artists, and is one of the cofounders of Def Jam Records, the Russell Simmons Music Group, Phat Fashions, and Rush Communications. However, perhaps the most notable thing about Russell Simmons is how he became the most affable candidate to lead the post-Civil Rights Movement, and has been often mentioned among possible candidates to run for mayor of New York City.

Simmons was born and raised in the Jamaica Queens section of New York, but moved to the more middle class neighborhood of Hollis Queens when he was eight. Both of his parents graduated from Howard University in New York, and Simmons grew up in a well educated, fairly affluent home. His father, Daniel Simmons, was a public-school attendance supervisor, and his mother Evelyn was a recreation director. They both tried to teach their children the best they could, but despite their middle-class status, Russell found himself being lured into the street culture that would define the early hip-hop movement.

Unlike his brother, who was interested in music and eventually became a rapper in the seminal group Run-DMC, Russell Simmons found that he always had the inclination of an entrepreneur. His early efforts focused on more illicit products, however, as Russell began selling marijuana throughout the neighborhood. Despite the illegality, Russell was able to develop and enhance his already natural business acumen. It became apparent to him that he enjoyed making money, but soon found that this sort of lifestyle was not the kind he wanted for himself.

The young Simmons joined a local gang called the Seven Immortals, and continued to sell marijuana and imitation cocaine. A few run-ins with law enforcement and a situation where he was forced to shoot at a potential robber convinced Russell to enroll at City College of New York, where he began majoring in sociology. He also began shifting his focus from street hustling to concert and artist promoting. While Russell was beginning to become more interested in music, he soon realized the next big thing was not the disco music that most clubs were blasting at the time, but instead something new, something called hip-hop.

Simmons began to spend more and more time working on his promoter career, and decided to drop out of CCNY-Harlem a few credits shy of his degree so that he could create his own company—Rush Productions/Rush Artist Management, which he presided over from 1977 until 1991. The first major artist that Simmons managed was his friend Curtis Walker, who rapped under the name Kurtis Blow. Simmons and Blow co-wrote his first big hit, the 1979 single "Christmas Rappin'." Shortly after this, Simmons agreed to represent his younger brother Joey Simmons's rap group. They did not have a name, so Simmons decided to give his little brother the moniker "Run" and named the group "Run-DMC." Little did they know that they were about to become the seminal group of the 1980s hip-hop movement. They were Simmons's first experiment in merging hip-hop with mainstream culture, as he signed a multimillion-dollar endorsement deal with the shoe and clothing company Adidas following their hit single, "My Adidas."

While Simmons helped guide his brother's group to prominence, he realized he needed a bigger platform to keep them and to lure other artists to hire him. In 1984, Simmons met a young Caucasian NYU student with a love for street music and punk rock named Rick Rubin—within a year Simmons and Rubin had created their own record label, which they ran out of Rubin's dorm room. They named the label Def Jam and funded it themselves until they secured their first big hit with LL Cool J's "I Need a Beat"—which led to a distribution deal with CBS.

At this point Russell had a platform for his artists, and his label had quickly become the pre-eminent hip-hop source in the world. He decided to enter into another realm of media when he turned his life story into a sort of fictional movie called *Krush Groove*. While the movie was wildly panned by critics for its qualities as a film, it was really just another platform to showcase his label's artists, and it quickly became a hip-hop cult hit. Simmons followed it up with another film, *Tougher Than Leather*. Through the 1980s and early 1990s, while Russell was the president of Def Jam, he signed and helped the careers of **Will Smith**, the Beastie Boys, Slick Rick, Public Enemy, and LL Cool J.

Another project that Simmons embarked upon during this period was the launch of HBO's Russell Simmons's Def Comedy Jam—a place where black comedians could perform standup routines on a national stage, and was host to a number of the greatest modern American comedians including Steve Harvey, Bernie Mac, Chris Tucker, Jamie Foxx, Chris Rock, Martin Lawrence, D. L. Hughley, and Cedric the Entertainer. By this point in the early 1990s, Simmons was already a massively influential figure; one who had managed to enhance and support this nascent hip-hop culture while also bringing it to the masses through mediums other than just music. The HBO special became one of the top rated programs on the network, and debuted those entertainers to the mainstream.

Not all was a success, as Russell faced two major disappointments that would have really launched his companies into another level and solidified him as the premier hip-hop Presario. The first was losing out on the rights to produce John Singleton's 1991 film *Boyz N' the Hood*—only because Columbia Pictures president Frank Price refused to do business with someone who wore a track suit and sneaks, according to Simmons. The second mistake was not paying enough attention to one of Simmons'—at the time—smaller clients, Will Smith. Smith left Rush Management, citing disappointment with the lack of attention he was receiving. He would go on to become one of the most powerful figures in popular American culture over the next decade. Def Jam would survive, and was able to put out popular artists like DMX, Ja Rule, Redman, Method Man, and the most valuable of all—**Jay-Z** (Simmons struck up a distribution deal with Jay-Z's Roc-A-Fella Records). Simmons had become a legend, especially in the world of hip-hop culture, despite selling his stake in Def Jam to Universal for $120 million in 1999; he would remain onboard as a chairman.

Simmons soon found that he wanted to move beyond the musical word into other avenues of business and entrepreneurship. While he had dabbled with bringing black comedians into the homes of many white viewers who normally would not have given them a shot—via his HBO show—Simmons felt that another aspect of hip-hop and black culture could appeal to a wider base as well, and that was clothing. In 1992, Simmons founded Phat Fashions, which he ran as CEO from 1992 to 2004. Phat Fashions was built on two lines—Phat Farm, a group of clothing for men, and Baby Phat, its female companion. Phat Fashions was to be, according to Simmons, a bridge between "street style and popular culture." The fashion line really became a major outlet for Simmons, and he grew more and more involved in designing and growing the company, especially after his wife began overseeing the women's line. The company grew 30 percent every year for the first decade, and while it did not turn a profit from 1992 to 1998, by 2002 Phat Fashions was making revenues of $265 million. In 2004, Simmons sold the company to the Kellwood Group for $140 million so the brand could be brought into more department and specialty stores. Simmons was quoted in the New York Times as saying, "They wanted to put me in the ethnic part of the department store. But Phat Farm's best-selling item is a pink golf sweater—its not a grass skirt or a dashiki." Like his Def Jam label, Simmons pioneered the urban clothing style, and other hip-hop magnates began following suit.

Simmons umbrella company, Rush Communications, had seen massive growth following the success of his Def Jam Comedy series on HBO, watching revenues climb from $31 million in 1993, to $65 million in 1994. Rush had some experience with film making dating back to Simmons's early work on his music films, but his company had the chance to work on a major motion picture in 1996 when it produced the film *The Nutty Professor*, a film starring Eddie Murphy, which was a run-away hit. The film cost $54 million to produce, but wound up grossing almost $274 million worldwide. Rush went on to produce *Gridlock'd* and *How to Be a Player*.

Rush Communications had Simmons's fingerprints all over it, and was quickly becoming an ever-expanding empire. The company began advertising in the mid 1990s, producing commercials for Coca-Cola and ESPN, and partnered with the Manhattan advertising firm Deutsch to form dRush. They began building Web sites, starting with 360HipHop.com, a Web site that was intended to be a hip-hop super site with music, reviews, articles, and more. Simmons became vice chairman of Black Entertainment Television, and began using the two companies to work together to provide greater access to his label's recording artists.

By the 2000s, Rush owned an energy soda called DefCon3, a sneaker company, and the spiritual successor to his Def Jam Comedy, Def Poetry Jam—an

HBO show that eventually went on to become a Tony-Award winning Broadway show in 2003. The concept was to showcase young urban poets the same way he showcased young urban comedians in the early 1990s. By 2002, Rush Communications was earning $550 million a year, and even had collaboration with M. Fabrikant & Sons jewelry to produce pieces using the Phat Farm, Baby Phat, and Simmons family brands. Simmons also worked on a wireless phone that he designed for Motorola that sold for $550, called the i90 and i95, which used his Phat Fashion brand. He pushed Rush into the financial services industry, creating a pre-paid debit card for people without access to credit or bank accounts, and a company called UniRush. UniRush teamed with Jackson Hewitt to provide tax preparation services for low-income families. Throughout all of this, Simmons managed to run a household with a wife and children in New York, and even became involved in political activism, something rarely seen in most modern hip-hop figures.

Making money was not Simmons's only concern; he was also a devoted family man and political activist. After meeting supermodel Kimora Lee in November of 1992, the pair dated until they married in December of 1998. Appropriately, Simmons little brother Joseph, who was "Reverend Run" from RunDMC, had become an ordained minister and oversaw the Simmons wedding. The couple had two children, Ming Lee and Aoki Lee, born in 2000 and 2002, respectively. The pair divorced in 2009 after a separation, but remain close and work together continually on the Phat Farm line. Simmons attributes a lot of his business success to his spiritual life. He is a devoted vegan, and he also practices yoga daily in the office and at home. He requires his employees to read Deepak Chopra's book, *The Seven Spiritual Laws of Success*, followed by a written report on the book. Simmons had always said that he did not want to work with people who only had money signs behind their eyes, but had a soul as well.

As Rush Communications became more and more profitable, Simmons began to become concerned that its only goal was to earn money. Simmons decided to rectify this by creating the Rush Philanthropic Arts Foundation and the Simmons Brothers Arts Scholarship. The foundation donated money to predominantly black public schools and gave scholarships to troubled black youths. Also, profits from Phat Farm and DefCon3 soda go to a slavery reparations fund. His philanthropic efforts have not received as much attention as his not-so-nascent political career, however.

In 2001, Simmons created the Hip-Hop Summit Action Network, a nonprofit group that meets around America to raise political awareness among young Americans, particularly urban youths. They are also an outreach program to get young people voting, and this platform gave Simmons quite a fair amount of political clout. He began writing for the Huffington Post on a regular blog feature, and Presidential candidates began courting his favor in 2004. John Kerry and Al Sharpton both had Simmons attend events in hopes of gaining his support for their campaigns. He ran a fundraiser for Hilary Clinton's senate campaign, and lobbied to overturn the three-strikes drug law in New York—known as the Rockefeller laws, they often give first-time offenders long-term sentences, something that has negatively impacted the urban community in no small way. He has campaigned with Governor George E. Pataki, and has campaigned for a larger school budget and to end the war in Iraq. Also, despite continued denials, Simmons's name is often mentioned as a possible candidate for mayor of New York City.

Simmons has already cemented himself as one of the brightest and most influential entrepreneurs in the country. As he continues to broaden his reach to philanthropic goals and political aspirations, Simmons will only see his influence broaden to different demographics. His passion, spirit and drive have found him success in many endeavors, and only time will tell what else Simmons will accomplish down the line, whether he becomes mayor of New York, or changes the dynamics in the inner city through his lobbying efforts and donations.

Adam P. Boyd
University of California, Los Angeles

FURTHER READING

Chang, Jeff. *Can't Stop, Won't Stop: A History of the Hip-Hop Generation*. New York: Picador Press, 2005.

Simmons, Russell. *Life and Def: Sex, Drugs, Money + God*. New York: Three Rivers Press, 2003.

Tommie Smith (1944–)
and John Carlos (1945–)

Tommie Smith and John Carlos embarked upon one of the world's most memorable protests just hours after winning the gold and bronze medals in the 1968 Olympic 200-meter race. As the "Star-Spangled Banner" played during their award ceremony, they removed their shoes, turned to their left to face the U.S. flag, and each thrust one fist into the air. White Australian Peter Norman, who won the silver medal in the same race, wore an Olympic Project for Human Rights (OPHR) pin to demonstrate his support. Smith and Carlos remained silent as the U.S. anthem played, allowing the symbolism of their actions to communicate for them; their removed shoes represented black poverty, Smith wore a black scarf around his neck to represent Black Pride, and Carlos wore a string of beads to commemorate black people who had been lynched. The two athletes bowed their heads in prayer, as they physically represented Black Power to the international community.

Their unprecedented protest was unwelcome. The crowd booed as the Olympians left the platform. The men's raised fists stirred controversy and deeply affected the athletes' lives; they risked their medals, futures, and even their safety to give voice to marginalized and oppressed African Americans, and particularly to black male athletes. Smith and Carlos left an indelible mark on the history of sports and the struggle for equality. The bravery and passion they exhibited on one of the world's largest and most celebrated stages truly make them icons, just as their superior skill and discipline made them Olympians and leading athletes of track and field.

Despite this act of solidarity, Smith and Carlos led distinct lives. They grew up in different areas of the United States. These separate backgrounds informed their opinions about their place in the world. Their personalities also greatly differed, pulling them in different directions throughout their lives. The distinctions did, however, pull them together for that race on October 16, 1968.

Smith was born in Clarksville, Texas on D-Day, the day that the Battle of Normandy began in World War II: June 6, 1944. He grew up in Acworth, Texas, a town of only 20 people. While his hometown was small, his family was not: he had 13 siblings, 11 of whom survived infancy. His parents were sharecroppers, and the Smith children helped their parents work in the fields. His parents valued work and education, and attempted to instill these values in their children. Smith attended a racially segregated, one-room school in Acworth, and his early educational opportunities were limited.

Smith's family moved from Texas to California while he was still young. The family's future employers paid to bring them west, and placed them in an agricultural labor camp where they worked to pay back the cost of their move. Smith developed his burgeoning athletic talent in the California school system, racing his older sister Sally through the fields their family worked and later in physical education classes at school. Smith also developed new confidence in his academic abilities.

As a high school student, Smith became a successful athlete. He played football and basketball, ran track, and lettered in all three sports every year of high school for a total of 12 letters. The student did well as a receiver in football, and was his school's all-time leading scorer. He did particularly well in track, however. His speciality was the 220-yard race, but Smith particularly made a name for himself with a different event. At a meet in his junior year, he ran the 440-yard race in 47.7 seconds, on his first try, which was the best time in the United States that year. The physical conditioning that Smith developed by working with his family in the fields provided him with both strength and endurance; the difficult work he'd performed with his family also provided him with the discipline necessary to improve his game.

While still a high school student, Smith also developed his political consciousness. Due to his athletic success and pleasant manner, his peers elected him student body vice president. While in office, he discussed the nature and effects of racism during a speech. His classmates were unprepared to hear this message, however, and did not receive it well. He later suggested that the student body, as well as the faculty of his school, felt betrayed by his comments as they differed from the happy outlook he normally displayed.

Smith's athletic success provided him with the opportunity to attend college. Though many schools solicited the icon-in-the-making, San Jose State University proved to be Smith's best option because it offered him an athletic scholarship while also keeping him close to home and his older siblings. Smith's scholarship at San Jose State allowed him to choose football, basketball, or track and field. After trying collegiate basketball for a season, Smith moved to track and field.

The strong track and field program at San Jose State proved to be the perfect training ground for Smith. Lloyd "Bud" Winter coached San Jose State's team; his aptitude for coaching and the talent he fostered at the school earned the team the nickname "Speed City." Though Smith injured his hamstring and spent most of his first season in recovery, he was still named athlete of the year by the U.S.A. Track and Field Foundation. Smith's athletic success continued. Although larger than his contemporary sprinters—at 6′4″ and 180 pounds— his strength and the lessons he learned at Speed City allowed him to use his size, along with strides measuring nine feet or more, to his advantage. He set world records during his subsequent years at San Jose State, and at one point held 11 simultaneously.

During these same years, John Carlos's childhood and adolescence also prepared him for the Olympic Games. Carlos was born in Harlem, New York, on June 5, 1945. He understood poverty just as well as Smith, and spent some of his childhood breaking into freight trains. The experiences of the two men were informed by different perspectives; both men experienced economic hardship, but the opportunities available to African Americans in Harlem were different from those available in Texas and California.

Carlos's academic and athletic talents provided him with the opportunity to improve his circumstances through education. In high school, he realized that he was a powerful student; he was gifted academically as well as athletically. He graduated from Machine Trade and Medal High School, and secured admission to East Texas State University (ETSU) on a full track and field scholarship. Carlos led his collegiate team to win the track and field Lone Star Conference Championship, providing the school with its first and only championship from this competition. After studying at ETSU for one year, the athlete transferred to San Jose State, the same school Smith attended. Carlos ran track at his new school under the guidance of Winter.

Circumstances and personality continued to keep Smith and Carlos apart. Though they both studied at San Jose State, they did not run for the school's team during the same years. By the time that Carlos qualified to run at Speed City, Smith had already completed the number of semesters in which a student might be eligible to participate in athletic programs. The athletes' backgrounds also provided them with contrasting perspectives. Smith's childhood in Texas and California shaped his opinions just as strongly as Carlos's childhood in Harlem shaped his.

The personalities of the athletes differed as well. Where Smith was calm and understated, Carlos was boisterous and exuberant. Smith's personality shone forth during his races, for example. He wore sunglasses in most races, in part to protect his eyes from the sun, but also due to shyness: he wished to hide his face from spectators even as his running seized their attention and set world records. Carlos, in contrast, felt comfortable with eyes upon him and, in Smith's opinion, frequently drew attention to himself.

> In those days reputation was a big thing. If you could win a game before you went out, win it. That could mean winning it in the papers by saying certain things or by not saying certain things. You got very crafty at the game.
> —Tommie Smith

The athletes' politicization reflected the times in which they lived. The Civil Rights Movement had reached a turning point by the time Smith and Carlos entered San Jose State. **Malcolm X** was assassinated in February 1965, shortly after Smith entered college, and race riots broke out throughout the United States later that summer as African Americans vented their feelings of outrage and hopelessness. **Martin Luther King, Jr.,** was assassinated in April 1968. The 1968 Olympics occurred during a time of great upheaval, and the activist sentiments held by Smith and Carlos did not develop in isolation.

Smith and Carlos participated in overt political activism through their years at San Jose State. Smith and teammate Lee Evans created the United Black Students for Action (UBSA) and became members of the organization's executive committee. They, together with Carlos, also studied with Dr. Harry Edwards, a sociology professor. Edwards, who had attended San Jose State himself on an athletic scholarship as an undergraduate, was Smith's first African American professor. He challenged his student athletes and taught them that their opinions mattered, even if many of their peers believed that they were only valuable for their physical abilities as athletes. The political thought developed by Edwards and the students at San Jose State was particularly masculinist; Smith and Carlos came to believe that expressing their opinions and standing up for their rights allowed them to reclaim black manhood. Edwards became the athletes' primary advisor during their final years at San Jose State.

The political expression of African American athletes shifted prior to the 1968 Olympic Games. **Muhammad Ali** made international news when he changed his name from Cassius Clay in 1964. He again shocked many when he refused to fight for the United States in the Vietnam War in 1966. His political resistance helped Smith and Carlos recognize that they, and not only politicians and traditional activists, possess political views. Ali's actions were part of a changing climate in which athletes realized that they were valuable for their athletic prowess and discipline, but also for their minds. African American athletes throughout the United States discovered their power during this era, and used the attention they received through athletics to change their sports as well as the nation. Smith and Carlos learned, by watching Muhammad Ali and listening to Edwards, that their thoughts mattered, regardless of their chosen profession.

The African American athletes preparing for the 1968 Olympics soon began meeting with one another, and these meetings attracted the interest of journalists. As the Games neared, the media also speculated on the athletes' plans. During a competition in Tokyo in September 1967, a Japanese reporter spoke to Smith. The icon, when questioned by the reporter, explained that he did not believe that African Americans were treated fairly in the United States. The reporter next asked him if he and other African American athletes planned to boycott the Olympics. Smith responded, "Depending upon the situation, you cannot rule out the possibility that we Negro athletes might boycott the Olympic Games." Smith's comments fueled the fears of those in the United States who already suspected that plans were underway to disrupt the 1968 Olympics. They believed that any protest or boycott on the part of African American athletes representing the United States would be a disruption to the proceedings and an embarrassment to the United States.

African American athletes continued to prepare for the Games and deliberate upon possible political action, but they did not prepare for the upcoming Olympics in isolation. They formally created the OPHR in October 1967, under the guidance of Edwards, to organize together and determine whether they should take formal action in the upcoming Games. The OPHR consisted primarily of men, however, as male athletes structured their political arguments around reclaiming manhood rather than around rights for men and women, or for male and female athletes. Smith and Evans served as spokespeople for the ambitious organization. Edwards and the athletes involved wished to use the Olympic Games and their notoriety in sports to fundamentally challenge the racism African Americans faced in the United States.

OPHR members sought to prevent the United States and sports institutions from using African American success in sports as proof that racism did not exist, or as evidence that African Americans were happy with their status in the United States. The men in the OPHR believed that their actions would demonstrate that even those few black people who were able to reach some level of financial success through sports were unhappy with the state of civil rights in the United States. The primary aims of the OPHR were threefold: to reinstate Muhammad Ali as the Heavy Weight Champion of the world, remove Avery Brundage as head of the U.S. Olympic Committee (USOC), and remove South Africa and Rhodesia from the Olympics.

The OPHR was ultimately unable to decide on a formal action that all athletes were willing to take. Some feared that a boycott would ruin their only chance to play in the Olympics. Others were concerned that participating in a boycott or protest would limit their opportunities to play professional sports, or prevent them from finding endorsements after the Games. Yet others were unconvinced that a formal protest was necessary, or worried about the harassment they believed they would face if they did participate. In the end, the OPHR decided that no formal boycott would be organized. Each athlete was left to decide his best individual course of action.

As the Olympic Games began, Smith and Carlos again demonstrated their physical abilities at the trial races. Carlos finished the 200-meter dash in 19.7 seconds and broke the world record for the race. His time was not recognized as a world record, however, because the athlete wore spiked shoes that were not allowed. Smith had a good showing as well, finishing the race in 19.9 seconds. Public speculation surrounding the athletes focused not only on political actions they might take before or during the Games, but also on their physical prowess and the upcoming 200-meter race.

The day of the 200-meter race and protest proved trying for both athletes. At the end of the semifinal heat, Smith pulled his left abductor muscle; his thoughts concerning how he might stage a protest after the race, in addition to his nervousness, distracted him and he slowed down too quickly crossing the finish line. He fell and was carried from the field. Winter, as well as Carlos and Evans, tended to Smith in the waiting room, icing the injury, until the final was less than one hour away. They took Smith back to the training field so that he could practice walking and running on the injury. He jogged briefly, learning that he could still maintain mobility despite the injury.

The race itself inevitably neared. Lanes were drawn by lot; Smith was placed in Lane 3 and Carlos in Lane 4, which are among the better lanes from which to race. The runners positioned themselves in their starting blocks. Carlos was ahead of Smith in position. The two men prepared to race, and soon heard the starter's whistles.

The race began as the gun fired, and Smith, Carlos, and the other runners took off. Smith intentionally held back through most of the race, as he feared that he could not run the length of the track at full power due to his injury. Believing he had 15 full strides available to him before he might re-injure himself or collapse, Smith waited until the last 60 meters of the race before running at full capacity. Carlos was about three meters ahead of him, but

Smith almost immediately surpassed him as he thundered by with his long strides. Carlos seemed to slow down, perhaps surprised that his injured teammate had suddenly entered his field of vision.

As Smith passed Carlos on the track, he knew that he would win the race. Elated to near the finish line first, he triumphantly raised his arms in the air. This slowed his progress in the race's final meters, but even so he finished the race at 19.83 seconds, winning the gold and setting his personal best in the event despite his injury. Norman and Carlos followed immediately thereafter, at 20 seconds, with Norman just beating Carlos for the silver.

Following the race, Smith, Norman, and Carlos awaited their awards ceremony and protest. Returning to their dressing room, Smith and Carlos finalized their plans for the protest in these underground rooms. Hours later, they staged their infamous protest during their medal ceremony. When the U.S. anthem played, the athletes turned toward their flag and thrust their fists into the air.

Neither Smith nor Carlos realized the full consequences of the protest that day. They both faced death threats in the months leading up to the 1968 Games, as had other members of the OPHR. Edwards even chose not to attend the Games, despite his efforts to serve as a mentor to the two athletes prior to the Games. Smith believed that Edwards failed to come to Mexico City because he feared the death threats that they each had received. The icons' protest meant that the two athletes would receive more death threats, as well as other repercussions.

Smith and Carlos were punished for their protest almost immediately. Brundage suspended them from the U.S. Team, and banned them from the Olympic Village. When the USOC refused to follow his orders, Brundage threatened to ban the entire U.S. track team. Smith and Carlos were subsequently expelled from the Games. The athletes also faced criticism from without the Olympic Village; their salute was described as "Nazi-like," "childish," and "angry." Few in the media were willing to acknowledge the motivation behind the gesture, and instead only focused on the fact that their protest embarrassed the image of the United States as a bastion of freedom and equality.

Both athletes struggled to resume their normal lives following the Olympics. Few people seemed to agree with their protest, and Smith and Carlos struggled to find jobs in California. They each experienced periods of stressful unemployment. While their difficulties were shared by many other black Americans, Smith and Carlos attributed these challenges to their participation in the Olympic protest. Their assumptions appear logical in light of the clear harassment they faced for their political activism.

Smith later recalled facing harassment upon his return to the United States. He worried about how he would be able to support his wife Denise and their son Kevin, and believes that the difficulties he and Denise faced during this time ultimately led to their divorce. Smith's extended family also faced pressure after his protest. His mother died of a heart attack in 1970, which he blames on the stress she experienced after receiving death threats and packages containing manure and dead rats. These deliveries were messages intended to frighten Smith's mother and punish her for raising a son who would challenge his place in the world by becoming successful and protesting institutionalized racism.

Some doors did open for Smith, however, and he continued his career in sports. He finished college and played professional football for three years with the Cincinnati Bengals. Following his last season, he petitioned the National Collegiate Athletic Association to return to track, though his request was rejected because of his status as a professional athlete. Boundaries between professional and amateur athletes are less rigid now, but they prevented Smith's return to track. Having earned a master's degree, he coached track at Oberlin College instead, and also taught sociology; he later taught sociology at Santa Monica College in California.

Smith received eventual acclaim for his athleticism. He was inducted into the National Track and Field Hall of Fame in 1978 and the California Black Sports Hall of Fame in 1996. In 1995, he coached the U.S. team at Barcelona's World Indoor Championships. He held 11 world records during his career, and set all-time bests including 10.1 seconds for the 100-meter dash, his Olympic 19.83 seconds for the 200, and 44.5 seconds for the 400.

Carlos similarly faced great difficulty following the Olympics. Immediately after the Games, he continued to pursue his talent in track and field. In 1969, he ran the 100-meter race and tied the pre-existing world record. He also had to support his family, however, and found that he faced harassment and threats similar to those that met Smith, as well as trouble finding employment. He did not finish his academic training at San Jose State, which compounded his problems finding a job that he found meaningful. He played football with the Philadelphia Eagles, but a knee injury prematurely ended his career.

More hard times fell upon Carlos. Kim, his wife, committed suicide in 1977. Carlos believes that the stress she faced from their economic hardship as they tried to raise four children, combined with fear stemming from the death threats they continued to receive, led her to end her life. Though these struggles appeared insurmountable, Carlos did not give up, but continued to search for a place in which he belonged.

> Athletes are human beings. We have feelings too. How can you ask someone to live in the world, to exist in the world, and not have something to say about injustice?
> —John Carlos

Carlos responded to this tragedy by turning his attention to others. He worked with a Los Angeles city councilperson, and founded the John Carlos Youth Development Program in 1977. Funding the program was a struggle; despite Carlos's success in the 1968 games, the controversy surrounding his protest, coupled with the fact that he founded the program long before athletes normally found financial success and corporate sponsorship, limited Carlos's opportunities to grow the program. He used a marketing position he landed with Puma to briefly fund the program.

Carlos also maintained his connection to sports. In 1982, he was hired by the Los Angeles Olympic Organizing Committee to bring inner-city organizations to the city's efforts to prepare for the 1984 Games. He still ran competitively as well, though age and lack of time for training limited his success. He became a counselor, in-school suspension supervisor, and track and field coach at a high school in Palm Springs in 1985.

Though Smith and Carlos eventually found stability and success, this safety took more than a decade to secure. They still communicate frustration over the loneliness they experienced during those years. The honors they now receive help them understand that their protest and courage are remembered and celebrated. The National Track & Field Hall of Fame, for example, inducted Carlos in 2003. That same year, students at San Jose State University announced plans, later finalized in 2005, to erect a 20-foot high statue in their honor.

The two men continue to accrue acclaim for their protest and the powerful athleticism with which they graced the Olympic stage. An exhibit about Speed City in 2007 honored San Jose State's former prowess in track and field, the efforts of former coach Winter, and the talent of the students who pursued the sport under Winter's guidance. Carlos also trained Charles Barkley, a former NBA star, to race in a somewhat staged competition against Dick Bavetta, one of the NBA's most popular, experienced, and well-conditioned referees, at the 2007 NBA All-Star Weekend.

Smith and Carlos are athletic icons and remarkable athletes. Just as remarkably, they helped change the connection between U.S. athletes and politics by demonstrating that athletes have political opinions. The courage and will that led them to win the Olympics and stage their protest also allowed them to survive the threats, criticism, and isolation they experienced in the ensuing years. Their talent, discipline, bravery, and commitment to something larger than themselves helped changed the world for the better.

Megan Falater
University of Wisconsin-Madison

FURTHER READING

Drake, Dick. "Tommie Smith & Lee Evans Discuss Potential Olympic Boycott." *Track & Field News*. November 1967. http://www.trackandfieldnews.com/display _article.php? id=1605 (accessed August 5, 2009).

Hartmann, Douglas. *Race, Culture, and the Revolt of the Black Athlete: The 1968 Olympic Protests and Their Aftermath*. Chicago: University of Chicago Press, 2003.

Maese, Rick. "A Courageous Act of Defiance." *The Montreal Gazette*, August 20, 2004, C4+.

Smith, Tommie, with David Steele. *Silent Gesture: The Autobiography of Tommie Smith*. Philadelphia: Temple University Press, 2007.

Zirin, Dave. "The Living Legacy of Mexico City: An Interview with John Carlos." *Counterpunch*, November 1/2, 2003. http://www.counterpunch.org/zirin11012003.html (accessed August 5, 2009).

Zirin, Dave. *What's My Name, Fool? Sports and Resistance in the United States*. Chicago: Haymarket Books, 2005.

Dreamstime

Will Smith (1968–)

Will Smith is, without a doubt, one of the most well-known movie stars on the planet. Smith began his career as a hip-hop artist who made the transfer to acting, beginning with a lead role on a TV show loosely based on his life, *The Fresh Prince of Bel-Air*. From there, Smith moved on to movies and has lit up the big screen, with his films grossing more than two and a half billion dollars throughout his career, winning multiple Grammys, and scoring multiple Golden Globe and Academy Award nominations.

Smith was born September 25, 1968, to Caroline, a school board employee, and Willard C. Smith, Sr., owner of a refrigeration company in a middle class neighborhood in West Philadelphia. Will was the second of four children, and was graced with a remarkable charm that has become a hallmark of his success throughout the years. At Philadelphia's Overbrook High School, Smith became so renowned for talking his way out of trouble that he earned the nickname "Prince." His youth in Pennsylvania was the very definition of a melting pot. Smith was raised Baptist, but attended a strict Catholic high school. He was liked by everyone, and quickly found that he had a knack for performing. As a youth in the early 1980s, Smith idolized Eddie Murphy and hip-hop icon Grandmaster Flash, inciting him to begin rapping, but also joined the Julia Reynolds Masterman Laboratory and Demonstration School in Philadelphia.

Smith's early focus was on music, however, and by age 16 he had cemented himself locally with his own unique style of comic-rapping, where his lyrics were intelligent, but often playful and free of obscenities. At a party, Smith met Jeff Townes, a local DJ who went by the name of DJ Jazzy Jeff. The two became fast friends and soon decided to hook up and form DJ Jazzy Jeff and the Fresh Prince. Despite being accepted to MIT on a pre-engineering scholarship, Smith got the approval of his parents to continue with his musical career. Smith and Townes began writing and recording music, but unlike their contemporaries they set their songs in a nonthreatening, family-friendly zone that included songs about girls, parents, school, and sports. "Girls Ain't Nothing But Trouble" and "Parents Just Don't Understand" were two of the group's number one hits that helped propel their debut LP *Rock the House* and the follow up *He's the DJ, I'm the Rapper* to double-platinum status and a first ever win for rap at the 1988 Grammys.

Smith's image as a middle-class rapper appealed to parents around the country, and was readily adopted by wary parents who wanted to appease their children's request for hip-hop but did not want to buy them music by Public Enemy or NWA. He attributed his success to the fact that he went to white schools for most of his life and then a black high school, and so he was able to speak to both groups and make them enjoy his music and his humor for different reasons. The success came quickly. Smith achieved all of this success in high school, and was a millionaire by the time he was 18. Smith would put out another record with Jazzy Jeff, *Code Red*, and win another Grammy for the track "Summertime" in 1991, but at this point Smith was beginning to turn his attention toward acting. He met a producer named Benny Medina in the 1980s, whom he collaborated with on an idea for a sitcom centering around his life in Beverly Hills and the surrounding area in California. They pitched the idea to NBC, and the network went for it, despite Smith never having acted before in his life.

Just like his life, the show centered around Smith leaving the inner city of Philadelphia and going to live in Bel Air, California. Smith joked, and still does, that he has always made up for average acting talent with an extreme work ethic. Smith said the first time he had to perform as an actor was the first day he set foot on the set, and that for the first half of the first season, the director and producers had to cut around the fact that he was mouthing the other actors' lines—a habit he formed because he was so concerned about failing that he had memorized the entire script.

The show was a runaway success, but Smith did not see a lot of the profits from having a hit TV show due to some financial mistakes he made following his teenage stardom. Smith underreported his income, and the IRS ended up moving to collect nearly $3 million dollars in back taxes. Smith was forced to forego some of his property, and 70 percent of his wages on *Fresh Prince* were garnisheed during his time on the show. Smith was a TV star, but he told an interviewer that his goal was always to be "the biggest movie star in the world" and he was about to do just that. Midway through his time on *Fresh Prince*, 1993, Smith took on a lead acting role in the small budget dramatic film, *Six Degrees of Separation*. Smith played the role of a homosexual street hustler, who falsely claimed he was the son of **Sidney Poitier** to work his way into New York's high society. Despite a lot of doubt about Smith, the movie was hailed by critics as an excellent movie and his performance was deemed extraordinary; the movie even received an Oscar nomination. Soon, Smith would turn his acting success into box office success.

The Fresh Prince of Bel-Air ran from 1990 to 1996, and ended because Smith had suddenly become one of the biggest stars on the planet. Smith's first big-time success came in his starring role in 1995's *Bad Boys*. With a production budget of about $19 million, the film was expected to meet with modest success. It was one of the first mainstream action movies with two black leads, and Will Smith and his agent carefully chose it. They believed that everything Smith did was a building block, and it was the appropriate thing to do at this point in his career. Smith was paid $2 million, and the film ended up earning $140 million worldwide—Will Smith was officially on the map.

For his next project, Smith had a tough choice to make. Producer Brian Grazer (*Apollo 13, Liar Liar, 8 Mile, The Da Vinci Code*) offered Smith $11 million to star in an action movie he had planned, but Smith and his business partner James Lassiter felt that it was too risky and, wisely, turned it down for a lead in the film *Independence Day*. The first of Smith's seven movies that had been released in July (earning him the nickname "Mr. July"), a*Independence Day* grossed more than $815 million worldwide, and was without a doubt one of the biggest movies of the 1990s. It led to a string of starring roles for Smith in the next few years as well.

Starting in 1995 with *Bad Boys*, Smith had at least one movie come out every year through 2009. 1997 saw Smith star alongside Tommy Lee Jones in the Alien-centric film *Men in Black*—a film that brought Smith's per-movie rate up to 5 million. *Independence Day* and *Men in Black* showed that Smith could easily handle action comedies; his wit, charm, and athletic build helped in action scenes and with all the one-liners his characters spit out. Right when Smith's career was reaching superstar level, he decided to return to his music career.

In 1997, after *Men in Black* came out and Smith sang the show's theme song, he released his first solo album, *Big Willie Style*. A worldwide hit that enjoyed the success of four number one singles ("Men in Black," "Gettin' Jiggy Wit It," "Miami," and "Just the Two of Us"), and it went on to sell more than 14 million albums worldwide, charting as the ninth best selling rap album of all time in the United States. The success of the CD lasted through 1998, and all the singles were accompanied by expensive music videos. Smith ended up becoming the only artist ever to receive two Grammies in the same category from the same album in two different years—he won Best Rap Solo Performance in 1997 for "Men in Black," and in 1998 for "Gettin' Jiggy Wit It."

The success of *Big Willie Style* would not be duplicated, and the follow-up, *Willennium*, which was released only two months after *Big Willie Style* finally disappeared from the charts, was met with unrealistic expectations. Smith had collaborated with the influential rapper Nas on his first solo album, but went with his old friend DJ Jazzy Jeff as the producer on his second. The album produced the hit singles "Wild Wild West" and "Will 2K," but the album ended up selling only two million copies in the United States and four million world wide—down greatly from the nine million domestic and fourteen million its predecessor had sold.

Smith released *Born to Reign* in 2002, an effort to move away from his comedic, party oriented music and into more artistic territory. The CD was not received very well, and only ended up selling a little more than 500,000 copies in the United States and was only certified Gold. The last CD Smith put out as of this writing, 2005's *Lost and Found*, was a commentary on Smith's lack of focus on his music career during his intense decade of acting, and how he had found his way back to his roots. The album also only had moderate success commercially (charting Gold, but no more), but critically was well received as Smith took on subjects like the state of rap—which he feels has reached an all-time low—his critics who say he is not black enough, and how he feels he has found his musical swagger again. The impetus for the album, though, was the decade-long string of block busters that Smith embarked upon after his initial success in *Bad Boys*, *Independence Day*, and *Men in Black*.

In 1998, Smith starred in *Enemy of the State*, a conspiracy thriller movie directed by Jerry Bruckheimer—a film that earned Smith $14 million dollars and grossed a quarter of a billion dollars worldwide. The following year, Smith made what he considers the biggest mistake of his career as he turned down the lead role of Neo in *The Matrix* in order to star in the somewhat box office bust, the wild west/sci-fi mash up *Wild Wild West*. George Clooney pulled out as his co-star at the last minute; the movie went on to lose money domestically, and was panned critically as well. Smith ended up apologizing to the original creator in a 2009 interview.

The spiritually infused golf movie set in the 1930s, *The Legend of Bagger Vance*, followed. The film was unpopular critically and also bombed in theaters, earning only $30 million worldwide. Smith was unsure of what his next film would be. Michael Mann was trying to put together a biopic on the famous Boxer **Muhammad Ali**, but Smith had turned down the role eight times. Finally, when Ali called and asked if Smith would do it, Smith accepted the role—he says he did not feel he could ever adequately portray Ali's skill and charisma.

Ali was a true labor of love. The film ended up running over budget, so Smith and Mann put in some of their own money to cover costs, although Smith did earn $20 million for the role. The movie was received warmly by critics, particularly regarding Smith's performance and his devotion to the role. While the film severely underperformed at the box office, losing about $30 million worldwide, Smith was rewarded with his first Oscar nomination for best actor. Following three underperforming movies in a row, Smith and his business partner decided it was time to do something that was guaranteed to make a profit. *Men in Black II* was the perfect film to recapture the box office magic, and despite being a near carbon copy of the original, the film earned more than $440 million worldwide. Smith raked in almost $60 million from the film, and was back on top of the box office world. He came back with another sequel the following summer in 2003's *Bad Boys II*, another critically panned, but commercially successful movie. Smith made almost $50 million from the film.

Smith broke the trend with the film adaptation of *I, Robot* in 2004, another sci-fi action movie where Smith is forced to battle sentient robots. It was also the first film where a vast majority of the film featured only Smith, carrying the film alongside computer generated effects. Will broke out of his patented action roles by doing voice over work for the animated DreamWorks movie *Shark Tale*, and a 2005 romantic comedy, *Hitch*—both films were massive successes and continued the trend of Will Smith commanding upwards of $20 million a film. Smith went with the Hollywood adaptation of Chris Gardner's remarkable life in *The Pursuit of Happyness*, where he starred alongside his son as a father and son who were evicted from their apartment as he struggled to succeed as a stockbroker. The film was another mega-hit, and he was nominated for his second Academy Award in the Best Actor category for his performance.

Another sci-fi movie, the post-apocalyptic *I Am Legend*, followed with Smith starring solo in nearly every scene of the movie. The film broke records for box office grossing that December, and made more than a half billion dollars worldwide. In 2008, he played a super hero in the critically disappointing *Hancock*, but that film made more than $600 million and cemented Smith as perhaps the most popular box office draw in the modern era. His most recent film, *Seven Pounds*, was more artistic and did not do as well, but still made a profit. Smith's career has gone from that of a solid television actor, to without a doubt one of the biggest stars on the planet. Smith's career has been so profitable that he is the eighth highest grossing actor of all time, with his 19 films averaging $133 million per film, domestically. Smith has numerous more other films in production, and his career looks like it will not be slowingly down any time soon.

Smith has been married twice, and has three children, yet despite his first marriage, he has been known as one of the most devoted family men in Hollywood. From 1992 until 1995, Smith was married to Sheree Zampino. They had one son, Willard Christopher Smith III, also known as Trey. Trey was the subject of Smith's son in the song "Just the Two of Us." Smith and Zampino were divorced in 1995 when the two simply said they were no longer in love. They married too young and went through money troubles the entirety of their marriage.

Smith remarried in 1997 to actress Jada Pinkett, and the two have been happily married ever since. Pinkett, determined not to let Trey lose out on a relationship with his biological mother, invited Zampino to live with the couple for a time while she got on her feet again. Pinkett and Smith had two children of their own, Jaden Christopher Syre, born in 1998, and Willow Camille Reign. Jaden starred with Will in *The Pursuit of Happyness*, and Willow was featured as Will's daughter in *I Am Legend*.

Smith has entered the production sphere, creating a TV show based on his life with his wife called *All of Us*, and creating a production company with his business partner called Overbrook Entertainment, which is currently working on a remake of Clint Eastwood's film *Play Misty For Me*. He also has a company with his brother Harry, called Treybell Development Inc., based in Beverly Hills, which works on building projects in inner-city Philadelphia. Politically, Smith has long been a supporter of the Democratic Party, and has even joked that he would be interested in running for President in a decade. Smith donated money to **Barack Obama**'s campaign, and President Obama has publicly stated that if there is ever a Hollywood film based on his life, he would like Smith to play the part—jokingly—because "he has the ears." The two have reportedly discussed a film based on the 2008 election. While still a young man, Will Smith has already conquered the music and acting realms. He owns one of the best selling CDs of all time, has become one of the top grossing actors of all time, and is transcending culture and genre across the world. He has truly become a shining example of success and is, without a doubt, an icon of black America.

Adam P. Boyd
University of California, Los Angeles

FURTHER READING

Berenson, Jann. *Will Power! A Biography of Will Smith*. New York: Spotlight Entertainment, 1997.
Robb, Brian J. *Will Smith: King of Cool*. New York: Plexus, 2002.

Spelman College

Spelman College

Originally founded in 1881 as the Atlantic Baptist Female Seminary, Spelman College is the oldest Historically Black College or University (HBCU) dedicated to the education of black women. For more than 125 years, Spelman College has served as a touchstone for black women, helping to reinforce the ideals for black womanhood. While it was labeled by many in the first 70 years of its existence as a "finishing school," Spelman and its sibling schools of **Morehouse College** and Clark Atlanta University were fertile recruiting grounds for civil rights activists during the 1960s and 1970s. Notable former students of its college, and now defunct high school, include novelist Alice Walker, playwright Pearl Cleage, activist Marian Wright Edelman, ambassador Aurelia Brazeal, and Alberta Williams King (mother of **Martin Luther King, Jr.**). Spelman's status as an important institution during the Civil Rights Movement, the most recognizable women-only HBCU, and myriad of influential graduates, merits its status an important icon of black America.

Located in Atlanta, Spelman is now a participant in the Atlanta University Consortium that includes Morehouse College and Clark Atlanta University. As of 2009, it had a student body of more than 2,100 students and a faculty of 174. At slightly fewer than 39 acres, Spelman has expanded extensively since its first year—1881—in the basement of the Friendship Baptist Church in Atlanta.

Spelman's status as an icon of black America is largely determined by its history. On April 11, 1881, two Baptist missionaries from the American Baptist Home Missionary Society, educated at the Oread Institute of Worcester, established a school for black women that would eventually become Spelman College. The missionaries, Sophia B. Packard and Harriet E. Giles, sought to eventually establish a liberal arts institution that would educate young women on a wide range of subjects including Latin, psychology, civics, and ethics. Initially, the school was comprised of two different departments, academic and normal. The normal department provided rudimentary education to young women who were unfamiliar with the basic educational skills of reading, arithmetic and writing. The academic department introduced more complex subjects than those listed above, but remained an ancillary part of the curriculum for more than a decade as the school concentrated on basic education. Along with the school's emphasis on piety and Victorian-era, lady-like behavior, these two departments accomplished the school's goal of educating the "head," the "hands," and the "heart."

Within a few years of the school's establishment, Packard and Giles inaugurated an industrial department that provided more practical skills like sewing, cooking, and other domestic arts. Yet, both Packard and Giles remained adamant in their desire to preserve the academic aspirations of their school, rather than submit to the more trade oriented approach that dominated black education during the nineteenth century. In many ways, their philosophy of education demonstrated the tension within the educational community between the ideas of **Booker T. Washington** and **W. E. B. Du Bois**. Packard and Giles, as well as other educators of the era, attempted to craft a path between the two philosophical giants by offering both trade and higher education.

Two years after its founding in 1881, the Atlantic Baptist Female Seminary moved out of the Friendship Baptist Church's basement and into a nine-acre property close to the church. A former hospital and four former barracks stood on the property, and these five buildings provided an environment much more conducive to learning than the church's dark and musty basement. In addition, the new facilities provided room for many of the seminary's students to live on campus. One year after the move, on June 8, 1882, Packard and Giles gave a presentation to a congregation in Cleveland, Ohio that included oil mogul John D. Rockefeller in the audience. Their passionate address touched Rockefeller, and after querying Giles and Packard on their commitment to the school, he donated $250 and pledged his future support. In 1884, Rockefeller donated another $5,000, ensuring the school's future existence as an independent school for women. Over the years, he and his family made good on his promise by donating millions to Spelman College, prompting Packard to change the seminary's name from Atlantic Baptist Female Seminary to Spelman Seminary on April 11, 1884, in honor of Mrs. Rockefeller's maiden name. The institution was renamed Spelman College in 1924.

By 1885, the school enrolled almost 650 students and housed nearly 250 on campus. It remained largely concerned with rudimentary education, but the higher education mission remained, and by 1894 Spelman began teaching classes on Latin and other college preparatory subjects. Packard and Giles sought to create black women leaders, but they were oddly quiet concerning many of the era's most controversial racial questions. While the school condemned lynching as "barbaric," it did little to actively confront the problem. Its characteristic silence was even more noticeable on the subject of reparations. In addition, while Spelman's mission was to create leaders, very few black women held leadership positions at the college for the first 50 years of its existence. These positions largely went to white women educated in Northeastern universities. It took more than 100 years after the college's founding for the first black woman, Dr. Johnetta D. Cole, to serve as its president.

Packard, Giles, and other school administrators were very much products of their times as they, in large part, clung to traditional beliefs concerning gender roles. A 1901 speech entitled "What Spelman Seminary Stands For," delivered by the American Baptist Home Missionary Society's secretary, General Thomas Jefferson Morgan, spelled out the school's vision. Spelman's goal was to, in short, do for black women what Vassar, Wellesley, and other women's colleges did for white women. These colleges reinforced gender roles and prepared women for their lives as housewives and moral leaders. Women educated as leaders would be influential in their homes and in their communities. Men, on the other hand, would remain primarily responsible for the material welfare of their families. For nearly 100 years, Spelman retained a somewhat undeserved reputation as a strict finishing school for black women that focused on forming good housewives.

Yet, during those 100 years, Spelman underwent a variety of dramatic changes. The school's third president, Lucy Hale Tapley (1910–1927), pushed for a renewed focus on teacher education. With the board's blessing, the school was renamed Spelman College in 1924 and, in the final year of her tenure, Tapley discontinued the elementary school, opting to spend Spelman's resources on other projects. Both of these actions emphasized the college's commitment to higher education. Tapley also expanded the grounds through the construction of buildings such as Sister's Chapel, which is still one of the largest buildings of the Atlanta University Center, seating more than 1,000 people. Under Tapley's administration, the College's curriculum ostensibly encouraged a more utilitarian education. Spelman received funding from the John F. Slater Fund for further developing its industrial education. In response to guidelines that came with the grant, the course catalog expanded to offer more courses in such practical subjects as cooking, sewing, millinery agriculture, and basketry. While these courses enjoyed broad enrollment from students across the college, few graduated with degrees in these types of industrial subjects. Instead, the trend was to broaden one's education with industrial courses, but major in teaching, nursing, or other academic subjects. Yet, managers from the Slater Fund expressed pleasure with the results, allowing the school to receive much needed funds and continue its goals. Following 17 years of service, Tapley stepped down in 1927.

Tapley's resignation led to the appointment of Mount Holyoake alumnus, Florence M. Read (1927–1953), as college president. Read's 26-year-long administration of Spelman led to a series of changes throughout the college, chief among them being the signature of an Agreement of Affiliation with Atlanta University and Morehouse College. This agreement set up a system of cooperation where Spelman and Morehouse served undergraduate students, while Atlanta University concentrated on graduate students. This consortium is now known as the Atlanta University Center (AUC). In addition to her work building relationships between outside schools, Read was an avid fundraiser, substantially increasing the size of Spelman's endowment, which exceeded $3 million by the end of her tenure.

Another of Read's significant contributions to Spelman's legacy is her strengthening of a decades-long Spelman tradition of recruiting lecturers and performers to the college. As Jim Crows laws often prevented black men and women from attending these types of performances, Spelman officials tried to make them available to the black community through campus performances. Many of these performers were the "leading lights" of what would come to be called the "Harlem Renaissance," and some would stay on as either lecturers or visiting professors. Read believed that exposing Spelman students to black leaders and intellectuals resonated with the college's goals and produced better students.

Following Read's retirement in 1953, Dr. Albert E. Manley became the first black male president of Spelman College. Manley, a graduate of John C. Smith and Stanford Universities, served as Spelman's president for 23 years. This era saw Spelman come into its own both as a place for social justice and as a prestigious academic institution. Manley worked tirelessly to upgrade Spelman's facilities and faculty.

The other defining theme of Manley's administration, the Civil Rights Movement, began shortly following his assumption of office. For more than 20 years, the AUC had served as one of the forming grounds for civil rights leaders. This list would eventually include such luminaries as Dr. Martin Luther King, Jr. (Morehouse), Ralph Abernethy (Clark Atlanta), and Ruby Doris Smith Robinson (Spelman). In keeping with the tradition of former students, members of the Center, particularly the ladies of Spelman, took interest in the movement. They participated in marches and sit-ins, and helped to organize the Student Non-Violent Coordinating Committee (SNCC).

Like many established black leaders of the era, Manley officially frowned on most of these activities. He encouraged his students to be patient and pursue their ends through legal means. Spelman students and faculty were reminded of the dangers of prison, the worries of parents and families, and their responsibilities as representatives of the college. Nevertheless, AUC students remained active in the Civil Rights Movement. As their first major action, AUC students published a manifesto in the major Atlanta newspapers on March 9, 1960, demanding an end of discrimination and full recognition of their worth as citizens and human beings. While Manley congratulated his students for articulating their views, he urged them to go no further.

Many Spelman students heeded his call, but others kept participating in a variety of protests. Led by history professor Howard Zinn, students conducted a sit-in at 10 different locations on March 15, 1960. Seventy-seven students were arrested and accused of breaching the peace, intimidating restaurant owners, conspiracy, and refusing to leave the premises. Additionally, six of the signatories of the manifesto were accused of the same counts. While none of the accused was convicted, the incident demonstrated the legal dangers of protesting and authorities' willingness to resort to legal measures to protect white privilege. Still, students continued to practice nonviolent resistance through sit-ins, picketing, and marches. On the day following the initial sit-ins, a group of AUC students founded the Committee on Appeal for Human Rights, and within two months, eleven students—some of them from Spelman—gathered on May 13 and 14 for the first meeting of what would become SNCC. These parallel organizations played vital roles throughout the Civil Rights Movement across the Jim Crow South, and both counted many Spelman students among their leadership.

Some of the Spelman community who participated in the movement found themselves disciplined not only by the forces of Jim Crow, but by the college's administration. One example is Gwendolyn Robinson, now Gwendolyn

Zohorah Simmons, who Manley accused of being a communist and expelled in 1965 following her arrest for her avid participation in marches and sit-ins. Robinson was reinstated due to student protests, but kept under strict probation. Shortly thereafter, she transferred out of the college. Another example is Zinn, one of the faculty leaders and mentors of many of the students involved in the Civil Rights Movement. Fired in 1963, he received no explanation for his firing from Manley or any other members of the administration. While these cases were more the exception than the rule, Spelman's administration still remained officially and vocally opposed to much of the nonviolent protests of the Civil Rights Movement.

While the Civil Rights Movement captured the nation's attention, Spelman continued its goals of educating the "head," the "hand" and the "heart." Part of this was Manley's introduction of study abroad opportunities to places in Europe and Africa that broadened students' horizons. Manley also substantially raised the profile of Spelman's fine arts program. The John D. Rockefeller, Jr. Fine Arts Center, completed in 1964, holds the Departments of Drama and Music, and has educated many award-winning performers. One of the most well known graduates of Spelman's Department of Drama and Music is playwright Pearl Cleage. While actress Keshia Knight Pulliam, best known for her role as Rudy Huxtable in *The Cosby Show*, graduated from Spelman, she earned a degree in sociology rather than drama. In addition to its work educating artists, Spelman also emphasizes the artistic contributions of and about women of the African Diaspora through the Spelman Museum of Fine Art. Past exhibitions have highlighted Atlanta, black women in cinema, and contributions from Spelman's faculty. To this day, both the Fine Arts Center and the Spelman Museum of Fine Art remain vital parts of fulfilling Spelman's educational goals, and Manley deserves credit for his work toward keeping the arts at the fore of Spelman's educational agenda.

Manley's retirement in 1976 led to the appointment of Dr. Donald M. Stewart (1976–1986). While some of Spelman's students still remained engaged in civil rights issues, Stewart's administration faced much less outward controversy than Manley's. During his tenure, Stewart started a variety of different academic programs and departments, including chemistry, women's studies, and computer science. Stewart also established a writing workshop, and began the Academic Computer Center in 1985. In 1979, Spelman formalized a movement to place alumni in positions of leadership when Marian Wright Edelman (class of 1960) was elected Chair of the Board of Trustees. During Spelman's 1981 centennial celebration, Beverly Guy-Sheftall and Jo Moore Stewart published an important history of Spelman College entitled *Spelman: A Centennial Celebration*. In his final year as president, Donald Stewart dedicated the Donald and Isabel Stewart Living-Learning Center, which serves as the honors residence hall, as well as a housing facility for visiting lecturers. Stewart stepped down in 1986 to accept the presidency of The College Board.

Following a six-month interim presidency by Dr. Barbara Carter, Dr. Johnetta B. Cole assumed the presidency from 1987 to 1997. Cole continued the College's legacy by establishing new programs and expanding the College's facilities. Cole immediately committed herself and the College to the goal of greater social activism and community integration, establishing an Institute for Community Service and building the Community Building that now bears her name. During her administration, more Spelman students became involved in community service than ever before. In 1991, the White House recognized the Spelman Community Service Program as Point of Light number 563. Spelman's commitment to community service was further enforced by visits from notable humanitarians including Nelson Mandela. Spelman received further financial recognition of its community service programs with an endowment from the Bonner Foundation for the Bonner Community Scholars Program in 1993.

The Bonner Foundation's gift was not the only funding Spelman received during Cole's tenure. A prolific fundraiser, Cole's presidency began with a $20 million donation from Camille and **William "Bill" Cosby** that was used for the construction of Camille O. Hanks Cosby Academic Center. By the end of her administration, Cole had raised more than $110 million for the university.

Cole's 1997 retirement marked another historical appointment with Dr. Audrey Forbes Manley who, on her inauguration, pledged to serve five years and act as the bridge to the twenty-first century. While as the first black woman president of Spelman College, Cole exemplified the school's goal to train black women leaders, Forbes Manley graduated from Spelman in 1955, making her the first alumna president in Spelman history. Packard's and Gile's goal for training black women leaders had come full circle. In addition, Forbes Manley was the former Deputy Surgeon General and Acting Surgeon General of the United States, as well as the wife of former president Albert E. Manley. Under her administration, Spelman added new grounds to its campus, further burnished its academic reputation, and improved its students' access to technology. In 1998, Spelman received a chapter of Phi Beta Kappa, the nation's oldest honor society. During the same year Spelman attained the number two ranking on the *Mother Jones* list of the top 10 activist colleges, further vindicating the work of Dr. Johnetta B. Cole. In addition, in 1998 Spelman became a provisional member of NCAA Division III, fielding teams in basketball, soccer, volleyball, cross country, golf, and tennis. In 2005, it was granted full status as a member of the Great South Athletic Conference, competing in the aforementioned sports as well as softball.

Spelman continued its service to the community with the establishment of the Spelman Independent Scholars Program in 2001. Members of the Program interview black elders in the community and across the nation to record and commemorate the memories of those who lived through the Jim Crow era and the Civil Rights Movement. Through a partnership with the University of Delaware, Spelman expanded its access to arts education. The two schools partnered in hopes of filling holes in their arts curriculum. In 2001, Forbes

Manley fulfilled her pledge to only serve five years by announcing her retirement during Spelman's October convocation ceremony.

Forbes Manley officially retired in 2002, and was named president emeriti. She was replaced by the current president, Dr. Beverly Tatum. Tatum brought a strategic plan to Spelman that included five goals: maintain and improve academic excellence, develop community leaders, improve Spelman's environment, increase the visibility of the campus community's accomplishments, and continue to offer exemplary customer service to all those touched by Spelman. Spelman has worked to accomplish these goals, even as it confronts the problems that universities across the nation are facing. Budget cuts, endowment losses, and increasing costs have forced many universities to find creative and innovative new ways to fulfill their goals.

In addition, as demonstrated by Spelman's internal conflict over the correct way to work for civil rights during the 1960s and 1970s, the College has dealt with a variety of controversies over the years. Chief among them is the long-running issue of colorism. While it is not as prevalent or blatant as the days of the "brown bag test," a skin-test that denied black women with a skin tone darker than a brown paper bag entrance to universities, parties, and sororities, colorism remains a significant enough issue for Spelman students that it is part of diversity training. As part of new student orientation, incoming students are expected to attend a seminar where they grapple with the themes of colorism, classism, sexual orientation, and religious diversity. Throughout the rest of their studies, Spelman students continue to discuss these themes in classes and college-sponsored lectures.

One of the most public examples of Spelman women's willingness to grapple with these issues came in response to a proposed visit to Spelman College by rap artist Nelly in 2004. Nelly scheduled an appearance at Spelman, hoping that his appearance at an influential HBCU would lead to greater minority participation in a nationwide blood marrow drive he organized in response to his sister's diagnosis of leukemia. While the drive went on as planned, Nelly did not appear because of a protest by Spelman students. Widely known for his graphic lyrics and music videos, in 2003 Nelly had released the music video for his song "Tip Drill" which showed black women participating in a variety of sexually explicit motions, including the swiping of a credit card through a woman's buttocks. This music video offended many Spelman students, and they organized a protest and a boycott. Nelly's cancellation provided a platform for Spelman students to present their concerns to a national audience. In the spring of 2004, seven Spelman women appeared via satellite on the *Oprah Winfrey Show* to present their arguments. Other leading figures of the black community joined the Spelman students in their condemnation of what they saw as the demeaning representations of black women in music, television, and other forms of media. While the protest garnered a significant amount of publicity, many Spelman students believe that misogynistic representations and lyrics remain commonplace.

While Spelman students have participated in the debates on civil rights, colorism, and misogyny, they have also been part of the public consciousness in other, less controversial, ways. During the six-season run of the television show *A Different World*, which chronicled the experiences of students at the fictional HBCU "Hillman College," series director-producer Debbie Allen made yearly pilgrimages to Spelman and Morehouse. In conversations with students from both colleges, she garnered new episode ideas and checked the veracity of her representation of an HBCU.

Over the years "Spelman women" and "Morehouse men" have shared more than conversations with television producers. Due to their proximity—the two campuses are separated by a single street—and Morehouse's status as a male-only HBCU, the two have enjoyed a special relationship for almost a century. Since 1936, a Spelman woman and a Morehouse man have been jointly crowned the king and queen of their schools' homecoming courts. Spelman women are the cheerleaders and dancers for Morehouse athletic teams, while Morehouse men are often recruited for theater productions put on by Spelman students. The bond created between the students of the two colleges remains strong long after graduation, as evidenced by the number of alumni networks shared by the two institutions.

Many Spelman graduates, such as humanitarian Marian Wright Edelman, have testified to the importance of Spelman for forming their consciousness and self-image. As a "safe place" free of expectations set by the opposite gender and whites, Edelman believes that Spelman allowed black women to develop to their full potential (Edelman, 118–119). In the sheltered community of Spelman College, black women have been and still are able to confront the stereotypes and expectations laid on them, and determine for themselves what it means to be a black woman. While Spelman is definitely not free of the influence of cultural baggage, it remains a place for black women to find themselves.

Therefore, in spite of issues within and without, Spelman continues to be a vital and dynamic force for education in the black community, as well as an institution committed to its mission of educating the "head," the "hands," and the "heart." Due to its role as an influential educational institution for black women, its historical significance during Reconstruction and the Civil Rights Movement, and its continued cultural relevance, Spelman College has attained the status of icon for black America.

John Rosinbum
Arizona State University

FURTHER READING

Edelman, Marian Wright. "Spelman College: A Safe Haven for Young Black women." *Journal of Blacks in Higher Education* 27 (2000): 118–23.

Graham, Francis D., and Susan L. Poulson. "Spelman College: A Place All Their Own." In *Challenged by Coeducation: Women's Colleges since the 1960s*, edited by Susan L. Poulson and Leslie Miller-Bernal. Nashville: Vanderbilt University Press, 2006, 234–56.

Guy-Sheftall, Beverly, and Jo Moore Stewart. *Spelman: A Centennial Celebration, 1881–1981*. Atlanta: Spelman College, 1981.

Lefever, Harry G. *Undaunted by the Fight: Spelman College and the Civil Rights Movement*. Macon: Georgia University Press, 2005.

Watson, Yolanda L., and Sheila T. Gregory. *Daring to Educate: The Legacy of the Early Spelman College Presidents*. Sterling, VA: Stylus Publishing, 2005.

Mary Church Terrell
(1863–1954)

Although Mary Church Terrell is not remembered by many people today, her activism and writings still shape conversations about gender and race. Terrell, an activist in the late nineteenth and early twentieth centuries, challenged Americans to acknowledge the experiences of black women. She supported black women by creating and maintaining private social services for them. She also advocated varied strategies over the course of her lifetime, including black self-help, interracial cooperation, and direct action. Terrell, a true icon of black America, worked tirelessly on behalf of all African Americans, particularly women.

The firstborn of her family, Terrell was born Mary Eliza Church, to Robert Reed Church and Louisa Ayers, in 1863. Her parents were former slaves, and her father was the son of his former master, but Mary and Robert Church worked hard to create lives that would not remind them or others of their former status. The Church family belonged to a class of elite African Americans in Memphis, Tennessee. While the black elite did not have the same financial resources as the white elite, Terrell had many advantages compared to other black people in Memphis. During Terrell's first years of life, her mother ran a salon for white women, which supported the family financially.

Robert Church invested in real estate during two yellow fever outbreaks in two consecutive years in Memphis. People fleeing the city for their health were desperate to sell their land in order to obtain the financial resources to support themselves elsewhere, so Church bought property at a very low price. He believed that people would return to the city after the scare passed, though many expected the city to be permanently abandoned. Church was correct, and accumulated so much wealth that, by the time his oldest daughter became a young adult, he was one of the wealthiest black men in the South.

Terrell's parents tried unsuccessfully to protect her from the realities of racism. Memphis in the mid-nineteenth century was a dangerous city for African Americans. The Church couple's divorce did not help matters, either. Louisa Church enrolled Terrell in school in Ohio, in the hopes of offering her better educational opportunities. There, the six-year-old girl became the only black child in her classes, and was exposed to racism without the buffer of her parents.

Concerned about her peers' opinions of her and other African Americans, Terrell decided to prove her race's competence by performing well in school. She also refrained from complaining about her loneliness and the physical distance that separated her from her family members, as she understood that her education was a unique opportunity for her. Although she believed that some of her peers treated her poorly because she was black, she continued to try to succeed academically. Terrell remained in school in Ohio throughout her childhood and adolescence, though she would spend summers with either of her divorced parents and her siblings.

After finishing high school, Terrell enrolled at Oberlin, one of the few colleges that admitted black women. Pushing aside the educational program usually offered to women, Terrell enrolled in the gentlemen's course, which focused on classics, for several years. She immersed herself in extracurricular activities, which were largely religious and literary organizations. She also enjoyed dancing. Terrell graduated from Oberlin College in 1884.

After graduating from college, Terrell returned to Memphis and lived with her father for one year. He wanted her to remain with him, where he could support her financially and ensure that all of her needs were met. Terrell balked at this idea, however; she was one of the first black women to earn a bachelor's degree in the United States, and she felt compelled to use her education to help other black people. Her family's financial resources and her education exposed her to notable African Americans such as **Frederick Douglass** and **Booker T. Washington,** and those meetings pushed her to consider following in their footsteps.

Many other elite black women during the Jim Crow era would feel similarly obligated to use their educations and professional skills to help their communities. The attitude with which Terrell approached her life is particularly noticeable here. She felt optimistic about the opportunities available to her. Although many careers and freedoms were denied to her, she focused instead on those that were available.

Terrell determined that she would work, despite her father's ability to support her indefinitely. She accepted a job at Wilberforce University in Ohio, and again traveled to that state. Her decision disrupted her relationship with her father, and they did not speak for nearly one year. Terrell was an industrious worker, teaching numerous courses. At the end of the school year, she was able to heal the rift that her employment created between her father and herself. After working at the university for one year, she moved to Washington, DC, and taught at M Street High School. She took additional classes at Oberlin while working in Washington, DC, and earned her master of arts in 1888. Robert Heberton Terrell, a Harvard-educated Virginian with a law degree from Howard, was her supervisor at this high school.

Mary Church Terrell's affection for Robert Terrell placed her in a difficult position. While she loved Robert, she struggled to reconcile her desire to work in the public sphere and societal conventions regarding gender roles. She feared that marriage would relegate her to the home and prevent her from making meaningful contributions to her community and nation. Undecided, Terrell went to Europe for two years, as her father had hoped; she was attracted to Europe because she believed that the continent did not have the same racism and sexism present in the United States, and that her ideas might consequently be taken more seriously there. In several countries in Europe, including France, Italy, and Germany, Terrell practiced the languages she had learned during her earlier education, and enjoyed time with visiting family.

She returned to the United States, and decided to marry Robert Terrell. She considered postponing the wedding after receiving a job offer to become the registrar of Oberlin, which was both a promotion and an opportunity that

Terrell believed neither Oberlin nor any other white university had offered a black person before. Accepting this offer would have meant separation from her fiancé, who had become the principal of M Street. She instead married Terrell in 1891 in Memphis, where her father happily made the ceremony a lavish event, much to his daughter's dismay.

Her marriage connected her to a prominent black man, but also shifted the opportunities available to her. Her husband, in addition to working as the principal of M Street, also practiced law in Washington, DC. He later taught law at Howard University, and served, from 1902 to the end of his life, as an appointed judge in the District of Columbia Municipal Court. Although Terrell's wedding united her with an accomplished husband, she lost work opportunities in marriage. Washington, DC did not permit married women to teach, so Terrell could not teach at M Street even though her husband was its principal. Early in her marriage, she lost three children shortly after their births, though in 1898 she gave birth to a healthy daughter named Phyllis while visiting her mother in New York. She and her husband also raised one of her nieces, Mary Louisa, beginning in 1905.

Terrell felt compelled to speak out publicly about racism shortly after she married. She had learned that Tom Moss, a prominent African American in Memphis who ran a grocery store that competed with the businesses owned by whites in the city, was lynched by a white mob along with several of his black business associates. This lynching, which also pushed another friend of Moss, **Ida B. Wells-Barnett**, into activism, shocked Terrell. She used her connections to, with Frederick Douglass, meet directly with the President of the United States, Benjamin Harrison, to discuss the lynching. Harrison did not take any action as a result of his meeting with Douglass and Terrell, however. Yet the meeting was remarkable in its display of Terrell's thought process; she believed that appealing to the President with the facts of the lynching would be enough to move the federal government into action. Terrell's action could be construed as naiveté, but she shared this mindset with other African Americans, including Douglass.

Terrell's activism soon shifted to organizational activity. She and many other Americans frequently created and joined clubs and other organizations, in which they worked with friends and other community members toward a common, shared goal. White and black Americans created such organizations, which were sometimes connected with their churches, but black women's organizations frequently assumed political as well as social purposes. Black women's clubs sought to challenge racism and supplement the resources available to a community that frequently lacked sufficient economic opportunities. These clubs also fostered pride in the black community by not only improving social conditions, but by improving black people's knowledge and consequently their ability to use available resources.

Terrell participated in the black women's club movement. She joined with other notable black women, including Anna Julia Cooper, to form in 1892 the Colored Women's League in Washington, DC. Terrell and the League's other founders argued that black women could work together to improve the conditions faced by the black community. Stressing self-help ideology, she encouraged black women to see themselves as the solutions to the problems created by racism and economic circumstances. Women from many different states joined the League, modeling their organizations after that created by Terrell and counting themselves as members of the larger League.

Many other black women's clubs were founded in the North; Terrell and these other founders collaborated to create an umbrella organization for each of these clubs. For example, other prominent black women, including Joseph St. Pierre Ruffin and Margaret Murray Washington, created the Federation of Afro-American Women in Boston. These women joined their organizations together to create the National Association of Colored Women (NACW). As the first president of the organization, Terrell stressed racial uplift. Indeed, the NACW adopted "Lifting as We Climb" as its motto, encouraging black women to lift other black people to better social and moral conditions as they themselves improved. The motto was positive and encouraged black women to believe that better circumstances were possible. By arguing that the end of racism was contingent on black women's status and treatment, Terrell shifted attention to black women's circumstances.

Racial uplift also placed a heavy burden on black women, however. People who advocated racial uplift in the late nineteenth and early twentieth centuries believed that black people should improve their material and social conditions by behaving in ways reminiscent of white middle-class ideals. These organizations stressed women's successful execution of gender roles, though a mother's responsibility was defined broadly and ranged from knowledge of child development to how to build houses. Conforming to these ideals would enable African Americans to prove to themselves and to white people that they were moral and capable citizens. Terrell explained in 1916 in a speech addressed to black women in Charleston at the Mt. Zion African Episcopal Methodist Church,

> We have to do more than other women. Those of us fortunate enough to have education must share it with the less fortunate of our race. We must go into our communities and improve them; we must go out into the nation and change it. Above all, we must organize ourselves as Negro women and work together. (White, 22)

Elite black women, according to the philosophy of racial uplift, must use their resources to improve themselves and all others who belong to the black community. Racial uplift implies that racism exists because white people believe that black people are morally and socially inferior. To lift the race up to the same moral standards held by white people, then, would end or disrupt racism by challenging whites' assumption regarding black people.

Yet the notion of racial uplift can be considered class-specific. Elite black women decided to improve the social conditions of their community and race by seeking to change the behavior of the black poor and working-class, in particular. Terrell explained, for example, that she feared that African Americans would be judged by the most ignorant black women, rather than by their educated, elite counterparts. Black women's clubs frequently targeted vices in their communities, and shut down, for example, gambling houses to stop black people's gambling. Black communities desired this change, however, and expected women such as Terrell to offer this service to other black people; black communities wanted elite black women to use their status and education in ways that would benefit everyone.

Terrell also worked with predominantly white women's organizations. Although not a member of the National Woman Suffrage Association, one of two primary organizations that advocated women's right to vote, Terrell regularly attended the bi-annual meetings held in Washington, DC from the 1880s. Through her attendance at these meetings, she met Susan B. Anthony. The National American Woman Suffrage Association, which was the product of a merger between two formerly separate suffrage associations, invited her to speak twice at their Washington, DC meetings, in 1898 and 1900. In the first of these speeches, she argued that black women face a far greater burden than white women and black men, because black women suffer from racism as well as sexism. This articulation of black women's experiences was remarkable. Terrell's commentary, and the venue in which she was permitted to speak, allowed her to challenge white women to acknowledge the different experiences faced by black women.

The members of the NACW determined to identify and meet the needs of black women to uplift them. Many black women worked to support their families or supplement their partners' incomes; Terrell and the NACW created kindergartens and nurseries to assist working mothers with childcare. They also created Mother Clubs to teach women how to better care for their children. By creating Mother Clubs, Terrell gained a greater awareness of the problems faced by other black women. She adapted the clubs to meet the social needs of black women, and encouraged the people who staffed these clubs to pay attention to the poor employment opportunities available to black men and women.

In addition, cognizant of the migration that many black women made on their own in this era from the South to the North, black women's clubs sought to help black women adjust to urban life, as many migrants came from rural areas in search of better job opportunities and freedom from Southern racism. Arrival in the North was disheartening to many women, who learned that white people and custom in the North were also racist. Some black women struggled to find employment after traveling from their homes to new cities. The black women's clubs sought to ameliorate some of this shock and struggle by connecting new arrivals with a larger community and, consequently, with better information and more opportunities.

Terrell also established schools to help girls and young women. The NACW sponsored schools that taught domestic science, which focused on mothering and homemaking, but also stressed the disciplined and scientific aspects of such work. Education in mothering, for example, would examine childhood development and stress the importance of proper parenting for children. Providing such instruction to women at a young age would, Terrell hoped, improve the next generation of the black community.

She and her club associates stressed a black feminism that prioritized women. By arguing that the fate of the black community rested with black women, Terrell made their circumstances and experiences uniquely important. Black women, who were frequently excluded from conversations about race in the nineteenth century, found a strategy through Terrell's comments that allowed them to articulate their thoughts and insist that their experiences were valid and integral to the black experience. Indeed, some of Terrell's associates would go so far as to argue that the black community could only be saved through the labor of black women, rather than through the work of black men and women.

Black women's clubs did encounter problems, however. John Hope, a prominent African American, spoke to Atlanta clubwomen, but criticized them for what he considered their unwomanly behavior. Arguing that black men, rather than black women, should concern themselves with the material progress of the race, Hope insisted that black women were limiting black men's opportunities by trying to assume this role themselves. Hope's comments deeply upset Terrell and other black women, who insisted that the fate of the black community continued to rely on their status as black women. Yet these attacks and counter-attacks revealed black people's fears regarding gender roles in a society that denied freedom to both black men and women.

Terrell's activism and financial resources allowed her to become a public figure in black America. She delivered speeches describing the racism that African Americans faced, and commented on their worth and value as human beings. By stressing the progress made by African Americans, Terrell hoped to demonstrate the injustice of a racism directed against worthy people. She authored articles on issues important to her community as well, including lynching and disenfranchisement, or the limitations placed on black men's opportunities to vote. No women could vote in federal elections before the passage of the Nineteenth Amendment in 1920, though many states would limit black women's opportunities to vote immediately after the ratification of that amendment.

Terrell had a very light complexion, and some people assumed that she was white. She learned to navigate others' assumptions of her race throughout the course of her lifetime, but she learned that allowing some white people to assume that she was white could work to her advantage:

> I have sometimes taken advantage of my ability to get certain necessities and
> comforts and I have occasionally availed myself of opportunities to which I was

entitled by outwitting those who are obsessed with race prejudice and would have withheld them from me, if they had been perfectly sure of my racial status. But never once in my life have I been tempted to "cross the color line" and deny my racial identity. I could not have maintained my self respect if I had continuously masqueraded as being something I am not. (Terrell, 471)

Some African Americans have strongly criticized the practice of passing, arguing that black people with lighter complexions enjoyed benefits unavailable to those who were darker and thus not mistaken as white. Terrell did not pass out of animosity or a desire to be white, however; she instead allowed other people to mis-identify her so that she might feel safer at select moments. This strategic maneuvering through others' racial categories highlights Terrell's intelligence.

Terrell's courage and honesty frequently led her to criticize others and to question herself. She certainly commented on the hatefulness of racists, but she also condemned white liberals who did not do enough to help black people. In addition, she challenged black men who did not support causes important to women, and she was unafraid to criticize black women. She also struggled with the irony of her personal life choices; while she encouraged black women to become better mothers and uplift the race by improving their families and homes, her life did not match what she preached. She spent much of her life traveling and speaking publicly, rather than remaining at home with her family.

As Terrell aged, she received much recognition for her lifetime of work. In 1929, Oberlin identified her as one of the 100 most successful graduates. She published her autobiography in 1940, sharing her thoughts on her upbringing and activism. When the Washington, DC branch of the American Association of University Women refused to let her renew her membership, she received the support of the national leaders of the organization, who forced her reinstatement in 1949. She also received honorary doctorates from several of the universities in which she and her husband had worked or enrolled.

Terrell's age, as well as the support she received from others, did not end her activist work. Her husband's health declined for years before his death in 1925, which caused her much grief. Her feelings did not deter her, however. She shifted her focus to segregation, and pushed to end the practice in Washington, DC, in particular. The chair of the Coordinating Committee for the Enforcement of District of Columbia Anti-Discrimination Laws, Terrell decided to create a test case that would bring the practice of segregation in the nation's capitol to the courts. In 1950, at the age of 86, she joined a sit-in at Thompson Restaurant in Washington, DC. When she and her fellow activists were denied service, they went to court. While the *District of Columbia v. John Thompson* case moved through the court system, Terrell continued to challenge segregation.

Terrell's politics again shifted. Facing whites' opposition to desegregation firsthand, she determined that her earlier strategy of racial uplift was unable to create the equality she had envisioned for African Americans. Instead, she worked with black youth to directly challenge and confront those who enforced segregation. The case brought about by Terrell's 1950 sit-in resulted in 1953 in a victory for the African American community, as the U.S. Supreme Court determined that segregated restaurants were unconstitutional.

Terrell's long life began before the end of the American Civil War and ended shortly after the 1954 *Brown v. Board of Education* decision, which some historians have used to mark the beginning of the Civil Rights Movement. She survived the entirety of the Jim Crow period, and struggled throughout her life to combat the racism to which she and other African Americans were subjected. She also recognized that black women's experiences were unique, however, and campaigned around issues that particularly affected them. Her strategies to combat racism evolved throughout this era, just as did those of other African American leaders.

Terrell devoted her life to helping black America. Although she did not need to work and might instead have lived in a privileged cocoon created by her father, she chose instead to organize on her behalf and for her community. She strategically used her social and economic privilege to help other African Americans throughout her entire adult life. Her activism created material benefits for black families; she created new resources such as kindergartens to assist families with limited options, and she encouraged black women to prioritize and uplift themselves. She also created a model for black women's clubs that influenced generations of clubwomen. The evolution of her politics demonstrated her thoughtfulness and adaptability, as well as her willingness to question herself. Terrell's lifetime of activism makes her an icon of black America.

Megan Falater
University of Wisconsin-Madison

FURTHER READING

Shaw, Stephanie J. *What a Woman Ought to Be and Do: Black Professional Women Workers during the Jim Crow Era*. Chicago: University of Chicago Press, 1996.

Terrell, Mary Church. *A Colored Woman in a White World*. Foreword by Debra Newman Ham, 1940. Amherst, NY: Humanity Books, 2005.

White, Deborah Gray. *Too Heavy a Load: Black Women in Defense of Themselves, 1894–1994*. New York: W. W. Norton, 1999.

The man over there says that women need to be helped into carriages and lifted over ditches, and to have the best place everywhere. Nobody ever helps me into carriages or over puddles or gives me the best place...

...and ain't I a woman?

Look at my arm! I have ploughed and planted and gathered into barns, and no man could head me ...and ain't I a woman?
I could work as much and eat as much as a man— when I could get it—and bear the lash as well ...and ain't I a woman?
I have borne thirteen children, and seen most of 'em sold into slavery, and when I cried out with my mother's grief, none but Jesus heard me ...and ain't I a woman?

Sojourner Truth   Abolitionist, 1851

Library of Congress

Sojourner Truth
(1797–1883)

Sojourner Truth, born Isabella Baumfree, advocated slavery's abolition, women's suffrage, and African American civil rights. Self-emancipated from slavery in New York in 1826, Baumfree became Sojourner Truth in 1843 after converting to Christianity and joining an evangelical Methodist movement. She began speaking to abolitionist gatherings in the 1840s, in an age in which even African American men spoke in public at their peril. She gave her most celebrated speech to an 1851 women's rights convention, making the argument that women deserved civil rights based on Christian principles and their hard work. During the Civil War and afterward, she worked for the relief of freedpeople, as the formerly enslaved were known. Her image became iconic after she began selling *cartes-de-visite* bearing her image as a dignified African American woman, but white amanuenses and authors largely crafted her public persona. Throughout her long career, she spoke before religious gatherings, abolitionist, and women's suffrage meetings, and after Emancipation advocated equality and reparations for former slaves.

Born enslaved in Hurley, Ulster County, New York, Isabella was the youngest of 10 or 12 children of Elizabeth "Betsey" and James "Bomefree" (or Baumfree). Like their owner Johannis Hardenbergh, the Baumfree family spoke Dutch. Isabella Baumfree lost most of her siblings to sale. She knew only one of her siblings, Peter, and when her second owner Charles Hardenbergh died, his heirs sold Isabella for $100 to John Neely in 1807 or 1808, along with a flock of sheep. The sale separated nine- or ten-year-old Isabella from her parents, and when she could not understand what the English-speaking Neelys demanded of her, she was beaten severely. "Now the war begun," Truth recalled of that time (Gilbert, 26).

Isolated from her family, Baumfree toiled in filthy conditions for a series of owners. After a year of labor and abuse in the Neely household, Baumfree became the property of the Schriver family of Kingston, for whom she did a variety of domestic and agricultural work. In 1810, she was sold again, this time to John Dumont. That began 16 years of hard work and maltreatment in the Dumont household, likely including sexual abuse by Dumont's wife Sally. Nevertheless, Baumfree tried her best to please the Dumonts, minimize her punishments, and preserve her dwindling self-esteem.

In about 1813 or 1814, an enslaved man named Robert attracted her attention and "an attachment sprang up" between them (Gilbert, 34). Robert's owner forbade the match and his sons beat him nearly to death after discovering the two together, which ended their romance. In about 1815, Baumfree married Thomas, another slave of the Dumont family. Thomas had already been married twice and had lost one wife to sale. Between 1815 and 1826, Baumfree gave birth to five children. She had the first, Diana, around 1815. Peter, named after her father, was born in 1821; Elizabeth, named after her mother, arrived in 1825; and Sophia was born a year later. Baumfree and Thomas may have had one more child, but it likely died in infancy or childhood. Despite being a woman and a mother, the Dumonts still worked her as hard as a man.

After Sophia arrived, Baumfree decided to become free. New York State law required that all slaves born before 1799 would be emancipated on July 4, 1827. Those born after, including Baumfree's children, would still have to serve a term of years in slavery. To inspire Baumfree to work harder before freedom, Dumont promised to manumit her one year early and move her and Thomas into a cabin together. After she seriously injured her right hand, however, Dumont broke his promise. Despite that, she did not leave at once, departing in late 1826. Taking baby Sophia, Baumfree went to live with Isaac and Maria Van Wagenen, who opposed slavery, for about a year.

During that time, Baumfree underwent a spiritual transformation. Her self-emancipation from the Dumonts coincided with an awakening to sin and salvation in Jesus Christ, a vision of whom she beheld. She dedicated herself to preaching, prayer, and enthusiastic worship. She embraced Methodist perfectionism, an all-encompassing devotion to God guided by Holy Spirit, or as she simply put it, "the Spirit" (Gilbert, 92). Baumfree recalled her growing faith as a "soul-protecting fortress," from the safety of which she struggled against fear, sin, and—in due time—slavery and its injustices (Gilbert, 71).

Almost immediately, her faith and perseverance were tested when her son Peter was taken from New York to Alabama. The impending New York emancipation gave slaveholders considerable financial reasons to sell enslaved people before they were set free. Despite being illegal, New York slaveholders cashed in on a lucrative slave trade to the Deep South. In 1826, Dumont sold Peter to a relative of his wife, who after bringing him to New York City sold him again after discovering that the boy of five or six was too young to complete his tasks. That owner sold him yet again, this time to another relative of Sally Dumont, who took him to Alabama, a thousand miles away. When word reached Baumfree, she immediately set out looking for him but got no sympathy from the Dumonts or anyone responsible for Peter's removal.

In an extraordinary move for the time, Baumfree went to court to get Peter back. Black women had nearly no civic status anywhere in the United States at the time, and Baumfree was still enslaved under New York law. Nevertheless, with the financial support of Ulster County Quakers and the legal assistance of two prominent Dutch lawyers, Baumfree sued the man who had taken her son. The proceedings took a year, during which she worked for one of the lawyers. She won the case and Peter returned, though evidence of his abuse was heartbreaking. Not yet seven years old, he had been scarred by the lash, kicked by a horse, and beaten by the man who took him south. Initially Peter was too traumatized to even acknowledge Baumfree as his mother, but she had won an unlikely victory against a white man and the family of her enslavers.

After reuniting with Peter in 1828, Baumfree headed south to New York City with two fellow Methodists, settling in Bowery Hill, where she worked for a family that shared her religious perfectionism. She would stay with them until 1832. In the city, she reconnected with siblings Sophia and Michael. She had never met Michael until then. Another sister, Nancy, died before she could meet her. Contemplating the enforced separations, Sojourner Truth later recalled asking, "What is this slavery, that it can do such dreadful things?" (Gilbert, 81). But she did not despair and gained a reputation for her zealous and inspirational preaching, especially during Methodist revivals in the city from 1829 to 1831. She preached with and at times was more popular than white Methodist revivalists. Baumfree had an authenticity and charisma that drew people to her, and she practiced a pious self-denial that many of her contemporaries lacked in their personal conduct. She preached the Gospel as she knew it and felt it, despite not having learned to read or write, which fit with perfectionists's emphasis on spiritual experience rather than theological disputation.

Though confined to wage work in the households of prominent coreligionists, Baumfree's vocation was preaching and converting. A number of revivals swept New York, which attracted charismatic and controversial preachers. By 1832, Baumfree was working for another Methodist perfectionist, Elijah Pierson, when she encountered Robert Matthews, also known as "the Prophet Matthias," who led a movement based on his prophesy that the world would end on July 9, 1836. By mid-1833, he led a separatist community called the Kingdom of Matthias outside of New York City. Baumfree came to live there in 1833, and while performing much of the domestic drudgery, she was subject to sexual abuse by a female member. When Matthias was charged with Pierson's murder, Baumfree stood by him and contributed her savings to his cause. She also won a slander suit against one of the Kingdom's former financial backers. After the murder trial, in which Matthias was convicted on lesser charges, the community fell apart.

Baumfree returned to New York City and her son Peter. She struggled to earn a living in the hard times following 1837. After getting in trouble with the law, Peter left on a whaling ship in 1839. Like most black women doing domestic work for white families, she lived isolated from a broader black community. Baumfree mostly worshiped in white-run churches and associated with charismatic clerics like Matthias rather than black civic leaders, temperance advocates, and abolitionists. Nell Irvin Painter comments that most black leaders "took their cues from the public realm, from politics and business, while she heeded the voice of the Holy Spirit" (Painter, 72).

In her mid-forties, Baumfree took stock of her life and decided that "every thing she had undertaken in the city of New York had finally proved a failure." As for the city, "she felt called in spirit to leave it, and to travel east and lecture" (Gilbert, 98–99). She left on the first of June 1843, traveling to Long Island, then to Connecticut, and became Sojourner Truth. The choice of name indicates her itinerancy working in the service of truth. There was more than just individual moral urgency to her rebirth and decision to leave the city. Truth had become an adherent of a Second Advent movement known as Millerism, after its leader William Miller, who prophesied the Biblical apocalypse in 1843. The Millerites were racially integrated, believing that in the end times, social distinctions of color and gender were irrelevant. Truth traveled up the Connecticut River valley and settled in the cooperative community of Northampton, Massachusetts.

Followers called the failure of Miller's prophesy the Great Disappointment, but Truth's exodus from New York and entry into the Northampton Association of Education and Industry would begin the work for which she would become famous. At Northampton, Truth met leading abolitionists **Frederick Douglass**, William Lloyd Garrison, Wendell Phillips, and a number of reformers including Sylvester Graham. Life at Northampton was austere. Dedicated to open-mindedness, however, it was also racially integrated. The Northampton founders rejected the prevailing political economy, but they sought to change it through moral and social reform. There Truth honed her voice and her speaking skills. Her preaching, praying, and declamations won her admiration, and reformers recognized her speaking potential. Douglass later commented that she was a "strange compound of wit and wisdom, of wild enthusiasm and flint-like common sense" (Painter, 98). The Northampton commune disbanded in 1846, but Truth stayed in the area.

Partly to tell her story and partly to buy her own home (after living in and working in the homes of so many others), Truth went to work on an autobiography, published as the *Narrative of Sojourner Truth* in 1850. Between 1848 and 1850, Olive Gilbert, also a former Northampton Association member, served as her amanuensis. Truth printed copies of her *Narrative* on credit, and then sold them to audiences who heard her speak. Slavery had left her without formal literary skills, a challenge that would heighten as her fame grew and others refashioned her words and image. Truth's *Narrative* is primarily a spiritual autobiography, and Gilbert emphasized both Truth's religious enthusiasm and her suspicions of the world. "Through all the scenes of her eventful life may be traced the energy of a naturally powerful mind," Gilbert wrote, "the fearlessness and child-like simplicity of one untrammeled by education or conventional customs—purity of character—an unflinching adherence to principle—and a native enthusiasm" (Gilbert, 121–122). In the spirit of Christianity, Truth ends her *Narrative* by forgiving former owner John Dumont after he repented and confessed the sinfulness of slavery.

Through her Northampton associations and publication of her *Narrative*, Truth broadened her network to include some of the most prominent reformers in America. After launching her speaking career in 1844, she spoke in 1845 in New York City to a convention of the American Anti-Slavery Society. In 1850, she addressed a women's rights meeting in Worcester, Massachusetts, which succeeded the 1848 Seneca Falls convention. Besides abolitionists like Garrison and Douglass, Truth associated with feminists like Amy and Isaac Post, and Lucretia Mott. As a formerly enslaved woman, Truth was in a tiny minority of abolitionist and women's rights reformers to be both African American and female. Even many radical abolitionists did not appreciate women speaking in public, and some feminists shared prevailing ideas about white supremacy.

Truth's oratory differed from most abolitionists and women's rights advocates because of her distinctive mix of homespun wit, broad Biblical repertoire,
and first-hand experience of slavery. In 1851, her reputation on the rise, she
toured the abolitionist and women's rights speaking circuit with radical British
reformer and Member of Parliament George Thompson. Truth stayed with the
Posts while speaking in western New York, which began a lifelong friendship.
Unlike in her previous associations with whites, Truth found Thompson and
the Posts to be free of racial prejudice. In May, Truth addressed a women's
rights convention in Akron, Ohio, in which she gave her most celebrated
address.

> I am a woman's rights. I have plowed and reaped and husked and chopped and
> mowed, and can any man do more than that? I have heard much about the sexes
> being equal; I can carry as much as any man, and can eat as much, too, if I can get
> it. I am as strong as any man that is now. As for intellect, all I can say is, if a
> woman have a pint and a man a quart—why cant she have her little pint full?
> I have heard the bible and have learned that Eve caused man to sin. Well if woman
> upset the world, do give her a chance to set it right side up again. (Fitch and
> Mandzuik, 107)

Garrison's *Liberator* reported, "The power and wit of this remarkable woman
convulsed the audience with laughter" (Fitch and Mandzuik, 143).

The 1850s were a time of great urgency for opponents of slavery, and Truth
became more vehement of her denunciations of slavery and of white people,
prophesying that a time would come when black people would have their
revenge. She compared the U.S. government to ill-fated kingdoms of the
Hebrew Bible, which had suffered God's wrath. To black audiences, she
preached uplift and economy. During the 1850s she traveled widely, west to
Indiana as well as around New York and New England. She sometimes toured
solo, and confronted one hostile gathering of Democrats by recalling that she
had nursed white babies as a slave. To shame them, she revealed her breast
as a symbol of her bodily connection to an institution of slavery in which black
women were forced to suckle white infants, often to the exclusion of their own
children. Instead of being a passive black woman on display at auction—
where enslaved women were subject to humiliation at the hands of white
buyers—Truth used her physical body as a powerful rhetorical image, calling
attention to her blackness as well as her womanhood. Those were images
few could attempt—and only Truth actually pulled off.

Truth was undergoing another religious transformation, this time influenced
by the Spiritualism of some of her friends in the reform movement. Spiritualism,
which included communication with the spirit world, was gaining popularity in
the mid-nineteenth century, and the Posts in particular were leaving their fervent
Quakerism for Spiritualism. In 1857, Truth left her house in Northampton,
Massachusetts, and moved to the Spiritualist community of Harmonia, in Battle

Creek, Michigan. Her daughters Elizabeth and Diana joined her, along with two grandsons.

During the Civil War, Truth rose to national prominence in large part because of how others used and to an extent manipulated her voice and image. In 1863, Harriet Beecher Stowe, author of *Uncle Tom's Cabin* and other popular anti-slavery melodramas, published an article, "Sojourner Truth, the Libyan Sibyl," which began with a fictionalized account of a visit Truth made to Stowe in 1853 seeking the author's endorsement of her *Narrative*. The article was widely read, and Stowe effectively remade the plain-spoken Truth into an exotic curiosity, "a full-blooded African," who spoke in an affected Southern accent, of the kind white audiences unfamiliar with Truth might expect of a former slave (Painter, 154). Stowe appeased white racial stereotypes by portraying Truth as a woman whose racial characteristics determined her temperament and outlook. That was not the first time Stowe had magnified Truth's reputation by bending the truth. In 1860, she published an account of Truth's supposed confrontation with Frederick Douglass years before at a meeting in Boston. Douglass was arguing that the only remedy for slavery and racism was violence, to which Truth reportedly responded, "Frederick, is God dead?" The actual exchange had taken place in 1852 in Salem, Ohio, and witnesses reported Truth asking Douglass, "Is God gone?" (Mabee and Newhouse, 83). Stowe enlarged and embellished the story in "The Libyan Sibyl." Stowe was not alone. Women's rights reformer Frances Dana Gage published her own version of Truth as a Southerner, recreating Truth's famous 1851 Akron speech. Gage recalled Truth asking, repeatedly, "Ar'n't I a woman?" Truth was upset at Stowe's characterization of her as an "African," but there was little she could do.

Truth did have one way to represent herself on her own terms, and in 1863 Truth began selling *cartes-de-visite* or baseball card-sized photographs featuring her portrait, usually sitting upright, in a domestic middle-class setting, with sewing in her hands. Photography as a consumer product took off during the Civil War, and so did Truth's trade in marketing her image. "I sell the shadow to support the substance," reads the caption of most of the cards. With few other sources of income, selling her photographs sustained her financially through much of the decade. Those images would become iconic.

During the Civil War, as enslaved African Americans freed themselves from bondage, Truth had a pressing agenda: assisting refugees fleeing war. In contrast to her pre-war aversion to politics, she embraced the Union cause and supported Abraham Lincoln. In 1864, Lincoln received Truth at the White House, though curtly. Her more palpable presence in Washington, DC that year was as an activist for decent treatment for freedpeople gathered in filthy and dangerous refugee camps. She also battled discrimination in public transportation, managing to get fired streetcar drivers who refused to accommodate black passengers. As part of the National Freedmen's Relief Association, and later the Freedmen's Bureau, she advocated for freedpeople's needs, speaking to former slaves as one who had known slavery. She also secured jobs for freedpeople and urged them to learn self-help and self-improvement, even if available employment was far away from home.

After Emancipation, as reform efforts shifted to voting rights, Truth remained a staunch and vocal supporter of women's rights. With feminists like Susan B. Anthony, Elizabeth Cady Stanton, and Frances Ellen Watkins Harper, she advocated universal suffrage, or voting rights for all adults. But Truth, like Harper, spoke for black women. They did not oppose the vote for black men, as some white feminists did, but Truth worried that without civil rights, black women would remain financially dependent, primarily upon husbands. She spoke as an African American woman who had to eek out a living without civic status. The women's suffrage movement split in the 1860s over the issue of whether to endorse gains made for African American men by the Fourteenth and Fifteenth Amendments. Truth tried to heal divisions, but joined the American Woman Suffrage Association, rival to Anthony and Stanton's National Woman Suffrage Association.

The culmination of her career as an advocate for freedpeople's relief was a plan to resettle the formerly enslaved in Kansas. By 1870, political will to aid freedpeople was dwindling, many former slaves were still refugees, and the tide of racial terrorism was rising nationally. With that in view, Truth looked to the government to give the formerly enslaved land and opportunity rather than continuing desultory assistance where they were. She enlisted supporters to gain signatures for petitions to Congress, and spoke extensively in favor of creating a reservation for African Americans in Kansas. The plan foundered for lack of support, but Truth enthusiastically supported the black Exodus to Kansas in 1879. Federal abandonment of Reconstruction and the rise of reactionary Democrats severely curtailed African American gains since Emancipation, and bloody violence compelled many to leave. She raised funds to help in the resettlement effort, which ended by 1880.

In part to pay for the care of her grandson Samuel Banks, Truth authorized a new autobiography in 1875, this time with fellow women's rights activist Frances W. Titus acting as her "scribe." The book did much to promote Truth as an icon without adhering to historical detail. Adding to the 1850 *Narrative*, Titus excerpted from Truth's "Book of Life." The 1875 *Narrative* included numerous exaggerations and represented her accomplishments through the prism of the public image crafted by Harriet Beecher Stowe and others. In representing her famous 1851 Akron speech, for instance, Titus repeats the phrase "ar'n't I a woman?" relying on Frances Dana Gage's distorted account of the event (Titus, 134, 256). Titus published an expanded posthumous edition in 1884.

By the late 1870s, Truth was in failing health, and despite plans to continue speaking and advocating for women's rights and freedpeople's resettlement, she remained near her Battle Creek home and daughters Diana, Elizabeth, and Sophia. Her early evangelical fervor had given ground to a thoroughgoing

Spiritualism. Truth died on November 26, 1883, recognized as an icon in her time.

Calvin Schermerhorn
Arizona State University

FURTHER READING

Fitch, Suzanne Pullon, and Roseann M. Mandzuik. *Sojourner Truth as Orator: Wit, Story, and Song.* Westport, CT: Greenwood Press, 1997.

Gilbert, Olive. *Narrative of Sojourner Truth, a Northern Slave, Emancipated from Bodily Servitude by the State of New York, in 1828.* Boston: Printed for the Author, 1850.

Mabee, Carleton, and Susan Mabee Newhouse. *Sojourner Truth: Slave, Prophet, Legend.* New York: New York University Press, 1993.

Painter, Nell Irvin. *Sojourner Truth: A Life, a Symbol.* New York and London: W. W. Norton, 1996.

Titus, Frances W. *Narrative of Sojourner Truth; a Bondswoman of Olden Time, Emancipated by the New York Legislature in the Early Part of the Present Century; with a History of Her Labors and Correspondence, Drawn from Her "Book of Life."* Boston: The Author, 1875.

Harriet Tubman (1822–1913)

Harriet Tubman, whose given name was Araminta "Minty" Ross, was born enslaved on a Maryland plantation in 1822. Tubman achieved international recognition within her lifetime by defying incredible odds in her escape from slavery and her heroic rescues of enslaved relatives and friends. For these audacious feats, Tubman earned the nickname, "Moses of her people." Tubman's exceptional commitment to the eradication of slavery continued as she served in the Union army during the Civil War as a nurse, scout, and spy. After the war, Tubman was devoted to the care of her extended family and disadvantaged African Americans. Like so many laudable figures, Tubman did not purposefully venture into African American iconography, rather she was an unlikely hero whose impetus was to escape slavery, free her family from bondage, and fight racial and social injustice. Tubman is now one of the most recognized African American icons of the nineteenth century.

Tubman grew up in the early years of a burgeoning country founded upon ideals of freedom and equality, yet mired in the opposing institution of slavery. Tubman was born on the Thompson plantation in Peter's Neck, Dorchester County, Maryland. In the decades leading up to the Civil War, Maryland became an intersection of Southern slavery and Northern abolitionism. The invention of the cotton gin in 1793 stimulated resurgence in the most brutal systems of chattel slavery in the South. At the same time, slavery in the North began to weaken as abolition efforts increased and Northern economies no longer supported the widespread use of slave labor. The slow eradication of slavery in the North led to a large population of free blacks in Maryland in the early nineteenth century. Growing up in this community meant that Tubman suffered from the brutal injustices inherent in slavery, but she also found hope for freedom within her associations with the free black community.

Tubman's family life was a remarkable example of tenacity in the face of unspeakable odds. Tubman's parents were enslaved by different owners, thus their marriage, not recognized by law, was as tentative as their respective slaveholders' inclinations. Anthony Thompson enslaved Tubman's father, Benjamin "Ben" Ross, who was a skilled lumberman. Mary Pattison enslaved Tubman's mother, Harriet "Rit" Green, who primarily performed domestic duties in slaveholders' homes. In 1801, Mary Pattison married her second husband, Anthony Thompson. This marriage led to Rit and Ben's union and by 1808, the couple had married and begun their family. Tubman was the fifth of nine children born to the unsanctioned marriage, suggesting the couple created some stability in their relationship. Despite their best efforts, however, Rit and Benjamin Ross had little control over the fate of their family. When Tubman was a very young girl, Rit and all of her children became the property of Edward Brodess, Mary Pattison Thompson's son by her first marriage. Brodess moved Rit and her children to Bucktown, 10 miles away from the Thompson plantation and Benjamin Ross. Though separated, the couple instilled in Tubman an intense sense of family loyalty. Tubman's dedication to her family was the primary focus of her life and prompted some of her most daring acts.

Tubman was acutely aware of the brutalities of slavery from the beginning of her life. Not only was her family fractured by their move away from Benjamin Ross, they faced an even more horrific separation when Edward Brodess sold three of Tubman's sisters to Southern slave dealers. For Tubman, these traumatic events were connected by the daily injustices she faced as an enslaved girl. One of her earliest recollections was of caring for her younger siblings while still a very young child, as Brodess forced Rit to abandon the children to perform domestic work in his house. This was a dangerous but pervasive circumstance of enslaved children. Tubman did not remain in this situation for long, however, as Brodess began to hire out her labor when she was a little girl. Many slaveholders capitalized on the labor of those they enslaved by "loaning" slaves to neighbors then receiving pay for the slaves's labor. When Tubman was about six years old, Brodess hired her out to James Cook who forced her to trap muskrats even when she became ill with the measles. After Tubman's illness progressed to the point of rendering her useless to Cook, he returned her to Brodess where she remained until she was well enough to be hired out again. Tubman would relive this series of events throughout her childhood. Tubman was homesick during her time away from her family. In addition to suffering from an early separation from her family, she experienced the cruelties of slavery at the hands of several slaveholders. One particularly brutal woman, Susan, forced Tubman to clean all day, and then sit up all night with Susan's baby. If the baby cried, Susan beat Tubman with a whip. Tubman bore the scars from these beatings on her neck for the remainder of her life.

Tubman's resilience in facing the pain and anguish she endured as an enslaved girl was remarkable. It is likely she garnered her will to resist white oppression in part by her mother's example. Tubman remembered that some time after Brodess sold her sisters, he attempted to sell one of Tubman's brothers. Rit circumvented the sale of yet another child by hiding her son. Rit defied Brodess's repeated requests to bring forth the child, hiding him for more than a month until she was certain her son was safe. This incident was probably only one of a series of strategic and common examples of resistance Tubman witnessed growing up.

Even as a young girl, Tubman employed various tactics to defy slaveholders' authority. In one instance, she bit a slaveholder when he whipped her. In another, she ran away to avoid a beating after she stole a piece of sugar. Perhaps like many enslaved girls, Tubman might have used other methods of resistance to white authority, such as refusing to work or indolence. By the age of 12, Tubman's defiance served to have her relegated to fieldwork. Tubman became skilled at such work and was said to prefer fieldwork as it allowed her some distance from whites who so callously abused her.

Tubman grew to a petite five feet, but her small frame veiled her incredible strength and ability to overcome excruciating trials. When she was still a teenager, Brodess again hired Tubman out to a nearby plantation. She worked primarily in the fields, though on one fateful day she accompanied the plantation's cook to a nearby dry goods store. This inconspicuous venture proved to forever alter Tubman's life when she interceded on behalf of an enslaved man running away from his overseer. Tubman stepped in front of the overseer in pursuit of the fugitive slave just as the overseer threw an iron weight toward the runaway. The weight hit Tubman in the head with such force that it impaled a piece of her shawl into the wound. Despite the gruesome nature of the injury and the gravity of her near fatal wound, Tubman was forced back to work on the plantation without any medical attention. Tubman became so ill from the injury and subsequent abuse and neglect, that the plantation owner returned her to Brodess, who immediately, and to no avail, attempted to sell her. She remained on the Brodess farm under the care of her mother until she recovered from the immediate affects of the injury.

Though her health improved somewhat during this time, Tubman never fully recovered from the injury. She suffered from headaches and would succumb to intense bouts of lethargy that have been attributed to narcolepsy or epilepsy. Along with the narcoleptic spells, Tubman, already deeply religious, began to have powerful visions, resulting in her reputation as a spiritual guide. Tubman's increased spirituality played a profound role in her adult life, and in her ability to escape and fight against slavery.

When Tubman was well enough to work again, Brodess hired her out to work with her father at John Stewart's lumber business. Once more, Tubman exhibited remarkable strength and skill performing the labor-intensive work of chopping and hauling wood. Her stamina and vigor was said to match that of the men with whom she worked. While working for Stewart, Tubman met and married her first husband, John Tubman, a free black, in 1844. When Tubman assumed her husband's last name, she also changed her first name from Araminta to Harriet. There is little extant information regarding the marriage, but it is known that the couple did not have children. Five years after they married a series of events prompted Tubman to make the difficult and courageous decision to escape slavery.

Tubman traversed the worlds of freedom and slavery on a daily basis. Her father, Benjamin Ross, gained his freedom in 1840, thus both her father and husband were free when Tubman began to seek her own freedom. Prior to escaping, Tubman sought legal means of acquiring her freedom by investigating the free status of her mother. In 1845, Tubman hired an attorney to investigate whether Rit and her children should have been granted their freedom per the will and testament of one of Edward Brodess's relatives. According to the will, the attorney determined Rit Ross should have gained her freedom at the age of 45. The Pattison family took advantage of the vagueness of the language of the will and opted to continue to enslave Rit and her children. Tubman was devastated by the discovery of this cruel deception. Left with no legal recourse to obtain her freedom, Tubman recalled that she began to pray for the conversion of Edward Brodess, with the hope that his newfound faith would prompt him to release Tubman and her family from slavery. When this failed, Tubman remembered praying for Brodess's death, which occurred shortly thereafter in March 1849. Tubman admitted she regretted praying for the slaveholder's death, though her primary concern became the looming threat of sale by Brodess's heirs. The imminent threat of sale, and the conflicting worlds of freedom and slavery within her own family, fueled Tubman's desire for freedom that had long since been ignited.

Having determined that she needed to flee while the possibility of a successful escape remained, Tubman utilized the already established Underground Railroad to gain her freedom in September 1849. Initially, Tubman's brothers accompanied her, but when they decided to back out, Tubman continued on her own. Tubman's daring escape consisted of a treacherous 90-mile journey through Maryland, Delaware, and Pennsylvania, that took her two to three weeks to complete. Tubman faced incalculable danger on the journey, as whites engaged in legal and informal systems of surveillance geared toward the capture and re-enslavement of runaways.

Tubman settled for a short time in Philadelphia, a known haven for runaway slaves. Philadelphia's free black population swelled in the decades leading to the Civil War, which allowed fugitives to incorporate themselves into the community. Though expanding in numbers, black Philadelphians faced intense racism resulting in the organization of black churches and social and abolition societies. They also formed informal networks of assistance to aid the constant influx of fugitive slaves. White abolition societies also worked to support former slaves as they began new lives in Philadelphia. Tubman found refuge within these groups and embraced newfound freedom. She worked briefly as a domestic before Tubman's family contacted her in 1850 to request her assistance in rescuing her niece, Kessiah Bowley, and Kessiah's two children, who were slated for sale. Tubman returned to Maryland and brought these family members to safety in December 1850. She returned for her second rescue mission in the spring of 1851, at which time she brought out a brother and two other men. Tubman's third rescue mission, in the fall of 1851, was especially difficult as she went with the express purpose of bringing her husband, John Tubman, to live with her in the North, only to find that her husband had remarried during her absence. Despite Tubman's profound disappointment at this discovery, she rescued 11 people on this mission, and determined to continue her work of emancipation. From this point on, Tubman embraced her role as a freedom fighter. For Tubman, freeing her people was a divine calling for which she would risk everything.

Tubman's successful rescue missions became widely known among abolitionists including William Still of Philadelphia, Thomas Garrett, the famous Underground Railroad stationmaster, and **Frederick Douglass**, who is thought to have housed the 11 fugitives from Tubman's third mission in his New York home. Tubman was also closely associated with the militant abolitionist John Brown, who was hanged for organizing the 1859 attack on Harper's Ferry, Virginia. Abolitionists provided funds and practical assistance for Tubman's freedom crusades. By the middle of the 1850s, Tubman began to speak publically at antislavery meetings, where she gained her reputation as "the Moses of her people," for her daring and triumphant rescue missions.

Because so much of the work of the Underground Railroad was conducted under the strictest secrecy, the breadth and depth of the network is still unknown. Abolitionists, including Tubman, employed various methods of relaying covert messages and moving fugitives along the network to freedom. Underground Railroad workers provided shelter, food, clothing, and sometimes transportation for Tubman and those she rescued. Tubman led runaway slaves through harrowing terrain along Underground Railroad routes through Maryland, Delaware, Pennsylvania, New York, and into Canada. Many abolitionists, including entire families, took extraordinary risks to aid fugitives. The second Fugitive Slave Act of 1850 increased these risks and emboldened slave catchers. Tubman, a fugitive herself, repeatedly took extraordinary personal risks to save her family and friends.

Tubman exhibited extreme skill and leadership when executing rescue missions. She traveled, mostly on foot, through harsh terrain and in grueling circumstances, all the while suffering from chronic health problems, including her random spells of unconsciousness. One extraordinary antidote exemplified her determination to ensure the safety of everyone under her stewardship. In the beginning of a rescue mission, one of the male runaways wanted to turn back. Tubman threatened to shoot the man, as she feared his weakness would lead him to relay information about the mission to slave catchers. Tubman was also known for her resourcefulness. She boasted of being able to dupe former owners and townspeople by her clever disguises when her rescue missions brought her back to her hometown.

Though the folklore surrounding Tubman's rescue missions claim she liberated hundreds of enslaved men, women and children, recent scholarship determines Tubman conducted 12 or 13 rescue missions that resulted in the freedom of approximately 70 individuals. Most of the people Tubman rescued were relatives. On one mission, Tubman brought out her parents, who were freed, but under suspicion in Dorchester County for assisting fugitives. There is also evidence Tubman provided information to 50 enslaved people that allowed them to navigate the Underground Railroad to freedom. For these brave acts, Tubman became known as one of the most famous conductors on the Underground Railroad.

Subsequent to rescuing her family, Tubman remained devoted to their care and safety throughout her life. After rescuing them from Maryland, she settled them for a brief time in St. Catherines, Canada. In 1859, Tubman and her family moved back to the United States, settling in Auburn, New York. Tubman made many friends in Auburn including William and Francis Miller Seward and Lucretia Mott's sister, Martha Coffin. Tubman purchased a home in Auburn in 1859 from William H. Seward. She mortgaged $1,200 for the house and seven acres, a financial burden she struggled with for the remainder of her life.

Members of Tubman's family, including her parents, lived in her Auburn home. Due to her rescue missions and work in the abolitionist movement, she had little time with her family in Auburn before the Civil War began in 1861.

Tubman's fierce quest to secure freedom for the enslaved led her to serve for more than two years in the Union army during the Civil War. Through her contacts with abolitionists, Tubman became acquainted with John Andrew, governor of South Carolina. Governor Andrew sent Tubman to Beaufort, South Carolina, in 1862. Working as a cook, laundress, scout, nurse, and spy, Tubman's service in the war reflected her resourcefulness and unyielding determination. While serving in South Carolina, Tubman developed important alliances with local Union army officers. Tubman tapped these friendships to support her endless efforts to provide food, shelter, clothing, and medical supplies for black soldiers and refugees. Tubman's association with Union officers also propelled her into the unlikely role of military combatant and spy. Her ability to mediate between Union military officials and freed slaves allowed her to garner invaluable intelligence from the black community. Tubman became one of the first women to lead a military campaign when she, along with Colonel James Montgomery, led the Combahee River Raid that resulted in the freedom of almost eight hundred slaves. Tubman ended her war service in Virginia as a nurse in a military hospital, where she campaigned for better conditions for African American soldiers. Despite her devoted service during the Civil War, the U.S. government denied Tubman remuneration for her service.

In 1865, the Thirteenth Amendment abolished slavery. However, Tubman and scores of other African Americans continued to suffer the oppressive effects of institutionalized racism. Tubman encountered this virulent bigotry immediately after her service in the Civil War. Returning from the war to her home in New York in 1865, a railroad conductor violently assaulted Tubman when she refused his request to move to the segregated smoking car. The conductor and two men wrestled with Tubman until they removed her to the smoking car, breaking her ribs and severely injuring her arm in the process. Other passengers joined in the affray by yelling racist insults at Tubman. Xenophobic incidents like these were the norm, rather than the exception, for African Americans as they navigated a society entrenched in suffocating racism.

During the years of Reconstruction, Tubman, though even more disabled by the conductor's attack, continued to struggle to support her extended family at her home in Auburn, New York. She was also active in community social work on behalf of freed African Americans. In an effort to raise funds to support her ever-growing household and to contribute to freedmen societies, Tubman, who remained illiterate throughout her life, collaborated with Sarah Hopkins Bradford, an author of several short stories, to write a biography. Bradford's *Scenes in the Life of Harriet Tubman*, published in 1868, was the first lengthy biography of Tubman and the first project in which Tubman made significant contributions. Tubman's friends assisted her efforts to raise funds for her social work by offsetting the printing costs of the biography. Tubman marketed the biography by telling stories from her life at the private meetings of social activists and friends, as well as at fairs organized to raise funds for freed African Americans. Tubman's biography was a helpful fund-raising project that allowed her to pay off some of her debts. Despite the failure of Bradford to provide an unadulterated account of Tubman's life story, the biography remains a valuable insight into Tubman's life.

It was also during this time that Tubman married one of her longtime boarders, Nelson Davis, at the Presbyterian Church in Auburn in 1869. Davis, a veteran of the Civil War, was a brick mason by trade, and he and Tubman ran a brickyard on her property for a number of years. In 1874, the couple adopted a baby, Gertie Davis. Tubman continued to grapple with the weighty burden of supporting her extended family, and eventually that of her husband, as his health declined due to tuberculosis. Tubman persistently tried to sustain the extensive household expenses she incurred in supporting various extended family, orphans, elderly, and indigent African Americans. For this reason, Tubman, along with influential friends, periodically petitioned the government for compensation for her service in the Civil War. It would not be until she applied for a widow's pension after the death of Nelson Davis in 1888, that the government considered Tubman's application. It would be another seven years before Tubman received a widow's pension in 1895, after the lengthy examination process the government imposed on African American veterans and their families.

The release of Bradford's revised biography, *Harriet, The Moses of Her People*, in 1886, came in an era of intensifying racial divisions. Tubman, a suffragist since the 1860s, witnessed the division of white and black activists over the issue of black male suffrage with the passage of the Fifteenth Amendment in 1870. Tubman was a member of Stanton's and Anthony's National Woman Suffrage Association (NWSA), and was personally associated with Susan B. Anthony. Members of NWSA rejected the campaign for all male suffrage at the expense of women's suffrage, and though Tubman's official stance on this volatile issue is unknown, it appears she leaned toward the views of the women's suffragists. Whatever her personal opinion was on the matter, Tubman was able to maintain friendships on both sides of the divided social activist groups created by the Fifteenth Amendment. After the release of *Harriet Tubman, The Moses of Her People* in 1886, Tubman began once again to speak at the meetings of local and national suffrage organizations, including the National Association of Colored Women (NACW). After an absence from public consciousness through the 1870s and into the 1880s, Tubman re-emerged as the heroic figure she had been during the abolition movement.

Tubman's social activism reflected an acute awareness of the racial disparity and oppression African Americans faced. Though she always maintained strong alliances with whites in her community and in activist circles, these associations did not shield her from the growing racism of the late nineteenth century. Tubman remembered the unyielding prejudice in Auburn when she attempted to purchase land to fulfill her dream of opening a home for elderly African Americans. The land auction officials challenged Tubman's winning bid, assuming that she, as an African American woman, would not be able to provide the funds for such a purchase. Tubman prevailed over the racist and sexist disputes of white auction officials by securing the mortgage for the land with the help of the African Methodist Episcopal Zion Church.

With her newly acquired land, Tubman, well into her sixties, began to work toward the dream of the much needed home for impoverished and elderly African Americans, which she wanted to name the John Brown Hall in honor of her martyred friend, John Brown. Tubman wanted the home to be a free refuge for the members of her community most in need of assistance. Just as she had with all of her other social projects, Tubman worked tirelessly toward her dream of the John Brown Hall home, but she was scarcely able to provide for her own household and the two mortgages for her home and the adjacent land. Therefore, Tubman was never able to make her dream a reality on her own. In the mid 1890s, Tubman donated the land to the A. M. E. Zion Church, with the request that the church follow through with the proposed John Brown Hall institution. Tubman's donation resulted in a contest between the black A. M. E. Zion Church members and Tubman's white friends over the management of the institution. The contest played out until Tubman officially transferred the property to the A. M. E. Zion Church in 1903, when the two sides came to a sufficient agreement to the terms of use of the land and Tubman's compensation. The project became a reality when it opened in 1908 as the Harriet Tubman Home for the Aged. The public opening of the home was a community celebration and tribute to Tubman, who had so selflessly served throughout her life. Tubman spoke of her life's work at the dedication ceremony, stating, "I did not take up this work for my own benefit . . . but for those of my race who need help. The work is now well started and I know God will raise up others to take care of the future. All I ask is united effort, for 'united we stand, divided we fall.' " (quoted in Humez, 2003, 106). When she could no longer care for herself, Tubman moved into the Harriet Tubman Home in 1911. She passed away at the home on March 10, 1913, after a yearlong struggle with pneumonia.

Tubman's iconic life became a symbol of African American and women's heroism, a legacy that continues to the present. Tubman's story is celebrated in monuments and museums throughout the United States and in Canada. In the twentieth century, Tubman's story was told primarily through children's books, which cemented some of the myths surrounding Tubman's iconic life in the public consciousness. Tubman has recently become the focus of serious historical investigation. Historians have clarified certain aspects of the folklore of Tubman's life, but in so doing, they have unveiled the complex woman who defied overwhelming odds in her quest for freedom and justice. Tubman's selfless service and ability to overcome adversity remain an inspiration to those who learn of her amazing life.

Kendra Kennedy
Arizona State University

FURTHER READING

Bradford, Sarah H. *Harriet Tubman: The Moses of Her People*. New York: Corinth Books, Inc., 1961. Originally published 1886.

Bradford, Sarah H. *Scenes in the Life of Harriet Tubman*. New York: W. J. Moses, 1869.

Clinton, Catherine. *Harriet Tubman: The Road to Freedom*. Boston: Little, Brown and Company, 2004.

Humez, Jean. *Harriet Tubman: The Life and the Life Stories*. Madison: University of Wisconsin Press, 2003.

Larson, Kate Clifford. *Bound for the Promised Land: Harriet Tubman, Portrait of an American Heroine*. New York: Ballantine Books, 2004.

Larson, Kate Clifford. "Tubman, Harriet Ross." In *Black Women in America*, edited by Darlene Clark Hine. Oxford: Oxford University Press, 2005.

Sernett, Milton C. *Harriet Tubman: Myth, Memory, and History*. Durham, NC: Duke University Press, 2007.

Ture, Kwame. *See* Stokely Carmichael (Kwame Ture)

Nat Turner (1800–1831)

Nat Turner is best known for leading a religiously-inspired slave insurrection in 1831 in Southampton County, Virginia. Turner's rebellion led to the death of at least 55 whites and approximately 255 blacks. It is arguably the most widely discussed slave insurrection in U.S. history. Turner's militancy succeeded in arousing mass hysteria in the antebellum South over the response of enslaved African Americans to his "call to arms" that fed fuel to the smoldering fire of slave rebellion and strengthened the South's resistance to rebellion that, 30 years later, erupted in the Civil War.

Nat Turner was born on October 2, 1800, in Southampton County, Virginia, to a father "whose name is unknown" and a mother named Nancy (Wood, 21). They were all enslaved by Benjamin Turner, a devout Methodist and farmer who had given them his surname of Turner. Nat Turner's father was born on the Turner plantation to a slave commonly referred to as "Old Bridget." His father escaped the Turner plantation when Nat Turner was a child. Benjamin Turner purchased Nancy in 1799, several years after many historians suggest she landed in Norfolk, Virginia, directly from Africa.

It was into this context that Turner was born, just a week before enslaved Gabriel Prosser was arrested for organizing an alarming slave insurrection designed to conquer Virginia's capital at Richmond. Five days after Turner's birth, Prosser and 26 co-conspirators were hanged in Richmond. In the Chesapeake and Low Country regions (i.e., Virginia and the Carolinas), this event was widely discussed as both a warning and an encouraging tale. The story made an immeasurable impact on young Nat Turner.

In 1809, Turner, his mother, and grandmother (along with five other slaves) were loaned out to work two miles from Benjamin Turner's estate on a 360-acre cotton plantation newly acquired by Benjamin's oldest son, Samuel. When Benjamin died the following year, Samuel became the legal owner of Turner and his immediate family, including his wife Cherry—somewhere between the years 1809 and 1822 Nat Turner had married. In 1822, this arrangement ended with Samuel's passing, leading to the sale and break-up of Nat Turner's family.

Thomas Moore purchased Turner as a prime field hand, to work on a farm in western Southampton County near Flat Swamp. Cherry became the property of Giles Reese on a small farm next to Thomas Moore's bigger farm. In 1828, the year when violent insurrection was imminent for Turner, nine-year-old Putnam Moore became his master in place of his deceased father Thomas. The latter half of the following year brought on more changes, as wheelwright Joseph Travis married Putnam's mother, Sally Francis, and moved onto the Moore plantation. In 1830, this farm became popularly known as "Travis place."

Contrary to several historical accounts, Turner was showing signs of becoming a local leader prior to his rebellion. That this happened is remarkable, if we consider the narrow bounds within which an enslaved person was able to express publicly his charismatic leadership without attracting vengeance from the politico-economic power structure. His effectiveness was also made possible through the power of black religion, seen as a force for social justice and an avenue for divine retribution. In 1830 Southampton County, 9,501 blacks lived in the area, 7,756 enslaved and 1,745 free, versus 6,573 whites. Outnumbered and protecting their investments, most Southampton County whites were quick to bestow severe punishment on any black person who dared to show any sign of opposing their dehumanization that would allow the black majority to overcome white authority. According to Thomas R. Gray's *The Confessions of Nat Turner* (1831), Turner was well aware of this.

As a youth, Turner's family and friends used to remark that he was destined "for some great purpose." From his youth, Turner could read and write, and as he matured he learned enough about religion that he sometimes functioned as a folk minister in small gatherings on Sundays: the day the enslaved were free from the burdens of work, which would explain Turner's freedom to "wander" around preaching to and teaching other slaves on the eve of his rebellion. To counteract the praise, which included his being privileged by his masters, Turner said he "studiously avoided mixing in society, and wrapped [himself] in mystery, devoting [his] time to fasting and prayer." This cloak of mystery makes Turner an elusive historical figure and is perhaps the reason why many scholars do not see much to indicate that Turner would ever lead an insurrection.

Turner was an average sized man for the 1830s, at least five feet and six inches in height, and 150–160 pounds. He had developed considerable physical strength from his manual labor. Turner was also very private. He had family in close proximity, and was "privileged" as a prime field hand on the plantations on which he served. Turner was not viewed by whites in Southampton County as a slave who would jeopardize his social standing as a top field hand. As simple as Turner implied in *The Confessions of Nat Turner*, his introverted-and-content public persona was a public mask of his making, in self-defense of his true intentions that included the possibility of rebelling against his oppressors in a divinely inspired capacity at an undisclosed future date.

Turner recognized the power of black religion as a force for social justice and divine retribution at a very young age. He is the product of a syncretic religious experience between African Religious Traditions and Christian Methodist, with the former coming from his mother and grandmother, and the later being indirectly acquired while listening in the shadows at church meetings in Benjamin Turner's home. Overheard at one of these church meetings was Matthew 6:33, which spawned young Turner's belief that Christianity could be a source of liberation for enslaved blacks. This revolutionary interpretation ran contrary to the traditional use of Christianity as a tool for masters continuing to justify black enslavement in the 1830s. From the meeting he heard, "Seek ye the kingdom of Heaven and all things shall be added unto you." From all indications, it was hearing this verse that planted in him the seeds of his placing African Americans in the Biblical context of enslaved Israelites.

In the Bible, enslaved Israelites were God's chosen people and *he* divinely empowered them to take their freedom and do away with the sin of their enslavement by violently defeating their masters. For Turner, people of African descent were America's enslaved Israelites. What plan God had for him, and how he, a young boy, was supposed to address black deliverance from slavery, he believed would be revealed at a later date, and Turner's task was to wait patiently for that day.

In 1823, it had been more than a decade since Turner heard the revelation of Matthew 6:33. In this year, while plowing, according to Turner a spirit began urging him to "Seek ye the kingdom of Heaven and all things shall be added unto you." From this point to 1825, he intensely contemplated that single verse and began sowing the seeds of rebellion among other enslaved blacks, by voicing his contempt for slavery. As this was happening, Turner records that he was taken back into his childhood to subliminal experiences presented to his mind. These were visions, but he was unclear how to assess what was being presented.

In 1825, Turner was at the crossroads of competing notions of liberation. One stressed individual freedom and the other stressed collective freedom. Collective freedom warned him that if an individual was free from bondage and others remained enslaved, then that individual was not really free because the *peculiar institution* of chattel slavery in America, ironically called "the land of the free," remained intact. As a matter of fact, during the antebellum period, most individual slaves who fled bondage were re-enslaved. Nevertheless, in 1825 Turner temporarily ran away from slavery, similar to the action of his father two decades earlier.

However, instead of leaving the Moore farm, he disappeared into the woods for a month and, surprisingly, returned with a rejuvenated sense of purpose. While at the crossroads in the woods, Turner reported that a spirit appeared admonishing him that his present flight was "directed to the things of this world, and not to the kingdom of Heaven, and that [he] should return to the service of [his] earthly master."

Crucial for Turner, as he sought to bring about a divine kingdom/nation for black liberation, was his relationship with other slaves who seemed open to becoming insurrectionists. Most of his peers were disappointed by his voluntary return to the Moore farm. Before rumblings about his return resulted in damage to his credibility as a disgruntled slave, Turner regained most enslaved blacks' trust and respect when he started having visions of a Judgment Day wherein slavery, as an evil, would be abolished by forces of good. In the first of his visions, Turner saw the following:

> White spirits and black spirits engaged in battle, and the sun was darkened—the thunder rolled in the Heavens, and blood flowed in streams—and I heard a voice saying, "Such is your luck, such you are called to see, and let it come rough or smooth, you must surely bear it."

In this vision Turner said he acquired knowledge on the inner workings of the universe such as the elements, "revolution of planets, the operation of tides, and changes of the seasons." This was followed by revelations of "drops of blood on corn"; "hieroglyphic characters and numbers" on leaves in the woods; men previously seen in the heavens were now materially manifested covered in blood; and the Holy Ghost revealed itself to Turner.

Turner, certain that he was chosen to bring an end to slavery, became devoted to the mission of bringing about a Judgment Day upon white people. This did not just include killing. In one instance in 1827 at Pearson's Mill Pond, Turner, a slave, baptized Etheldred T. Brantley, a white "alcoholic overseer on a nearby plantation" (Darity, 467). This happened before an interracial crowd in which Brantley asked Turner to baptize him after supposedly hearing about Turner's recent vision. What then transpired was a dramatic transformation in Brantley, in which he gave up slavery and repented through fasting and prayer for nine days until healed from a skin condition where "blood oozed from the pores of his skin."

From 1825 to 1829, Turner's revelations became more immediate and intense, calling for action and the right time to do so. Such was the case on May 12, 1828, when a vision told Turner regarding the Day of Judgment against slavery that "the time was fast approaching, when the first should be last and the last should be first." He was also told to conceal this information until he received a sign. In late February 1831, Turner interpreted an eclipse of the sun as his cue to "arise and prepare [himself], and slay [his] enemies with their own weapons." This signaled Turner's move from contemplation and self-isolation toward organizing an actual insurrection. To this end, he had the greatest confidence in fully disclosing his plan of divine retribution to fellow slaves Henry, Hark, Nelson, and Sam.

July 4, 1831, was the original date when Turner's rebellion was supposed to begin. It was rescheduled because Turner was sick. By this date he was calling his insurrection his "work of death." After several aborted starts, Turner and company made Sunday, August 21, 1831, the day that the rebellion began. During that afternoon the insurrectionists had a secluded two-hour dinner in the woods at Cabin Pond near Travis's place. Together they intended to create a plan and arm themselves to do God's work. At the dinner, three new insurgents, named Will, Austin, and Jack, arrived.

The conspirators agreed that no white person, no probable slavery sympathizer was to be spared, regardless of age or gender. Their work of wrath began about 2 a.m., at the farm of Joseph Travis, Turner's master. Not to alarm any member of the Travis family, Turner entered his master's home by climbing a ladder and sneaking through a second-floor window to unlock the downstairs front door from the inside and stole Travis's guns and ammunition before the band murdered the family of six. It was agreed that Turner should deal the first death blow to his master's head. In the dark, Turner's hatchet missed Travis's skull, which woke him. As he called out for his wife, Sally Francis, Will

"The Executioner" murdered them both with an axe. They died in bed as did the three other sleeping family members including Turner's 12-year-old master, Putnam Moore. Initially they ignored the Travis's crying baby. The group looted the Travis home for money and ammunition and had gone some distance from the farm, forgetting the baby. However, they recalled their initial agreement that no white-and-free person was to be spared; and they returned to dispatch the child.

Following a brief celebration at Travis's barn, Turner marched his army off to the adjacent Francis farm 600 yards away. Salathul Francis had no family. Instead of sneaking into his home, Turner sent two of their party, Sam and Will, who were known to Francis. They knocked on his door and claimed to have a letter for him. This convinced him to open the door, which resulted in his being beaten to death outside of his home. From here, Turner's forces split up and silently marched in the dark, brutally casting Judgment on the families of Reese, Turner, Peebles, Newsome, Edwards, Francis, and Barrow, to name a few of their victims. These families lived miles apart. As Monday sunrise drew near, local residents were becoming informed about this alarming rebellion.

Simultaneously, Turner's army was growing. In response to hearing of an open rebellion to free enslaved African Americans, blacks tired of their oppressed conditions were willing to go to war for their freedom. At sunrise Turner had 15 men; by 10 a.m. he had 40 men; and 50 to 60 men by noon. At sunrise, nine rebels rode horses. The further away white families like the Bryants lived from the Travis farm, the better their chance to fight the rebellion, or flee (as most did). This was the case with the Porters and Harrises who successfully fled; unlike, however, Mr. Doyle, who was caught and killed while attempting to escape along a road. By 9 or 10 a.m., on the way to Levi Waller's home, Turner's rebellion had temporarily taken command of the streets of Southampton County. Now commanding 40 men, he put 15 to 20 of his best soldiers on horseback in the front of his army and sent them to murder and/or contain white Southamptons in their homes, filling them with terror, until they got around to killing them. After the Whitehead killings at the crack of dawn, this tactic of "blitzing" white people and their property with deadly intentions prevented Turner from directly engaging in the actual killings. He became solely a general, managing his messianic war, and once in a while viewing "the mangled bodies as they lay, in silent satisfaction, and immediately start[ing] in quest of other victims."

Turner's armed insurgency came to an abrupt end in the pursuit of capturing Jerusalem, Virginia, where they hoped to restock on weapons and ammunition, and recruit more troops. Jerusalem was the largest nearby town, and Turner's army was growing and needed better arms, not dull axes, swords, and clubs. They headed for Jerusalem after murdering a worker named Drury, along with the Williams and Vaughan families.

The tide for the rebels turned at the James W. Parker farm, which was just three miles from Jerusalem. Approximately 50 insurgents convinced Turner to stop their march to kill the Parkers. Turner's suspicions that the Parkers had escaped was found to be true. Not only did his army lose valuable time on their way to Jerusalem, the white militia had enough time to build a strong counter attack force. After regrouping, on Turner's way back to the main road, his forces encountered a militia of 18 white men in a field. Temporarily alarmed by this event, Turner's forces readjusted, became recomposed, and forced the white militia into retreat 200 yards over a low hill. On the other side of this hill, the white militia regrouped and joined a militia from Jerusalem. They were well-armed and succeeded in wounding several insurgents, sending most rebels scrambling. Turner, determined to reach Jerusalem with 20 men, attempted to enter the town through the rear, three miles below, in a private location at the "Nottoway River at the Cypress Bridge" (Wood, 28). Here he discovered militia forces had organized into an imposing presence all over town.

Now in retreat, Turner's forces quickly dissolved. Still hopeful of bringing forth Judgment, Turner's army retreated back into their old neighborhood to recruit, kill and loot. The success of this was minimal, because Turner's community was nearly deserted after earlier insurrection. Moreover, the few whites in the area, including the Blunt family, were protected by Major Thomas Ridley's armed militia at his plantation.

At this point, Turner's forces were reduced to three (himself, Jacob, and another slave named Nat). The white militia had taken command of his old neighborhood, including the Travis farm. The militia was looking for insurgents and their anonymous leader. (An accurate description of Turner would not be available until mid-September.) In the meantime, the rebels hid in the woods until night, and then Turner sent Nat and Jacob to search for his "disciples": Henry, Sam, Nelson, and Hark. Nat and Jacob never came back. Suspicious they would tell white officials of his location, Turner left the woods and concealed himself in a man-made hole that he called a "cave," "under a pile of fence rails in a field" on the Travis farm. He lived in this location for six weeks with a $500 reward for his capture, residing in his cave during the day, and at night gathering food and intelligence. On one late October night, a dog found Turner's hiding place and took his meat while he was out. Several nights later, the same dog found Turner in the cave and started barking. Two men of African descent, who were accompanying the dog, approached the hole. They ran from Turner after he pleaded that they be silent about his location. Turner concealed himself in a new hole on the Travis farm until he was discovered on October 30 by local farmer Benjamin Phipps, who was out on slave patrol. Armed with a loaded shotgun, Phipps took away Turner's dull sword and escorted him to Southampton County Jail.

On November 5, Turner was sentenced in Southampton County Court to execution. Six day later, in Jerusalem, he was hanged, skinned and surgically dissected. However, prior to his execution, Turner dictated his "confession" to physician Thomas R. Gray. From this interaction, Gray published

The Confessions of Nat Turner. This text, more than any source, has provided the most material pertaining to Nat Turner and his rebellion. From it, people have viewed Turner as either a prophet or fanatic. This, of course, depends on one's interpretation, and taking into account that Gray was both fascinated and repulsed by Turner's smart, candid, and calm demeanor following the mass murder of white people in Gray's own community.

Most abolitionists such as William Lloyd Garrison referred to Turner as a prophet and emancipator who, although his tactics were more radical and violent than theirs, believe that his overall strategy to end U.S. slavery converged with their own objective in doing the same. In contrast, slave masters and slavery sympathizers such as Gray dismissed Turner's "organic abolitionism" and publicly ridiculed him as a religious fanatic to downplay the rebellion's true impact: that most white people were finally being forced to see slavery for what it was, morally wrong and driven by racist-greed, and that people enslaved were intelligent, courageous, and willing to assert their natural right to freedom using any tactic at their disposal, including bloody violence.

Turner's rebellion led to the death of at least 55 whites, and generated a climate of hysteria that lasted decades in the United States, especially the South. This led to Virginia's state legislature seriously contemplating an end to slavery, only to retain it in a close vote and to instead support policies severely curtailing black freedom and abolitionist free speech. The state also executed 55 African Americans, banished suspected slave insurgents, and acquitted only a few. Neighboring North Carolina also tried and executed blacks suspected to be insurgents connected to Turner's rebellion. Finally, in a fit of hysteria, white mobs from Virginia to Georgia in the South, to Tennessee in the West, murdered around 200 black people suspected to be slave rebels. Most of the accused were innocent victims with no connection to Turner's rebellion, leaving one to wonder if looking for Turner insurgents was a cover for the use of mob violence to purge "radical" elements from the ranks of the enslaved.

Turner's 36-hour apocalyptic uprising made the American abolitionist movement nationally relevant, and forced many white Americans to choose a side on slavery. This, along with David Walker's *Appeal*, and the rise of U.S. abolitionism, were defining moments in the coming of chattel slavery's end—following the U.S. Civil War and the ratification of the Thirteenth Amendment in 1865. Turner's rebellion happened at a crucial moment in U.S. history. The 1830s decade was a period in which slavery was expanding and the nation was industrializing, democratizing white men only, and moving westward through the conquest and the mass murder of Native Americans. With every stolen mile, new states and territories emerged through the Missouri Compromise of 1820; until this formula no longer worked in the 1850s. This led to increasingly flawed strategies to maintain the North-South divide in a failing effort to prevent to the violent breaking-up of the Union.

In closing, Turner's rebellion led to the death of more than 350 Americans, and to states such as Virginia betraying their first instinct about slavery by refusing to voluntarily end their peculiar institutions without bloodshed. Driven by huge profits, greed, and the rule of white supremacy, the consequence of this deferment to human freedom eventually resulted in a "Judgment Day" called the U.S. Civil War, in which more than 600,000 Americans died at the hands of other Americans, a bloodbath that finally ended most forms of legalized enslavement and temporarily cleansed the nation's soul.

Herbert G. Ruffin II
Syracuse University

FURTHER READING

Aptheker, Herbert. *Nat Turner's Slave Rebellion: Including the 1831 "Confessions."* Mineola, NY: Dover Publications, 2006.

Clarke, John Henrik. *William Styron's Nat Turner: Ten Black Writers Respond.* Westport, CT: Greenwood Press, 1987.

French, Scot. *The Rebellious Slave: Nat Turner in American Memory.* Boston: Houghton Mifflin Harcourt, 2004.

Gray, Thomas R. *The Confessions of Nat Turner: The Leader of the Late Insurrection in Southampton, Virginia.* Whitefish, MT: Kessinger Publishing, 2004.

Greenberg, Kenneth S. ed. *The Confessions of Nat Turner and Related Documents.* New York: Bedford/St. Martin's, 1996.

Greenberg, Kenneth S. *Nat Turner: A Slave Rebellion in History and Memory.* New York: Oxford University Press, 2004.

Oates, Stephen B. *The Fires of Jubilee: Nat Turner's Fierce Rebellion.* New York: Harper Perennial, 1990.

Sernett, Milton C., ed. "Section II: 'Slave Religion in the Antebellum South.' " In *African American Religious History: A Documentary Witness.* Durham, NC: Duke University Press, 2004.

Turner, Nat. *The Confessions of Nat Turner: The Leader of the Late Insurrection in Southampton, VA: Electronic Edition.* North Carolina Collection, University of North Carolina at Chapel Hill. http://docsouth.unc.edu/neh/turner/turner.html.

Tuskegee Airmen

The Tuskegee Airmen is the collective name of the first African American pilots to serve in the U.S. armed forces. Also known as the "Red Tails" after the stripes of red paint that decorated their planes, this group of dedicated and determined young men enlisted, despite a popular belief that black men lacked intelligence and patriotism. Comprising the 332nd Fighter Group of the U.S. Army Air Corps, and its four squadrons, the 99th, 100th, 301st, and 302nd, the Tuskegee Airmen served and flew with distinction during World War II. As the only African American pilots in combat at this time, the Tuskegee Airmen felt a strong sense of duty, not only to serve their country, but to prove that African American servicemen were just as capable as their white counterparts. In that respect, the Tuskegee Airmen had dual pressures. Aside from the inherent pressures of military training and combat, these African American pilots were subject to Jim Crow laws and a very racially segregated military that treated them as inferior and denied them access to many privileges afforded to whites. By enlisting and serving in these conditions, the Tuskegee Airmen countered America's racist attitudes by demonstrating a genuine willingness to put their lives on the line for a country not willing to do the same for them. These men knew that only if they performed well in battle would their existence and persistence in a role that they had previously been excluded from be solidified. Despite the immense pressure to perform and the many attempts to exclude and devalue their service, the Tuskegee Airmen met, if not exceeded, the expectations and goals of every challenge placed before them, as they carried with them into each battle the hopes and dreams of equality, both for themselves, and for their 13 million African American countrymen.

African American presence in the military was highly controversial. At a time when many states were still operating under Jim Crow, and a time where many political leaders still embraced segregation politics, it is no surprise that the military had many of these same constraints. However, many leaders fought for the right of African Americans to rise to the status of officer. Their efforts, combined with the urgency of war, led to the creation of an all-black combat unit. This was forced by a series of legislative moves in the U.S. Congress in 1941. Even before the program officially began, there were attempts to shut it down. The War Department, consisting of numerous individuals who were very reluctant to accept African Americans into their ranks, set up a hard-to-meet set of standards that would exclude anyone without a minimum level of flight experience or with higher education. However, even under these attempted restrictions, the Air Corps received a large number of applications from qualified black men. Many of these applicants were participants in the Civilian Pilot Training Program at Tuskegee Institute, which had been training qualified individuals in the program since 1939. Additionally, what the War Department did not account for was that, unlike in World War I, many African Americans now had the ability to receive, and had received, their high school diplomas. A large number also were either in college, or already had earned baccalaureate degrees.

After the initial screening of applicants, those possessing the necessary intellectual and physical qualifications began as aviation cadets, being trained initially as single-engine pilots. If this training was successful, cadets continued to be trained as twin-engine pilots, navigators, or bombardiers. These airmen were trained at Tuskegee Army Air Field (TAAF) in Tuskegee, Alabama, thus yielding the collective name "Tuskegee Airmen" to the pilots that trained there. The formation of the 99th Fighter Squadron marked the official start of the Tuskegee program in June 1941. Thirteen members made up the first class, only five of which successfully completed the nine-month training. For this, they received Army Air Corps silver pilot wings. One of these five, and perhaps the most famous, was Captain Benjamin O. Davis, Jr., one of the very few black West Point Academy graduates at that time. He would command the 99th Fighter Squadron, and later the 332nd Fighter Group. The remaining four were commissioned second lieutenants.

The successful completion of the training program was no easy task. Upon entering the program, cadets were subject to numerous tests, including both intellectual and psychological exams. To conduct these tests, the U.S. Army Air Corps established the Psychological Research Unit 1 at Maxwell Army Air Field, Montgomery, Alabama, among other units around the country. Psychologists involved in this research used many of the first standardized tests in an attempt to put the right people in the right job. For example, tests of dexterity were done to determine which cadets would be best trained as navigators, bombardiers, and pilots. But the selection of these roles was only a small part of the picture. An entire unit consists of much more than the pilots. A service arm is needed to support any unit, and the 99th was no exception. Grounds crew, mechanics, engineers, medical support, radio repairmen, etc., were all operationally integral to the ability of any Army Air Corps flying squadron or ground unit to be fully functional. Until TAAF had the facilities to support training of such unit support in 1942, much of the training was conducted at Chanute Air Base in Rantoul, Illinois.

The Tuskegee Airmen, in a way, were the firsts of many firsts for African Americans serving in the U.S. military. Because of the strict racial segregation rules, a separate set of flight surgeons, in addition to all of the other supporting personnel, was needed to support the Tuskegee Airmen. This would be the first set of non-white flight surgeons to be trained for the U.S. Army. From 1941 to 1949, 17 flight surgeons served with the black pilots, all products of one of the earliest racially integrated training courses in the Army. Regardless of the role they served, enlisted African Americans were subject to the same qualification standards as all other military personnel. However, they were not afforded the same consideration when it came to access. Blacks were not allowed to enter military clubs, or dine or drink. If it was available, they could sometimes order from a window, but that was a best-case scenario. They were also banned from the places where white soldiers trained and relaxed. In the case of the military, separate but equal only referred to the testing and qualification measures, not to the day-to-day existence of these men.

In total, 992 pilots would graduate at TAAF from 1941 to 1946, all of which received commissions and pilot wings. Navigators, bombardiers, and gunnery crews were trained at other military bases. Of these pilots, 450 served overseas. The first unit to go overseas, the 99th Pursuit Squadron, also known as the 99th Fighter Squadron, was deployed to North Africa, specifically French Morocco, in April 1943. Under the command of Colonel Davis, the 99th commenced combat operations from Tunisia, and attacked its enemies in Tunisia, Sicily, and the island of Pantelleria. While operating in North Africa, the Tuskegee Airmen and respective ground crews were still subject to much segregation, enforced by Colonel William W. Momyer, the leader of the all-white 33rd Fighter Group. Despite success on the campaign, so much so that enemy forces in Pantelleria surrendered in fewer than nine days due to the aerial attacks that made invasion unnecessary, the 99th received criticism, not commendation, from Momyer. He told media sources in the United States of the 99th and their failures to be courageous and competent. This news spread rapidly, in sources such as *Time* magazine, and resulted in a House Armed Services Committee hearing to determine whether or not the Tuskegee Airmen were fit for duty. As a result, President Roosevelt ordered an evaluation of all Mediterranean Theater P-40 units, and found that the 99th was equal to the other units.

Less than a month later, the 99th would continue to demonstrate its worth, earning its first Distinguished Unit Citation and escorting B-25 medium bombers for an attack on Castelvetrano, Italy. During this operation, pilots were countered by enemy fighters. On that day, July 2, 1943, Lieutenant Charles B. Hall secured the first aerial victory for any African American in the U.S. Armed Forces by shooting down an enemy aircraft. The 99th, assigned to the Twelfth Air Support command, remained in Italy for about a year, moving to various locations, and preparing for and supporting the Allied invasion of Sicily and surrounding areas. Late January 1944, the 99th would again have a significant chance to solidify its value. Anzio was raided by German warplanes, and 11 of the 99th squadron's pilots would shoot down enemy fighters during a 48-hour period. Included in these 11 pilots was Hall, taking down his second and third aircraft. Of the eight fighter squadrons involved in the raid at Anzio, 32 enemy aircraft were shot down; the 99th took down the most, with 13. The closest all-white squadron took down seven, demonstrating that, contrary to what many wanted to believe at the time, black pilots could perform just as well or better than their white counterparts. After a couple of smaller enemy invasions over the course of January 27–February 7, 1944, the 99th brought down more planes, bringing their unit total to 18.

Between February and May 1944, an influx of Tuskegee Airmen would reach the Mediterranean. With a number of new pilots trained and ready for duty, a new fighter group, the 332nd, was formed. Composed of all-black pilots and commanded by former 99th commander Colonel Davis, the group consisted of three separate squadrons, the 100th, 301st, and 302nd, and was joined in May by the 99th. This was the U.S. Armed Forces's first all-black fighter group. The 332nd joined the 15th Air Force as escorts for heavy strategic bombing raids of a number of countries, including attacks in Austria, Czechoslovakia, Germany, Hungary, and Poland. Seven such escort groups accompanied the Fifteenth. In June 1944, the 332nd was put into action, escorting bombers on a raid in Munich, Germany, where they encountered, in route, 20 enemy fighters. Four members of the 332nd shot down five enemy planes that day, but also faced the group's first casualty. A Distinguished Flying Cross was awarded to Colonel Davis because of his bravery and leadership on June 9, 1944. Later that summer, the 332nd would down 36 enemy aircraft in July, making this the highest number the group had scored in a single month. Twelve of these hits came on an attack on July 18, where the Tuskegee Airmen would break another record for aircraft shot down in a single day, previously at 10. Many attribute this increase in success to a change in equipment, as the group was now flying P-51 Mustangs, the plane which is most commonly associated with the Tuskegee Airmen, instead of P-40 Warhawks, P-39 Airacobras, or P-47 Thunderbolts, which they had previously flown.

During this time, the 332nd earned the nickname "Schwarze Vogelmenschen" from its enemies, which translates into "Black Birdmen." The Allies preferred the names "Red Tails" or "Redtail Angels," based on the stripe of paint placed on the unit's aircraft to indentify themselves from the six other groups accompanying the 15th, all of which had their own colors. The popularity of the 332nd with white bomber groups also spread, as many of them requested the "Red Tails" as their escort, based on their impressive record.

The remainder of 1944 was relatively slow. Only a few enemy craft were encountered in August, and the same for September. On October 12, 1944, the most action of that fall was seen, as members of the 332nd shot down nine enemy aircraft in a battle that was low to the ground, with altitudes as little as 100 feet. For most of the winter, until March of 1945, few to no encounters with enemy aircraft were made. Thirteen of the group's 16 March scores were achieved on March 31, 1945, when the 332nd exceeded its already-held, single-day record of 12. April was also a successful month for the Tuskegee Airmen, and marked their last victory on the 26. By the end of the war, the Tuskegee Airmen completed 1,578 missions and flew 15,533 sorties. The program at Tuskegee graduated 992 pilots, 450 of which were deployed overseas. The "Red Tails" recorded 32 prisoners of war and a total of 66 killed in action. They shot down 112 enemy aircraft, securing the record for the most shot down in a single day, 13. The 332nd proved that it was just as, if not more capable, than any of its all-white peer groups. Among the many accolades of the group were one Legion of Merit, one Silver Star, two Soldier Medals, eight Purple Hearts, 95 Distinguished Flying Crosses, 14 Bronze Stars, and 744 Air Medal and Clusters. On March 29, 2007, the Congressional Gold Medal was awarded to roughly 300 surviving Tuskegee Airmen and their widows, by then President George W. Bush, and is now on display at the Smithsonian Institution.

During the war, and even still today, many believed that the Tuskegee Airmen never lost an escorted bomber in battle. The claim appeared for the first time in press on March 24, 1945, stating, "332nd Flies Its 200th Mission Without Loss," as a headline in the *Chicago Defender*. This headline, along with claims that bombers were lost in battle, caused much controversy. Many suspected racially motivated, and not fact-based intentions were behind many of the counter claims. Because of this, the Air Force, in late 2006, conducted a reassessment of the unit's history. In the report published by the Air Force on March 28, 2007, it was declared that there were indeed bombers, up to 25, who were shot down by enemy fire while being escorted by the 332nd. In fact, the report claims, a bomber was actually shot down on March 24, 1945, on the day the claim of 200 missions without loss was published. Even today, this record remains highly contested. A historian from the Air Force Historical Research Agency confirms the loss of up to 25 bombers, while a professor at the National Defense University claims that in his research of more than 200 mission reports, he found no bombers lost to enemy fire. But, there is a difference between bombers being lost and being lost to enemy fire. Regardless of whether bombers were lost, lost to enemy fire, or not lost at all, the Tuskegee Airmen proved themselves to be incredibly worthy of respect, producing results in each mission, and more importantly, paving the way for many African American military personnel and operations. A January 26, 2008, article in the *St. Petersburg Times* discusses how record keeping in World War II was not as exact as it is today, so the record will remain controversial. In that same article, Bill Holloman, one of the Tuskegee Airmen who now leads the group's history team and who has spent his own money on researching the record of the 332nd, believes that whether or not the record is perfect, the story of the Tuskegee Airmen is really about a group of dedicated men who fought discrimination and adversity to become a distinguished group of pilots who served their country. A fellow "Redtail," Charles Hardy, stated "Let's face it . . . we had one hell of a record any way you look at it."

The record of the Tuskegee Airmen may be contested, but their abilities were without reproach. Despite all of this success and recognition, racism still ran strong. Through 1946, airmen were trained at the Tuskegee Army Air Field, with black women being allowed to enter the program in some support field capacities. Despite the still-existing segregation and few advancement opportunities presenting themselves for African Americans, black men and women continued to train diligently to serve their country. After returning from the war, the 332nd competed in an annual All Air Force Gunnery Meet in Las Vegas, Nevada. And they won. In 1948, President Harry S. Truman ended segregation in the military with Executive Order 9981, which advanced equality of treatment and opportunity in all of the U.S. Armed Forces. This placed an increased demand on Tuskegee Airmen, as many were highly sought after to participate with the newly formed U.S. Air Force, who had already planned to racially integrate its efforts. This was a big step in early attempts toward racial integration in the United States.

While spending time overseas, many of the Tuskegee Airmen experienced their first exposure to a world where legalized segregation did not exist, and returned to the United States with a heightened sense of dedication to advance equality for all African Americans. World War II caused many people, both black and white, to ask critical questions about equality for all citizens. The Tuskegee Airmen played a key role in advancing many of these questions, and did so by staying actively engaged in the military or in other segments of society. Some went on to teach at institutions of higher learning and flight schools. Many continued to be leaders, and continued to fight for equality in their daily lives. One such airman was Lincoln J. Ragsdale.

Lincoln J. Ragsdale was a Tuskegee Airman who continued to battle for racial equality long after the war was over. Commissioned as a second lieutenant in November 1945, Ragsdale proudly served his country and supported the African American fight for equality and civil rights, a battle that he would continue fighting until his death in 1995 at the age of 69. Upon completing his service and returning home after the war, he realized how much of an impact he, and the other airmen, had made in the black community. As Ragsdale stated in *The Arizona Republic* in a 1983 interview,

> I remember when we used to walk through black neighborhoods right after the war and little kids would run up to us and touch our uniforms, "Mister, can you really fly an airplane?" The Tuskegee Airmen gave blacks a reason to be proud.

The experiences he had in the war and serving as a Tuskegee Airman influenced his leadership in the civil rights movement. He served as the head of the Phoenix, Arizona branch of the National Association for the Advancement of Colored People, and was a predominant face of the civil rights movement in the Southwest.

Today, those who are still living continue to make appearances at numerous locations, from sporting events to classrooms, the White House to community centers, and making an impact on each community they touch. As an example, four of these men flew to Balad, Iraq, in 2005, to speak to active duty airmen serving in the then-current incarnation of the 332nd, representing a linkage between the past and the present. One of the men who spoke to these service men and women was Lieutenant Colonel Lee Andrew Archer, Jr., who recently passed away on January 27, 2010. Archer, a fighter pilot who flew 169 combat missions, gained much notoriety during a dogfight on October 12, 1944, where he shot down three German fighters in a matter of minutes. Despite his successes and dedication to his country, flying more than double the number of missions as the average pilot, he returned home and was welcomed by signs pointing "Colored Troops" in one direction and "White

Troops" in another. Not to be deterred by a genuine desire to serve, he remained in the armed forces until his retirement in 1970. After speaking to the 700 servicemen in Iraq, Archer told *The Associated Press*, "This is the new Air Force ... black, white, Asian, Pacific Islanders, people from different parts of Europe. This is what America is."

Many monuments and other forms of recognition have been designated to honor the Tuskegee Airmen. The Tuskegee Army Air Field, where the pilots trained, is now the official Tuskegee Airmen National Historic Site. A postage stamp initiative is underway to create a commemorative design in honor of the airmen. A monument at the old Walterboro Army Airfield in Walterboro, South Carolina, showcasing a bronze bust and concrete monument, is on display at the location where many of the African American military aviators were trained for duty. Randolph Air Force Base honors the Tuskegee Airmen, keeping the "Red Tails" of T-1A Jayhawks flying through efforts by the 99th Flying Training Squadron. The city of Atlanta, Georgia officially named a portion of State Route six in honor of the Tuskegee Airmen, which, appropriately, serves as the main path into the Hartsfield-Jackson International Airport. Yet another memorial exists in Lancaster, California, near Edwards Air Force Base. Indeed the Tuskegee Airmen are forever embedded in the history of the United States.

Today, more than 100 pilots from the original 992, and 200 ground personnel from approximately 15,000, are still alive, and many regularly attend the annual Tuskegee Airmen Convention, hosted by Tuskegee Airmen, Inc. This organization has detailed records of the Tuskegee Airmen, and functions as a voice for those men who served and continue to serve the United States. Destroying the belief that African Americans lacked intelligence, diligence, and courage, the Tuskegee Airmen met and exceeded all expectations that were set before them as the first black pilots in the U.S. Armed Forces. The immense pressure these men were under, from both their military responsibilities and their dedication to represent the hopes of millions of African Americans in the United States, did not deter them from accomplishing both missions. On January 20, 2009, more than 180 surviving Tuskegee Airmen attended the inauguration of **Barack Obama**, the first elected African American President. The feeling was reiterated by retired Lieutenant William Broadwater, a Tuskegee Airman, "The culmination of our efforts and others' was this great prize we were given on Nov. 4. Now we feel like we've completed our mission."

Jill S. Schiefelbein
Arizona State University

FURTHER READING

Dalfiume, Richard M. *Desegregation of the U.S. Armed Forces: Fighting on Two Fronts, 1939–1953*. Columbia: University of Missouri Press, 1969.

Dryden, Charles W. *A-Train: Memoirs of a Tuskegee Airman*. Tuscaloosa: University of Alabama Press, 1997.

Dudziak, Mary L. *Cold War Civil Rights: Race and the Image of American Democracy*. Princeton, NJ: Princeton University Press, 2000.

Haulman, Daniel L. *112 Victories: Aerial Victory Credits of the Tuskegee Airmen* (condensed version). Air Force Historical Research Agency. March 31, 2008. http://www.tuskegeeairmen.org/uploads/AerialVictories.pdf (accessed March 3, 2010).

Motley, Mary Penick. *The Invisible Soldier: The Experience of the Black Soldier, World War II*. Detroit: Wayne State University Press, 1975.

Osur, Alan M. *Blacks in the Army Air Forces during World War II: The Problem of Race Relations*. Washington, DC: Office of Air Force History, 1977.

Sandler, Stanley. *Segregated Skies: Black Combat Squadrons of World War II*. Washington, DC: Smithsonian Institution, 1992.

Scott, Lawrence P., and William M. Womack, Sr. *Double V: The Civil Rights Struggle of the Tuskegee Airmen*. East Lansing: Michigan State University Press, 1994.

Tuskegee Airmen, Inc. *Who Were the Tuskegee Airmen?* http://tuskegeeairmen.org/Tuskegee_Airmen_History.html (accessed March 1, 2010).

Alice Walker (1944–)

Alice Tallulah-Kate Walker was born Alice Malsenior Walker in Ward Chapel, a neighboring community to Eatonton, Georgia, on February 9, 1944. As a novelist, poet, short story writer, essayist, anthologist, educator, publisher, humanist, feminist, and activist, Walker is simultaneously one of the most celebrated and feared persons in the world of letters. Walker's preeminent work is the epistolary novel *The Color Purple*. It was published in 1982, and won her the Pulitzer Prize for Fiction and The American Book Award. The novel's success birthed Walker's international acclaim, and set her into the crosshairs of some members of the African American community who saw the book as an attack on black men. Walker responded to the criticism, not with an apology, but by producing more provocative works and living a life committed to causes she holds dear to her heart. As a woman who has published more than 35 works of nonfiction, poetry, short-story collections and novels, Walker is one of the most accomplished American writers.

Her works are required readings across liberal arts disciplines, as she covers a breadth of subject matter. Her activism earned her the "Humanist of the Year" award from the American Humanist Society in 1997. On December 6, 2006, she was inducted into the California Hall of Fame located at The California Museum for History, Women, and the Arts.

Born the youngest of eight children of Willie Lee and Millie Tallulah (Grant) Walker, Alice Walker was part of a family rich with dignity, but meager in resources. Her father was a dairy farmer and sharecropper, and her mother supplemented their modest family income working as a maid. Not wanting her daughter tethered to the life of a sharecropper, Walker's mother enrolled her into first grade at the age of four. Her family was steeped in the oral tradition or story telling, which influenced Walker to begin writing as young as eight years old.

Walker's view of the world, both literally and figuratively, would be shaped by a tragic childhood accident. In 1952, during a game of cowboys and Indians with her brothers, Walker was shot in the right eye with a BB gun. In an attempt to cover up the incident, she conspired with her brothers to keep the shooting a secret. Walker lost sight in her right eye as a result of not receiving treatment. The scar tissue covering the eye would not be removed until she turned 14. However, the event impacted her perspective on honesty and dealt a blow to her self-confidence. Understanding that the bullet had injured her eye and the cover up exacerbated her blindness, Walker committed to truthfulness in her life. The disfiguring scar tissue rendered Alice shy, and led her to embrace reading and writing poetry as a means to cope with her isolation.

Her formal education journey began at East Putnam Consolidated, a school formed by her father. In due course, she attended Eatonton's Butler-Baker High School, and graduated as valedictorian of her class in 1961. In the fall of 1961, Walker enrolled in Atlanta, Georgia's historically black women's school, **Spelman College**. The climate of race relations in the United States was experiencing a shift due to the emergence of the Civil Rights Movement.

She became active in the nonviolence movement, and became recognized as a student activist. Walker's participation was rewarded when she was chosen to be one of Spelman's select students to attend the World Youth Festival in Helsinki, Finland in 1962. The group of students received an honor prior to attending the festival. Walker and her peers were guests of Coretta Scott King, wife of civil rights icon **Martin Luther King, Jr.**, at the King household in Atlanta, Georgia.

Ironically, while attending Spelman, an all-black women's college, two of her biggest influences were white men. Two Spelman professors, Howard Zinn and Staughton Lynd, were key figures and mentors in Walker's life. Zinn, historian, activist, and author, influenced Walker with his lessons and advocacy of civil disobedience. Lynd, a historian and activist in his own right, encouraged Walker to excel academically. After completing two years at Spelman, Walker transferred to another women's college, Sarah Lawrence in Bronxville, New York. She graduated with a Bachelor of Arts in Liberal Arts in 1966.

Professor Lynd's mother, Helen Merrell Lynd, was one of Walker's first mentors at Sarah Lawrence. Poetry professor Muriel Rukeyser served as a model for Walker's future as both an artist and activist. As a journalist, Rukeyser had covered the trial of the Scottsboro Boys, nine African American boys falsely accused of raping a white woman in 1931. Rukeyser recognized potential in Walker's writings, and submitted her short story, "To Hell with Dying" to **Langston Hughes**, who published it in *The Best Short Stories by Negro Writers: 1899–1967*. The short story was based on an experience Walker had which had her contemplating suicide. While at Sarah Lawrence, Walker became pregnant and strongly considered suicide. She sought the aid of a college friend who assisted her with a safe but illegal abortion. This experience sent her into a one-week writing frenzy that culminated in, "To Hell With Dying," and the poems in her book of poetry, *Once: Poems*.

Upon graduation, she worked briefly for the New York City Welfare Department before heading back to the South to participate in the Civil Rights Movement. She relocated to Mississippi, a place where she had spent the summer of 1965 participating in voter registration drives. Working for the NAACP Legal Defense Fund, she took depositions from blacks who had been evicted from their homes for attempting to register to vote. While there, she became romantically involved with a young white Jewish attorney for the NAACP Legal Defense Fund, Melvyn Rosenman Leventhal. Walker, not wanting to continue the tradition of the black mistress of a white man in the South, proposed to Leventhal, and he accepted. As much as an act of romantic love, as an act of civil disobedience, the two wed in 1967 in New York City, then settled in Jackson, Mississippi. The act invited scrutiny, from both blacks and whites, as interracial marriage was both taboo and illegal in Mississippi. They settled into a three-bedroom home once owned by civil rights activist Marian Wright Edleman. Their union produced their daughter Rebecca Grant Levanthal (Walker), born in 1969.

The two worked tirelessly for the Civil Rights Movement while fending off threats from the Ku Klux Klan and other white supremacists. Levanthal handled cases that lead to the desegregation of public schools in Mississippi. The two relocated to New York in 1974. They began to experience difficulties in their marriage, and divorced in 1976. Walker would later comment that the divorce was necessary to write about such wild and free women that appear in *The Color Purple*. Walker and Leventhal decided a joint parenting model would be best for raising Rebecca. She would spend two years with each parent. Rebecca would later publish a book—*Black, white, and Jewish: Autobiography of a Shifting Self* (2002)—detailing her unorthodox upbringing.

While in Mississippi, Walker established herself as a writer within academia. She accepted an offer from Jackson State College to serve as a Writer-in-residence in Black Studies in 1968–69. Subsequently, she was Writer-in-residence at Tougaloo College in Tougaloo, Mississippi from 1970 to 1971. From 1972 to 1973, Walker was Lecturer in Literature at two Massachusetts schools, Wellesley College and University of Massachusetts. At Wellesley she became a pioneer. As a lecturer at Wellesley, Walker created one of the first courses on African American women writers.

At this early stage in her career, Walker was extended awards and accolades normally reserved for seasoned writers. In 1966, she was Bread Loaf Writers Conference Scholar. She was both a Merrill Writing Fellow and McDowell Colony Fellow in 1967. A National Endowment for the Arts grant was bestowed upon her in 1969. The Radcliff Institute Fellowship followed in 1971. At the tender age of 28 Walker received an honorary PhD from Russell Sage College. In the same year, 1972, she delivered the convocation address at her alma mater, Sarah Lawrence College. Her book *In Love and Trouble: Stories of Black Women*, earned her the Richard and Hinda Rosenthal Award from the National Institute of Arts and Letters in 1974.

Not limiting herself to the academy, in 1973 Walker joined the staff of *Ms. Magazine* as an editor. Following her divorce from Leventhal, Walker relocated to Northern California to begin a new chapter in her life. Once settled in the Bay area, in 1978, she began a romantic partnership with Robert Allen, editor of *Black Scholar*. This partnership would endure 13 years. The role Allen played in her life during their relationship can be seen in her essays in *Anything We Love Can Be Saved: A Writer's Activism* (1997). Walker settled in the small town of Mendocino, California, and became an instructor of African American studies at Berkley in 1980.

Through all of her various transitions in career and family, Walker maintained her commitment to her childhood pastime of story-telling, writing fiction. Her first novel, *The Third Life of Grange Copeland*, was published in 1970. The book is set in Georgia and chronicles the saga of the Copeland family from the 1920s until the early 1960s. The book tackles the destructive effects of the life of a family forced to eke out an existence as sharecroppers. Grange Copeland's "lives" take him from a violent adulterous husband, then neglectful father, to a loving grandfather left to deal with the consequences of his previous incarnations.

In 1976, Walker published *Meridian*. This book is set in the 1960s and 1970s, and centers on the coming of age of Meridian Hill. Meridian is a college student involved in the Civil Rights Movement who becomes romantically involved with fellow activist Truman. They have a topsy-turvy relationship that includes an unwanted pregnancy, abortion, and heartbreak. Truman eventually weds a white civil rights worker while Meridian recommits herself to the ideals of the movement following the death of one of the movement's icons. The unwanted pregnancy, subsequent abortion, and the interracial union of civil rights workers are all themes which occurred in Walker's real life.

Those two books established Walker as a novelist; however, *The Color Purple* catapulted her from literary notoriety to popular acclaim. *The Color Purple* brought Alice Walker to the forefront not just for its literary merit, but also for the variety of groups it managed to rub the wrong way. Some African American males felt the book was an assault on them, while some women were offended by the role sexual experience played in female identity formation. Others took issue with the use of grammar and dialect of the characters. A mother in California wanted the book banned from public libraries.

The Color Purple is an epistolary novel held together by the main character Celie. As with her previous novels, the setting is in Walker's home state of Georgia. Walker's story centers on a young poor black woman surrounded by a colorful cast of characters used to tell the story of a person being broken and then made whole again. The story boldly tackles such taboo subjects as incest, domestic violence, same sex partnerships, and questioning the existence of God. *The Color Purple* presents the readers with characters who go through a redemptive process to find wholeness. Key to the story is the ability of women to find comfort, and a source of healing and love, from one another.

The Color Purple earned Walker both the Pulitzer Prize for Fiction and the National Book Award. A few years later, music producer Quincy Jones purchased the novel's film rights. After receiving Walker's blessing, Steven Spielberg was set to direct the film. The film served as the acting debuts for two individuals who would go on to become icons in their own right, Whoopi Goldberg and **Oprah Winfrey**. The movie also starred seasoned actor, Danny Glover. **Quincy Jones** scored the film and composed the music for the soundtrack. The film, released in 1985, received 11 Academy Award nominations, but did not go without criticism. The movie became a portal for various interest groups to revisit previous dialogues. Ultimately, Walker would document her trials and tribulations of making *The Color Purple* into a film in a book titled *The Same River Twice: Honoring the Difficult*. Despite the "difficulties," in 2005 Scott Sanders, former president of Mandalay Entertainment, organized a group of investors to create the musical *Oprah Presents: The Color Purple*, which opened to sold-out crowds on Broadway and across the nation.

Because she is a successful novelist, some have forgotten that Walker is also an accomplished poet. She has published several poetry collections including, *Revolutionary Petunias and Other Poems* (1973), *Horses Make a Landscape More Beautiful* (1985), and *A Poem Traveled Down My Arm: Poems and Drawings* (2003). Walker writes in a free form style, rarely using rhyme. Some poems appear to be streams of consciousness, while others illuminate her beliefs and thoughts about issues. She often addresses themes such as race, gender, matters of the soul, and political commentary.

Another less known venture of Walker's is her writing of children's books. Her first publication for children, *Langston Hughes: American Poet*, appeared in 1974. This seems a fitting tribute, as Langston Hughes provided Walker one of her first breaks by publishing her short story, *To Hell With Dying* (1988), which served as the title of her second children's offering. This book, as well as *Finding the Green Stone*, a story about finding one's inner strength, (1991) featured illustrations by Catherine Deeter.

The empowerment of women and spirituality play major roles in Walker's writing and in her work as an activist. Often cited as a feminist, Walker considers herself a womanist. She is credited with coining the term, "womanist." In her book, *In Search of Our Mother's Garden: Womanist Prose*, she explains that the word is used to describe the experiences and perspectives of women of color. This perspective reflects itself in the strong resiliency of black female characters in Walker's novels. In her life, most of her work has been as an advocate for issues concerning women of color.

Spirituality is interwoven into Walker's life as well. Some critics have classified Walker as New Age. Naysayers took issue with the first epitaph of the book reading "To the Spirit." Walker has been open about her unique embrace of spirituality that includes the Buddhist practice of *tonglen*—taking in the bad and sending out the good. One of her first ventures into non-Western spiritual practices came in the 1970s while researching Voodoo as practiced by Southern blacks. This quest led her to the book *Mules and Men* by **Zora Neale Hurston**.

Hurston's impact on Walker was profound. Hurston was a female writer, folklorist, and anthropologist most famously known for her novel *Their Eyes Are Watching God*. Hurston was a key figure of the Harlem Renaissance who died penniless in 1960. In Hurston, Walker found both a kindred spirit of an African American female writer and an individual unashamed of the traditions and folklore of African people. After learning about Hurston's dying in poverty, Walker absorbed the lesson of not having to be dependent on anyone for her well being as an artist. In 1973, Walker and scholar Charlotte D. Hunt located Hurston's unmarked grave in Pierce, Florida, and placed a headstone with the inscription "Zora Neale Hurston/ 'A Genius of the South'/ 1901—1960/ Novelist, Folklorist/Anthropologist." In 1975, Walker wrote "In Search of Zora Neale Hurston" for *Ms. Magazine*. This article, along with other works by Walker, revived interest in Hurston's work. Walker also edited

I Love Myself When I Am Laughing . . . and Then Again When I Am Looking Mean and Impressive: A Zora Neale Hurston Reader (1979).

Walker's novels following *The Color Purple* served as platforms for her to share her perspectives on indigenous spirituality and advance awareness of her advocacies. *The Temple of My Familiar*, Walker's novel following *The Color Purple*, contained strong spiritual themes. Published in 1989, it served as a platform for Walker to address her broadening spiritual beliefs including reincarnation, pantheism, and karma. *Possessing the Secret of Joy* (1992) was a protest novel challenging the practice of the female circumcision. The clitoridectomy was a practice Walker became aware of while traveling in Africa as a college student. Walker and others who want to see an end to the practice refer to it as female genital mutilation. Some readers were shocked to learn of such a practice, while others saw Walker as meddling in a tradition that has served as rites of passage for centuries within certain cultural groups.

Walker's advocacy against the practice manifested itself into a documentary film, *Warrior Marks: Female Genital Mutilation and the Sexual Blinding of Women* (1993) with filmmaker Pratibha Parmar. Walker also published the companion reader of the same title. One of her most heartfelt discoveries was that this practice is carried out against women by women. *Warrior Marks*, the book and documentary, are just two examples of Walker's activism. Walker was arrested in 1987 at the Concord Naval Weapons Station in California while protesting the U.S. government's shipment of weapons to Central America. Being a strong supporter of Cuba's Fidel Castro, she rejected President Clinton's invitation to the White House in 1996 because she disagreed with the U.S. embargo against Cuba. She has made humanitarian aid trips to Cuba and Palestine in an effort to show her solidarity with the peoples of those nations. And on the eve of the Iraq War in 2003, she was arrested with members of Code Pink for crossing police lines during an anti-war rally.

Walker's open exploration of aboriginal religious practices, feminism, and humanitarian issues have made her a highly sought after speaker by groups and institutions committed to creating a more diverse spiritual and intellectual landscape. Some of these lectures and graduation addresses are included in her 2006 nonfiction publication *We Are the Ones We Have Been Waiting For: Inner Light in a Time of Darkness*. Walker's commitment to embracing traditional practices has yielded her speaking engagements from the African-American Buddhist Conference, the Midwives Alliance of North America and the International Association of Black Yoga Teachers. She has delivered commencement addresses to graduates of Agnes Scott College and California Institute of Integral Studies. Her speeches are peppered with her observations on popular phenomena, advocacy of indigenous practices, humor, and the reciting of poems. More conventional circles have not been as inviting to Walker, nor her boundary-pushing message. *Alice Walker Banned* (1996) recounts Walker's battles with censors.

In 1994, two of Walker's essays "Am I Blue?" and "Roselily" were removed from a statewide test for 10th graders. The essays were disallowed for being "anti-meat eating" and "anti-religious," respectively. *The Color Purple* consistently tops lists of most censored books. Walker's experience with being persona non grata allowed her to empathize with imprisoned journalist Mumia Abu-Jamal as she penned the forward to his book *All Things Censored* (2000).

Throughout her career, Walker has been able to maintain a reputation that brings her both censorship and praise. She considers herself not just an American, but also a citizen of the planet, and in many regards has been embraced globally. Her works have been translated into more than two dozen languages, and her books have sold more than 10 million copies. Her activism ranges from ensuring that medical supplies reach Palestine to advocating vegetarianism. In December 2007, Walker's archive was established at Emory University. The archive features Walkers journals, scrapbook, drafts of her early works of nonfiction, photographs, her notebooks, and quilt she created while writing *The Color Purple*. The exhibit opened in April 2009. Following the election of **Barack Obama** as the 44th President of the United States in 2008, Walker published an open letter referring to his election as "a balm for the weary warriors of hope." Walker resides in Northern California and continues her works of activism.

Lasana O. Hotep
Arizona State University

FURTHER READING

Bates, Gerri. *Alice Walker: A Critical Companion*. Westport, CT: Greenwood Press, 2005.

Smith, Evelyn. *Alice Walker: A Life*. New York: W. W. Norton & Company, 2004.

Swick, David. "We Live in the Best of Times." *Shambhala Sun*, May 2007.

Walker, Alice. *Anything We Love Can Be Saved*. New York: Ballantine, 1997.

Walker, Alice. *The Color Purple*. New York: Harcourt Brace Jovanovich, 2003.

Walker, Alice. *Meridian*. Fort Washington, PA: Harvest Books, 2003.

Walker, Alice. *Once*. Fort Washington, PA: Harvest Books, 1976.

Walker, Alice. *In Search of Our Mother's Gardens: Womanist Prose*. Fort Washington, PA: Harvest Books, 2003.

Walker, Alice. *The Third Life of Grange Copeland*. Fort Washington, PA: Harvest Books, 2003.

Walker, Alice. *We Are the Ones We Have Been Waiting for: Inner Light in a Time of Darkness*. New York: New Press, 2007.

Madam C. J. Walker Collection, Indiana Historical Society

Madam C. J. Walker
(1867–1919)

Born into a family of former slaves in the South, Madam C. J. Walker worked for decades at low-paying jobs before she recreated herself. She eventually became the head of a vast empire of hair care products for African American women, in the early twentieth century. From an annual income of approximately $500 a year as a laundress, to $3,000 in 1907, $34,000 in 1913, and a net wealth of approximately $600,000 when she died, Walker worked tirelessly to over-come a difficult childhood and often poverty-stricken young adulthood, to become one of the most successful African American women in business. More than just a success in business for herself, she provided jobs to countless other black women, developed products directed at a black female audience, and led an adult life that few Americans of any race, particularly poor black women from the South, could dream of at that time.

Despite trappings like an $80,000 dollar home in New York, the ability to travel not just across the United States but to countries around the world, and a daughter known as A'Lelia Walker, the Joy Goddess of Harlem, who wore fancy clothes and attended wild parties in New York City, Madam Walker maintained a commitment to helping charities and the fight of the African American population for equality. She once said, "I am not a millionaire, but I hope to be some day, not because of the money, but because I could do so much then to help my race." This sentiment, combined with her success in business when so few blacks, much less black women, were able to do so, and the fact that her business developed a product directed at the much underserved African American community, is why Madam C. J. Walker is still recognized as an important figure not just in African American history, but in women's history and business history.

Walker's childhood and early adulthood mirrors that of many African Americans from the South in the years following the Civil War and the end of slavery. Born to formerly enslaved parents, Walker spent her first few years in Madison Parish, Louisiana, a rural part of the state. Following the war, her parents Owen Breedlove and Minerva Anderson remained on the plantation of their former owner. When that man died in 1865, the Bureau of Refugees, Freedmen, and Abandoned Land confiscated the plantation. This allowed the Breedlove family to remain on the land, lease it from the Bureau, and continue raising cotton.

This is the world in which Madam C. J. Walker was born. Of course, at that time her name was not C. J. Walker, and it was not preceded by the formal "Madam." That moniker developed over the course of her life. A famously private person, and someone who concealed much about her past, a great deal about her life is unclear, especially in areas relating to her youth, young adulthood, and numerous marriages.

Although not born into a life of comfort, Walker's family supported itself through farming. One of several children, it is believed that Walker's parents gave her the name Sarah Breedlove. Her life soon changed forever when her mother died around 1874. By 1877, her father, too, had passed away. By the tender age of 10 Walker found herself an orphan, a difficult and often dangerous position for a young African American woman in the Deep South.

Despite this turn of events, Walker was not entirely without family. She relied on her older sister Louvenia for support. The importance of family remained a constant throughout Walker's life, and was an important component of many black families during this time. In an often hostile environment and with few job opportunities, family provided the support necessary to find work and housing.

Much of this section of Walker's life is unknown, but it is clear that within a year of her father's death, she traveled with her sister—who was somewhere between 14 and 18 years in age—and brother-in-law from the Louisiana Delta to Vicksburg, Mississippi. Although still in the South, this move across the river meant a big change for both sisters. No longer in their small, country town, they had to adapt to city life. More importantly, they had to learn to live on their own and support themselves without the protection of their parents.

Even though young—approximately 10 years old—it is during this early period that the tenacity and independence of Walker emerged. The small family ran a laundry business, and Walker helped by undertaking any work she was able to handle as a young girl. However, life with her sister grew increasingly difficult as there was little money or food. Struggling to live in the often-abusive household of her brother-in-law, Walker moved out at the age of 14 and married a man named either Jeff or Moses McWilliams. Then known as Sarah McWilliams, a name she only used for a short time, Walker soon gave birth to a baby girl in 1885, when she was about 17 years old. Named Lelia McWilliams, this girl too would adopt a new name later in life, and eventually would develop as a social figure and a business heiress of sorts in New York during the Harlem Renaissance.

Still unaware that she eventually would start a business empire built around hair products, own numerous homes across the country, and fund her daughter's future extravagant lifestyle, Walker continued to struggle as a young wife and now mother in the South. However, the perseverance that later would prove to be an asset in her business and already had helped her survive the death of her parents and a difficult move from her childhood home, again showed itself.

By the time she was 20 years old, her husband had died, which left Walker again alone. More than alone really—now with a small daughter to support, Walker could not turn to her sister Louvenia as she had years before as a girl. Instead, she took matters into her own hands and moved to St. Louis in 1887. In this new environment, Walker again relied on family ties to help in her adjustment. An older brother lived in the area and ran his own barbershop. Although Walker was not involved in this business at first, it rather prophetically provided a glimpse into her future.

Certain characteristics, like hard work and a devotion to family, remained central parts of her life in St. Louis, just as they would remain for her entire life and business career. Despite her brother's involvement in the hair business,

Walker initially began working in laundries, relying on the skills she learned from her sister and brother-in-law in Mississippi.

More than just a focus on work and family, though, another important aspect of Walker's life emerged at this time—her belief in charity and activism. Although she later met important black leaders such as Booker T. Washington and certainly had an interest in promoting black rights, particularly those of women, and in supporting certain causes and charities, these activities rarely are what she is remembered for today. Still, Walker maintained a long-standing interest in these issues and received her first introduction to them in her early years in St. Louis while attending church. Her first chance at public speaking came through her involvement with the church's Sunday school, and this led to other charitable work on a small scale.

While many people with money think little of doing this kind of work, Walker was committed to helping her community and people around her at a time when she herself earned little money. She worked as a laundress, and moved almost constantly to raise her daughter in the best environment possible, but still found a small amount of additional time and money to give back to those around her.

In 1893, things changed once again for Walker and her daughter. The brother she remained close to for almost six years in St. Louis died. Like the stressful times that caused Walker to marry for the first time in Mississippi, Walker again found herself without the vital family support that she needed, and shortly thereafter married a man named John Davis. Very little is known about this union, and it clearly was not a happy marriage. Despite their problems and her refusal to mention him publicly once she began her business, they were still listed as married eight years later in 1901, and had Walker's now 15-year-old daughter Lelia living with them. They apparently also had two children together, but both died young. Perhaps due to all of these factors, Walker is listed separately as Sarah M. Davis in a 1901 directory, and John Davis later claimed that by 1903 she had abandoned him.

In addition to these struggles in her married life, Walker also was dealing with the growth of her daughter. High-spirited and rarely interested in school or work, Lelia was now a teenager and ready for high school. Unlike Walker, who was orphaned at a young age and forced to work for her survival, Lelia benefitted from her mother's unswerving devotion. Even when they had little money, Walker focused on giving her daughter the comfort and safety that she herself rarely felt when growing up. Perhaps because she never had to struggle in the same way, Lelia did not apply herself in school and often seemed to abuse her mother's good faith in her. Although this is one possible explanation of their mother-daughter relationship, it also is likely that Lelia simply struggled to live up to her mother's dominant personality and seemingly unending supply of energy for work.

While later in life when her hair care business was doing well Walker found few people she could trust and often felt let down or taken advantage of by employees and family members, she never appeared to feel this way about her daughter. Part of this devotion can be seen early on during Walker's marriage to John Davis. During this time, Lelia took the entrance exam for high school, but failed. Despite this failure and her general lack of interest in school, Walker found enough money to send her to a boarding school in Tennessee. At a cost of $7.85 for the first month's room and board in 1902, Lelia began her studies there as a seventh grade student at the age of 17, but only stayed there for one year before returning to St. Louis in 1903.

During this first major separation from her daughter, Walker seemed to benefit from the extra time it provided and began her entry into the world of hair care products for African American women. More than just additional time on her hands, however, Walker also felt a personal connection to the topic. Not only did she have some limited experience with hair through her brother's barbershop, but she also faced her own difficulties with poor hair and scalp conditions.

Like many other African American women at the time, Walker suffered from a poor diet and health. This, in addition to current hair care practices, impacted the condition of her hair and scalp. Despite suffering from problems including dandruff, dryness, bald spots, and hair breakage for 15 years, it was not until 1905 that she began using a product called Wonderful Hair Grower, which was one of several products directed at a black audience. Products like this often relied on a potent mixture of sulfur or lye and cayenne pepper, a combination that rarely alleviated any of women's symptoms, and instead often exacerbated them.

While hair salons and products had long been directed at a white audience, black women often were denied entrance to these establishments and required a different set of hair-care practices and products for their hair. By the late 1880s, a women named Rebecca Elliott became one of the first people to market hair products to the black population. Her System of French Hair Care, based in Indianapolis, was well-known throughout much of the country. To sell the products, she ran a group of agents who sold her products (much like Mary Kay sales people today) door-to-door, and she also offered a mail order service.

Many others, mostly African American women, soon followed Elliott into the hair business. Although they tried to differentiate their products, many offered variations of the same formula and often branched out on their own after starting as selling agents for another company, thus learning some trade secrets and luring away customers. This is exactly the tactic used by Walker, who appeared to first start as an agent for a woman named Annie Turnbo. This transition occurred around 1905, a time when she was suffering from her own hair problems, but also because she was getting older and no longer wished to do the hard labor of working in a laundry.

Annie Turnbo offered not just a job for Walker as an agent, but a sort of role model as a black woman in business. Even though she came from Chicago, the urban Midwest, which was unlike Walker's rural Southern upbringing, and had advantages like family and school, she also was a woman who decided to create her own product, move to a new city, and relentlessly promote her product to different markets. Although it is unclear if Turnbo and Walker ever met in person during these early years, Turnbo certainly provided both a personal and business model for Walker to follow, and Walker certainly took note.

Turnbo was born in Chicago in 1869, around the same time as Walker. She developed her hair care products, and in 1902 decided to move to St. Louis to try selling her products there and prepare for an exhibition at the upcoming World's Fair, which would be held in town. Unlike other hair care products that often relied on a base of lye combined with ingredients like meat drippings, to oil and straighten the hair, Turnbo believed that these products actually caused dandruff, hair loss, and burning skin rather than helping the symptoms. She created her own Wonderful Hair Grower and a liquid shampoo made of a sage and egg rinse base. Although there is little scientific evidence to show that this combination actually could lead to hair growth, it certainly would not have had the same negative effects as applying lye, meat fat, and cayenne pepper to the hair and scalp.

Upon moving to St. Louis, Turnbo found a community ripe for her business. As mentioned previously, few white-run hair salons permitted black customers, and in 1902 the city directories listed only one black female hairdresser in contrast to more than 20 black barbers. Despite the room for both a female hairdresser catering to the black population and a market ready for a less abrasive hair-care product, Turnbo also faced some resistance to her career choice. A hairdresser was not seen as a very desirable position, but even more so her focus on the business world received greater criticism because few women, particularly black women, ran their own businesses at this time. Walker, too, soon faced much of the same criticism, and she worked actively to change the business environment for black women through her involvement in the National Negro Business League and the National Association of Colored Women.

While their relationship during this early period remains unclear, Turnbo and Walker became staunch adversaries once Walker entered the hair-care business with her own product. Much of the contention between the two lies in the murky origins of Walker's product. Some believe that she relied on her past relationship with barbers, her own hair problems, her familiarity with ironing while working in laundries, and repeated tests on her daughter Lelia to create her own formula. Other accounts suggest that she took some of Turnbo's product to a druggist who examined the product and gave her the list of ingredients. From there she simply reproduced the product under her own name and swept the market with clever advertising and keenly timed moves to different parts of the country.

Walker herself provided her own version of events, one that differs from both of these more likely turn of events:

One night I had a dream and in that dream a big black man appeared to me and told me what to mix up for my hair. Some of the remedy was grown in Africa, but I sent for it, mixed it, put it on scalp, and in a few weeks my hair was coming in faster than it had ever fallen out. I tried it on my friends; it helped them. I made up my mind to sell it.

While a dream may have occurred at some point, and while she likely tested her product before its use, it is more likely that Walker's version is meant primarily for a good story and as an editorial piece for publicity coverage. Even Walker herself changed this story over the years. Later she pointed not to a magical dream and secret African ingredients, which never seemed to be a part of her products, but to "dedication, hard work, and perseverance" as the keys to her success.

A shrewd businesswoman, Walker's account often changed, depending on the audience. If meant for advertising, she used the more fantastic version of the dream, and relied on claims of great, almost miraculous success, even using images of Lelia's adopted daughter—who was part Native American—to demonstrate the abilities of her products. However, if directed at the black community, business leaders, and particularly black women in business, she relied on tales of her humble beginnings and continuous hard work. For instance, her address in 1912 at the 13th Annual Convention of the National Negro Business League, included the statement, "I am not ashamed of my past. I am not ashamed of my humble beginning. Don't think because you have to go down in the washtub that you are any less a lady!" This showed her own success and devotion to work, but it also intended to encourage other black women to see business as an option to change their current circumstances.

Perhaps more importantly, though, her candid discussion of her humble beginnings and constant toiling pointed to her own struggles in life. This made Walker's success more impressive, yes, but those early experiences also are part of what molded her into the person she became—someone who was not afraid to use and rely on connections, someone not afraid of hard work, someone used to difficult times. How hard was it for Walker to survive a scathing editorial from Turnbo when she already had overcome becoming an orphan at the age of ten, an abusive brother-in-law, the deaths of two of her own children, and the back-breaking work at laundries? This is why it is important to understand Walker's childhood and life prior to her business. First, her business did not really begin until her late thirties; much of her life was spent in just a struggle to support herself and her daughter. Furthermore, these early struggles made her who she was. Her dedication to hard work and her commitment to charitable endeavors helped her company grow successfully. Walker's life prior to her involvement in hair products developed the person who is remembered today as the doyenne of African American hair care, not competitors or even predecessors like Annie Turnbo who also ran successful companies.

Although Walker at times referred to the prophetic dream that led to her involvement in hair care products, the reality was far more complex and slow to develop. Around the same time that Turnbo arrived in St. Louis in 1902, Walker also began to be involved in hair care for African American women. In St. Louis she started selling products door-to-door, whether her own or Turnbo's remains a little unclear. Along with selling the products, she offered demonstration where she would straighten and curl people's hair. Clearly interested in more than just a hair growth formula, Walker offered a wider array of services from the beginning by focusing on both hair growth products and straightening techniques using the hot comb, which she did not invent but eventually improved on. This more holistic approach is what separated her from other hair care companies and selling agents at the time, and led to Walker's interest in hairdressing—not just selling—and to the eventual founding of a beauty school in her daughter's name.

Even if she began as an agent for Turnbo and sold her products, Walker soon began marketing her own products and services. Her formula included sulfur (the secret ingredient), petroleum, beeswax, copper sulfate, carbolic acid, coconut oil, and perfume with violet extract to cover the smell of the sulfur. It is thought that early testing of this potent product on her daughter caused her to suffer extensive hair loss, which helps explain why Lelia adopted the eccentric look of wearing a turban to cover most of her head as she grew older.

Within a few years, several important changes occurred and heralded the rise of Walker's own business. In 1905 or 1906, she moved from St. Louis to Denver, and the 1906 Denver city directory listed Walker as a hairdresser, quite a change from her position as a laundress for many years prior to that. Although the directory uses the name Mrs. McWilliams even though no marriage certificate exists, Walker seems to have married C. J. Walker in 1906. This marriage was pivotal in several ways. First, it marked the arrival of the name she soon adopted and that would make her famous. Second, C. J.'s experience as a journalist helped the couple develop a successful advertising campaign to promote Walker and her products.

Rather than relying on word-of-mouth to spread information about her product, Walker relentlessly used more modern forms of advertising. Although she herself was interested in self promotion, it is clear that much of the understanding of the media and its usefulness came from her husband's experience as a journalist. In 1906, early in their relationship, he published a short article about Walker and her burgeoning business for a local paper in the African American community. Once people grew more familiar with her name, services, and products, Walker released a cleverly hidden marketing ploy in late 1906 or early 1907:

> We regret to say that Mrs. McWilliams Walker, who has done so much for the
> ladies of Denver and so truthfully demonstrated her ability to grow the hair, will

be with us no more after May 18th, as she expects to tour the West and teach her wonderful method to the hundreds whom she could not reach in Denver. Mrs. Walker has done what others have failed to do, and will leave many witnesses in Denver to testify to same.

With no apparent plans to move at this time, this seems to be nothing more than a marketing scheme, likely organized by her husband, to encourage business. Just as she began to use advertisements to promote her business, she also adopted the title "Madam," or at times "Madame." It is unclear why she did so, but it seemed to add more clout to her name and hair products. Although this title gave the appearance that she was adopting a more noble air, she never completely abandoned her past, often referring to her days as a laundresses and by continuing to help poorer relatives and community members. The name "Mme" rather than "Mrs" helped her stature in the community and business world. However, it, like the multiple homes and nice clothing that she later would purchase, also were reminders to herself that she was a success. In fact, it likely was one of the few ways she could relish her accomplishments because she rarely spent time away from the company even though she struggled with poor health, like many others in the African American community, because of the previous deprivations in her life.

In 1907, she finally followed through with the move she announced almost a year earlier. Always looking for better markets, this time she targeted Pittsburgh, Pennsylvania, which she saw as a prime location between the large African American communities and potential markets in the East and South. At the age of 40, Walker no longer was young or healthy, but she did not let this stop her. Still, the transition proved to be difficult for her on a personal level and as a business woman. Unlike the Southern and Western cities where she lived before, Pittsburgh had a long-established community of black elite families who rarely welcomed newcomers into their mix. Additionally, the city already had a well-known black hairdresser who catered to the wealthy African American women. Always a shrewd business woman, Walker located her business close to the well-known hair salon, but offered a different set of products. Rather than opening her own shop that would compete directly with the existing store, Walker sold her formula of hair grower, offered a mail order business for other products, and promoted the use of hot combs. In this way she was able to make a small name for herself in Pittsburgh and double her income from the year before by earning a total of $6,672 in 1908.

Despite all of this success, Walker realized that she would remain a small business unless she could open her own factory. When real estate in Pittsburgh proved too pricey, she moved to Indianapolis in 1910. Unlike Pittsburgh, with its elite black community and established hairdressers, Indianapolis at that time only had four black hairdressers and none of them were well-known. She immediately established shop and started advertising in local papers. Walker also began the transition from hairdresser to larger distributor by moving into direct sales of her hair products and into the sales of hot combs. This was the beginning of the Walker Manufacturing Company.

Unlike in Denver where she allowed her husband C. J. to have an important role in the business and left him largely in charge of advertising, in Pittsburgh and Indianapolis, Walker became increasingly involved in all aspects of her business. Perhaps because of this desire or perhaps because of other problems within the marriage itself, her relationship with C. J. crumbled just as her business began to grow. In 1910, she made more than $10,000 and bought a house worth the same amount, which was signed for in just her name. She also began constructing a factory and offices behind her home, and hired two men as her lawyer and business manager. Likely because of her difficult and often short-lived relationships with most men in her life, she had usually relied on female employees and staff. These two men remained the two exceptions to this rule for much of Walker's business career.

Shortly after the factory opened in 1911, Walker incorporated her company and gave places on the board of directors to herself, her daughter, and her husband. Likely because she understood her daughter's lack of interest in the business and because she saw the growing problems in her marriage, she kept all of the stock options in her own name. This proved to be a wise move, because the couple divorced in 1912. Although he argued that some of the company's success was from his work, which was true, the court found him at fault for the divorce due to extramarital affairs, and granted him no money. Although unsuccessful on his own, he tried to bank on his experience with the company and his by then well-known name by starting "C. J. Walker's Wonderful Hair Preparations" just a few days after the divorce. Rather than view him with disdain, Mme. Walker gave her ex-husband some money to help start his competing business.

As a testament to her work ethic and singular devotion to her company, Walker undertook additional projects during the dissolution of her marriage and the emergence of her company as a successful public entity. Not yet involved in the plight for African Americans rights, Walker recognized the important leaders at the time, and targeted her energy on Booker T. Washington. She first wrote to him in 1910 to ask for financial backing in building her first factory. Washington already had released statements condemning whitening creams and other beauty products that helped black women look white. He probably perceived the hair care business, especially with its focus on hair straightening, in a similar vein and viewed it with disdain, which helps explain his lack of response to her request. Undeterred by his silence, Walker wrote Washington again in 1911 with an invitation to visit her home and factory whenever he was in Indianapolis. This time Washington replied, but only with a short note, and showed little interest in visiting her.

When these attempts to receive Washington's recognition went nowhere, Walker decided to travel to his home in Tuskegee, Alabama. Under the pretense of wanting to speak at the annual farmer's conference held there, she asked Washington to allow her to speak, which he grudgingly did. By this time in 1911 and 1912, Walker was earning more than $1,000 a month, and ran a staff of more than 950 agents selling her products across the country, in addition to her mail order business. She rightly recognized Washington's dismissive treatment of her, and tried yet again to gain not just his attention but his approval and validation of her business, something she deemed necessary. She traveled to the 1912 National Negro Business League annual convention in Chicago. This time when Washington ignored her request to speak, she started talking without his introduction. Despite this unorthodox approach, her ability to stand up to Washington, one of the most powerful leaders of the black community at the time, paid off, because when she started talking about her business and the money she earned, people listened.

Just as she took sole control of her business through its stock options and she stood up to powerful men like Booker T. Washington, she continued to do things her way in other areas of her life. As an example, in the early 1910s, the YMCA in Indianapolis was trying to raise money for a new building in the black part of town and was having a difficult time. At a public event for the building, Walker committed $1,000 to the project and helped encouraged other community leaders to give as well. This was a large amount of money at the time, and approximately 10 percent of her annual income. Perhaps because of the undeniable size of this gift and the fact that she was the first African American woman to make a donation of this amount, Booker T. Washington finally accepted an invitation to stay at her home for the opening of the YMCA building in 1913.

Flush from this success and from the increasing profits of her company, Walker purchased a home in New York City, and established a hairdressing school named Lelia College on the first floor of the home. Her daughter ostensibly ran the school but more often focused on friends and parties. To be closer to her daughter, the only family Walker really had, Walker soon split her time between Indianapolis and New York. She was earning approximately $34,000 a year by 1913, and gave her daughter an allotment on which to live. However, Lelia, who by then went by A'Lelia, routinely overspent on luxurious clothes, lavish parties, and expensive home furnishings, and while Walker remained a strict manager of her business, she always was much more generous with her daughter. Even though her business manager often suggested otherwise to both of them, neither Lelia nor Walker did little to curb Lelia's spending habits.

Of course, Lelia was not the only one spending money. Walker, too, began to make larger purchases as she earned more money. By 1914, she owned three brownstones in New York City in addition to her home in St. Louis, and then put down a deposit on a 20-room mansion in Queens. Fearful that the home and property were not worth the advertised price, her business manager spent several years trying to end the deal.

In 1916, when Walker extracted herself from the home in Queens, the Walker Manufacturing Company had more than 3,000 employees and was the largest African American owned business in the country. Because of this success, Mme. Walker finally was able to buy the property for the place she would view as her home. From a family of poor cotton farmers and former slaves in the Louisiana Delta, Walker now purchased land in the Palisades of New York, where she was surrounded by some of the richest white people in America. Unlike many wealthy neighborhoods at the time, which used racial covenants to keep black buyers out, no restrictions existed in this neighborhood, mostly because it was never thought that a black person would be able to afford a home there. This home, which she named Villa Lewaro, was completed in 1918, and Walker immediately moved in.

Lest it seem that Walker used all of her money on homes and furnishings, it must be understood that Mme. Walker is remembered today for more than her business savvy. In the years between 1913 and 1918, she also increased her charitable activities. Ever looking to Booker T. Washington despite his continual rebukes, Walker established a scholarship to help students at Tuskegee attend classes without having to work. She also hoped to start an industrial school in Africa. Walker spent several years looking for collaborators on this project, and left the project money in her will.

Although Walker at times was involved in the National Association for the Advancement of Colored People (NAACP), particularly their anti-lynching campaign, and joined the advisory board of the Circle of Negro War Relief during World War I, Walker generally was active on a more individual level. Much like her early reliance on family ties to survive, she helped those whom she met. Several examples of these more personal projects include raising money for a young black harpist to attend school, suing a movie theater for charging her more money for a ticket because of her race, and donating money to help save **Frederick Douglass**'s house from decay and demolition. She also received many letters from distant family and strangers alike, asking for her help. She felt obligated to do so, but often kept them on a strict budget as a way to monitor the expenditures.

In 1916, she started the Mme. C. J. Walker Benevolent Association, which was made up of all of her agents, and held competitions for the most new members, highest sales, and biggest charitable donations. While she certainly encouraged her employees to sell more, she also helped instill the value of giving back and reinforced this company priority through an annual meeting with all employees.

By 1916, all of her work, personal commitments, and other activities began to take a toll on her health. Walker suffered from numerous health problems, likely ranging from high blood pressure to diabetes and kidney disease, and doctors recommended that she cease making public appearances and end her involvement with the company. While she agreed to limit her travels and asked for more help in running the company, she refused to stop working altogether. In 1918 alone, Walker attended the National Association of Colored Women where she made an address on the opening night, led a discussion the next day, and gave a separate talk about her business. She also held the second annual meeting of agents from her company, and gave several speeches for the NAACP. That same year she continued her interest in Africa by attending the National Race Congress in 1918, an action that put her name on the "Negro Subversives" list of the Military Intelligence Division.

The following year she made a final trip to St. Louis to give a talk, but fell ill shortly after arriving. Finally acknowledging that the end was near, she asked to return home and died just four weeks later, on May 24, 1919, at Villa Lewaro. Her beloved home served as her home for only a little over a year, but Walker had been able to see it in all of its glory. The company continued to grow for several years, with sales of $486,762 in 1919 (equal to $4.8 million today) and $595,353 in 1920 (more than $5 million today). Following what likely would have been Mme. Walker's own instincts, the company expanded and built a new factory in 1928 at a cost of $350,000.

Unfortunately, this opening fell right before the Great Depression, during which the company struggled to survive. Sales dropped to less than $200,000 in 1930. Although still a great deal more than Walker earned initially, it was a serious blow following the huge expenditure of the new factory. To survive these difficult years, the company was forced to sell the contents of Walker's beloved home. In 1931, the same year that Walker's daughter Lelia died of a cerebral hemorrhage, the company put Villa Lewaro itself up for sale.

Even though she and her daughter both died at the relatively young ages of 51 and 46, respectively, and despite the struggles of her company after her death and the eventual sale of her palatial home, Walker's legacy and her company survived long after she did. The company based its headquarters in Indianapolis in its original building from 1927 until the company was sold in 1979. Today, both the company house and Villa Lewaro belong to the National Register of Historic Places. Only a small number of landmarks relate to African American history, and even a smaller number are tied to homes and businesses owned by black women. Several books document the life of Madam C. J. Walker, one of them written by her great-great-granddaughter, and numerous children's books use her life story to inspire future generations to pursue their dreams and overcome any hurdles they may encounter. Mme. Walker's dying words supposedly were, "I want to live to help my race." She worked tirelessly to do this in her life, and through her charitable contributions, presence on the National Register, and accounts of her struggles and successes, it has been ensured that her legacy will continue well into the future.

Elyssa Ford
Arizona State University

FURTHER READING

Bundles, A'Lelia. *On Her Own Ground: The Life and Times of Madam C. J. Walker.* New York: Scribner, 2001.

Bundles, A'Lelia. *Madam C. J. Walker.* New York: Chelsea House Publishers, 1991.

Colman, Penny. *Madame C. J. Walker: Building a Business Empire.* Brookfield, CT: Millbrook Press, 1994.

Due, Tananarive. *The Black Rose: The Dramatic Story of Madam C. J. Walker, America's First Black Female Millionaire.* New York: One World, 2000.

Lowry, Beverly. *Her Dream of Dreams: The Rise and Triumph of Madam C. J. Walker.* New York: Alfred A. Knopf, 2003.

Booker T. Washington (1856–1915)

Almost immediately following a five-minute speech that he delivered on September 18, 1895, at the Cotton States and International Exposition in Atlanta, Georgia, former slave and founder of Tuskegee Normal and Industrial Institute Booker Taliaferro Washington became black America's white-appointed leader, spokesperson, and representative. In this carefully calculated and widely praised speech, Washington offered temporary remedies to the so-called Negro Problem that did not disrupt the white South's racial hierarchy. He humbly instructed blacks to remain in the South, to continue working as agricultural laborers, to coexist harmoniously with whites, to embrace vocational and industrial education, and to abandon struggles for political and social equality. Washington reassured Southern whites that they would be "surrounded by the most patient, law-abiding, and unresentful people that the world had seen," and accepted segregation, declaring: "In all things that are purely social we can be as separate as the fingers, yet, one as the hand in all things essential to mutual progress."

With his famous 1895 oration, Washington, the "trickster" and interracial mediator, executed a plan that he would employ with minor alternations during the next 20 years of his life. He wore what Paul Laurence Dunbar dubbed "the mask," presenting himself as a non-threatening "safe Negro" to gain financial and political support and resources from powerful whites. Washington, who adjusted his speeches, writings, and propaganda depending upon his particular audience, used his position as the white-appointed black spokesperson of the Progressive Era, and more importantly the millions of dollars that he was able to solicit, to run Tuskegee Institute, to fund its many practical reform projects that aided thousands of poor Southern blacks, and to strategically undermine and challenge white supremacy without appearing to do so.

Between 1895 and 1915, Washington wielded so much power and influence within African American communities and influential white circles that in his classic *From Slavery to Freedom* (1947) historian John Hope Franklin called this period, an era that historian Rayford W. Logan later dubbed "the nadir" of black American life, "The Age of Booker T. Washington." Washington was among the few black celebrities of his time to achieve national and worldwide fame. Though hated by more than a few white supremacists, in 1901 Washington became the first African American to dine in the White House. He had tea with Queen Victoria in England; he received honorary degrees from Yale, Harvard, and Dartmouth; he advised Presidents William McKinley, Theodore Roosevelt, and Howard Taft; and he received funding from various benevolent organizations and was supported by wealthy white industrialists and businessmen turned philanthropists, including J. D. Rockefeller, Collis P. Huntington, J. P. Morgan, Henry H. Rogers, George Eastman, Robert C. Ogden, William H. Baldwin, John Wanamaker, Julius Rosenwald, and Andrew Carnegie, who in April 1903 pledged $600,000 in U.S. steel bonds to Tuskegee.

Washington remains an enigmatic historical figure and icon. For some, his life "up from slavery" embodies the Horatio Alger "rags to riches" success story and he represents positive attributes of black economic independence and self-help. At the same time, for others he epitomizes a conservative, materialist post-antebellum era Uncle Tom. Today's high school and college students tend to perhaps know Washington best for founding Tuskegee Institute, now Tuskegee University; his famous "Atlanta Compromise" speech; his classic and enduring autobiography *Up From Slavery* (1901); his tumultuous relationship with **W. E. B. Du Bois**; and his controversial approach to confronting white supremacy in the Jim Crow South. Since his death, Washington's leadership has been widely debated. The historical scholarship on Washington is exhaustive, rich, and diverse, and in the new millennium alone 10 books have been published on Washington that claim to offer new and nuanced analyses. A large group of African American intellectuals, scholars, and historians still consider Washington a power-hungry accommodationist who stifled the black struggle for civil and political rights, equality, and liberation. A much smaller school of revisionist historians have begun to more adamantly reject negative portrayals of Washington's leadership and legacy, instead highlighting the challenging historical context that shaped his decisions and actions, his behind the scenes attacks on lynching, discrimination, and segregation, as well as his pragmatism, utilitarianism, and practical self-help and uplift programs.

Washington's legacy has been symbolically invoked and memorialized in many ways. The numerous buildings on Tuskegee's campus that were constructed by students, teachers, and staff members are the most obvious fruits of Washington's accomplishments. In 1922, sculptor Charles Keck's *Lifting the Veil of Ignorance*, a large bronze statue of Washington figuratively emancipating a kneeling slave as Lincoln does in Thomas Ball's 1876 *Freedmans Monument*, was erected in the center of Tuskegee's campus. In 1929, Liberia's first agricultural and vocational school was founded and named in honor of Washington. In 1940, Washington became the first African American to be depicted on a U.S. postage stamp, and between 1946 and the early 1950s, he was the first African American to be featured on U.S. money, a memorial half-dollar silver coin. In 1956, Washington's birthplace in Franklin County, Virginia, was designated a National Historic Site, and since the Civil Rights Movement several other spaces have been named in his honor. For five decades, scholars have had access to the Booker T. Washington Papers (approximately 375,550 items) housed at the Library of Congress Manuscript Division, the largest collection of primary source materials on an African American historical figure. Equally noteworthy, following his death thousands of black males have been named after Washington, including Booker T. Jones, organ and piano player for once popular Memphis Soul band Booker T. and the M.G.'s, and former World Championship Wrestling and World Wrestling Entertainment Heavyweight Champion Booker Tio Huffman, whose ring names include Booker T., Booker, and King Booker. Countless elementary, middle, and high schools as well as other institutions have also been named after Washington. In the new millennium, many black conservatives have claimed the Tuskegee, and organizations like the Chicago-based Heartland Institute have called upon African Americans to return to Washington's philosophies of self-help and entrepreneurship.

Born a slave when the nation's most pressing and controversial issue was slavery, Washington opened Tuskegee Institute on July 4, 1881, with about 30 students, three teachers, and two crudely constructed log-cabin structures. When he died on November 14, 1915, Tuskegee Institute had more than 100 buildings, 2,345 acres of land, 185 teachers and staff members, 1,527 students, and an endowment of at least $2 million. For the first two decades after graduating from Hampton Normal and Agricultural Institute in 1875, Washington devoted his life to uplifting Southern rural blacks through the platforms of economic self-help, vocational and industrial education, interracial cooperation, and "character building." Members of Du Bois's Talented Tenth, Tuskegee graduates were expected to become educational reformers and cultural missionaries. For the last two decades of his life, Washington strategically presented himself to various publics in different ways. Convinced of the U.S. government's failure to help blacks during the post-Reconstruction era, Washington called upon blacks to focus on uplifting themselves with a self-help materialist ethos that placed social and political equality on the back burner. He ultimately believed, or at least hoped, that their success would eventually gain them their civil rights that he secretly fought for from time to time. Washington's approach to African American uplift was multidimensional, complex, and unstatic, and the circumstances of his early years and upbringing help explain his oftentimes hard to decipher character and actions.

Washington was born on April 5, 1856, in Hales Ford, Virginia, on the farm of his owner James Burroughs, a small yeoman farmer who in 1861 owned 10 slaves and approximately 200 acres of land. Washington's worth amounted to $400. Washington's resourceful mother, Jane, was a cook and house-servant for the Burroughs family, and Washington's father could have been one of several white men, including James Burroughs, Ben Hatcher, or Josiah Ferguson. As an enslaved child, Washington performed small tasks and chores. He recalled being provided with meager clothing and food rations, and once witnessed his uncle being whipped. Until she died in the summer of 1874, his mother cared from him and her other children to the best of her ability.

Following the Civil War, in 1865 a nine-year-old Washington, his mother, his older brother John, and his younger sister Amanda migrated by foot and wagon 200 miles to Malden, West Virginia, to live with Wash Ferguson, Jane's husband. Between 1865 and 1872, Washington worked in Malden's salt and coal mines, and all of his earnings were taken by his stepfather. An exploited victim of child labor, Washington worked long hours, taught himself from a Webster's blue-back speller, and eventually attended school after working mornings in the mines. On the first day of school when he was asked what his name was he adopted the last name Washington, symbolically severing his ties to slavery while creating a new identity for himself. While in the small industrial river town of Malden, Washington met two significant teachers: William Davis, a Freedman's Bureau teacher from Ohio, and white New Englander Viola Ruffner. Washington briefly attended night school under Davis's guidance at the Tinkersville School, and then he worked as a domestic servant and gardener for Ruffner, making about $5 per month, all of which was taken by his stepfather. A former school teacher, Ruffner reinforced many aspects of New England culture, such as thrift, cleanliness, promptness, and self-help, encouraging his desire to become educated and teaching him the fundamentals of grammar and "standard" English. In September 1872, Washington ventured 500 miles to Hampton Normal and Agricultural Institute in Hampton, Virginia, and between 1872 and 1875, he attended Hampton under the direction of Samuel C. Armstrong, who became a father-like figure to him and later recommended him for the principalship at Tuskegee. Though he received a scholarship during his first year at Hampton, he also worked as a janitor to pay his school fees. At Hampton, he learned brick making and the importance of personal hygiene, and studied the Bible, rhetoric, and public speaking, as well as the basics of reading, writing, history, geography, and arithmetic. A model student and member of the debate club, in 1875 he delivered one of Hampton's graduation speeches and participated in a staged debate. Washington's performance was praised by a writer for the *New York Times*.

After graduating from Hampton, Washington returned to Malden, operating from 1875 until 1878 a day and night school with close to two hundred students, more than a few of whom later attended Hampton. In 1877, he drew upon his experiences working as the secretary of the Malden Republican organization in 1869, and briefly became involved in a movement to relocate the capital of West Virginia. While in Malden, he also briefly studied law. Influenced by a "call" to preach, in the fall of 1878, Washington enrolled in Wayland Baptist Theological Seminary in Washington, DC. After six to eight months, he left Wayland because of what he described as a snobbishness and elitist attitude that permeated the student body. A rural Southerner at heart, Washington probably also experienced a discomforting sense of culture shock in this new urban environment. Though later in his life he traveled extensively throughout the Northeast and the nation, Washington routinely spoke out about the vices of urban life.

In 1879, he delivered Hampton's commencement address, and beginning in the fall of 1879 he began teaching at Hampton. Washington began by overseeing Hampton's night school, the "Plucky Class," and was then charged with overseeing the education and acculturation of approximately 75 Native American students. As a result of the bargaining strategies of former skilled slave Lewis Adams and an enthusiastic recommendation from Armstrong, in the spring of 1881 a 25-year-old Washington was hired as the first principal of Tuskegee Normal and Industrial Institute, Macon County, Alabama. In June, Washington ventured to Tuskegee to assess the situation, recruit students, and mobilize the black community as he had done years earlier in Malden. A grassroots leader in the making, he intimately interacted with the poor blacks of Macon County, deciphering their most pressing educational and cultural needs. Though Alabama allotted Tuskegee $2,000 to hire and pay teachers, this was not enough to maintain the type of institution that Washington envisioned. For $500, he soon purchased an additional 100 acres of land, with three buildings in need of repair. In 1882, Washington married Fanny M. Smith, who until her death two years later, worked tirelessly for Tuskegee. In 1882, under Washington's guidance, the students constructed Tuskegee's first major building, Porter Hall, a three-story Victorian home that served multiple purposes, including a dormitory for female students. The money that was used to construct Porter Hall, as it was the case for nearly all of Tuskegee's buildings, was donated by a wealthy white philanthropist.

During its first decade, Tuskegee grew significantly. By 1890, Tuskegee was valued at $100,000, included more than 600 acres of land, had more than 400 students, 25 teachers, and more than five new major buildings constructed by student labor. More than 10 industries were offered to Tuskegee students, such as farming, brick making, blacksmithing, carpentry, printing, sawmilling, sewing, wheel righting, shoe making, canning, and cooking. Resembling Hampton's curriculum, students enrolled at Tuskegee were trained in the basics of vocational and industrial education, studied grammar and composition, history from a Eurocentric perspective, geography, language, and especially cleanliness and personal hygiene. The "gospel of the toothbrush," economic self-sufficiency, "working with the hands" in a dignified manner, redemptive suffering, self-sacrifice, and the Protestant work ethic were central to Washington's philosophy. Life for Tuskegee students, who were regularly occupied from 5:00 a.m. until 9:30 p.m., was very demanding and strict. A micromanager in today's terms, Washington routinely weeded out students who violated the school's many rules. Although routinely characterized as a trade school, Tuskegee students were ultimately trained to become teachers who embraced the Progressive Era reform ethos. While the vast majority of Tuskegee students came from the South, a small group of students came to study at Washington's school from throughout the African and Asian diasporas.

Washington's first wife (Fanny) died in 1884, leaving him with the daughter they named Portia (born in 1883). One year later, Washington married Hampton graduate Olivia Davidson. She gave birth to two children, Davidson and Booker, and was essential to Tuskegee's early success and fund-raising efforts. In the spring of 1889, Davidson, who suffered from respiratory problems, died. In 1890, Washington hired Mississippi native and Fisk graduate Margaret Murray as lady principal, and in 1892 Murray, who founded the Tuskegee Woman's Club and later served as president of the National Association of Colored Women, became Washington's third wife, helping him raise his family and run Tuskegee while he spent approximately six months of every year fund-raising across the nation, especially in the Northeast. In 1899, with a $40,000 deficit, Tuskegee faced great financial challenges. Yet, the first half of the 1890s were quite prosperous for Washington's school. In 1895, Tuskegee had about 2,000 acres of land and 800 students.

After helping convince Congress to fund the Cotton States and International Exposition in Atlanta, Georgia, on September 18, 1895, Washington delivered his famous oration that catapulted him into the position of a black leader. On February 20, 1895, **Frederick Douglass** died, leaving a void in black leadership that Washington eagerly filled. Following his "Atlanta Compromise" speech, his popularity skyrocketed, influential whites funneled resources to Tuskegee, and Washington continued to travel on fund-raising trips. While he was away, his personal secretary Emmett J. Scott and his wife Margaret kept him informed about Tuskegee's daily operations.

During the two decades from 1895 until 1915 when Washington reigned as the most powerful black man in the United States, he faced opposition from white nationalists and black activists, developed a wide variety of grassroots reform projects emanating from Tuskegee for the Southern black masses, created and supported several organizations, orchestrated an intricate system of propaganda, and selectively and secretly fought for blacks' civil rights. While Washington's conciliatory position won over many whites throughout the nation, more than a few Southern white nationalists like politicians James K. Vardaman, J. Thomas Heflin, Tom Watson, Ben Tillman, and racist novelist Thomas Dixon, Jr. opposed him. During the early 1900s, Washington's life was threatened upon more than one occasion; he received many death threats after he dined in the White House with Theodore Roosevelt. When Roosevelt visited Tuskegee in 1905, New York City detectives went to Tuskegee to protect Washington from rumored assassins. Progressive white reformers who founded the NAACP in 1909 were opposed to Washington mainly because of his failure to speak out against lynching and disenfranchisement and because of the power that they perceived he misused.

While Washington had many black allies and millions of African Americans flocked to his speaking engagements, he was not elected a preeminent leader by black communities throughout the nation. Many influential African American leaders challenged Washington not only because he was hand-picked by white America as black America's leader, but because he endorsed industrial education while belittling classical education; told "darky jokes" to his white audiences; placed the burden of solving the so-called Negro Problem on blacks' backs: advised blacks to not protest for their political and social rights; refused to consistently and publicly denounce lynching and racial violence, Jim Crow segregation, and disenfranchisement; and because Washington sometimes ruthlessly used his power to squash his opposition. In "Of Mr. Booker T. Washington and Others," a chapter in *The Souls of Black Folk* (1903), Du Bois publicly chastised Washington. In July of the same year, William Monroe Trotter and his followers turned one of Washington's National Negro Business League events in Boston into a riot, clearly demonstrating to white America that

Washington did not have unanimous support within the black community. Founded in 1901, Trotter's *The Guardian* criticized, denounced, and lampooned Washington in no uncertain terms. Other black activists who spoke out against Washington included **Ida B. Wells-Barnett**, W. Calvin Chase, Henry McNeal Turner, Mary Church Terrell, Charles W. Chestnutt, Pauline Hopkins, Kelly Miller, William H. Councill, William H. Ferris, Archibald Grimké, and members of Du Bois's Niagara Movement. Washington was so concerned with his opposition that from January 6 to 8, 1904, he organized a clandestine peace-making meeting at Carnegie Hall with close to 30 black male leaders, the majority of whom supported him. Washington's plans did not pan out; influential black leaders, namely Du Bois, Trotter, and Wells, continued to forcefully denounce his leadership.

Washington initiated a wide array of practical educational uplift programs for the poor Southern black masses. In 1883, he opened up a night school at Tuskegee primarily for adults that, by 1900, had 400 students. Between 1892 and 1915, Tuskegee hosted its annual Negro Conferences. Washington and his staff, and eventually thousands of Southern rural farmers, discussed the evils of the mortgage system and sharecropping, and the value in owning land, saving money, building schools, raising their own crops, remaining in the South, and following moral codes of living. In the 1890s, Washington also established programs like the Dizer Fund and the Southern Improvement Association to help black farmers purchase homes and farms at low interest rates. At Tuskegee's Farmer's Institutes and "Short Courses in Agriculture," farmers learned the basics of scientific agricultural work and how to maximize the production of cotton, the care of poultry, and the proper preparation of the land. Participants organized fairs and received diplomas, awards, and prizes. Scientist **George Washington Carver**, who arrived at Tuskegee in 1896 and often had problems following Washington's orders, was instrumental in these activities. In 1898, Carver began distributing free practical farming manuals to black farmers throughout Macon County. In 1893, Washington created a summer Bible school for adults, and Margaret Murray began organizing Mother's Meetings, small conferences where women in the community discussed motherhood, household management, and respectability.

Beginning in 1906, Washington educated poor farmers in Macon County and other nearby towns on how to improve their crops with the Jesup Agricultural Wagon, also known as the Moveable School, the "Farmer's College on Wheels," and the Farmer's Cooperative Demonstration. Renamed the "Booker T. Washington Agricultural School on Wheels" after Washington's death, with this effort Washington took the school directly to rural peoples. In 1910, Washington organized his outreach programs under an Extension Department that, among other things, distributed practical farming guide bulletins titled the *Messenger* and the *Negro Farmer*. With building materials and funding from Sears and Roebuck genius Julius Rosenwald, in 1912 Washington began to create the Rosenwald School Program, constructing about 80 schools for African American children in rural areas near Tuskegee. Washington established several landowners farming colonies and demonstration centers, such as the Hill Taylor Project, Greenwood Village, Baldwin Farms, and a short-lived project in Hilton Head. Washington was also a Pan-Africanist. In the early 1900s, he sent several Tuskegee students and teachers to Togo, West Africa for a short-lived experiment in cotton growing. From March 21 to 27, 1915, expanding upon earlier programs such as a 1908 five-day-long conference on tuberculosis at Tuskegee, and a 1914 conference on public health, Washington initiated National Negro Health Week. Under Washington's leadership, Tuskegee printed materials and sponsored lectures dealing with disease prevention and better health practices.

Washington founded organizations as well. In 1882, he founded the Alabama State Teachers Association, a first of its kind, professional racial uplift organization for black teachers. Promoting black economic nationalism, empowerment, entrepreneurship, and networking, in 1900 Washington established the National Negro Business League. Washington also actively supported the Negro Organization Society of Virginia and the National Urban League, and gave money and encouraged donations to Fisk and Howard.

Washington publicized and legitimized his approach to black uplift programs with an elaborate system of propaganda, dubbed by his opponents "The Tuskegee Machine." Between the early 1880s and his death, Washington delivered thousands of planned and impromptu speeches before black and white audiences throughout the nation, and he also employed black and white photographers to visually document his and Tuskegee's accomplishments while simultaneously countering stereotypical images of blacks in the mainstream media. With the help of ghostwriters and scholars, between 1896 and 1915, Washington published 13 books (including two autobiographies, an African American history narrative, a biography on Frederick Douglass, several collections of essays, speeches, and inspirational quotations, and one study comparing Southern rural blacks with poor rural Europeans), and countless essays in mainstream U.S. newspapers and magazines. To the dismay of many of his African American critics, Washington also subsidized and bought off the editors for influential black newspapers and magazines, including the New York *Age*, the Washington *Colored American*, the Boston *Colored Citizen*, the *Colored American Magazine*, *Alexander's Magazine*, and the *Washington Bee*. *Up from Slavery* (1901) was Washington's most influential book. Not only did it empower its many black readers, such as **Marcus Garvey**, but it also helped expose Washington's program to potential donors, especially those in the North.

Although Washington did not consistently protest for blacks' civil and political rights, and mandated that Tuskegee students embrace Americanism and remain apolitical, he selectively spoke out for blacks' rights and secretly funded court cases combating discrimination. Before his "Atlanta Compromise" speech, Washington only openly challenged racial discrimination a few times because he feared making his school a target for white supremacist hatred. In an 1885 essay in the Montgomery *Advertiser*, Washington condemned the treatment of Tuskegee staff members on a segregated train in Alabama. In 1896, Washington voiced some opposition to the *Plessy v. Ferguson* decision in the Washington *Post* and *Our Day*, and condemned lynching in the Minneapolis *Journal*. In 1899, Washington covertly fought against segregation and disenfranchisement in Georgia. In 1900, he secretly contributed money to combat Louisiana's grandfather clause. In 1903 and 1904, he secretly funded two major legal cases against voter discrimination in Alabama. In 1906, he paid a lobbyist to challenge laws upholding railroad segregation across the nation. Between 1908 and 1911, Washington supported the struggle against Alabama's oppressive anti-black contract-labor laws. By 1912, Washington became more assertive in speaking out against racial prejudice and segregation, as exemplified in his 1912 article in *Century*, "Is the Negro Having a Fair Chance?" Between 1912 and 1915, Washington spoke out against lynching in more direct and clear terms. In the year of his death, he worked to defeat a bill that sought to ban immigrants of African descent from entering the United States, and a month after he died, his most critical assessment of segregation and anti-black violence was published in the *New Republic*, "My View of Segregation Laws."

Because of his grueling work ethic, Washington's health began to cause him problems when he was only 29 years old. In 1885, he became so ill that he had to seek treatment and rest for several weeks. Beginning in the 1890s, Washington suffered from stress, migraine headaches, chronic indigestion, elevated blood pressure, and most likely diabetes. On March 19, 1911, in New York, a white man nearly beat Washington to death because he claimed that he was a thief who was attempting to sexually assault his wife. Nonetheless, between 1911 and 1915, Washington engaged in intense speaking tours in Texas, Florida, and Louisiana. Washington never fully recovered from being attacked, and by late 1914, Washington became very ill. On November 4, 1915, Washington died in his home at age 59. In May 2006, medical doctors reviewed Washington's medical records and determined that he did not die from what his white Southern doctors called "racial characteristics" or syphilis, but instead from high blood pressure that was close to double that which is considered normal.

Pero Gaglo Dagbovie
Michigan State University

FURTHER READING

Bieze, Michael. *Booker T. Washington and the Art of Self-Representation*. New York: Peter Lang Publishing, 2008.

Brundage, W. Fitzhugh, ed. *Booker T. Washington and Black Progress*. Gainesville: University of Florida Press, 2003.

Caroll, Rebecca, ed. *Uncle Tom or New Negro?: African Americans Reflect on Booker T. Washington and Up from Slavery One Hundred Years Later*. New York: Harlem Moon, 2006.

Dagbovie, Pero Gaglo. "Exploring One Century of Historical Scholarship on Booker T. Washington." *Journal of African American History* 92 (Spring 2007): 239–64.

Denton, Virginia Lantz. *Booker T. Washington and the Adult Education Movement*. Gainesville: University of Florida Press, 1993.

Jackson, David H. *Booker T. Washington and the Struggle against White Supremacy: The Southern Educational Tours, 1908–1912*. New York: Palgrave Macmillan, 2008.

Norrell, Robert J. *Up from History: The Life of Booker T. Washington*. Cambridge, MA: The Belknap Press, 2009.

Smock, Raymond W. *Booker T. Washington in Perspective: Essays of Louis R. Harlan*. Jackson: University of Mississippi Press, 1988.

Denzel Washington
(1954–)

Denzel Hayes Washington, Jr., one of the great and most popular actors of the late twentieth and early twenty-first centuries, has created a life for himself and his family—as well as a model for other aspiring actors—based on integrity, passion, hard work, and responsibility to self and others. For decades, Washington's name has appeared at the top of producers's and directors's wish lists for the actor to star in a lead role in their films. At first glance, it would appear that Washington has confirmed the "American Dream": a young, intelligent, virtuous African American man from humble origins works hard, endures a few barriers, and eventually begins the pathway to fame, wealth, and eternal happiness for himself and his family. Upon closer inspection, however, Washington also becomes a much more complicated, intriguing, and critical character; a man who is never afraid to speak his mind, to offer powerful social critique, to push Hollywood to employ black people in the film industry, and to give to organizations that share his visions. A review of his films demonstrates that Washington evades simplistic categorization and instead uses his career in the film industry for a multitude of purposes.

The first black male to consistently compete for roles with white males, Washington has demonstrated to both the film industry and movie-going America that a black actor can play a leading role in a big-budget blockbuster movie as well as a white actor. He continues to earn these roles because he has proven that he can perform better than his competitors—and because the major companies learned quickly that they can make millions of dollars in the theaters. Washington, in addition to pursuing and earning big-budget roles, has continuously throughout his career selected films he deemed to be important to black America. Films that explore major themes and issues in African American history and society have attracted Washington, and he has also selected films that expose racial injustice and complicated realities. These films and their social justice themes can be empowering to people of color, because systems of power that privilege some, at the expense of others, are exposed. In addition, Washington, because of his status as a film superstar, has created a space in popular culture for complex and controversial racial topics to enter the mainstream. Denzel Washington, by making big-budget films and racially-conscious critical films, has used his celebrity power to bring attention to racial issues in American society and history.

Throughout his career, Denzel Washington has expressed his distaste for the ideas that fans, journalists, and academics project onto him, confusing him with his characters. He maintains that he is an actor, and as an incredibly talented artist, he becomes characters with whom people can identify. Washington refuses to be typecast, continually takes on challenging and different roles, and evades others's abilities to figure out who *he* is as a person, other than a brilliant artist and actor, a loving and supportive husband and father, and an intellectual with a critical analysis of society and culture.

Washington dislikes being qualified as the best black actor of his generation. He points out that too often the term black is used as a modifier, a categorizer, rather than as a way to recognize orientation, experience, and identity. He also rejects the notion that he speaks for an entire race of people, or the so-called black community, and is frustrated by the perception that a large and diverse people can somehow be reduced to a single worldview. He reminds the media and his fans that he does not speak for everyone, but he does speak for himself, and many people, regardless of color, can agree—or disagree for that matter—with his perspectives. At the same time, however, Denzel Washington has redefined the ways in which black Americans are portrayed in film, and has expanded the job opportunities for people of color throughout the film industry. One of Washington's deepest beliefs is that the definition of success is helping others; Washington's body of film as well as what he represents in American society as an actor and a role model has helped many others.

Denzel Washington credits the adults in his childhood with helping to shape him into the person he became. He was born the middle of three children to Denzel and Lynne Washington on December 28, 1954, in Mount Vernon, New York. In the 1950s, Mount Vernon, which bordered the Bronx, consisted of a diverse, middle-class community of primarily West Indian American, Irish American, Italian American, and African American families. Washington's father worked two jobs, in a department store and at the water department, and also preached on Sundays as a Pentecostal minister. His mother, a former singer, worked as a beautician. Denzel, his older sister Lorice, and his younger brother David, grew up in a strict, disciplined household that included a limited exposure to television and the movie theater. The Washingtons only permitted their children to watch approved religious films like *The Ten Commandments* and *King of Kings*, as well as selected Disney films.

Washington's parents worked long hours to support their family, and the Boys Club in Mount Vernon became the place where he would begin to dream big and believe those dreams would come true. The head of the Boys Club, Billy Thomas, encouraged the boys to do well in school, to play sports, and to remember the community they came from: boys who went on to college would send Thomas pennants to hang in the gym to encourage younger boys to work hard to go to college. From a young age, Washington also learned how to earn money—and that it could be fun to earn money. His mother found him a job cleaning up at a barbershop owned by her friend Jack Coleman, where he would also find the time to hustle patrons at the shop. In addition to keeping the barbershop clean, Washington would run errands for clients, like dropping off their dry cleaning, to earn additional income. In the barbershop, Washington learned his first lessons about acting. Coleman turned into a "master of ceremonies," and a bevy of characters would come through the shop, presenting themselves in their varied and eccentric roles, and often telling terrific stories. Washington's education in the classroom and by hitting the books was critically strengthened from his experiences at the Boys Club and at the barbershop.

Denzel Senior and Lynne Washington divorced when Washington was 14 years old. Reflecting later in life on their divorce, Washington realized that it made him angry, and he began a period where he got in a lot of fights. Family and religion were central to the Washington household. When he perceived one to crumble, Washington rejected the other, although he has since become religious again. The experience also left a lifelong impact on Washington; he determined to be in a healthy, strong marital relationship and to uphold his responsibilities to his marital partner and his children. But at the age of 14, Washington rebelled. He snuck out of the house to hang out with his friends, many of whom were getting into drugs and criminal activities. His mother recognized the potential trouble brewing, and found a partial scholarship for her son at Oakland Academy, a prep school in upstate New York. Lynne Washington also believed she should contribute to his private education, and took pride in her ability to help pay for such an expensive education. She worked hard to support the family with her business investments, including the beauty shop that she owned and operated. This was another important lesson for young Washington, the empowerment that came with working hard to help those you care about so they have the opportunity to also work hard and dream big.

In addition to the basketball court, the gridiron represented another place where Washington learned lifelong lessons during his childhood. Washington's role models and favorite footballers were Jim Brown and Gale Sayers, two African American superstar players, and Washington himself developed into a good player. The well-rounded high school student also excelled as a musician, playing the piano, and in theatrical performances while at YMCA summer camps. He walked on to both the football and basketball teams in college, but athletics represented just one facet of Washington's collegiate experience, a place where he determined to try out everything college had to offer. This near-picture-perfect story did include some setbacks.

Washington graduated from high school in 1972 and matriculated to Fordham University in the Bronx. To pay for tuition, Washington took out several loans and also began an after-school program for the children of working single parents at a church in Manhattan. After a semester in which he earned poor grades, Washington dropped out of school, worked a number of jobs, and received the wake-up call that he better get back into school and this time actually apply himself. He returned to Fordham with a new dedication to academics, determining to double major in journalism and drama. He also continued to pursue his interests in athletics and the arts; he continued to play on the university's football and basketball teams, wrote a lot of poetry, and performed on the stage in student productions including *Othello* by William Shakespeare.

Faculty on campus immediately recognized Washington's skill as a thespian, and encouraged him to pursue a career in acting. In 1977, while still in college, Washington won a role in the made-for-television movie *Wilma*, about the life and track career of Wilma Rudolph. Washington graduated from Fordham, received a degree in journalism, and moved to San Francisco to enroll in American Conservatory Theatre (ACT), where he bused tables in a restaurant to pay for his acting education. At ACT, Washington learned to expand the elements of education to be an actor. He studied dance and scene design in addition to his classes in acting. Acting classes introduced him to sense-memory, awareness of body movements and environment, the "Method" of emotional immersion in a role, and technique and the intellectual approach to a part. Washington trusted his instincts to take the best from each theoretical approach to acting rather than dedicating himself to one method, a decision that has contributed to his well-rounded acting abilities. Although invited back for a second year at the highly competitive school, Washington left ACT after his first year to pursue a career in the film industry. He moved south to Los Angeles, crashing at his cousin's house while he searched for jobs. Despite his training and talent, Washington lacked experience and found it very difficult to find quality work. He decided to return to New York to gain some experience on the stage before embarking on a film career. In New York, he crossed paths with Pauletta Pearson, with whom he worked on *Wilma*, and the two began to date.

Washington found the incredibly competitive theater scene to be quite frustrating in the late 1970s, with so many talented young actors vying for roles. Although Washington received offers for movie roles, he turned them down because they portrayed black men in negative stereotypical ways, most often as junkies, drug dealers, or pimps. Washington chose unemployment in the theater scene over meaningless and potentially harmful roles on the big screen, recognizing that if he took those roles early on in his career he would never be able to break through to leading male roles. He finally decided to appear in a film, a social comedy entitled *Carbon Copy*, released in 1981. In the film, directed by Michael Schultz, and co-starring George Segal, Washington played the illegitimate son of a white corporate executive played by Segal. The movie bombed at the box office, and Washington missed the matinee on day of the film's release because he was waiting in the unemployment line for a much-needed check. Pauletta Pearson helped Washington through these difficult times, and although he believed his acting career had been squashed, she continued to encourage him toward his goals.

In the meantime, the pragmatic Washington found work at an urban recreation center, where he would teach sports and theater to local kids. A week before the programs were to begin, however, Washington received the great news that he had earned the role of **Malcolm X** in a play he had auditioned for at the Henry Street Settlement Arts for Living Center, *When the Chickens Come Home to Roost*. Washington remembers his time as Malcolm X at the Federal Theatre to be his most rewarding and favorite role on the stage. He also found work in a series of parts in various small black theater companies, including the Negro Ensemble Company's production of *A Soldier's Play*, Lonne Elder's *Ceremonies in Dark Old Men*, and Richard Wesley's *Mighty Gents*.

Washington began to take television roles, and made the transition from the New York stage to network television work smoothly in the early 1980s in

License to Kill and *Flesh & Blood*. He continued to reject movie role offers of pimps and drug addicts, and had his first big break when Bruce Paltrow, a producer working for NBC, wanted Washington to play a central role on a dramatic series set in a teaching hospital in Boston, St. Eligius. Washington was cast as Dr. Philip Chandler on the hit series *St. Elsewhere*, and stayed with the show for its entire run beginning in 1982. Washington played the complicated character well, and was pleased that Dr. Chandler did not conform to either a negative stereotype or an idealized cliché that could be just as damaging. Washington portrayed Dr. Chandler as an intelligent doctor who, rather than being perfect, was a human being with flaws and problems just like everyone else. He developed a large fan base, and used his popularity to earn more acting jobs. During summer breaks from the taping of the series, Washington took roles in films that did not conform to his image on the hit series. Fearful of becoming pigeon-holed and typecast into a single character, he took on the part of a villain in the film *Power*, directed by Sidney Lumet, and other roles in films including the critically-acclaimed *For Queen and Country* and *Cry Freedom*.

Just as Washington's acting career began to blossom, so did his personal life. Washington and Pearson married in the summer of 1983, and after the second year with *St. Elsewhere*, the couple decided they were financially ready to have children. John David was born in 1984, and the Washingtons allowed their baby to appear in an episode of *St. Elsewhere* in a maternity ward scene. Washington also purchased a brand-new car for his mother, something he had wanted to do for a long time. Although his career was just beginning to take off, he supported his wife and young family. Pauletta had dreams and artistic ability, too, and Denzel ended up turning down his first major magazine cover and feature story to support his wife, who had sacrificed her career for a few years while she supported their first son and her husband worked. The interview for the cover story happened to be the same day as Pauletta Washington's return to the stage to perform in concert. Instead of meeting the journalist for the interview, Denzel cancelled to watch baby John as his wife rehearsed, and to be there for her backstage before the show to calm her nerves. She receiving a standing ovation for her vocal performance, and her proud husband knew that he had made the right choice. For Denzel Washington, family would always come before his acting career.

In addition to his family-first orientation, Washington also had a driving work ethic. Rarely did the young actor sit around and wait for directors and producers to call and offer roles in big pictures. He proactively searched out projects, especially art films, and films with talented directors, small companies, and tight budgets, but meaningful storylines. Even after his first Oscar nomination for his role in *Cry Freedom*, Washington never sat back waiting for big-time offers, and at times returned to Broadway to star on the stage.

Washington won his first Oscar, in 1989 for Best Supporting Actor, playing "Tripp," a runaway slave in *Glory*, a film based on the **54th Massachusetts**

Colored Regiment that fought for the Union during the Civil War. Denzel Washington's 1989 Oscar win reflected a historic change taking place in Hollywood. Not only were black actors beginning to have so-called crossover appeal with larger audiences regardless of race, black writers and directors were also producing films of critical acclaim that appealed to mainstream audiences and also portrayed black characters in complex roles. **Spike Lee**'s *Do the Right Thing*, John Singleton's *Boyz N the Hood*, and other films broke ground, opening the way for other filmmakers and providing a new generation with films and themes constructed by black people. Thirteen years after his first Oscar, Washington became the first African American male to win for Best Actor in a Leading Role, awarded to him for his performance as a corrupt cop in *Training Day*. Washington's performances had earned him highest recognition from the Academy of Motion Picture Arts and Sciences. During the 1990s and 2000s, he was one of the most sought-after actors in Hollywood.

Washington has a personality that balances a desire for wealth, on the one hand, and personal integrity on the other. The "X-factor" in the equation is his confidence: Washington believes he is a good actor and deserves a big paycheck for his work, but at the same time he is grounded in his identity and understands his role to carefully select only the characters that diversify his portfolio, benefit black people, and demonstrate the power of complex characters in film. Washington successfully balances his hopeful desires with a grounded reality. He has always maintained to the press that he desires racially nonspecific roles, and avoids films that address racism. Despite his claims to never pursue roles for political or social reasons, Washington's arguable best work has come in socially conscious projects with powerful storylines and messages of social and racial justice. His performances in so-called nonracially specific big budget films often take on additional nuance and meaning because of his identity as a black man. In addition, Washington carefully selects roles in big-budget productions to make sure he is cast in positive roles, either as a doctor, a lawyer, an officer of the law, or a journalist. As any talented artist inevitably discovers at some point in his or her career, the way in which people interpret the art may be quite different from the creator's intentions—that is what makes the art beautiful and powerful. Moreover, Washington simply can occupy both positions: he can certainly desire to be the best at his craft regardless of race, while simultaneously making films that create positive images about and for black people.

While Washington has successfully played characters either intended to be white or categorized as racially nonspecific roles, sometimes casting a black man in a role has provided unintended consequences that have enhanced the power of the film's story. The best example of how Washington's identity as a black man has provided added meaning to a film is award-winning *Philadelphia*. Starring as legal counsel for a man—played by Tom Hanks—wrongfully terminated from his job because he is gay and has AIDS, Washington's transformation from a hateful, fearful bigot into an empathetic, justice-seeking friend is enhanced because the character is an African American man. For example, Washington examines a key witness who works as a paralegal at Hanks's former firm. The woman, who is multiracial and has African ancestry, answers Washington's questions concerning whether she had ever personally experienced discrimination or bigoted comments in the workplace. She tells a story about how the partners in the firm mentioned that she should wear "less ethnic" and "more American" earrings to fit in better at the firm and to appeal to important clients. Although a subtle moment, Washington and the woman hold their eye contact slightly longer than normal, and the audience feels a moment of shared experience and empathy between the actors. The more obvious deeper meaning, of course, is that an African American lawyer represents his homosexual client who suffers from AIDS; clearly a black person in the United States has experienced a fair share of discrimination in a lifetime and may want to rally behind a cause of social justice.

Films like *Crimson Tide*, *The Pelican Brief*, and *Courage Under Fire* have created another consequence for Washington, whether intended or unintended. By playing racially nonspecific characters, Washington has played a major role in integrating the big screen. He has demonstrated to audiences of color and white audiences that a black actor can play any role; that, like all other human beings, black people come from diverse backgrounds and have countless life experiences, political positions, and worldviews; and that Denzel Washington is positioned among the top few actors of all time.

Washington's fame has also made him a race leader, whether he wanted to take on the position of leadership or not. Washington became involved in the anti-apartheid movement to protest oppression in South Africa when he played Biko in the film *Cry Freedom*. In the summer of 1988, he was scheduled to appear at a benefit concert to support Nelson Mandela in England at Wembley Stadium. He had also accepted an invitation to take part in a celebrity tennis tournament at Windsor Green, a fundraiser for the prince. While in New York a few days before his departure for England, Washington attended a musical about Mandela's efforts in South Africa entitled *Sarafina!*, and was deeply moved by the experience. Some of the actors had lived in South Africa and bore visible scars from the apartheid system that included racial violence. After the show, Washington met with actors backstage to congratulate them on their powerful performance. Struck by the fact that many of the young performers called him "Biko," his name in *Cry Freedom*, Washington realized he could not negotiate a middle path by appearing at both a Mandela benefit concert and a tennis tournament to raise funds for the British aristocracy, the very people who had refused to attend the premiere of *Cry Freedom* and who refused to rally behind the anti-apartheid movement. He instantly canceled his plans to attend both events and only took part in the benefit concert for Nelson Mandela.

Scholars and critics have generally agreed that Washington's good looks and abilities as a leading man in the line of the romantic, masculine gentleman positioned him to break through the color line by becoming the first black man to be a popular, mainstream sex symbol—a Hollywood heartthrob for all fans regardless of race. What makes Washington so appealing in addition to his good looks and skill as an actor is that confidence—that X factor, again—that is totally devoid of arrogance or egotism, but grounded in charisma, morality, and a passion for justice. At the same time, however, some scholars and critics have noticed and given much attention to Washington's series of movies where he stars opposite white female leads, and the films either present Washington in asexual roles or never include love scenes involving romantic intimacy. Washington has skillfully sidestepped gossip and rumors that he has asked interracial love scenes to be removed from scripts by stating that historically people become obsessed with situations where black men and white women are involved romantically, and that over-attention to one scene would ultimately take away from the purpose and messages of the film. In films like *The Pelican Brief*, where he co-stars with Julia Roberts, *Courage Under Fire*, with co-star Meg Ryan, and *The Bone Collector*, with co-star Angelina Jolie, Washington never shares an intimate scene with his female leads. He and Meg Ryan never appear together, because Ryan's character is dead, and he plays a detective paralyzed from the neck down in his film with Angelina Jolie. Some stories surrounding *The Pelican Brief* assert that Washington initiated the decision to have intimate scenes between him and Roberts deleted, although these rumors have not been confirmed. Other telling situations include when Washington passed on playing the title role in a film version of *Othello* in 1995 (played by Laurence Fishburne), and when he dropped out of 1992's *Love Field*, a film that included a love scene with blonde-hair, blue-eyed Michelle Pfeiffer. The question remains whether Washington avoided romantic scenes with white female actors because of fearful executive producers, statistical data that demonstrated the bigoted nature of general audiences, or Washington's own personal beliefs.

Washington takes considerable risks in films below the production and distribution levels of the major commercial blockbusters, however; and these films often explore the themes of power and oppression in black history and society. For example, Washington has taken roles in four powerful Spike Lee films, *Mo' Better Blues* (1990), *Malcolm X* (1992), *He Got Game* (1998), and *The Inside Man* (2006). He also sees a space for social justice films with powerful messages in blockbuster movies, and has utilized the power of his celebrity to get important films made with big budgets and for mass distribution. In films like *The Hurricane* and *Remember the Titans*, Washington has played black men who represent the intersections of race, power, and oppression, and often, how people can work together to overcome oppression with acts of social and racial justice. In recent years, this has meant crossing over to producing and directing. In 1990, Washington and Flo Allen partnered to head a production company that developed projects for Tri-Star Pictures, and in 2002 and 2007, Washington directed his first films, the critically-acclaimed *Antwone Fisher* and *The Great*

Debaters, both based on true stories of young black people who overcome their odds to achieve. In his most recent major production film in which he plays a real person, *American Gangster*, Washington plays Frank Lucas, one of New York's major historical crime bosses, reminding Americans that black people have been everywhere historically, even as prominent members of organized crime.

While Washington has significantly contributed to major changes for black people in the film industry, he acknowledges that Hollywood still has a long way to go. For example, Washington has expressed his frustrations with the inability of young black actors, young black women in particular, to find work. In interviews following both *Antwone Fisher* and *The Great Debaters*, Washington mentioned that while his young stars have been acclaimed for their "breakthrough" performances, "breakthrough" would mean that they will find work easily in the future, and that may not be the case. In addition, Washington has vocalized his displeasure with the fact that he must appear in the films he directs to get proper funding and distribution.

In addition to his appraised skills as an actor, Washington's good looks and well-rounded values have also received much attention. His appeal comes from his audiences's and fans's abilities to relate to him as a real person, while at the same time also seeing him as a top celebrity. His commitment to his family, his integrity, and his work ethic provide an admirable combination to which many people aspire. The Washingtons have four children (John David, born in 1984; Katia, born in 1987; and twins Malcolm and Olivia, born in 1991). The family lives quietly and away from fans and media in the outskirts of Los Angeles. Washington repeatedly states that family is more important to him than anything else in life, and has provided the foundation for everything that he does. The Washingtons present an image quite rare in Hollywood in the late twentieth and early twenty-first centuries: a loving husband and wife who are also good parents to their well-adjusted, intelligent, athletic, goal-oriented children. Washington understands the power of his family to affect impressions of black America, both as role models and also as an example of a strong, loving, successful black family. In 1995, the family traveled together throughout Africa, and Denzel and Pauletta renewed their vows before Desmond Tutu. Oldest son John David Washington signed with St. Louis Rams as a running-back in 2006 after a collegiate career at Morehouse College, and Katia graduated from Yale University. The twins both entered college in the fall of 2009; Malcolm is attending Penn University and plays on the basketball team, and Olivia is in acting school at New York University. The children learned from a young age that their father worked hard to be successful, and that they would work to enjoy success in life as well. Denzel and Pauletta have enjoyed a long marriage of 27 years. In addition to being a good husband and father, Washington also enjoys working with children and promoting youth organizations. He has coached Little League baseball, and has served as a national spokesperson for the Boys and Girls Clubs of America, the very organization he grew within during the 1960s.

Denzel Washington has redefined and expanded the ways in which black Americans are portrayed in film. These black actors, including Washington, Morgan Freeman, Danny Glover, James Earl Jones, and later **Will Smith** and Jamie Foxx, appeal to all audiences rather than segments of the population, and therefore have impacted general perceptions of African Americans in U.S. society. By no means is this a light burden to bear, and Washington backs away from the idea that he alone is affecting, making, and changing the history of race relations and perceptions of black America. While some scholars and critics have interpreted this position to be a celebration of "rugged individualism" over "community loyalty," Washington should not be placed alongside advocates of colorblindness and the bootstraps mentality. Rather, scholars should find the nuanced sophistication of Washington's position to be one of pride as a black man, pride as an actor, and the confidence to take on a diversity of roles to benefit American society. Washington continues the legacy of the "race man," the man in the black community who works for the benefit of his people, but in a twentieth- and twenty-first-century context that expands the beneficiaries of his race work to include the multiracial, multiethnic society that is the United States.

Victoria L. Jackson
Arizona State University

FURTHER READING

Brode, Douglas. *Denzel Washington: His Films and Career*. Secaucus, NJ: Carol Publishing Group, 1997.

Nickson, Chris. *Denzel Washington*. New York: St. Martin's Paperbacks, 1996.

Parish, James Robert. *Denzel Washington: Actor*. New York: Ferguson, 2005.

Reid, Mark. *Black Lenses, Black Voices: African American Film Now*. Lanham, MD: Rowman & Littlefield, 2005.

Sheridan, Earl. "Conservative Implications of the Irrelevance of Racism in Contemporary African American Cinema." *Journal of Black Studies* 37, no. 2 (November 2006): 177–92.

Washington, Denzel with Daniel Paisner. *A Hand to Guide Me: Legends and Leaders Celebrate the People Who Shaped Their Lives*. Des Moines, IA: Meredith Books, 2006.

Wooten, Sara McIntosh. *Denzel Washington: Academy Award-Winning Actor*. Berkeley Heights, NJ: Enslow Publishers, 2003.

Ida B. Wells-Barnett
(1862–1931)

For three decades spanning approximately 1890–1920, Ida Bell Wells (Wells-Barnett after her marriage) dedicatedly worked to better the life situations of people of African descent and women living in the United States. To work to benefit her people, Wells-Barnett's efforts can be grouped into two major categories. On the one hand, she took on the enormous task of exposing the propaganda and correcting the falsities espoused by the white, often Southern, press and politicians. She dedicated herself to the goal of correcting white, mainstream beliefs concerning African Americans, which spanned from the innocent—yet ignorant—to the virulently racist. On the other hand, Wells-Barnett passionately devoted her energies to community-building, helping to organize institutions and services to assist African Americans. An underlying, foundational belief in humanity drove Wells-Barnett in her many activities; this passion for human dignity provided Wells-Barnett with her unwavering, uncompromising positions on every cause she took on. Without hesitation, she spoke her mind to Southern whites, Northern white liberals, and African Americans with whom she disagreed. Her fearless, articulate, and outspoken nature, during a time of oppression and violence often considered the nadir of African American history, makes Ida B. Well-Barnett an icon of black America.

Ida B. Wells was born to parents who were enslaved in Holly Springs, Mississippi, on July 16, 1862, during the Civil War. Holly Springs represented both rural and urban lifestyles in the nineteenth century, with cotton plantations and an iron foundry for the Mississippi Central Railroad representing the two primary forms of employment. Ida's father, Jim Wells, worked as a carpenter in the city. He was the progeny of the man who enslaved him and Peggy, one of his enslaved workers, who lived on a plantation in rural Tippah County, Mississippi. When Jim turned 18, Mr. Wells brought him to the city to apprentice him out to a man named Bolling, who owned a carpentry business. A young woman, Lizzie, worked as Mr. Bolling's cook. She had grown up one of 10 children in rural Virginia, and was sold through the slave trade to Mississippi. Despite countless efforts, Lizzie never successfully located her family in Virginia after she was sold to Mr. Bolling. Jim and Lizzie married during the Civil War, and after the war Jim Wells opened his own carpentry business. His business flourished after the destruction brought by the war, and Jim Wells became a prominent member of the Holly Springs community. He belonged to the masons and became a master mason, and served on the first board of trustees of Rust College (later Shaw University), a freedmen's college established in 1866. Lizzie Wells took care of their eight children, and young Ida, the oldest of her siblings, assisted her mother in their upbringing and education.

Jim and Lizzie Wells taught their children that their responsibility as free, young African Americans was to learn as much as they possibly could. Ida Wells's first memories included reading the newspaper to her father and a group of his friends, and she took classes at Rust College from a very young age. The young married couple did not shelter their children from the truth about slavery, and Lizzie especially talked to her children about the atrocities committed during slavery. Lizzie felt that it was her duty as a mother to inform her children about the nature of their grandparents's relationship. Although Mr. Wells had died, Peggy, Jim's mother, continued to live and take care of the widow Polly Wells, the woman who had formerly held her in slavery. Lizzie told young Ida the truth about Peggy and Polly's relationship, and did not hide from her that Polly had taken vengeance on Peggy the day after Mr. Wells died, by whipping her. In the summers, young Ida would stay with her grandmother and "Miss Polly" out in the country, and these memories deeply impacted her worldview, her opinions of race relations, and her desire to always expose falsities about the past to promote the truth.

In the summer of 1878, while young Ida visited her grandmother in the country, tragedy struck Holly Springs and the Wells family when a yellow fever epidemic took many lives, including both of her parents. Against the warnings of friends and family, Ida Wells, understanding her role as the oldest child, returned to Holly Springs to care for her siblings as the new head of the household. She discovered a home in which the youngest child had died, and two more children suffered from the disease. In an early example of her courage and bravery, Wells, only a teenager, determined to care for her family and successfully fought against the local Masons's decision to split up the children and place them in foster homes. A local white doctor supported her decision, and helped Wells care for her family by protecting her family's money in a safe downtown. He also made sure a nurse from the Howard Association (an organization to help fight the epidemic) stayed in the Wells household, even if no children were sick. Later in her life, Wells-Barnett recalled that her relationship with Dr. Gray represented her first exposure to a humane and sympathetic white man.

To earn money to support her family, teenage Wells, with help from the Masons, found a job as a teacher at a country school six miles outside of Holly Springs, which paid $25 per month. She traveled to the school by mule, taught Monday through Friday, and returned to her house for the weekend to wash, iron, and cook a week's worth of meals for her siblings. After a few months of this exhausting schedule, Wells accepted an offer from an aunt to move to Memphis so that she could continue to teach, but her aunt would care for the children. Wells took a position at a country school in Shelby County, Tennessee, and after passing an examination, she moved to a better-paying teaching job in the city schools of Memphis.

Before she transferred to the city school, however, Wells fought her first battle against racial discrimination, this time in the form of segregated public transportation. At the age of 22, in 1884, Wells rode the Chesapeake & Ohio Railroad from Memphis to Woodstock to travel to her teaching job. When a conductor on the train told her she must move to the smoking car from the ladies' car, she refused. When the man attempted to physically force her to move, she bit him. Only when two other train employees came to the conductor's assistance, were they able to move Wells. However, the train was stopping at a station, so Wells decided to get off the train rather than suffer the humiliation of riding in the smoking car, and immediately returned to Memphis to find a lawyer to sue the railroad.

Although she did not learn the significance of her actions until many years later, Wells became the first black plaintiff in the South to sue in a state court after the repeal of the Civil Rights Act by the U.S. Supreme Court in 1883. She had originally determined to employ a black lawyer, but the case stagnated and she later learned that he had been paid off by the Chesapeake & Ohio. Finally, with a new white lawyer, her case went to trial in circuit court, and Wells was awarded $500 in damages from a sympathetic Judge Pierce, who had fought for the Union and had moved after the war to Tennessee from Minnesota. The victory did not last, however, because the state supreme court reversed the lower court's decision upon an appeal by the railroad. Rather than gaining $500, Wells now had to pay more than $200 in court costs. When the U.S. Supreme Court overturned the Civil Rights Act, however, the justices reasoned that African Americans were not wards of the federal government but citizens of their respective states. This meant that African Americans should appeal to state courts rather than federal courts to seek justice. Wells had attempted to do just that, and the success of her case would have been precedent-setting. Instead, with the Civil Rights Act repealed, and with Southern states that failed to provide legal justice to African Americans, black people in Southern states found themselves without a venue to seek justice.

Ida B. Wells learned another hard lesson from her battle with the railroad when the black community of Memphis failed to rally behind her. She realized that her fellow African Americans did not recognize her fight as a race matter, and she determined to raise her own consciousness as an African American to help others develop their race consciousness. Frustrated with black preachers who did not provide practical advice, and realizing that she had never read a book by or about African Americans, Wells joined a lyceum of mostly teachers who met weekly to conduct literary and musical exercises, to practice their oratory and debate skills, and to develop their writing in essay competitions. The group published their works in the weekly paper, *Evening Star*, and Wells soon took over as its editor. Soon, Memphis pastors asked Wells to publish for their churches' weeklies as well, including Baptist Reverend R. N. Countee's *Living Way*, and within the next few months black newspapers throughout the country began to publish Wells's articles. Although she kept her job as a teacher to earn a salary, Wells discovered her true passion in writing about issues pertaining to African Americans. Signing her articles with the pen name "Iola," she wrote in a plain, common-sense tone that appealed to people who saw her as a friend who cared, rather than as an uppity, educated woman who spoke down to the people of her race.

The blurring of the difference between unequal segregation and equal separation always troubled Ida B. Wells, and established her as an early proponent of racial pride and Black Nationalism. Her first experience with the issue came in Visalia, California, in 1886. Wells had traveled to California to visit an aunt after an excursion to Topeka, Kansas, with the National Education Association. Her aunt convinced her to stay and teach the small black population in the area; however, the community resented her efforts because a black teacher in a black school meant that the community would self-segregate their children from the white, Native American, Mexican, and Mexican American children who all attended school together. Wells did not understand why a separate school was an issue, if her skills and the school's facilities were equal or even better than the school already functioning; however, she respected the black community of Visalia's wishes and eventually returned to Memphis. This tension between separate and unequal, and separate and equal, would form a major theme in Wells's public career and personal convictions.

Wells returned to Memphis to teach, but felt constrained by the profession; fortunately a new opportunity emerged when Reverend William J. Simmons of the American Baptist Home Missionary Society offered to hire her as a correspondent at the wage of one dollar per letter, weekly. Although she continued to work as a teacher, Wells happily accepted her first paid, professional job as a writer. For three years she wrote for the paper, represented the American Baptists at press conventions as their first female representative, and earned her unofficial title as the "princess of the press." In her position with the American Baptists, Wells first met many of the men and women she would later spend much of her career working alongside, including **Frederick Douglass**. Wells enjoyed writing for the church organization, but knew she one day wanted to be an owner and editor of a major weekly or even daily newspaper.

The opportunity arrived in 1889, when Reverend F. N. Nightingale and J. L. Fleming, the owners of *Free Speech and Headlight* in Memphis, invited Wells to write for their newspaper. She negotiated a deal as editor and equal owner (one third of the newspaper) with the two men. Almost immediately, Wells jumped into controversy, eager to push her community's buttons. One of her very first editorials criticized the lesser facilities and teachers of the segregated black schools in Memphis, where she also taught. The controversial editorial resulted in her failure to be re-elected to her teaching position by the Memphis school board after seven years of service. Wells held no regrets, however, because she would always choose to speak out about racial injustice. If she lost a job in the process, it made no matter to her; she would continue the fight.

Wells immediately demonstrated some of her skills as a journalist in her early years writing for the *Free Speech*. In her first summer with the paper, she traveled to Mississippi to investigate and expose how the state's new "Understanding Clause" worked to disfranchise African American potential voters. Her travels through Mississippi, Arkansas, and Tennessee also spread the word of her newspaper, developed her connections throughout the South, and expanded both her subscription lists and her contacts for new correspondents. In her first year, the newspaper's circulation grew from a modest 1,500 to more than 4,000. In addition to her ability to bring the black community together through her paper, Wells also demonstrated her fearless, outspoken, confident nature with the pen. In her first year with the *Free Speech*, in addition to exposing the injustice of the "Understanding Clause," Wells took on black preachers and conservative, accommodationist African Americans. She was unafraid to comment on a black preacher's hypocritical acts of adultery despite threats from an alliance of preachers to boycott her paper; instead of giving into the alliance, she published their threat and listed all of their names. Wells also chastised **Booker T. Washington** in an editorial for publishing comments critical of Southern African American leaders in Northern white newspapers. Even if his charges were true, she wrote, he should not make those criticisms in white papers, but should work with black Southern leaders to hone their skills. Ida B. Wells, pen name "Iola," showed no fear of anyone, and never compromised her work to expose racial injustice and to help African Americans.

While Wells toured Mississippi, prominent white citizens of Memphis, including local law enforcement officials, lynched three African American grocery store owners, Thomas Moss, Calvin McDowell, and Henry Stewart. Their business, People's Grocery Company, served the black community of Memphis and provided competition to the business of a local white grocer who desired total control of the market. Moss had also worked as a letter carrier, and enjoyed the status of a prominent citizen of the black community of Memphis before his murder. Wells was good friends with Moss and his wife Betty, and was godmother to their daughter Maurine. In early March 1892, white men raided the grocery store and in the ensuing shoot-out, white men had been shot, injured, and killed. Authorities imprisoned Moss, McDowell, and Stewart, and tensions rose in Memphis as white mobs gathered outside the jailhouse on consecutive nights. On the night of March 9, the mob broke into the jail and lynched the three men, and then proceeded to ransack the People's Grocery Store, stealing all the food and products, and destroying the building. Upon hearing of the lynching and racial violence in her hometown, Wells rushed back to Memphis to help her community.

Ida B. Wells's actions in Memphis following the lynching would influence her worldview for the rest of her life, and would make her a national and international celebrity. In her editorials for the *Free Speech*, she heeded the words of Moss from prison before his death, and encouraged the black community of Memphis to leave the racially hostile city and move west. Hundreds of Memphis citizens departed by wagon train and railway for Oklahoma Territory, and Wells traveled with them to report on the new settlements as a way to extinguish the propaganda promoted by white newspapers in Memphis that worked to keep African Americans—and their labor—in the city of Memphis. Meanwhile, African Americans who remained in Memphis enacted a general strike, boycotting the streetcars and ceasing to work in the service jobs that provided for white citizens of Memphis. Representatives of the City Railway Company, which was losing significant income from the boycott, attempted to pressure Wells to write an editorial telling her readers to ride the streetcars. Rather than give in to pressure, however, Wells instead published a transcript of her conversation with the railway representatives and continued to encourage the boycott. Ida B. Wells had never been naïve; she knew the danger of her position, yet she had also always been comfortable with her cause and the reality of the possibility of her death. After the lynching, she bought a pistol, arguing that it was better to die fighting against injustice than to die without a fight. Furthermore, she reasoned that if she could take one lyncher with her, it would even up the score just a bit.

The anticipated violence came in late May, when a white mob of "leading citizens" ransacked the office of the *Free Speech*, destroying the press and the office, and leaving a note stating that anyone who tried to publish the paper again would be punished by death. Wells had been in Philadelphia at the time for the African Methodist Episcopal Church (A.M.E.) general conference, and J. L. Fleming, her professional partner and the paper's business manager, had been warned by a white friend and managed to escape the city before the attempted lynching. Wells understood that returning to Memphis would be impossible if she wanted to live and to prevent further violence against the black community, and decided to stay in New York, where she took a position at the *New York Age*, negotiating an equal ownership of the paper with T. Thomas Fortune and Jerome B. Peterson. Wells embarked on her lifelong mission of exposing the truth about racial violence through the telling of the real stories of lynchings, which were becoming more numerous and horrific.

Although exiled from the South, Wells did not fear Southerners, racists, or her own death. At the same time, however, she believed in the necessity of, and held the confidence required for, self defense. She kept her pistol on her person at all times when she went out in public, understanding that many white people in the North and most white people in the South had a deeply vested interest in keeping black people in an underclass and an economy based in service and labor industries. Confident, intelligent, business-oriented men and women like Wells became the targets of mob violence and lynching because they disrupted the order of white supremacy. As Wells discovered the contextual environments of the lynchings she investigated throughout the Southern—and later Northern and Midwestern—states, she uncovered the real motivation behind lynching. Rather than the professed defense of "white Southern womanhood" and punishment of "black rapists," lynchings served in Wells's words as "an excuse to get rid of Negroes who were acquiring wealth and property, and thus keep the race terrorized and 'keep the nigger down' " (Wells-Barnett, 64). Wells realized she must investigate and report the details of every lynching to expose the truth behind the mob violence, and published a series of editorials in the *New York Age* that were reprinted in periodicals throughout the Northeast.

In addition to a driving desire to investigate the nature of lynching that sought to extinguish any form of black economic independence and political power, Wells wrote extensively on the brutality intrinsic to Southern white culture. While white Southern propaganda filled the minds of Americans with images and myths of savage, sexualized black male criminals, Wells described the "cold-blooded savagery of white devils under lynch law" (Wells-Barnett, 70). Her descriptions of lynchings never failed to leave out the details of the horrific acts of mutilation, slow and pain-inflicting torture, and murder by hanging, firing squad, or fire committed by white men and boys, sometimes even women. She also noted the community nature of the event, and how men, women, and children of all ages came to the watch the spectacle and entertainment of a lynching, some envied participants and spectators even taking home "souvenirs."

Writing under the pen name "Iola" or "Exiled," Wells added to her editorials another layer of analysis concerning the hypocritical nature of the Southern world order. She made sure to document when officers of the law took on prominent roles in a lynching, noting that proper procedures of law and order had been violated when the accused are killed without a trial or a guilty verdict. She also made connections between the reign of terror in the South and the failure of Reconstruction laws to protect black citizens, to provide for equal citizenship rights for African Americans, and to prevent white people from re-establishing white economic, political, and social supremacy based on differential access to resources. She explained how a culture of violence worked to prevent black challenges to the racial status quo. Wells even took on the subject of sexual relations between black and white folk, noting the historical intersections of power, race, and gender in the Southern states that allowed white men to have access to black women, no matter the woman's interest, yet warned black men with the threat of violence and death, and white women with the threat of social stigma and banishment, should the two ever desire each other. Wells's assertion that Southern black men and white women did in fact have consensual, romantic relationships was a shocking revelation in the late nineteenth-century United States.

Wells discovered that many of her Northern black readers and friends believed the lies espoused by Southern propagandists, and determined to eradicate the mythology surrounding lynching in the North to organize key allies to return real law and order to the South. Her writings reached an expansive audience, but after an experience giving a testimonial in Lyric Hall in New York, she realized she could better appeal to people's emotions and rally them into anti-lynching action through public speaking. For the next 30 years, she wore a gift received at that first speaking engagement in 1892, a gold brooch in the shape of a pen, at all special events and occasions.

Ida B. Wells's first testimonial also marked an important moment in history: the beginning of the club movement among black women. A committee of more than two hundred women volunteered to meet and to organize the speaking event at Lyric Hall, and after the success of the program that also included music and speeches before Wells's featured testimonial, the women determined to continue their organizing efforts as the Women's Loyal Union. The organization spread to other cities throughout New England, including Boston and Providence, where black women came together to serve their communities and to promote social, political, and economic justice. Wells toured these cities and spoke at events organized by the club's women, as well as events organized by white women.

In Philadelphia, Wells met Catherine Impey, a British woman who attended her lynching speech and made a connection between Wells's work and her own as the editor of *Anti-Caste*, a magazine published in England to advocate for the people of India. The friendship and partnership between Wells and Impey began what would become the worldwide campaign to end lynching in the United States. Impey invited Wells to England, Scotland, and Wales, to give her speeches and to provide the impetus for British organizations to issue condemnations of lynch law, to organize anti-lynching committees, and to provide enough moral and organizational pressure on U.S. politicians to put an end to lynching and mob violence for good.

Wells's speeches throughout the United Kingdom touched on much more than lynch law; she described in detail the nature of Southern society that oppressed African Americans while privileging white Americans. The themes of her speeches covered restrictive laws and Jim Crow segregation; anti-intermarriage sentiments; ballot box hostility, threats, and the murders of black men who attempted to vote; and the "color line" that segregated church services, provided separate and unequal education for children, and stratified the professions, trades, industries, and public transportation and accommodations. Then her detailed descriptions of the horrors of lynchings, like the most recent lynching in Paris, Texas, and the failure of appeals to the U.S. Congress, provided the emotional power to motivate her crowd of former antislavery groups to now take on the cause of anti-lynching. She spoke extensively of the "silent indifference" of many white liberals in New England, and hoped her new friends in the United Kingdom would provide the impetus for a powerful anti-lynching movement to create legislation to end lynching forever.

Wells returned to the United States in the summer of 1893 only to continue west to Chicago to visit the Columbian Exposition. The World's Fair attracted thousands of international visitors, and Chicago and the United States made sure to show the best the city and the country had to offer as a place of progress, liberty, freedom, and innovation. Wells located her good friend Frederick Douglass, who had attempted and failed to have African American participation in the World's Fair. Instead, politicians from the nation of Haiti, who, unlike the African American contingency, were granted a space in the fair, asked Douglass to work in their building based on their relationship with Douglass when he had worked as an ambassador to their country. Douglass and Wells had met a year earlier, when Douglass traveled from Washington, DC, to Philadelphia to hear and to meet the woman who singlehandedly began the campaign against lynching. During their time in Chicago, Douglass and Wells published a pamphlet entitled *The Reason Why the Colored American Is Not in the World's Columbian Exposition*, and distributed more than 10,000 copies from a desk in the Haiti building.

Wells, like the majority of African Americans and many Northern white Americans, held great respect for Douglass; however, she was unafraid to disagree with the race leader. The organizers of the Chicago fair decided they would have a "Negro Day" to highlight the contributions to the Americas made by people of African descent. Wells, offended by the segregated nature of the event, opposed it and refused to participate. Douglass, however, endorsed "Negro Day" and spoke in a featured program. Although she respected Douglass's position, Wells would not compromise her own beliefs even when a man she deeply respected chose to do something she felt was wrong. Another example of Wells's confidence in her own positions, and her fearlessness to speak out against those she believed had wronged, came when she returned to England the following spring, 1894. Many of the engagements she booked had been with religious organizations, and many of the people in her audience idolized temperance leader Frances Willard. She spoke and wrote about the Christian leader while in the United Kingdom, noting that Willard believed and endorsed the lies concerning lynching put forth by Southern propagandists. Reflecting on the segregated nature of religion and Women Christian Temperance Union (WCTU) chapters, Wells remarked that Willard was "no better or worse than the great bulk of white America on the Negro Question" (Wells, 208).

Before her second voyage across the Atlantic, however, Wells determined to make Chicago her new home. During the World's Fair, she had been exposed to work done by the Tourgee Club, a black men's club that published a column on civil and political conditions in the Chicago *Inter-Ocean*, and opened its doors on Dearborn Street to receive prominent African Americans visiting the fair. Its founders named the club to honor Judge Albion W. Tourgee, a Union soldier who stayed in the South during Reconstruction and published on the subject. The Tourgee Club set up a Ladies' Day that went unattended until Wells became the first guest speaker toward the end of the fair, and saw that the women of Chicago were completely unorganized. Wells decided to stay in Chicago and to set about developing women's clubs throughout Illinois. The Chicago Women's Club, later named the Ida B. Wells Club to honor its founder and first chairperson, formally organized that fall, 1893. Five months later, when Wells prepared to embark on her second trip to England, she accepted a position as a paid correspondent to write for the Chicago *Inter-Ocean* during her six months of travels.

What made Wells's testimonials and detailed descriptions of the atrocities of lynchings so powerful and emotionally compelling was that she spoke unabashedly to her audiences at a time when women rarely spoke of things of such a violent nature. More importantly, despite her early efforts, lynchings were becoming more common in the Southern states and were spreading to states in the Midwest and the Northeast, including New York, Ohio, Minnesota, and even Illinois and Pennsylvania—the host of the World's Fair to demonstrate progress and enlightenment in the Americas and the home state of Abraham Lincoln, as well as the Quaker State. Southern journalists—particularly those writing for the *Memphis Daily Commercial*—and politicians did not let Wells's words go uncontested. Georgia Governor Northern, for example, wrote a letter published in newspapers throughout England that responded to Wells's anti-lynching agitation, questioning her integrity as a reputable source. Their efforts proved futile as the vast majority of British folk already committed to anti-lynching organizations did not waiver in their positions.

Wells's anti-lynching campaign in England forced Americans to pay attention and to listen to her arguments. Not only did the number of lynchings begin to decline after peaking in the mid-1890s, but prominent Americans like Frances Willard no longer defended or condoned lynching—most likely for fear they would be called out by Ida B. Wells, who now enjoyed international recognition. Most importantly, however, Wells had successfully located and utilized a space to publicly expose and undermine the lies justifying lynching in the first place.

Wells returned to Chicago in the summer of 1894, immediately embarking on a domestic tour that took her from the East Coast throughout the Great Plains and all the way to San Francisco, to continue to raise money and awareness for anti-lynching efforts. While in Rochester, New York, Wells bonded with Susan B. Anthony, who sprang from her seat during one of Wells's lectures to answer a question concerning why African Americans did not leave the South in larger numbers if they were being terrorized. Anthony reminded her audience that conditions in the North were not much better for black people. Wells stayed as Anthony's guest during her time in Rochester, and confronted her on the position of the women's movement that had continually sacrificed black women at the altar of expediency. Another example of her fearless ability to speak her mind, Wells told Anthony she was wrong when she appeased her Southern white sisters by refusing to allow African American participation in the Women's Equal Suffrage Association in Southern states. Anthony earned back Wells's respect, however, when she expressed that she understood Wells's opinion. After her anti-lynching tour, Wells immediately took off for another series of speeches, this time as the member of an unprecedented movement to elect a woman to the board of trustees to the University of Illinois. She returned to Chicago in early 1895 absolutely exhausted, both physically and financially.

After years of travel and public appearances, Wells believed she was ready to settle down and have a family. She and Attorney Ferdinand L. Barnett married in June of 1895 at the Bethel Church in Chicago. Friends from all over the country, members of the press, and women's club and political organization members attended the wedding and reception, thrown by the Ida B. Wells Club. When friends and activists learned that she planned to give up her anti-lynching campaign, many expressed dismay and disappointment, not understanding her exhaustion and much-needed break. Even during her moment away from the public, Wells continued to shape history. Despite her efforts, anti-lynching remained controversial in the United States, and propagandists worked overtime to defame Wells-Barnett and to rouse up fear of black male rapists and monsters. To defend Wells-Barnett, and by extension, what they termed "Negro Womanhood," black women's clubs organized a meeting and sent out a press release with a unanimous endorsement of her agitation against lynching. The meeting of the three thousand women in 1895 at Faneuil Hall in Boston marked the beginning of the National Association of Colored Women's Clubs (NACW). The women moved to meet in 1896 in Washington, DC, to organize nationally.

Although F. L. Barnett and Ida B. Wells-Barnett welcomed their first son in March of 1896, Wells-Barnett had already re-entered her working life with three roles, as a journalist for the *Conservator*, a paper she now owned after purchasing it from her husband, as the president of the Ida B. Wells Woman's Club, and as a public speaker. After the birth of their second child, Wells-Barnett determined to commit herself to the profession of motherhood, giving up her newspaper work and her club presidency. Before she resigned, however, she worked to establish a kindergarten at Bethel Church, jumpstarting the public kindergarten movement that spread from Chicago throughout the country. Later on, collaborating with Jane Addams, Wells-Barnett continued her advocacy for integrated education by successfully extinguishing efforts by editors at the *Chicago Tribune* to promote segregated schools.

Wells-Barnett still felt committed to ending lynching, because the acts of community violence continued. Two years later, in 1898, Wells-Barnett and her allies recognized an opportunity for a federal intervention to stop lynchings once and for all. In Anderson, South Carolina, earlier that year a white mob had lynched a black postmaster, a federal employee. Wells-Barnett and a group of lawyers traveled to Washington, DC, to present resolutions to the president and to members of Congress. The committee successfully gained a meeting with President Theodore Roosevelt; however, the United States declaration of war against Spain in Cuba made all other actions frozen until the end of the war. Later in the year, when President McKinley failed to mention and condemn the Wilmington race riot, where white mobs attacked and killed black people and burned their businesses to the ground, the Afro-American Council passed a resolution condemning the president and determined to hold its first annual meeting in Chicago in 1899.

Wells-Barnett attended events at both the Afro-American Council meeting and the NACW, which had conveniently decided to hold its annual meeting to coincide with the inaugural meeting of the Afro-American Council. After years of frustrations concerning the absence of a powerful African American organization to successfully fight lynchings and now also race riots after events in Tulsa, Atlanta, and other cities, Wells-Barnett and the black leaders who gathered to organize the Afro-American Council began to gain confidence that they were beginning to effect positive change. That organization was realized

10 years later at a conference in New York in 1909. Frustrated by Booker T. Washington's industrial education program, **W. E. B. Du Bois** and other leaders who did not want to put limitations on the possibilities for African Americans met to choose a committee of 40 that would create the new organization. Although Wells-Barnett's name originally appeared on the list of 40 for her leadership in anti-lynching, Du Bois decided at the last minute to leave her name off of the list, a devastating blow to the woman who had dedicated her life to improving conditions for African Americans. Although not a member of the committee, Wells-Barnett's years of race work significantly contributed to the establishment of the organization that would be named the National Association for the Advancement of Colored People, or the NAACP.

As a black woman who was always drastically outnumbered in her organizational and club work, by black men and by white men and women, Ida B. Wells-Barnett had to deal with issues of both race and gender. Rather than becoming embittered or even the positive alternative, which would have been throwing herself into caring for her children that now numbered four, Wells-Barnett returned to Chicago to work for the black people of her home city. She taught Bible classes to young black men, and realized she could develop a program to help the men develop skills, find work, and stay away from crime and out of prison. She helped the men organize the Negro Fellowship League, and took a job as an adult probation officer, the first black woman in the city of Chicago to do so, to complement her work at the social center and employment office on State Street that the Negro Fellowship League occupied. The facility also offered rooms for rent. Wells-Barnett recognized the pressing need for such an institution in a city where thousands of Southern black people were migrating in increasing numbers.

Wells-Barnett's lifelong mission to end the lynchings of black people, however, still required her efforts. After lynchings and racial violence in Springfield and Cairo, Wells-Barnett determined to force the state of Illinois to pass and enforce legislation that would work to end the reign of lynch law in the state. While investigating the context of the Springfield lynching, she realized the central role played by sheriffs who allowed men to be taken from prisons and lynched. Her organizing efforts in the state capital helped to pass a law that would remove from office any sheriff who allowed mobs to kidnap and murder imprisoned men. Soon after the state of Illinois passed the law, another white mob lynched a black man in Cairo, and the state removed the sheriff from his position. Sheriffs removed from office under the new law, however, had the right to argue their case for reinstatement before the governor. Understanding the precedent-setting nature of this first hearing, Wells-Barnett and her colleagues organized to speak before the governor to make sure the sheriff would not be reinstated. After her investigations throughout the South, Wells-Barnett knew that laws on the books were meaningless unless they were enforced. Illinois Governor Deneen decided not to reinstate the sheriff, setting a precedent in Illinois and ending lynching in the state for good. Sheriffs knew they had to protect black men in their prisons, no matter the hostilities of the white mob outside.

By 1920, Ida B. Wells-Barnett had dedicated more than 30 years to improving the life situations of black people, and realized that it was her time to retire from her race work. Never complacent, Wells-Barnett understood the importance for African Americans to know their rights and responsibilities as citizens, and especially to learn the real histories and contexts of events. Indeed, almost prophetically, Wells-Barnett wished for a true history of the events in the years following the aftermath of slavery, and the failure of Reconstruction laws to assist black people and to stop the reassertion of white supremacy in the Southern states. Just three years after her death in 1931, W. E. B. Du Bois published *Black Reconstruction*, the very history she desired.

Ida B. Wells-Barnett is an icon of black America because, at a time considered to be the nadir of African American history, she fearlessly devoted her life to the cause of anti-lynching. In addition to exposing the falsities espoused to uphold white supremacy and racial violence, she also worked to build communities. Through her tireless efforts in building organizations and women's clubs, and working to provide educational, religious, housing, and recreational services to the community, Wells-Barnett helped to create the institutional support for black migrants new to the cities. Many people, black and white alike, did not know what to make of the confident, pistol-carrying woman who believed in self-defense, integrity, and human dignity. Later generations of black activists are indebted to the woman who can be considered the godmother of militancy. In her words, "Eternal vigilance is the price of liberty."

Victoria L. Jackson
Arizona State University

FURTHER READING

Bay, Mia. *To Tell the Truth Freely: The Life of Ida B. Wells*. New York: Hill and Wang, 2009.

Collins, Patricia Hill. *On Lynchings: Ida B. Wells-Barnett*. Amherst, NY: Humanity Books, 2002.

Giddings, Paula, J. *Ida: A Sword among Lions: Ida B. Wells and the Campaign against Lynching*. New York: Amistad, 2008.

Harris, Trudier, ed. *Selected Works of Ida B. Wells-Barnett*. New York: Oxford University Press, 1991.

Royster, Jacqueline Jones, ed. *Southern Horrors and Other Writings: The Anti-Lynching Campaign of Ida B. Wells, 1892–1900*. Boston: Bedford Books, 1997.

Schechter, Patricia A. *Ida B. Wells-Barnett and American Reform, 1880–1930*. Chapel Hill: The University of North Carolina Press, 2001.

Wells-Barnett, Ida B., and Alfreda M. Duster, eds. *Crusade for Justice: The Autobiography of Ida B. Wells*. Chicago: University of Chicago Press, 1970.

Cornel West (1953–)

Cornel West is a highly regarded intellectual in African American studies, philosophy, and religious studies. His scholarship inspires academics and non-academics alike, and he has revitalized African American Studies programs at two prestigious universities in the United States. His writing and commentary highlight the important intellectual contributions made by enerations of African Americans to philosophy and religion, thereby challenging racist assumptions that black Americans have not participated in these important endeavors. West's activism and academic pursuits have made him an important commentator on African American life in the United States, a well-known contemporary American philosopher, and an icon of black America.

Cornel West was born in Tulsa, Oklahoma, on June 2, 1953. His parents had access to good educational opportunities, and both graduated from Fisk University. West's mother, Irene Bias West, was an elementary school teacher and principal, after whom a school was later named. West's father, Clifton L. West, Jr., was an administrator in the U.S. Air Force. Cornel was not an only child; he had one brother, Clifton L. West III, and sisters Cynthia and Cheryl West. Cornel's grandfather was a Baptist minister, and the family raised young Cornel within this religious tradition. West joined the church at the age of eight when he was old enough to request membership. One of his grandmothers was a domestic worker for more than four decades, and West later remarked upon her ability to courageously thrive in an occupation that might have challenged her sense of dignity.

West's parents moved frequently, but Cornel finished school in a black neighborhood in Sacramento, California. Despite the prestige he gained as an adult through his work in universities, he did not always have a pleasant time in school. When his third-grade teacher slapped him, he hit her back. He was expelled for this self defense. Nevertheless, West found welcoming opportunities in his youth. He participated in sports, which helped him to build discipline and a sense of community. This feeling of community was likely important to West in part because of the number of times that his parents uprooted him to move to new areas.

West became an activist early. In elementary school, he led classmates in a protest against discrimination; he and the group stopped saluting the American flag in an expression of their discontent. His leadership skills continued to develop, and he was elected the president of his high school class in Sacramento. He led protests at his high school to add Black Studies to the curriculum. Such political consciousness did not appear overnight, however; West also worked with the Black Panther Party (BPP). This organization influenced West's politics, and it is from the BPP that West learned more about democratic socialism and black internationalism. West also drew upon the writing and speeches of **Martin Luther King, Jr.** and **Malcolm X**. Black music influenced West as well, and the works of John Coltrane and James Brown were particularly meaningful to him. As his political consciousness grew, he volunteered in BPP soup kitchens to help feed hungry children and families. These experiences compelled West to develop his politics as well as his connections to his community.

West entered Harvard University on a scholarship in 1970. Remembering his earlier political education, West worked with the local chapter of the BPP and volunteered to serve children breakfast. Studying with liberal philosopher John Rawls at Harvard, West read the writing of thinkers including **W. E. B. Du Bois**, Karl Marx, Søren Kierkegaard, Anton Chekhov, and Friedrich Nietzsche. West found that he was fascinated with modernity and Western philosophy. His studies and political activism pushed him to broaden his horizons.

While the cultural environment of Harvard in the 1970s did not embrace the style, modes of thought, or mannerisms of West's upbringing, he did not let this discrepancy deter him from his goals. Instead of trying to conform to the academy, West determined to use the academy for his own political and intellectual purposes. He worked to excel at his studies, but he refused to be ashamed of who he was, even if he felt like a minority at the school. West also found religion to be important to his academic thought, and believed that religious issues should be discussed in political circles. He graduated magna cum laude in just three years with a bachelor's degree in Near Eastern Languages and Literature, having learned to read Hebrew, Aramaic, and Greek in his studies of the Bible and classic literature.

West enrolled in graduate studies at Princeton University, which then had the best philosophy department in the United States. Here he closely studied pragmatism, a school of philosophical thought developed in the United States in the nineteenth century. Pragmatists believe that ideas must be understood within the context of their consequences. Truth does not exist on a higher plane outside of the real world in pragmatic thought, but instead is relative to the world in which truth-seekers exist. West's study of pragmatism legitimized his desire to connect the academy with the rest of life.

West finished his academic training quickly while also advancing his activist and academic career. He earned his master's degree from Princeton in 1975, and his doctorate in philosophy from the same university in 1980, when he defended his dissertation entitled "The Ethical Dimensions of Marxist Thought." While earning this final degree, West taught at federal prisons in New York and at Union Theological Seminary. At this seminary, he continued to explore and share his ideas regarding liberation and black theology, and worked with other important figures of black religious thought, including James Cone. A convergence of Christianity (particularly Roman Catholicism) and Marxist theory, liberation theology stresses Christians' political commitment to helping the poor and oppressed. West's graduate studies and work provided him with opportunities to combine his political and academic ambitions.

Upon completing his dissertation, West continued to teach at Union Theological Seminary and other schools. He published *Prophesy Deliverance!: An Afro-American Revolutionary Christianity* in 1982. Twenty years later, he commented that this remained his favorite of the works he had published.

Prophesy Deliverance! offered an intellectual examination of black Christianity, Marxism, and philosophy. Arguing that Americans should embrace a combination of prophetic Christianity and progressive Marxism, West highlighted the ways that these traditions might help black Americans, in particular.

In *Prophesy Deliverance!*, West argued that prophetic Christianity supported black America for centuries, and that black Christians used religion to critique their circumstances from as early as the eighteenth century. Black Christian religious leaders continued to advocate for the black community by challenging racism and classism through religious discussions and actions. This commentary was extended in the 1970s by black Christian theologians (and other liberation theologians) to critique the harms committed against black America by capitalism. Here, West argued, a Marxism that addressed racial disparity might intersect with prophetic Christianity. West's first book set forth a potential political and religious solution to the problems facing black America.

West's contributions to the academy focused on the importance of ideas. West noted in an interview with bell hooks (pen name of Gloria Jean Watkins) that ideas can generate pleasure, as they do for those who possess the opportunity and desire to pursue academic work, but that ideas can also buttress or challenge power. Indeed, from West's protests in high school to create space in the curriculum for Black Studies, to his work as a professor who seeks to share intellectual thought with audiences within and without the academy, West has spent his life concerned with the power that surrounds ideas.

West began teaching at Yale Divinity School in 1984, where he earned a full professorship in a briefer period than did many of his academic peers. He briefly returned to Union Theological Seminary in 1987, but was recruited to teach at Princeton University in 1988. There, he served as a professor of religion and director of the university's Afro-American Studies Program for several years. Given that West only completed his dissertation in 1980, his rise to become the director of Princeton's Afro-American Studies Program might be described as meteoric.

A life in the academy did not save West from encountering racism, however. He noted in *Race Matters*, which was published in 1993, that he was pulled over by a police officer while driving, on what he described as a false allegation of cocaine trafficking. In an effort to demonstrate that the charge was untrue, the scholar identified himself as a professor. The officer responded by calling himself the Flying Nun and addressing West with a racial epithet. In addition, West reported that he was pulled over three times in just his first 10 days at Princeton as he drove through residential neighborhoods.

West continued his political career, however, and published *The American Evasion of Philosophy: A Genealogy of Pragmatism* in 1989. This work examines pragmatism in the context of gender, race, and class. This work is particularly significant because the history of pragmatism is traditionally limited to only white male thinkers such as John Dewey and Richard Rorty.

West's work acknowledges the contributions made by men and women of color, and white women, to American philosophy. West published numerous other books, including *The Ethical Dimensions of Marxist Thought*, which was a revised version of his doctoral thesis, in 1991; *Breaking Bread: Insurgent Black Intellectual Life*, which he co-authored with bell hooks in 1991; and *Jews and Blacks: Let the Healing Begin* in 1995 with Rabbi Michael Lerner.

West is perhaps best known for *Race Matters*, which was published in 1993. This nonfiction bestseller remains an important classic in discussions of race in America. More than 500,000 copies were sold by 2009. This brief collection of essays remains a ground-breaking, foundational text in African American Studies. In it, West offers a series of essays on issues that he revisited throughout his career. He commented on the challenges black Americans face in a modern and postmodern world, the complex relationship between the black and Jewish communities in America, and black sexuality.

Having reached a high point in his career, West was a competent and desirable academic, and other universities wished to pull him into their programs. Henry Louis Gates, Jr., who became the director of Harvard University's Department of African American Studies in 1991, successfully recruited West in 1993. West left Princeton to teach at Harvard in 1994. He became the first Alphonse Fletcher, Jr. University Professor in 1998. Endowed professorships such as this are important honors for tenured academics that offer prestige and additional financial and institutional resources. This professorship also provided West with greater flexibility in teaching, and he offered courses in African American Studies, religion, and philosophy.

While West might have rested on his laurels at this point in his career, he determined to remain politically engaged. He spoke in support of the Million Man March in 1995, but he was criticized for his involvement by many who felt uncomfortable with the Nation of Islam. In 1997, he participated in President Bill Clinton's national conversation about race, in which racially diverse groups of leaders met to speak about race and racism. These leaders, including West, advised President Clinton on potential policies that might help all Americans, and served a symbolic role simply by advising the sitting President on race. These acts pushed West further into the national spotlight, drawing attention to his ideas and his published work.

In addition, West sought to share intellectual ideas with audiences that normally would not have easy access to them. He released a hip-hop album in 2001 under the Artemis Records label, in which he offers commentary on the state of black America. Entitled *Sketches of My Culture*, West's album had measured success. More importantly, the album was an innovative effort to reach out to the public, and particularly to young people. West strikingly also found in this album an opportunity to combine his love of music with his commentary on black America and modernity.

West's public outreach during his career as a tenured professor has extended considerably farther than a single hip-hop album, however. He frequently tours the United States and globe to share his lectures to non-university audiences. In the course of one particularly active year, he offered nearly 150 lectures. Traveling to offer this many lectures is a time-intensive process, and for this reason, even some academics who consider themselves activists offer few lectures simply because they cannot juggle frequent appearances with their teaching, research, and family responsibilities. West is richly rewarded for his non-academic work, but he argues that it is his sense of democracy that compels him to push beyond the walls of the academy.

When West lectures, he frequently draws from current events to help audiences understand his ideas. He used Americans' reaction to the terrorist attacks on September 11, 2001, and the tragedy of Hurricane Katrina, for example, as teaching moments. Many Americans responded to the terrorist attacks in 2001 with horror and fear. Yet West argued that these feelings are similar to those experienced by African Americans everyday. Having lived with the random terror of racism and white supremacy for centuries, African Americans, in West's opinion, have important insights to offer to other Americans. He likewise argued that Americans must accept the connections between the tragedy of Hurricane Katrina in New Orleans and African Americans' experience of slavery, lynching, and the racist criminal justice system.

Although West continued to remain a highly visible scholar-activist, his position at Harvard soon became controversial. A conflict with Lawrence Summers, then the president of Harvard, prompted him to leave the university to return to Princeton. In a private meeting, Summers reportedly criticized West's activities outside of the academy, including his hip-hop album, and suggested that his time might be better spent in new original research that might produce a scholarly publication. In addition, Summers is said to have trivialized West's academic work, and charged the icon with grade inflation.

West defended his work at Harvard, though he decided to leave the university. He later insisted that his argument with Summers was not about ego, but instead about whether academics should make their work accessible to all Americans. Indeed, West argued years before his conflict with Summers even began that not all academics are intellectuals; academics limit themselves to a small range of scholarship that is only relevant to other professors and advanced students, while intellectuals address issues that concern the entire public. Controversy surrounding Summers was not limited to only West, however; prior to resigning as president of Harvard, Summers suggested in 2005 that most of the university's top academics in science and engineering were men because of varied aptitude levels between men and women, thus implying that women do not become top professors at the university because they, as a group, are less capable than men.

The dispute between West and Summers continued to gnaw at West, who faced serious illness. Near the end of this controversy, West underwent surgery to treat prostate cancer. He had worried that he only had a few more months to live before he would succumb to cancer. Following the surgery, he commented on Summers's delay in contacting him to wish him a speedy recovery, and noted that the president of Yale, in contrast, had contacted West in a timely manner. West's comments imply that Summers was unconcerned about his health, and betray the icon's frustration regarding the state of his relationship with the Harvard president.

Responding to the mistreatment he received from Summers, West left Harvard and returned to Princeton in 2002, where he received an endowed position as the Class of 1943 University Professor of Religion. From this professorship, West continues to expound on black culture, philosophy, and religion. He recently published *Hope on a Tightrope*, which emphasizes that much more work must be done, beyond the election of Obama, to secure the liberation of men of color, all women, and gays and lesbians. Commenting on modernism, West argues that African Americans were historically excised from the modern state even as they lived within it; he believes that this has provided African Americans with a powerful fluidity that allows them to live within and without the modern world.

West's scholarship is unique in its conversational tone. Rather than dictate to other academics and readers, West creates opportunities for others to dialogue with him; he considers his conversations with others to be similar to the jazz he loved as a child. This collaborative approach is evident in the books he co-authored with other academics, including *Breaking Bread* and *Jews and Blacks*. His approachable commentary also surprises many listeners for its mixture of academic and vernacular styles. West frequently notes, for example, that people are "featherless, two-legged, linguistically conscious creature[s] born between urine and feces" (West, *Hope*, 28). Such comments emphasize our common humanity and shared state of embodiment. They also bring intellectual discourse down to a realistic level, as humans may be dignified, but they are also organisms subject to the physicality of human bodies.

West's soaring career has earned him other opportunities not available to most scholars. He played the role of Councilor West in *The Matrix Reloaded* and *The Matrix Revolutions*, which were both released in 2003. Appearing in the extra features to *The Ultimate Matrix Collection*, West explained the intellectual ideas raised by the film trilogy. Most academics appear only in documentaries, but West's work in the trilogy is congruous with his teaching philosophy and desire to share his ideas. In addition, West's fame as an academic has earned him opportunities to make appearances on television shows such as *Real Time with Bill Maher*; he has also made an appearance on *The Colbert Report* to promote *Hope on a Tightrope*.

West's political and activist work continues to earn him criticism. Other academics criticized West for his efforts to engage in controversial conversations outside the academy, in particular. Some critics express discomfort with West's conversations with Jewish leaders, while others worry about his conversations with leaders of the Nation of Islam. West's political and economic ideologies, including his position as Honorary Chair of the Democratic Socialists of America, also give some individuals pause.

West's political involvement has led him to comment on **Barack Obama**'s candidacy and presidency. West supported the candidate's bid for president beginning in 2007, when many African American leaders remained disinterested or distrusting of Obama. Speaking at a rally for Obama in November 2007 in Harlem, West urged voters to accept the candidate for who he was, rather than idealize him into something he could never become. This cautionary reminder of Obama's humanity exemplified West's scholarship; even politicians as talented and eloquent as Obama are human and have the failings and frailties common to all people. Following Obama's election, West belatedly validated the debates regarding whether Obama was "black enough" by seeking to determine whether the candidate would defend the oppressed rather than the oppressors.

Yet beyond questions of Obama's blackness, West and some other African American leaders express discomfort with the generational shift that the younger man's election represents. In preparation for a documentary, West traveled in 2008 with Tavis Smiley and nine other African American leaders on a bus tour in Tennessee on the 40th anniversary of the assassination of Martin Luther King, Jr. Smiley arranged for their tour of King's last days to be videotaped for a documentary entitled *Stand*. West explained that the purpose of the documentary was to foster black men's self-respect, which might be built up by watching 11 male African American leaders discuss political and social issues. The documentary offers important insight into the thoughts and lives of several black leaders, but it also serves as an implicit criticism of Obama through its design.

The very tour documented in *Stand* demonstrates the ideological and strategic differences between West's cohort and Obama. While West and other leaders toured Tennessee to remember King's last days, Obama battled through a particularly lengthy Democratic primary season in which he and Hilary Clinton fought for the party's nomination. On the anniversary of King's assassination, West complained on the *Huffington Post* that Obama's absence from Memphis, Tennessee, was disappointing. He suggested that Obama's "quest for power" had prevented him from keeping a "commitment to truth" (West, "On Obama Not Going to Memphis"). West expected Obama to observe a ritual that would satisfy the black community, and particularly an older generation within the black community, during the most trying period to date of Obama's political career.

West's suggestion that Obama had disappointed him by continuing to campaign underscores a misunderstanding between younger and older generations of black leadership. West acknowledged in *Stand* that a generational shift was occurring in African American leadership; speaking to his friends during the filming of the documentary, West explained as follows:

> Everybody knows Obama ain't charismatic vis-à-vis Martin or Malcolm or Medgar. But he's turning all these people on. Because he got a different group now. They got a different constituency now. Just like Alicia Keys don't move

my mama. But Mahalia [Jackson] does. That's right, cause Alicia got a different group now. (*Stand*)

West clearly explained that the politics and style of leadership had shifted in the twenty-first century. Yet his comments on the *Huffington Post* suggest that he still struggles to accept this shift and the priorities of younger African American leaders.

Later in 2008, West critiqued Obama's presidency before the latter man had yet taken office. In *Hope on a Tightrope*, which was published before Obama was inaugurated, West cautioned Obama to remain accountable to the Americans who need his help. He complained, for example, of Obama's cabinet choices and suggested that they indicated a continuation of traditional politics rather than the change that Obama had promised. Indeed, Obama's nominations of Larry Summers, Rahm Emanuel, and Hillary Clinton, for example, were criticized by many for being too reminiscent of Bill Clinton's administration. Further, West's history with Summers in particular may have contributed to his frustration following Obama's nomination of the former president of Harvard. Nevertheless, these concerns remain part of a larger, unresolved issue facing black America.

West remains hopeful for Americans' future and that of the nation's first black president. His commentary on the tension between the younger and older generations of black leadership demonstrate that, even as he is swept up in this conflict himself, he is intelligent and analytic enough to understand that the future of the black community and its leadership are in flux. West believes that his role in relation to Obama is to push the president to remain accountable to African Americans and equality; while some might argue that such a role creates an imposition upon a younger generation of leadership, West would likely argue that this role permits the younger generation to better understand the needs and concerns of their elders. West's analysis of the generational change in leadership, developed in the midst of this conflict, provides tools that allow Americans to better understand these changes.

Despite his outreach to the public, West keeps much of his personal life private. He has married three times; his frequent lectures likely complicate his relationships, as they demand that he travel throughout the United States and abroad. This travel also limits the time that he might have spent with his children. He is the father of son Clifton Louis and daughter Zeytun, and was stepfather to Nelson Hernandez during one of his marriages. He also has one grandson.

West is an important philosopher and voice in the United States. He seeks to improve the lives of all people, while lifting up people of color, women, gays and lesbians, and those who are oppressed by a combination of identities. He also stresses, as do new waves of academic thought, that whiteness, maleness, and heterosexuality should be studied and understood as closely as blackness and the experiences of other people of color, femaleness, and alternative sexualities. Although his agenda for liberation does not identically match that of other African American leaders, his hopes for America nevertheless parallel those of black Americans. West's concern for all people, his courageous intellectualism, and his efforts to share his ideas with all who will listen, truly make him an icon of black America.

Megan Falater
University of Wisconsin-Madison

FURTHER READING

Hooks, Bell, and Cornel West. *Breaking Bread: Insurgent Black Intellectual Life.* Boston: South End Press, 1991.

Smiley, Tavis. *Stand.* DVD. Smiley Group: Hay House, 2009.

West, Cornel. *Hope on a Tightrope: Words & Wisdom.* Carlsbad, CA: SmileyBooks, 2008.

West, Cornel. "On Obama Not Going to Memphis." *Huffington Post*, April 4, 2008. http://www.huffingtonpost.com/cornel-west/on-obama-not-going-to-mem_b _95179.html (accessed August 14, 2009).

West, Cornel. *Prophesy Deliverance!: An Afro-American Revolutionary Christianity.* Louisville, KY: Westminster John Knox Press, 2002.

West, Cornel. *Race Matters.* New York: Vintage Books, 1994.

Williams, Serena. *See* Venus Williams and Serena Williams

Dreamstime

Venus Williams (1980–) and Serena Williams (1981–)

Since 1994, Venus and Serena Williams have stood at the vanguard of professional athletic achievement, advocacy for racial and gender equality, and innovation in the business, interior design, and fashion worlds. The Williams sisters stunned the world with their domination of professional tennis. Their physical strength and will to win set them apart from their peers. The key to their games are fast serves and strong returns that exhaust their opponents; it has been these skills, and their desire to excel, that fueled their rise in the rankings in both women's singles and women's doubles competitions. Still under 35, speculation abounds as to which of the sisters will ultimately prove to be the most successful player in the long-term. No matter who registers the most victories, garners the most awards, or makes their mark in the world beyond the tennis court, the Williams sisters have already cemented their collective, unsurpassed legacy of excellence and achievement.

The sisters' path into professional tennis and celebrity status was plotted before their birth. Their father, Richard, loved to watch tennis on television, and he envisioned a time during which his yet-to-be-born children would compete at the highest levels of professional tennis onscreen. His first three daughters did not become tennis players, but Venus and Serena Williams took to the game almost immediately. Venus Ebone Starr Williams was born on June 17, 1980, in Lynwood, California, and Serena Jameka Williams was born on September 26, 1981, in Saginaw, Michigan. When the sisters were still toddlers, their father and Oracene (Brandi) Williams, their mother, introduced them to tennis. For six hours a day they played with shabby rackets and useless balls against a wall or on a pot-holed court. The two sisters were subjected to a grueling regimen as their father dissected his tennis manual and shouted instructions. They learned well, and the siblings began to compete before the age of five.

Venus and Serena Williams were not yet teenagers when invitations to national training camps began arriving in their Compton, Los Angeles, post office box. By the time the pair became teenagers, their father had withdrawn them from the junior circuit, but he later enrolled them in the professional tour after a brief hiatus. He was criticized for taking them out of school, but he justified his actions by saying that the sisters would be best served by concentrating on the most important area in which they were straight "A" students. The teenagers initially played in private professional events because they were too young to compete in World Tennis Association (WTA) events. Nevertheless, their games improved dramatically.

Venus Williams was the first to come of age, and made her mark in professional tennis in October of 1994. After 1994, the WTA did not allow 14-year-olds to compete in all tour events, although "phase-in" clauses allowed some to play in a limited number of events. The elder sister turned pro before the new rule went into effect, so the new limit did not affect her opportunities to play. Her first tournament was the Bank of the West Classic in Oakland, California, where she showed a good deal of promise in a loss to

Arantxa Sanchez-Vicario, who was then ranked No. 2 in the world. For her first two years on the pro tour, Williams stayed out of the limelight and kept up with her high school studies, not making her debut at a Grand Slam until the 1997 French Open.

Venus Williams was a success that year. In 1997, she became the first unseeded woman ever to reach the final of the U.S. Open, and the first African American woman to do so since Althea Gibson won back-to-back championships in 1957 and 1958. Though the icon lost in the finals to Switzerland's Martina Hingis, the 17-year-old, No. 1-ranked player in the world, she saw her own ranking shoot up from No. 66 to No. 25 in only one day. The highlight of that tournament, and the year, however, was the infamous "bump" that occurred during the Irina Spirlea and Williams semifinal. The two collided during a changeover. Williams's father later said that the incident was initiated by Spirlea and racially motivated. Richard Williams described his daughters as "the ghetto Cinderellas of the lily-white tennis world," in part because the "bump" would not be the first or last time that he and his daughters called attention to what they considered to be racist treatment on the circuit.

Despite the racism and on-court challenges that they faced in 1997, the Williams sisters flourished. Venus Williams started out the 1998 season well, beating Hingis in a tournament in Sydney, Australia, and reaching the quarterfinals of the Australian Open after defeating her younger sister in the tournament. Though she lost to Lindsay Davenport in the singles draw, the elder sister teamed up with Justin Gimelstob to win the mixed doubles championship. She won her first WTA singles title at the IGA Tennis Classic in March, and went on to score a big win at the Lipton International, defeating Anna Kournikova of Russia (another of tennis's highly-touted up-and-comers) and Hingis. The Lipton win propelled Venus Williams into the top 10. She finished 1998 with a great record in the Grand Slams, reaching the quarterfinals of the French Open and Wimbledon and the semifinals of the U.S. Open. She also set the record for the fastest serve ever recorded by a female player in a main draw match, at 129 miles per hour.

Despite her impressive record and growing confidence, Venus Williams had yet to achieve the accolade she dreamed about her whole life: a Grand Slam victory. Serena Williams, who the sisters' father once claimed would be the better player of the two, became a pro four years earlier in her first, non-WTA event, the Bell Challenge in Vanier, Quebec, in October 1995. She reached her sister's goal first, however, when she won the 1999 U.S. Open. Serena Williams had played sporadically, and did not meet with much individual success until 1997, when her ranking shot up from No. 453 to 304. After beating Mary Pierce and Monica Seles at the Ameritech Cup in Chicago, she jumped to No. 100 in the world. In July 1998, she won the mixed doubles title at Wimbledon with Max Mirnyi, and by August she improved to No. 21. In October 1998, Serena Williams beat her sister for the first time in the finals of the Grand Slam Cup in Munich, Germany.

Serena Williams won her first WTA tour singles victory in early 1999 at the Open Gaz de France in Paris. That win began an incredible season of five singles titles in 48 matches. In September 1999, the 17-year-old athlete defeated Hingis in the finals of the U.S. Open, becoming the first African American woman to capture a Grand Slam singles title since Gibson, who won five Slam events in the late 1950s. The following day, Serena and Venus Williams, who reached the semifinals of the singles draw before losing to Hingis, teamed up to win the doubles title. Both victories took place at the Arthur Ashe Stadium in Flushing Meadows, New York, which was named for the last African American to win a major tennis title, in 1975 at Wimbledon. The sisters also teamed up to win doubles titles at the French Open and the U.S. Open in 1999, becoming the first and only sister team to win a Grand Slam doubles title in the twentieth century.

The Williams sisters finished the 1999 season ranked in the top five in the world. Still, the higher-ranked Venus Williams finished off the 1999 season ranked No. 3 in the world, and was the second highest-paid player in terms of prize with career earnings of nearly $4,600,000. Serena Williams finished the season well too, as the third highest-paid player. The next year the glory belonged to her sister, although it did not appear that way initially. Both sisters got off to a slow start in 2000 due to injuries, and in April, Richard Williams announced that his older daughter was contemplating retirement. Just a few months later, however, Venus Williams began a winning streak that took her all the way to Wimbledon, where she grabbed a Grand Slam title of her own, beating both Hingis and her younger sister in an emotional semifinal match, before dominating defending champion Davenport in the finals. Just one day later, the icons teamed up to win the Wimbledon doubles title.

I believe that athletes, especially female athletes in the world's leading sport for women, should serve as role models. The message I like to convey to women and girls across the globe is that there is no glass ceiling.   —Venus Williams

The sisters' success continued. On September 9, 2000, Venus Williams met Davenport again in the finals of the U.S. Open, where she won her 26th straight match and became the first woman to win two Grand Slam titles in one year, as Hingis had done in 1997. Venus and Serena Williams also captured the doubles title. In the fall of 2000, both athletes represented the United States at the Olympic Games in Sydney, Australia, alongside Davenport and Monica Seles. Continuing her amazing winning streak, Venus Williams became the only other woman besides Helen Wills Moody (in 1924) to capture gold in both singles and doubles in the same Olympiad. The sisters won their 22nd straight doubles match in the finals at the Olympic Games.

As their celebrity grew, they were reminded, however, that many people still viewed them as inferior by virtue of their race. Early in 2001, in Indian Wells, California, an injured Venus Williams withdrew from her semi-final against her younger sister 10 minutes before the match began. During the tournament's final against Belgium's Kim Clijsters, crowds jeered and booed Serena Williams. She believed that this reception was racially motivated. The sisters' father also noted that he and Venus Williams were called "niggers" by members of the crowd as they made their way to their seats at the 2001 tournament:

> When Venus and I were walking down the stairs to our seats, people kept calling me nigger. One guy said: "I wish it was '65 [a reference to the 1965 Los Angeles race riots]; we'd skin you alive."

The pain created by this tournament lives on; the Williams sisters have boycotted Indian Wells ever since.

Venus and Serena Williams did not let such racist behavior deter them, however, and they remained a remarkable force in the tennis world. In July 2001, Venus Williams successfully defended her Wimbledon title, beating Davenport in the semifinal, and Belgian player Justine Henin in the finals. She had an even more eventful U.S. Open, beating the resurgent Jennifer Capriati in the semifinals before facing Serena Williams in the finals in the first meeting of sisters in a Grand Slam final since 1884. The elder athlete's maturity served her well in the all-Williams match up, as she beat Serena Williams in two sets to win her second consecutive Open title. The younger Williams sister handled an up-and-down season in 2001, but still reached a high point at the U.S. Open in September, where she had commanding victories over Davenport and Hingis in the quarter- and semi-finals, respectively.

2002, however, would belong to Serena Williams. She opened the year defeating Justine Henin to win the Gold Coast tournament. The icon reached the quarterfinals of the Australian Open, and defeated Venus Williams in the finals of the French Open, Wimbledon, and U.S. Open. The string of victories catapulted Serena Williams to the top of WTA tour rankings, while her sister dropped to second. Serena Williams won seven singles titles in 2002, a career best, and in February 2002, she became the top-ranked player in the world and the first African American player to secure that spot since the computer rankings began in 1975. Despite Venus Williams's fall in the international rankings, she and her sister won the 2002 Wimbledon doubles title for the second time.

The sisters' professional and personal lives were not without challenges, however. Venus Williams started the year by losing to her sister in the 2003 Australian Open final. During a semifinal match against Clijsters at Wimbledon in 2003, she suffered a severe abdominal injury that required medical attention during the match. Venus Williams rebounded to win that match, but lost the final to Serena Williams. The Williams sisters also experienced personal tragedy in 2003, when older sister Yetunde Price was murdered in Compton, California, on the morning of September 14, 2003. The era of domination by the Williams sisters appeared to close out after their sister's murder. Following Wimbledon, both sisters suffered injuries that kept them out of competition for the last half of the year.

The sisters returned to the tour somewhat rusty, and were inconsistent on the court. Venus Williams rebounded from a tough start to reach the 2004 Wimbledon final. She lost a controversial second round match to Croatian Karolina Sprem. The umpire of the match, Ted Watts, awarded Sprem an unearned point in the second set tiebreak, casting a cloud of doubt over Sprem's victory and putting his job security on the line. He was fired immediately after the match.

The sisters improved the following year. At Wimbledon in 2005, Venus Williams defeated defending champion Sharapova in a semifinal. This marked the sixth consecutive year that at least one of the Williams sisters reached the final, and it was the elder sister's fifth appearance in the Wimbledon final in the past six years. In the longest Wimbledon final in history, Williams was down match point at 6–4, 6–7(4), 5–4 (40–30) before coming back to defeat top seeded Lyndsay Davenport. This was Williams's third Wimbledon singles title, and the first time in 70 years that a player won after being down match point during the women's final. In addition, as the 14th seed, Williams was the lowest seed to win the women's singles title in Wimbledon history. She also reached the quarterfinals at the 2005 U.S. Open. In the fourth round, she defeated Serena Williams for the second consecutive time. In the quarterfinals, she lost to Clijsters, who went on to win the tournament. *Tennis Magazine* ranked Venus Williams 25th and Serena Williams 17th on their list of the 40 Greatest Players of the Tennis era that year.

Serena Williams cemented her own championship legacy between 1999 and 2007. After suffering a series of setbacks and facing limited success against a series of opponents, she logged some remarkable victories and returned to full form at the 2007 Australian Open, where the unseeded Williams defeated fifth-seeded Nadia Petrova of Russia in the third round. This was Williams's first win over a top-10 player since her defeat of Lindsay Davenport in the 2005 Australian Open final. In the fourth round, the icon defeated the 11th-seeded Jelena Jankovic of Serbia. She then defeated 16-seeded Shahar Pe'er in the quarterfinals and 10th-seeded Nicole Vaidisova in the semifinals. In the final, Williams dominated top-seeded and then-second ranked Maria Sharapova in just 63 minutes to take her third Australian Open singles title. The victory elevated her ranking from 81st to 14th in the world. It also marked the first time either Williams sister won a Grand Slam singles title in the absence of the other's participation in the same tournament. Serena Williams dedicated the win to her deceased sister. This return to success was her 16th career Grand Slam title, pushing her career totals to six women's doubles titles, three mixed doubles titles, and eight singles titles.

By 2006, Venus Williams also established herself as one of the all-time greats of professional tennis. Playing with a white Wilson (K) Factor limited-edition racket, featuring 22-carat gold leaf laid into the frame, a resurgent Venus Williams won her first six singles matches at Wimbledon in 2006, and reached the final for the sixth time. She clinched her fourth Wimbledon Title on July 7, 2007, with a decisive, unreturned 124-mph serve into the body of her opponent, Marion Bartoli. Seeded No. 23, Williams beat her own 2005 record as the lowest women's seed to win Wimbledon. During the ceremony, she said that her little sister inspired her to win. By claiming her fourth Wimbledon title, Venus Williams joined an elite group of champion tennis players, including Billie Jean King, Martina Navratilova, and Steffi Graf as the only women to win four or more Wimbledon ladies' singles titles in the Open Era.

Despite their dominance, Venus and Serena Williams continue to face racism and sexism on and off of the court. As recently as March 2007, the sports world was rocked by news that Serena Williams was subjected to racist heckling by a male spectator at the Sony Ericsson Open. The individual shouted to Williams to "hit the ball into the net like any nigger would." She reported the racist abuse to the umpire during her third-round victory against Czech Lucie Safarova, and the racist heckler was eventually removed from the stadium. Williams later explained,

> I was shocked. I couldn't believe it. It threw me off. I shouldn't have let it bother me because growing up in Compton, in Los Angeles, we had drive-by shootings, and I guess that's what my dad prepared me for, but I'm not going to stand for it.

Zina Garrison, a former Wimbledon finalist with close links to the Williams family, also suffered occasional racist abuse during her playing days. Garrison said that, even for someone as mentally strong as Serena Williams, racist insults are still extremely hurtful.

The mistreatment that Venus and Serena Williams face on the court is unfortunately not unique. Women of color who enter sports that are usually considered nontraditional for people of their race and sex are often confronted by social conventions that limit their access and opportunities. Their physical appearance, intelligence, intentions, and commitment are often questioned. Women of color, through their very existence, also force others to rethink conceptions of race, gender roles, and femininity. Inflexible definitions and conventions for race and femininity limit opportunities for women such as the Williams sisters. Women of color who enter a non-traditional sport are often criticized for not conforming to norms and patterns established by a society dominated by whites and men. Women who decide to participate in traditionally male sports, or female athletes whose physical appearances diverge from the norm, risk being stereotyped as less feminine or lesbian. For example, Venus and Serena Williams are regularly described as very muscular or "masculine" in build. The force with which they play has been likened to that of their male peers. Descriptions of the sisters frequently comment on their gender, even when journalists are not masculinizing them by describing their build. Venus and Serena Williams are not identified as athletes in some descriptions, but instead as female players. Their skills and athleticism alone are insufficient for these journalists, who instead insist on comparing the sisters to men in their sport.

To be the "other" in contemporary society is to be non-white, working-class, or non-male. Insinuated, built-in preferences for members of the dominant community are nearly invisible to the very people who benefit from them. As a result, they help fuel a cycle of racial, gender, and class discrimination under a veneer of ignorance and altruism in some of the most powerful institutions in American culture, which play large roles in reflecting and shaping popular culture and stereotypes. The media, in particular, acts as a unifying agent by fostering one-dimensional classifications of race, gender, and class, in addition to its tendency to turn its back on and misrepresent specific groups. The U.S. institution of sports also exhibits a problematic history with race, gender, and class. Even though the sports industry explicitly highlights the masculine ideal, it also creates race and class disparities with the help of the media.

The media's coverage of Venus and Serena Williams does not reflect the women's dominance and celebrity. The tennis stars receive fewer endorsements than many other tennis players, particularly their blonde (and blue- and green-eyed) counterparts. Their dark and muscular appearances stand in stark contrast to Western notions of beauty and femininity, which have changed little since the Middle Ages. Ironically, when female athletes of color *are* complimented for deploying their physiques and strength, commentators often cite their "natural" or "inherent" ability. These compliments suggest that their race, as opposed to their knowledge of the game and work ethic, are responsible for their success.

> I was shocked. I couldn't believe it. It threw me off. I shouldn't have let it bother me because growing up in Compton, in Los Angeles, we had drive-by shootings, and I guess that's what my dad prepared me for, but I'm not going to stand for [racist behavior].   —Serena Williams

Serena and Venus Williams have devoted a great deal of time and energy to refuting negative stereotypes about African Americans and women, and they have fought to eradicate institutional inequities within professional tennis. Like Billie Jean King, who came before them, the Williams sisters were not content to work only as ambassadors for athletic excellence. They also revealed themselves to be crusaders for equality and justice. The icons long objected to the unequal prize money awarded to men and women at Wimbledon and the French Open. Despite decades of lobbying by tennis pioneer Billie Jean King and others, in 2005 the French Open and Wimbledon still refused to pay women's and men's players equally through all rounds. Venus Williams met with officials from both tournaments in 2005 to argue that female tennis players should be paid as much as males. Although WTA tour President Larry Scott listened to Williams's demands, he refused to reverse the policy. The turning point for female tennis players came on the eve of the 2006 Wimbledon championship, when Venus Williams published an essay in *The New Times*. Williams accused Wimbledon of standing on the "wrong side of history":

> I [would] like to convey to women and girls across the globe that there is no glass ceiling. My fear is that Wimbledon is loudly and clearly sending the opposite message.... Wimbledon has argued that ... they [men] work harder for their prize money.... In the eyes of the general public the men's and women's games have the same value.... I intend to keep doing everything I can until Billie Jean's original dream of equality is made real. It's a shame that the name of the greatest tournament in tennis, an event that should be a positive symbol for the sport, is tarnished. (Williams, "Wimbledon Has Sent Me a Message," June 26, 2006)

Many listened to Williams's comments. British Prime Minister Tony Blair and members of Parliament publicly endorsed Williams's arguments. Later that year, the Women's Tennis Association and UNESCO teamed for a campaign to promote gender equality in sports, asking Williams to lead the campaign.

Efforts to secure gender equality in tennis, led by Venus Williams, produced change. Under enormous pressure, Wimbledon announced in February 2007 that it would award equal prize money to all competitors in all rounds. The French Open followed suit a day later. In the aftermath, French Tennis Federation president Christian Bimes admitted he was "particularly sensitive" to Williams's remarks. The athlete ultimately became the first woman to benefit from the equalization of prize money at Wimbledon by winning the 2007 tournament. Wimbledon awarded her the same amount as the male winner. After winning her second round match at Wimbledon in 2007, Williams responded to critics' claims that she was the sixth most likely woman to win Wimbledon. She explained that it was okay, because, if she were to have listened to critics, she never would have made it out off Compton to make it to the posh Palm Beach Gardens area of Miami, Florida.

Venus and Serena Williams diversified their professional endeavors, and made their mark in business, interior design, and the world of fashion. Venus Williams is a businesswoman and Chief Executive Officer of interior design firm V Starr Interiors, located in Jupiter, Florida. Her company garnered prominence by designing the set of the "Tavis Smiley Show" on PBS, the Olympic athletes' apartments as a part of the U.S. bid package for New York to host the 2012 Games, and the interiors for residences and businesses in the Palm Beach area. In 2007, she partnered with retailer Steve & Barry's to launch her own fashion line, EleVen. Her business success, coupled with her athletic victories, make her a force in multiple fields. It is not surprise that the *Ladies Home Journal* named her one of the 30 most powerful women in America.

For her part, Serena Williams also established herself as an icon. She too transcended the success and notoriety of the sports world to garner fame and power in business and fashion. Williams is well known for her distinct, color-ful outfits, on and off the court. In 2002, she created an on-court stir when she wore what appeared to be a leather cat suit at the U.S. Open. She again stunned onlookers at the 2004 U.S. Open when she wore a denim skirt and boots. She soon developed her own special line of shoes and clothing with athletic apparel giant Puma. Currently she has her own brand with Nike.

The Williams sisters also made their presence known through entertainment. Serena Williams became the center of attention and reached a new level of exposure at the London premiere of Pierce Brosnan's new film, *After the Sunset*, in November, 2004. She wore a candy apple red dress with sheer fabric over her breasts that created a near-topless effect at the gala. The younger icon also oversees the production of her own line of designer clothing called Aneres (her first name spelled backwards), which she plans to sell in boutiques in Miami and Los Angeles. In 2001, the sisters appeared on *The Simpsons*. Serena Williams also posed for a *Sports Illustrated* swimsuit issue, and has a lucrative career in advertisements. MTV announced, in April 2005, plans to broadcast a reality show around the lives of the sisters, but the show was ultimately aired on ABC Family. Serena Williams appeared on a number of television sitcoms, including *My Wife and Kids*, *ER*, and *Law & Order: Special Victims Unit*.

Despite their inevitable rivalry and busy schedules, the Williams sisters remain close friends. Raised as devout Jehovah's Witnesses, both were home-schooled by their mother and earned their high school diplomas. The athletes are also graduates of the Art Institute of Florida, where they studied fashion design. Their love for tennis and their competitive spirit brought the sisters closer together rather than driving them apart. When Venus Williams won her first Wimbledon grand slam in 2000 against Lindsay Davenport, the sisters sat up until 2:00 a.m. celebrating, and then went on to win the women's doubles the next day. Their affection for each other has also contributed to allegations of match fixing against their high-profile, image-conscious father; critics accused Richard Williams of orchestrating his daughters' careers to maximise their collective financial potential and titles. This accusation has never been substantiated.

Such intense scrutiny by critics, combined with the sisters' struggles against racism and sexism, do not cause them as much pain as witnessing the losses and disappointments of their own family. The violent murder of their sister Yetunde, and the sadness they feel when they witness one another's professional tennis losses, are in some ways more taxing than attacks they face from those outside their family. For example, when Venus Williams won the Wimbledon title for the second time in 2001, and returned during the same season to defend her U.S. Open title in a historic sibling showdown, her victory was bittersweet. She explained her mixed feelings regarding the title win as follows:

> I don't feel like I've won. I just hate to see Serena lose, even against me. I'm the big sister. I make sure she has everything, even if I don't have anything. I love her and it's hard.

By 2007, although still experienced and intimidating players on the circuit, the siblings seem to be slowing down. Their father suggested that the icons were losing interest in the sport. Despite this, Serena Williams secured her third Australian Open singles title and her eighth Grand Slam singles title in 2007. For her part, Venus Williams said of her last major win, "I knew my destiny was to be in the winner's circle." On the tennis court and beyond, Venus and Serena Williams emerged as towering championship athletes, adroit businesswomen, and international celebrities. They are truly African American icons of sports.

Matthew C. Whitaker
Arizona State University

FURTHER READING

Beard, Hilary, Venus Williams, and Serena Williams. *Venus and Serena: Serving from the Hip: 10 Rules for Living, Loving, and Winning*. Boston: Houghton Mifflin, 2005.

Donaldson, Madeline. *Venus and Serena Williams*. New York: First Avenue Editions, 2003.

Hodgkinson, Mark, "Serena 'Shocked' by More Racist Abuse." *Telegraph.co .uk* (March 4, 2007). http://www.telegraph.co.uk/sport/main.jhtml?view =DETAILS&grid=A1YourView&xml=/sport/2007/03/28/sthodg28.xml (accessed September 10, 2007).

"Little Sister, Big Hit: Williams Family Surprise—Serena Williams Wins the U.S. Open." *Sports Illustrated*, September 20, 1999.

"Party Crasher: Venus Williams Shakes Up Tennis." *Sports Illustrated*, September 15, 1997.

Schafer, A. R. *Serena and Venus Williams*. Kentwood, LA: Edge Books, 2002.

"Serena Williams—Awesome: The Next Target the French Open." *Sports Illustrated*, May 28, 2003.

Williams, Venus. "Wimbledon Has Sent Me a Message: I'm Only a Second-Class Champion." *New York Times*, June 26, 2006.

Oprah Winfrey (1954–)

On the opening of her $40 million school for girls in South Africa, one reporter summed Oprah Winfrey up as follows:

> The planet's most watched talk show host, one of America's most successful magazine publishers, a billionaire, an Oscar-nominated actor, the most important black philanthropist in the US and, according to several assessments, the most influential woman in the world. (Meldrum)

As an icon of black America, indeed, the entire United States, Winfrey is associated with some of the most dominant values and ideas in contemporary American popular culture. Among these, Winfrey represents a version of the American Dream narrative made famous in the rags-to-riches dime novels of nineteenth-century Unitarian minister and writer, Horatio Alger. The American Dream, according to Alger's formulation, is available to anyone, no matter how disadvantaged or powerless, no matter how modest one's origins. If one perseveres, if one always does right and does one's best, then, through honesty, hard work, and determination, one can overcome any obstacles along the way and triumph to build one's own American Dream against the odds. Winfrey's personal legend, constructed and retold over the course of her long career, is a contemporary Horatio Alger progress narrative, or bootstraps myth, of upward transformation from humble beginnings against difficult odds, to extraordinary success through individual strength of mind and hard work.

The Queen of Talk TV was born in Kosciusko, Mississippi, the illegitimate child of Vernita Lee and Vernon Winfrey in 1954. When her mother migrated to Milwaukee, Winfrey was left in the care of her grandparents. Though uneducated herself, Winfrey's grandmother, a strict disciplinarian, taught her granddaughter to read the Bible and to write by the time she was three. As a very young girl, Winfrey performed recitations at Sunday school. At six, she left her grandparents' farm to live with her mother. Winfrey excelled in school, skipping ahead from kindergarten to first grade, and again from second to third grade. Shuttled back and forth between her mother in Milwaukee and her father in Nashville, at age nine Winfrey was raped by a 19-year-old cousin, and until age 14 close male relatives and family friends sexually abused her. The abuse ended when Winfrey's mother attempted to place her daughter, who had become an uncontrollable delinquent, in a juvenile detention home. Turned away because the home was full, Winfrey was sent, instead, to live permanently with her father in Nashville. There she gave birth to a premature son, who died not long after. Under her father's guidance, Winfrey became an honor student again. She graduated from East Nashville High School, with a scholarship for her speaking ability to attend East Tennessee State. While a 16-year-old senior in high school, Winfrey began her broadcasting career by reading the news at WVOL radio for $100 a week. So began Winfrey's rise to celebrity.

Winfrey's life story reflects the idea, highly valued in American culture and made famous by Alger's novels, that material success results from dogged individual determination. This theme of transformation is fundamental to any understanding of Winfrey as an American icon. With a wide array of public images, Winfrey embodies the protean nature of an icon. She is malleable and open to multiple interpretations. Winfrey's persistence and long-time success result from, and reflect, her adaptability. In fact, change is a major theme on *The Oprah Winfrey Show*, which has itself undergone major transformations from time to time. For example, in 1996 Winfrey restructured her show, moving away from the tell-all, knock-down-drag-out daytime talk format of competitors such as Jerry Springer. She sought to reinvent *The Oprah Winfrey Show*, which she frequently calls "change your life TV," so that it would be more inspirational. In keeping with this theme came "Oprah's Angel Network," Winfrey's national effort to encourage viewers to make charitable contributions and to do volunteer work. A 1997 episode of *The Oprah Winfrey Show* launched the Angel Network, which began as a call to donate spare change to scholarships given by the Boys and Girls Clubs of America. Prompting gifts of both money and time, Winfrey organized volunteers to build homes for Habitat for Humanity. By 2009, according to its Web site, the Angel Network had collected more than $80 million in public donations to support a variety of causes in the United States and across the globe, from hurricane recovery, to Indian Ocean tsunami relief, to building schools in rural China and Kwa-Zulu-Natal, South Africa. Oprah's Angel Network teamed up with Free the Children to launch O Ambassadors Clubs, a school-based program of instructional resources and extra-curricular activities that encourage students to learn about and to raise funds to address poverty, education, health, and sustainable development. Winfrey brought philanthropy to prime time in 2008 with *Oprah's Big Give*, an eight-episode reality series devoted to charitable giving. Hosted by Nate Berkus, the show provided funds to contestants, who were challenged to invent creative ways to grow their resources to dramatically affect a stranger's life within five days. In its first week, the show was second only to *American Idol*, but steadily lost viewership as its run continued.

Practicing what she preaches, Winfrey donates millions out of her own pocket each year to support her interests. While Oprah's Angel Network is supported through public donations, the Oprah Winfrey Foundation is funded entirely by Winfrey herself, who personally selects not-for-profit organizations for grants. Winfrey put $36 million into the fund in 2006. Reflecting her commitment to education and to African causes, a third foundation, The Oprah Winfrey Operating Foundation, gives exclusively to the Oprah Winfrey Leadership Academy for Girls in South Africa. Created at Nelson Mandela's request, the school opened in 2007. Its goal is to serve 450 students in grades 7 through 12. In its first year, the school was tainted by scandal after a dorm matron was charged with abusing students. Thirteen counts, including indecent assault and criminal injury were lodged against Tiny Virginia Makopo. Bringing to mind her own experience of childhood sexual abuse, Winfrey responded, "It has shaken me to my core." Casting the story, characteristically, as one of both personal trauma and inevitable triumph, Winfrey continued as follows:

> This has been one of the most devastating, if not the most devastating, experiences of my life [...]. As with all such experiences, there is always something to be gained, something to be learned. At the core of me is a belief that all things happen for a reason no matter the devastation, and this too shall pass. (Perry)

While Winfrey is sometimes criticized for giving overseas to support causes such as the Leadership Academy, her charitable donations fund causes in the United States as well, such as a 2008 contribution of $365,000 to the Ron Clark Academy in Atlanta, Georgia. Winfrey also supports Mississippi's Jackson State University, Morehouse College, and Spelman College. Winfrey's philanthropy is not limited to historically black institutions, however. In 2007, Fox News reported a $1 million donation to Miss Porter's School, a tony finishing school in Farmington Connecticut. Though Winfrey sent her nieces there, the racial makeup of the school remains mostly white, boasting Rockefellers, Vanderbilts, and Jacqueline Onassis Kennedy among its graduates. The Oprah Winfrey Leadership Academy for Girls is modeled on the elite education offered by Miss Porter's.

After restructuring, doing well by doing good—another Horatio Alger trademark—became an enduring theme on *The Oprah Winfrey Show*, woven into the program's fabric of entertainment, self-improvement, and social reform. Winfrey's celebrity thus combines with the ideologies of self-improvement and cultural uplift to promote the American ideal of upward transformation. Winfrey's message of change-your-life TV aligned in 2007 with another prominent African American change agent, then Senator **Barack Obama**. While Winfrey has hosted other political figures on her show, for the first time she endorsed a candidate for the U.S. presidency. Criticized for not voting in previous primaries, Winfrey joined Obama on the campaign trail, appearing at rallies in Iowa, New Hampshire, and South Carolina. Studying the strength of Winfrey's political influence, researchers at the University of Maryland later concluded that Winfrey's endorsement of Obama added one million votes during the primaries and caucuses. Another study of the democratic primary, conducted at the University of Wisconsin-Milwaukee, found that Winfrey's support lead participants to say that they would be more likely to vote for Obama and to see him as more likely to win the nomination. Winfrey's endorsement for Obama, however, may have come with a cost. Along with a decline in circulation of *O, The Oprah Magazine*, *The New York Times* reported in 2008 that ratings for *The Oprah Winfrey Show* had slipped for the third year in a row, this time because Winfrey had alienated some of her audience of mostly white, middle-aged women, many of whom supported Hillary Clinton. Winfrey's support for Obama, however, fit with her own image and interests. As *The New York Times* observed:

Certainly, on a meta-level, there is a harmony between Ms. Winfrey and Mr. Obama, both in outlook and promise. They both speak of the politics of hope. They speak of change and spiritual renewal. Ms. Winfrey's philosophy carries the promise of self-improvement, and her endorsement, by extension, could carry the promise of nation-improvement. (Seelye)

From the Greek word for "image," an *icon* has, as its core, a visual representation, and media images of Winfrey reflect the American ideology of rags-to-riches-and-recognition. For example, in 1997, Winfrey appeared on the cover of *LIFE* magazine. In a smart red suit, she smiles broadly, looking directly at readers, holding an antique leather-bound volume with pages edged in gold. The title announces, "The secret INNER LIFE of America's most powerful woman: OPRAH Between the Covers." Like so many other accounts of Winfrey's life, this one expands the legend of this American icon. The article's title presents the major themes of her Cinderella fairy tale: secrets, intimacy, power, and education.

Turning to the story inside, however, one is confronted with a very different figure from the confident, relaxed, happy, and successful adult Winfrey on the cover. Filling the entire left-hand page is a stark black and white kindergarten class photo of Winfrey, grim-faced, staring blankly at the camera. Opposite, against a black background, is a quotation from her interview with *LIFE*. Winfrey's words offer a personal revelation, perhaps the single most distinguishing feature in the creation of this African American icon, and the hallmark of *The Oprah Winfrey Show*: "No one ever told me I was loved. Ever, ever, ever. Reading and being able to be a *smart girl* was my only sense of value, and it was the only time I felt loved" (Johnson, 45). The *LIFE* article illustrates that, in a sense, Oprah is herself a book. Put another way, her life is a carefully crafted story. Her progress narrative is told and retold in popular newspaper and magazine articles, television shows such as Winfrey's *Arts and Entertainment Biography*, and biographies such as Norman King's *Everybody Loves Oprah! Her Remarkable Life Story* and Nellie Bly's *Oprah! Up Close and Down Home*. As Winfrey has gradually revealed her life story on her show and in the popular media, fans have learned, over time, how education and hard work have led to her enormous fame and fortune.

As a poor African American girl growing up in the South during the civil rights era, among the obstacles Winfrey faced were her race and gender. At 19, she became the youngest person and the first African American woman to anchor the news at Nashville's WTVF-TV. As the first black billionaire in the United States and the first African American woman to join the *Forbes Magazine* list of the world's richest people, Oprah symbolizes the possibility of overcoming the double jeopardy of being black and female in a country whose history is plagued by discrimination against both. With rankings based on both earnings and fame, in 2008, Oprah Winfrey topped **Tiger Woods** as number one on the *Forbes* list of 100 most powerful celebrities. Winfrey is associated not only with Horatio Alger's theme of triumph over adversity, but also with the prevailing concerns in the United States of racial and gender equality. Winfrey's life story is extraordinary, both for the proliferation of obstacles set against her and for her soaring achievement. For some, such a story provokes hope and optimism. At the same time, this American icon, like others, simultaneously incites the opposite reaction. Winfrey may also be seen as a potentially detrimental stereotype of African American women as invulnerable, indefatigable, persevering, and enduring against great odds without negative consequences. The American myth of the tough, strong black woman, able to withstand any abuse and conquer any obstacle, sets an impossible standard that may lead ordinary women to take on overwhelming responsibilities, to ignore the physical and emotional costs, never seeking or receiving assistance.

Winfrey also represents media imperialism and commercial domination, communicating widely, not only across the United States, but also across the globe. She is mistress of all she surveys. Host of the highest-rated talk show in television history, with an estimated 49 million viewers each week in the United States, and broadcast internationally in 117 countries, Winfrey also established and owns its production company, Harpo Studios. She is creator of *Dr. Phil*, the successful spin-off of *The Oprah Winfrey Show*, and co-founder of the cable television network Oxygen Media. Winfrey's media empire has continued to grow with the creation of OWN: The Oprah Winfrey Network, a cable channel created in collaboration with Discovery Communications. Winfrey's dominion extends to film, as both actor and producer, with her best-known role as Sofia in Steven Spielberg's 1985 *The Color Purple*, for which she received an Academy Award nomination. As founder and editorial director of *O, The Oprah Magazine*, Winfrey is a major player in print media. According to her Web site, Winfrey's electronic presence is also vast, with Oprah.com averaging 96 million page views and 6.7 million unique visitors per month. The site receives an average of 20,000 e-mails each week. As the most important celebrity entrepreneur of our time, communicating extensively and marketing her fame in diverse media, Oprah stands for the American regard for the power and influence of the individual.

Herein lies a paradox in the iconography of Oprah Winfrey. On the one hand, her global influence via nearly every available medium is unparalleled. On the other, Winfrey simultaneously represents the ordinary, constructing the impression, highly valued in American culture, of "just folks." Winfrey is at once a larger-than-life celebrity and a regular gal. Anyone who has struggled to lose weight can relate to the Oprah who, in 1988, pulled a little red wagon filled with 67 pounds of fat onto the stage of her talk show and proudly showed off her size-10 Calvin Klein jeans. In 2009, after gaining 40 pounds, Winfrey said, "I'm mad at myself. I'm embarrassed. I can't believe that after all these years, I'm still talking about my weight." She continued, "When it comes to maintaining my health, I didn't just fall off the wagon. I let the wagon fall on me." By framing her acknowledgement in terms of her trademark personal revelation—another Oprah moment of truth—Winfrey highlights her moral authority: "It's all about telling the truth. I just believe that you're always better off if you just come clean" ("Oprah Reveals the Truth"). Sharing her struggle with her weight, yet again, reinforces Winfrey's bond with viewers. Just as she has done since the early days of her show, Winfrey reveals her personal traumas and tribulations, coaxing celebrity guests of her show and ordinary people alike to do the same. As a result, regular folk identify with Winfrey. This identification was illustrated, for instance, when Winfrey proclaimed, "Free speech not only lives, it rocks," after jurors rejected a multimillion-dollar defamation lawsuit by Texas cattlemen, prompted by Winfrey's caution during an episode of her show against the threat of mad cow disease ("Oprah: 'Free Speech Rocks' "). To critics, the accusation that Winfrey's remarks led to a cattle market plunge that caused $11 million in loses underscores the danger of placing too much power and influence with the individual, who may use that authority irresponsibly. For fans, Winfrey's story is emblematic of the American desire to see the little girl or guy triumph, David-over-Goliath fashion.

Likewise, in 2005, Winfrey reminded the world of the paradox of her celebrity—ordinariness. Thanks to rapid-fire, round-the-world Internet news and Web logs, the story of Oprah snubbed by upscale Paris boutique, Hermes, rose immediately to the status of myth, with multiple contradictory versions quickly circling the globe. This incident draws attention to the fact that Winfrey is not "just folks," attempting to dash into the Hermes shop on Faubourg Saint-Honore, a street lined with famous designer shops frequented by wealthy tourists and the well-to-do. At the same time, the story reminds us of the possibility that any African American may find herself similarly unwelcome in a tony boutique. The Hermes fracas brings to mind early episodes of *The Oprah Winfrey Show*, long before her online Oprah Boutique, with its exclusive Oprah's Book Club Pajamas for $64, in which Winfrey tackled the Ku Klux Klan or traveled to Forsyth County, Georgia, to ask local citizens why, for more than 75 years, they refused to allow a black person to live in the county. Winfrey's studio confirmed a version of the story that suggests a racist motive for barring her entrance. Harpo Productions compared Winfrey's experience to the film *Crash*, which explores racial intolerance in Los Angeles, tracking the heated intersections of a multi-ethnic cast of characters. Whatever the facts of the Hermes rebuff, anyone who has experienced racial hostility may connect with Winfrey's plight, an ordinary, everyday experience for many Americans.

By contrast, other versions of the Hermes incident cast Winfrey as an arrogant, wild-spending celebrity diva, rudely insisting on entrance even though Hermes had closed for the evening. While fans may view Oprah as a successful American capitalist, who, through hard work, has earned the privilege to spend without guilt, to critics, Winfrey's yearly "Oprah's Favorite Things" list of high-end products such as $312 hand-painted tea service, or a $465 Burberry quilted jacket, reflects and promotes the message that buying more and more brings happiness. A product endorsement by a celebrity of Oprah's status creates demand where no genuine need exists. To critics, such conspicuous consumption leads to global conformity and social alienation. It also has a detrimental effect on the environment and the world's poor.

Essential to Oprah as icon are multiple and contradictory interpretations such as these. To fans, Oprah is a sacred cow. But the very status of icon invites both adoration and satire. Artist Bruce Cegur illustrates both points of view in his digital print of Oprah as religious icon. One image, "The Crucifixion," shows Winfrey as a glowing Aunt Jemima figure hanging on a cross of steer horns. Cegur's image, he offers, may be interpreted both negatively and positively, as a symbol of spiritual power, community leadership, an African American woman's strength and authority. Superimposed over this figure is a wider, glowing female form, which pokes fun at Winfrey's weight-loss struggles. At the same time, Cegur suggests that this image may also represent the struggle faced by black women for respect and recognition. Beneath this figure is one the artist titles "The Last Supper," a stylized version of Leonardo Da Vinci's famous painting, lampooning Oprah, seated center, in the place of Christ, surrounded by Book Club guests and other famous women television talk show hosts. The label above reads, simply, "SYRUP," which reminds us that critics view Winfrey as a gifted actor, master of the con, and trafficker in base sentimentality and empty psychobabble.

However we interpret Winfrey as icon, she has perhaps influenced American popular culture most by making the personal public, by sharing the private details of her life, and, at the same time, persuading her guests to do likewise. As she has risen in popularity, Winfrey has disclosed more and more details of her life, more and more secrets. These details stress her extraordinary success against daunting barriers, while they emphasize her human frailty. As a result, viewers of *The Oprah Winfrey Show* may feel that Oprah is both television's richest entertainer and also "just like me." A 1986 *Woman's Day* article quotes Winfrey as saying, "People out there think I'm their girlfriend; they treat me like that. It's really amazing" (Tornabene, 50). Likewise, popular biographies of Winfrey promulgate her reputation for intimacy. Bly quotes the *Washington Post*'s characterization of Winfrey's distinctive style among talk show hosts: "If Jane Pauley is the prom queen, Oprah Winfrey is the dorm counselor [...]. People want to hold Barbara Walters's hand. They want to crawl into Winfrey's lap" (52). Readers of Winfrey's biographies know, for example, the "inside" story behind the public story of Winfrey's weight loss battle. They know not only the Winfrey who dragged a load of fat across stage, but also the Winfrey who secretly binged on a package of hotdog buns bathed in syrup. This imagined intimacy is the hallmark of Winfrey's career. On her show, Winfrey enters the personal space of guests, touches them, sustains lingering eye contact, and appears to listen carefully when they speak. Such behaviors establish a sense of sympathy and sociability between Winfrey and her guests and viewers. Viewers invite Winfrey into their homes—their own private spaces—and in return she brings them the private lives, not only of her guests, but also of herself. In short, Winfrey uses intimacy strategically to attract and maintain audience interest and loyalty. Telling a secret about oneself, as Winfrey sometimes does, breeds affection and loyalty because such a revelation both reflects and engenders trust. Not only do viewers feel they can trust Winfrey because of the intimacy she constructs, but they may also feel flattered, in a sense, and therefore closer to her, because she trusts them with the details of her personal life.

In this way, *The Oprah Winfrey Show* challenges notions of what "counts" as evidence in public debates and gives voice to women whose sentiments, interests, and concerns might otherwise go ignored. Winfrey's message of individual empowerment resonates strongly with her mostly female audience. This message is one that led popular culture critic, Steven Stark, to compare Winfrey to Mr. Rogers. While acknowledging that "the mission is to sell us something, which is the goal of all commercial television: 'I buy; therefore, I am' is the theology of most TV," Stark calls Winfrey "another rather old fashioned TV performer when you think about it, who, while not formally trained in religion, has turned her show into a similar kind of uplifting ministry of empowerment, in her case, for women rather than children." While critics deride Winfrey's brand of therapeutic talk TV as treacle, the force of that sensibility is illustrated in the vehement responses to a 2000 article in the *Washington Post*. In the "Style" section, well known for its sardonic wit, staff writer Libby Copland offers a mocking critique of *The Oprah Winfrey Show* in "Our Lady of Perpetual Help: In the Church of Feel-Good Pop Psychology, Spiritual Rebirth Means Starting at O." Indeed, as an American icon, Winfrey has become an image with sacred significance. In this case, Winfrey is depicted as a satirical religious icon, with flowing white robes, a star-topped staff in hand, a twinkling halo about her head. Winfrey is the Goddess of New Age spiritualism, which takes individual empowerment as its central tenet. Surrounding "Our Lady" in monks' robes are four self-help "experts" who once frequented her show. Gary Zukav, Dr. Phil, Suze Orman, and Iyanla Vanzant appeared regularly to offer strategies for changing one's life for the better.

One week after Copeland's "Our Lady" critique of Winfrey, three letters defending Winfrey's aim to improve both the lives of individual viewers and the communities in which they live appeared in the Op-ed section of the *Post*. One fiery response takes Copeland's "sarcastic Oprah-bashing" to task for ignoring Winfrey's good works—and her ability to inspire generosity among viewers. Kathleen Summers writes, "Your June 26 Style article charges her television show with encouraging self-absorption and simplistic guruism but conveniently leaves out a major theme of the Oprah show: charitable giving and volunteerism" (A23). As Copeland's piece and the responses to it demonstrate—and as the long-time popularity of *The Oprah Winfrey Show* illustrates—there is a significant place for the sensibility Winfrey advocates on her show. She speaks to the desire for hope, optimism, and the power of positive thinking to improve one's life, fundamental values in American culture. Winfrey's optimism, of course, is viewed by some as naïve and self-aggrandizing, but the history and power of its appeal are essential to understanding twenty-first-century American popular culture and Oprah Winfrey as a representative icon.

R. Mark Hall
University of North Carolina at Charlotte

FURTHER READING

Bly, Nellie. *Oprah! Up Close and Down Home.* New York: Kensington, 1993.

Johnson, Marilyn. "Oprah Winfrey: A Life in Books." *LIFE* (September 1997): 45–60.

King, Norman. *Everybody Loves Oprah: Her Remarkable Life Story.* New York: William Morrow, 1987.

Meldrum, Andrew. " 'Their Story Is My Story': Oprah Opens $40m School for South African Girls." *Guardian.co.uk*, January 3, 2007. http://www.guardian.co.uk/media/2007 /jan/03/broadcasting.schoolsworldwide (accessed April 25, 2009).

Miller, Matthew, ed. "The Celebrity 100." *Forbes.com*, June 11, 2008. http://www.forbes.com/2008/06/11/most-powerful-celebrities-lists-celebrities08-cx_mn_0611c_land.html (accessed April 1, 2009).

"Oprah: 'Free Speech Rocks': Texas Cattlemen Lose Defamation Suit." *CNN.com*, February 26, 1998. http://www.cnn.com/US/9802/26/oprah.verdict/ (accessed April 15, 2009).

Pease, Andrew, and Paul R. Brewer. "The Oprah Factor: The Effects of a Celebrity Endorsement in a Presidential Primary Campaign." *International Journal of Press/Politics* 13, no. 4 (2008): 386–400.

Perry, Alex. "Oprah Scandal Rocks South Africa." *Time.com*, November 5, 2007. http://www.time.com/time/world/article/0,8599,1680715,00.html (accessed April 1, 2009).

Stevie Wonder (1950–)

Stevie Wonder was born Stevland Hardaway Judkins on May 13, 1950, in Saginaw, Michigan. He is one of the finest musicians, songwriters, and producers of the Rock and Roll era. Wonder began his career as a child prodigy on the fledgling Detroit-based label, **Motown Records**. Wonder's rise to the top of the charts paralleled Motown's ascendency to a preeminent place in American culture. In the 1970s, Wonder branched out, becoming one of the first artists on the Motown label to record full length albums. Both aesthetically pleasing and socially conscious, Wonder's "classic" albums displayed his exuberant, soulful voice, his virtuosic keyboard and harmonica playing, and his keen skills as a songwriter and producer. Wonder's string of albums in the 1970s garnered widespread critical acclaim while appealing to a wide range of listeners. He became the first artist to win the Grammy for Album of the Year on three occasions: 1973 for *Innervisions*, 1974 for *Fulfillingness' First Finale*, and in 1976 for *Songs in the Key of Life*. Over the course of his career, Stevie Wonder has sold 100 million albums. He has worked as an activist against poverty, hunger, and racism throughout the world. Stevie Wonder is one of the most beloved figures in the history of American popular music.

Stevland Hardaway Judkins was born in the manufacturing and lumbering center of Saginaw, Michigan, to Calvin Judkins and Lula Mae Morrris Hardaway Judkins. Calvin Judkins bounced from job to job, spending much of his time as a street hustler. Judkins's inability to provide for his six children forced his wife to earn money in any way she could, including prostitution. The struggles of the Judkins family worsened when Wonder, their third child, went blind as a baby. Wonder was born prematurely. While in an incubator, doctors discovered that his retinas never attached to a connective blood vessel inside his eyes, rendering him blind for life. Wonder's blindness proved a serious strain on his mother. Lula Hardaway Judkins was an intensely religious woman. She brought her blind son to a series of faith healers, including Oral Roberts.

Lula Morris Hardaway walked out on her abusive, hard-drinking husband when Wonder was four years old. She moved her six children south to Detroit, and changed their last name to Morris, her father's last name. Wonder and his siblings were forced to fend for themselves while their mother worked a full-time job. To pass the time, the blind Wonder listened to the radio constantly. He took up the harmonica at age five and the piano at age seven. He also began singing in the church choir as a young child.

Fortune smiled upon Wonder at age 11. A cousin of The Miracles' Ronnie White heard Wonder fooling around with some friends on a street corner in Detroit's Black Bottom neighborhood. White's cousin immediately told the Motown star of the exuberantly singing and harmonica-playing child he had heard that day. Ronnie White found Wonder, and set up a meeting for the boy and his mother with Motown Records' founder Berry Gordy. Gordy signed the boy and put him to work with producer Mickey Stevenson, who nicknamed him "Stevie Wonder." Gordy added "Little" to the moniker to emphasize the child prodigy aspect of his talent.

Gordy rushed his new signee into their Hitsville U.S.A. studio on West Grand Boulevard in Detroit. Wonder recorded the effervescent single "I Call it Pretty Music, But the Old People Call it the Blues," which made little headway on the charts. He recorded his first full-length album in spring 1962, *The Jazz Soul of Stevie Wonder*. Wonder co-wrote two of the album's 10 tracks with Motown tunesmiths Henry Cosby and Clarence Paul. Later that year, Wonder recorded *A Tribute to Uncle Ray*, an album of covers of fellow blind musician and friend **Ray Charles**'s songs. Neither full length album garnered much popular interest.

Wonder's first major hit came from a live recording of "Fingertips," a song from his first album, at a Motor Town Revue (a traveling concert series consisting of Motown artists) in 1963. "Fingertips Part 2," as the hit single was titled, featured Wonder's exuberant harmonica playing. The single reached number one on the pop charts in the summer of 1963. Wonder's third album, *Recorded Live: The 12 Year Old Genius*, included the hit single, and reached number one on the pop album charts. He followed up the success of the album with several minor hits in 1963 and 1964.

The teenaged star took time off from recording in the mid 1960s to study at the Michigan School for the Blind. Dropping "Little" from his name, Wonder returned to the studio and recorded the dynamic, danceable top five hit "Uptight (Everything's Alright)." The single featured boisterous horns, thundering drums, and an adult-sounding Wonder belting out some of the most ebullient, heartfelt vocals in the history of soul music. In 1966, he made his first foray into socially conscious music, recording a top 10 hit version of Bob Dylan's "Blowin' in the Wind." Gordy steered the young singer away from such songs. He wanted Motown to stay above the fray politically in the increasingly tumultuous 1960s. Wonder thought this position untenable. Like his friend **Marvin Gaye**, he sought out greater autonomy from the Motown family's direct oversight of his career.

Sixteen-year-old Stevie Wonder co-wrote (with his mother, among others) his next major hit, "I Was Made To Love Her," in 1967. Wonder sings with evangelical fervor on the love song, displaying remarkable maturity for an adolescent. Around this time, Wonder helped write the Miracles' iconic single "Tears of a Clown," a number one hit single and arguably their best known song. Wonder followed up the success of "I Was Made to Love Her" with his exuberant, up-tempo version of "For Once in My Life," (1968) a song recorded as a ballad by The Temptations a year earlier. Gordy disliked Wonder's version of the song, but other Motown executives convinced him to release it as a single. "For Once in My Life" stormed up the charts in late 1968, reaching number two behind label mate Marvin Gaye's "I Heard It Through the Grapevine." The ballad "My Cherie Amour" scored Wonder another top five hit in 1969. "Yester-Me, Yester-You, Yesterday" and "Heaven Help Us All" also reached the top 10 in 1969. In 1970, Wonder reached number two on the charts with the soul masterpiece, "Signed, Sealed, Delivered," a song that pointed toward his move toward funk in the 1970s.

In the midst of Wonder's titanic success as a singles artist in the late 1960s, he released an ambitious instrumental album on which he played harmonica, drums, and keyboards. Gordy, recognizing the album's lack of potential commercial appeal, agreed to release it only if it were placed under a pseudonym. *Eivets Rednow* (1968), which is "Stevie Wonder" backwards, sold poorly but provided Wonder with the artistic freedom he had desired for years. In the 1970s, Wonder used the money he received from his trust fund (his 1960s earnings were held in trust until his 21st birthday in 1971) to purchase his own studio, form his own music publisher, Black Bull Music, and record independently of the Motown infrastructure, though he resigned to the label in 1971 at a significantly higher royalty rate than his peers at Motown. Wonder's friend Marvin Gaye, who battled Motown for more control over the direction of his career and content of his music, inspired the young performer to drive a hard bargain with the label and pursue his own musical vision. Gaye's classic album *What's Going On* (1971) moved away from Motown's singles-only aesthetic in favor of the full length LP as a form of artistic expression. Simultaneously political and emotive, *What's Going On?* inspired Wonder to pursue a similar aesthetic in his subsequent recordings.

At the age of 20, Wonder married soul singer and songwriter Syreeta Wright. Wright first worked at Motown as a secretary before scoring a record deal after an audition with the label's famed Holland-Dozier-Holland songwriting team. Wright was four years Wonder's senior. She recorded a pair of superb albums under his tutelage, *Syreeta* (1972) and *Stevie Wonder Presents: Syreeta* (1974). Wright sparked Wonder's lifelong interests in African literature and spirituality as well as an interest in Eastern philosophy. Unfortunately, Wonder's desire for Wright to take on traditional domestic roles clashed with her desire to retain her personal independence. Their marriage ended in divorce less than 18 months after it began.

Wonder recorded the first of his five "classic" 1970s albums, *Music of My Mind*, in late 1971 and early 1972. *Music of My Mind* displayed Wonder's multiple talents as a performer. He composed the songs, produced the album, and played virtually every instrument on the album. Though *Music of My Mind* only reached number 21 on the Billboard pop album charts, it received widespread critical acclaim. The album features early synthesizer work, but electronic sounds never dominate actual instruments on the cohesive recording. The ethereal "Superwoman (Where Were You When I Needed You)," the funky ballad "I Love Every Little Thing About You," and the sweet "Happier Than the Morning Sun" are among the album's standout tunes.

Talking Book (1972), the follow-up to *Music of My Mind*, garnered Wonder further critical acclaim while proving more commercially successful. The album combined social/political commentary, tender love songs, and several funk classics which were capable of rousing even the most staid people to get out on the dance floor. The number one single "Superstition" features some of Wonder's funkiest keyboard work, most clever lyrics, and most exuberant vocals. "You Are The Sunshine of My Life," which also topped the pop charts, is an achingly beautiful ballad that displays the intense pathos in Wonder's voice. *Talking Book* reached number three on the pop albums chart and earned Wonder his first Grammys. "Superstition" won the Grammys for Best R&B Song and Best Male R&B Vocal Performance. "You are the Sunshine of My Life" won the Grammy for Best Male Pop Vocal Performance.

Innervisions (1973) delved further into many of the social issues he addressed in *Talking Book*. "Too High" delves into the dangers of drug use and its impact on the quality of life in urban areas. "Higher Ground" is a funky philippic against urban poverty, the war in Vietnam, political corruption, and racism. The song reached number four on the pop charts. "Living for the City" tells the tragic story of a black Southerner who migrated north to seek out better opportunities, but is faced with the perils of urban poverty, violence, and a degrading working life. The song earned him his second straight Grammy for Best R&B Song. "He's a Misstra Know-It-All" lampooned President Nixon. *Innervisions* is a simultaneously ambitious and sonically arresting recording. It shows the young performer's simultaneous outrage at the state of the nation and earnest desire to build a new America upon the principles of love and community. It produced several top 20 hits and earned Wonder the Grammy for Album of the Year, making him the first Motown artist to win that award.

Shortly after the release of *Innervisions*, Wonder was critically injured in an automobile accident in rural North Carolina. While on tour in August 1973, a log that fell off a truck smashed through the front windshield of the tour van. Wonder, who was seated in the front passenger seat, was hit by the log, which put him in a coma for four days. After several months of rest and recuperation, Wonder returned to the stage for a March 1974 comeback show at Madison Square Garden.

In July 1974, Wonder released *Fulfillingness' First Finale*, which focused more on the sensual than the political. Again, Wonder played virtually every instrument on the recording (he received some fine background vocals from the Jackson 5 and Deniece Williams, though). The lovely "Too Shy to Say" and "They Won't Know When I Go" deal in the mysteries of love and loss. The hit single "Boogie On, Reggae Woman" is a catchy, Caribbean flavored novelty song. The chart topping "You Haven't Done Nothin" takes on Richard Nixon again, indicting him for war crimes and apathy toward the poor. *Fulfillingness' First Finale* topped the pop album charts and earned Wonder five Grammys, including the award for Best Male R&B Vocal Performance and Best Male Pop Vocal Performance. Wonder also won his second Grammy for Album of the Year. The following year, Album of the Year winner Paul Simon (*Still Crazy After All These Years*) thanked Wonder in his acceptance speech for not releasing an album in 1975.

The double-album *Songs in the Key of Life* (1976) arrived in record stores more than two years after *Fulfillingness' First Finale*. Many fans consider *Songs in the Key of Life* Wonder's definitive statement as an artist. Wonder spent countless hours in the studio perfecting the album. Initially slated for a fall 1975 release, the album came out in September 1976. It quickly took the top spot on the album charts, where it spent 14 weeks, then went on to go platinum 10 times over. *Songs in the Key of Life* opens with the gorgeous "Love In Need of Love Today," a triumphant suite which implored listeners to seek out love instead of hate. Wonder performed the song on the 2001 *America: A Tribute to Heroes* telethon following the September 11th attacks. The funky "Have a Talk with God" has become a staple of many contemporary Christian musicians' repertoires. "Isn't She Lovely," a song Wonder wrote about his newborn daughter Aisha (Yolanda Simmons, Wonder's girlfriend at the time, is the mother of the child), has been covered by numerous artists. The joyful song is considered a contemporary American standard. The funky, autobiographical "I Wish" reached number one on the pop singles chart. The album's other chart topper, "Sir Duke," was Wonder's homage to the recently-departed jazz legend Duke Ellington. *Songs in the Key of Life* navigates the range of human emotions as well as any album ever recorded. Wonder won his third Grammy for Album of the Year for the masterful recording.

Following the release of *Songs in the Key of Life*, Wonder took a hiatus from recording. He spent a great deal of time with his young family. Wonder studied African history and literature. He promoted antipoverty efforts in Africa. In 1979, Wonder released the predominately instrumental, synthesizer-laden soundtrack to the documentary *The Secret Life of Plants*. The album sold well, though not nearly as well as his single-filled 1970s albums. A year later, Wonder released *Hotter Than July* (1980) which re-established him as a major pop star. The reggae-esque "Master Blaster (Jammin')" reached number five on the pop charts. The album includes lovely ballads "Lately" and "Did I Hear You Say You Love Me" as well as the impassioned "Happy Birthday," a tribute to **Martin Luther King, Jr.** and a call to establish King's birthday as a national holiday. Wonder followed up on the success of *Hotter Than July* with a 1982 duet with Paul McCartney, "Ebony and Ivory." The duet with the former Beatle called for racial harmony between blacks and whites. Though panned by many critics as a facile, sentimental take on complex social issues, the song resonated with audiences, reaching number one on the Billboard pop singles charts and remaining there for seven weeks.

Wonder faced the wrath of critics and an enthusiastic response from fans again in 1983 with his number one hit single "I Just Called to Say I Love You," a song which appeared on the soundtrack to the Gene Wilder film *The Woman in Red*. The song featured a 1980s style drum machine and a straightforward synthesizer hook. Wonder received an Academy Award for Best Original Song for "I Just Called to Say I Love You." Critics decried Wonder's apparent move away from a more "authentic" soul in favor of a less nuanced pop sound. Wonder stated that he was not making a conscious move away from soul music. He was simply recording the music which came to him at the time. Moreover, Wonder was one of the first mainstream artists to embrace the synthesizer in the early 1970s. The fact that he incorporated more modern synthesizers into his music in the mid-1980s should not have been a surprise.

In the mid-1980s, Wonder took part in a series of all-star charity events aimed at merging activism and artistry. Wonder joined the Ethiopian famine relief super group USA for Africa, which was organized by Quincy Jones, Michael Jackson, and British rocker Bob Geldof. Jones arranged and produced the group's epic single "We are the World," which featured a brief duet between Wonder and Lionel Richie. "We are the World" skyrocketed to number one in both the United States and Great Britain in Spring 1985, helping to raise nearly $100 million for famine relief in Ethiopia. Later that year, Wonder participated in the recording of "That's What Friends Are For," a charity single recorded by the American Foundation for AIDS Research. "That's What Friends Are For" featured Elton John, Dionne Warwick, and Gladys Knight, among others. The single reached number one on the pop charts in January 1986, raising tens of millions of dollars for AIDS research.

During the late 1980s and 1990s, Wonder released albums at an increasingly infrequent pace. In 1987, he released the album *Characters*, a foray into smooth jazz. Audiences did not respond to the album as enthusiastically as many of his earlier releases. *Characters* peaked at number 17 on the album charts. Only one of the singles, "Skeletons," reached the top 20. Critics continue to bemoan the artist's move away from the kind of soul music he recorded in the 1970s. Many fans viewed Wonder's soundtrack to the 1991 **Spike Lee** film *Jungle Fever* as a comeback artistically. "These Three Words" served as the film's love theme for the interracial love affair between co-stars Wesley Snipes and Annabella Sciorra. The soundtrack includes a number of funky instrumentals which showed off Wonder's always remarkable skills on the keyboards.

Wonder became an elder statesman in the music industry during the 1990s. In the previous 20 years, he had received a number of lifetime achievement awards. In 1989, he was inducted into the Rock and Roll Hall of Fame during his first year of eligibility for the honor. Wonder received a Lifetime Achievement Award from the Grammys in 1996. To date, Wonder has won 25 Grammys, including three for Album of the Year. In 1999, Wonder received the Kennedy Center Honors along with Judith Jamison, Victor Borge, Jason Robards, and Sean Connery.

In recent years, many major artists have called on Wonder to perform duets. During the late 1980s, **Michael Jackson** and Stevie Wonder traded duets on their 1987 respective albums *Bad* and *Characters*. In 1997, he teamed up with singer, songwriter, and producer extraordinaire Babyface on the anti-domestic violence ballad "How Come, How Long." Wonder and Babyface received a Grammy nomination for the song. In 1999, Sting called on Wonder for a duet on the top 10 single "Brand New Day," the title track to the former Police front man's new album. The song served as the theme to CBS's morning program, *The Early Show*, for a number of years.

Many hip-hop and R&B artists have found Wonder's extensive catalog to be fertile material for samples, demonstrating Wonder's profound influence on urban audiences. Performers who grew up with Wonder as a musical constant in their lives have found inspiration in his catalog, which seems to have a song to express every feeling a human can experience over the course of a lifetime. Perhaps the most prominent sample of Wonder's music came in 1995 when west coast rapper Coolio sampled "Pastime Paradise" from *Songs in the Key of Life* for "Gangsta's Paradise," which appeared on the soundtrack to the Michelle Pfeiffer film *Dangerous Minds*. "Gangsta's Paradise" was the number one selling single of 1995. Wonder performed the song with Coolio at the 1995 Billboard music awards. **Will Smith** has frequently made use of Wonder's songs for his samples. Smith used "I Wish" on his 1999 hit "Wild Wild West," the title track to the 1999 film *Wild Wild West*.

In 2001, Stevie Wonder married Kai Milla, a New York fashion designer. The couple has had two children, Kailand Morris and Mandla Kadjay Morris. The new love in Wonder's life inspired him to return to the studio and record his first full-length album in more than a decade. *A Time to Love* (2005) featured a number of duets, much like Wonder's recordings during the 1990s. Wonder performs duets with Kim Burrell, Kirk Franklin, En Vogue, Prince, India Arie, and Paul McCartney, as well as a duet with his daughter Aisha Morris. *A Time to Love* is filled with gorgeous love songs. It received widespread critical acclaim, and reached the top five on the Billboard album charts. Wonder received a Grammy for Best Male Pop Vocal Performance for the single "From the Bottom of My Heart."

Less than six months after the album's release, Wonder took another hiatus from recording following the death of his mother, Lula Hardaway Morris, in 2006. Wonder had been making a number of high profile appearances in the wake of *A Time to Love*'s release, including at Super Bowl XL in Detroit and on an episode of *American Idol*. Wonder returned to the public eye in August 2007, following a long, intense period of grieving over the death of his mother. The *A Wonder's Summer Night* theatre tour in Summer 2007 featured the singer performing many of his classic songs. In 2008, Wonder performed a European leg of the tour.

Stevie Wonder continued his work as an activist and artist on behalf of the presidential candidacy of **Barack Obama**. Wonder performed at the Democratic National Convention in Denver on the night Barack Obama accepted his party's nomination for President of the United States. The nearly 100,000 attendees at the massive outdoor rally, a first in convention history, gave Wonder numerous ovations for his superb performance. Wonder drew the most applause for his concluding song, "Singed, Sealed, Delivered I'm Yours," a staple of Obama rallies throughout 2008. Wonder used his stardom to bring attention to Obama and raise money for the young candidate. On January 20, 2009, Wonder performed "Brand New Day" with

Sting at one of the inaugural balls held in honor of the new presidency of Barack Obama.

Clayton Trutor
Boston College

FURTHER READING

Davis, Sharon. *Stevie Wonder: Rhythms of Wonder*. London: Anova Books, 2006.

Early, Gerald. *One Nation under a Groove: Motown and American Culture*. Ann Arbor: University of Michigan Press, 2004.

George, Nelson. *Where Did Our Love Go?: The Rise and Fall of the Motown Sound*. Urbana: University of Illinois Press, 2007.

Lodder, Steve. *Stevie Wonder: A Guide to the Classic Albums*. San Francisco: Backbeat Books, 2005.

Love, Dennis. *Blind Faith: The Miraculous Journey of Lula Hardaway, Stevie Wonder's Mother*. New York: Simon and Schuster, 2002.

Werner, Craig. *Higher Ground: Stevie Wonder, Aretha Franklin, Curtis Mayfield, and the Rise and Fall of American Soul*. New York: Crown Publishers, 2004.

Tiger Woods (1975–)

Tiger Woods was born Eldrick Tont Woods on December 30, 1975, in the city of Cypress in Orange County, California. Tiger was a nickname he was given at an early age in honor of South Vietnamese Army Colonel Vuong Dang "Tiger" Phong, a close friend of Lieutenant Colonel Earl Woods, Tiger Woods's father. Tiger Woods is the finest professional golfer in the world. He has won more money on the Professional Golf Association (PGA) Tour than any player in history, approximately $85 million. He is on pace to win more major championships and tour events than any player in history. Entering the 2009 season, Woods won 14 majors and 65 tour events. Woods is an exemplar of consistency. By 2009, he had only missed the cut at five professional tournaments in his career. No other golfer is even close to matching this mark. More than just a world class golfer, Woods is a cultural icon and a marketing icon. His endorsement deals with Nike, Buick, Gillette, Accenture, EA Sports, and Gatorade, among others, make him one of the most lucrative brands in the sporting world. He is one of the most widely recognized athletes in the world, and possibly its wealthiest. Woods's multi-racial background in a sport historically dominated by whites has accentuated his notoriety throughout his career. His remarkable success has helped increase golf's popularity among people of color exponentially. Woods's uniqueness has also given him a distinct cultural cachet, which has helped bring in many younger fans to the sport. Tiger Woods is the quintessential twenty-first-century American icon. Like President Obama, Woods is living proof of the potential opportunities for people of all backgrounds in a multicultural America.

Eldrick Tont "Tiger" Woods is the only child of Lieutenant Colonel Earl Woods and Kultida "Tida" Punsawad Woods. The couple met in 1969 in Bangkok, Thailand, while the Lieutenant Colonel was serving overseas during the Vietnam War. The couple settled in Southern California following Lt. Col. Woods's retirement from the Armed Forces. When Eldrick Tont Woods was born in 1975, he joined in the Woods household two half-brothers and a half-sister from his father's previous marriage. Woods was raised in middle class, suburban Southern California. His father had put golf clubs in his hands well before his first birthday. Early in his retirement, Lt. Col. Woods had taken up golfing as a leisure activity. By the time of his son Tiger's birth, he was a full blown golf fanatic. The local golf courses, like the Woods' family neighborhood, were predominately white. The half-African American, one-quarter American Indian, one-quarter Chinese Earl Woods stood out on the links of Southern California. His young son—whose mother is half-Thai, one-quarter Chinese, and one-quarter Dutch—drew just as much attention, though less for his race than his prodigious play at a young age. In May 1982, six-year-old Tiger Woods hit his first hole in one.

Standing out did not dampen Earl Woods's enthusiasm for the game. It did not keep his young son from developing into a child prodigy, either. In 1978, two-year-old Tiger Woods appeared with his father on the *Mike Douglas Show*. The little boy carried a set of golf clubs twice his size out on stage and proceeded to put on a display of his skills with the driver. Jimmy Stewart and Bob Hope, Douglas's guests, awed at the young Woods. Douglas put Bob Hope, a long-time star of Pro-Am golf tournaments, up to a putting contest with Woods. Woods missed his putt, settling for a tap-in that drew roars of applause from the crowd. Hope refused the challenge, fearing the young golfer would defeat him. Throughout his boyhood, Woods put on similar displays of his golfing abilities on both local and national television, including the *Today Show*, *Good Morning America*, and ESPN's *SportsCenter*.

Woods began playing competitively at age eight. He competed in the 1984 Junior World Golf Championships in San Diego. The youth competition was designed for children aged nine and ten, but Woods's father secured him an exemption to play in the tournament. The young righty shocked the field and won the tournament at the famed Torrey Pines Golf Course. Woods repeated as champion in 1985. He went on to win four consecutive Junior World Golf Championships from 1988 to 1991. Sixteen-year-old Tiger Woods, six-time Junior World Golf Champion, split his time between the golf course and school. This may have put a serious strain on many students, but Woods remained at the top of his class at Anaheim's Western High School. Upon his graduation in 1993, Woods's classmates named the Stanford-bound young man the "Most Likely to Succeed" in their graduating class.

At age 14, Woods competed in the 1991 U.S. Junior Amateur Golf Championship. He became the tournament's youngest winner. He defended his title in 1992 and 1993, winning the tournament in a dominan fashionin both instances. He remains the only golfer to win the Championship on multiple occasions. In 1994, Tiger Woods competed in the U.S. Amateur Championship, the most prestigious amateur tournament in the country. Woods won in a shocking come-from-behind victory against favorite Trip Kuehne at TPC at Sawgrass. To this day, Kuehne says the psychological impact of his defeat at the hands of Woods derailed his professional career. Woods defend his title in 1995 and 1996, making him the only player to win the Amateur Championship three consecutive times, and only one of three players to win the tournament three or more times. The other triple winners are golfing legends Bobby Jones (1924, 1925, 1927) and Jack Nicklaus (1958, 1959, 1961).

Woods spent two years in Palo Alto, California, at Stanford University, majoring in economics. He was voted an All-American Golfer in his freshman year, winning three of the thirteen tournaments he entered with the Stanford Cardinal. As a sophomore, he won eight tournaments, including the Pac-10 Championship and the NCAA Individual Golf Championship. Arizona State edged out Stanford for the national championship. Woods dropped out of Stanford following his sophomore year to pursue a professional career. The 20-year-old golfer was already a well-known, heavily-hyped figure to PGA fans by the time he joined the tour full-time in 1996. His success as an amateur and collegiate golfer proceeded him.

> There are still golf courses in the United States that I cannot play because of the color of my skin. I'm told that I'm not ready for you. Are you ready for me?
> —Tiger Woods

Woods entered the PGA Tour with unprecedented hype. The corporate marketing machine which emerged in the 1980s to sell the products of **Michael Jordan** had been fine tuned by the time Tiger Woods arrived. Before Woods won a thing on the PGA Tour, Nike transformed Woods into a household name with their "I Am Tiger Woods" campaign, using the golfer's likeness to sell spikes, Woods's now iconic red polo shirt for Sunday final rounds, his black Nike swoosh hat, and a range of new Nike golf merchandise. Woods signed a $40 million deal with Nike soon after he acquired his PGA card in 1996. Tiger Woods has been the face of Nike since the retirement of Michael Jordan from basketball. Every year, Nike finds a new way to make use of its lucrative Tiger Woods brand in advertising.

The young golfer did not disappoint. In 1996, Woods played competitively in a number of major tournaments. He won the Las Vegas Invitational and the Walt Disney World/Oldsmobile Classic. Woods finished 24th in earnings in 1996. This was a remarkable showing, considering that he played in only 11 tour events for the entire year. *Sports Illustrated* named Woods their 1996 Sportsman of the Year, primarily for his cultural significance.

Tiger Woods emerged as golf's biggest star in 1997. He opened the PGA Season with a victory at the Mercedes Championships in Hawaii, easily outpacing his competition with a 14-under for the tournament. An unprecedented crowd gathered in Augusta, Georgia, the weekend of April 13, 1997, for the Masters Tournament. Arnold Palmer had always had a large, enthusiastic fan base, but nothing like the throngs of new fans who filled the galleries at the Augusta National Golf Club. They chased Woods from hole to hole, bringing a new energy to typically subdued PGA Tour events. Woods did not disappoint. He entered the final round with a solid lead over veterans like Tom Kite and Tom Watson. On Sunday, Tiger blew away his competition, building a massive lead over the field. Woods ended up with an 18-under, defeating his next closest competitor by a Masters record 12 strokes. The 1997 Masters offered the first evidence of the now widely held assumption that Tiger will always win a major if he takes a lead into Sunday. His competitiveness and clutch play makes him an unstoppable force when victory is in sight. Thus far, Woods is 14–0 when he takes a lead into Sunday at a major. Tiger Woods's walk to the 18th green at Augusta at the 1997 Masters has become one of the most iconic moments in the history of golf. The thousands of supporters who came to see Woods honored him with ovation after ovation as he neared his first victory in a major.

Resentment of Woods began even before he achieved stardom on the PGA Tour. Some PGA fans disapprove of his cocksure demeanor or his displays of frustration on the links. Some of his peers were jealous of his endorsement money. Others believed the young golfer had not paid his dues, but was already reaping unprecedented rewards. Some players and fans argue that the Tour has become beholden to Woods. A tournament's success is now predicated entirely on whether or not Woods chooses to play in it. Some resentment of Woods amounts to simple racism. The first widely publicized, racially charged incident related to Woods took place in the aftermath of Woods's first victory at the Masters. Former Masters' champion Fuzzy Zoeller stirred up a great deal of controversy with the racially charged comments he made about Woods's victory. Traditionally, the reigning Masters' champion selects the menu at the next year's Masters' Club Dinner. Zoeller told reporters to tell Tiger not to put fried chicken or collard greens on the menu. Several of Zoeller's sponsors dropped him. Zoeller later apologized personally to Woods for the comments, which Woods says he did not take personally.

Following his win at the Masters, Woods was called on by numerous corporations to endorse their products. The 22-year-old golfer accepted offers to endorse everything from cars to watches to breakfast cereal to video games. Advertisers matched Woods's sleek play on the golf course with the contours of the Buick LeSabre. Woods served as Buick's primary pitchman between 1999 and 2008, when General Motors' financial troubles forced the company to part ways with most of their celebrity spokespeople. The *Tiger Woods PGA Tour* video game franchise became a big hit for Electronic Arts (EA) Sports. Sales of the game have rivaled those of all other sports video games except John Madden NFL Football games. EA's *Tiger Woods* video game has gone through 12 annual editions, selling in the millions of copies. All of these distractions may have led to Woods's relative lack of success in the second half of the 1997 and 1998 PGA Tour seasons. Woods's vocal detractors described him as in a slump or, even worse, a one hit wonder.

Woods answered his critics in 1999. With the help of coach Butch Harmon and new caddy extraordinaire Steve Williams, Woods honed his short game and improved the accuracy of his always substantial drives. Woods scored victories at the Memorial, the Buick Invitational, and the Motorola Western Open before winning his second major, the PGA Championship. The 1999 PGA Championship took place at the Medinah Country Club, just north of Chicago. On the opening day of the tournament, the flamboyant Spanish golf sensation, Sergio Garcia, took a two-stroke lead over a cluster of competitors. Woods himself sat four strokes behind the leader after round one. On day two, Woods shot a 66, leaving him two strokes off the pace of new leader Jay Haas. Woods tied for the lead after the third round with Canadian Mike Weir. On Sunday, Woods played steady on the links while

Weir collapsed on the back nine. Garcia staged a furious comeback on Sunday afternoon, but Woods held off the Spaniard by one stroke to capture the PGA Championship. Later that year, Woods won his second PGA Player of the Year Award. (He won his first in 1997. In all, he has earned the honor nine times.) Woods was also named the Associated Press's Male Athlete of the Year for the second time.

In 2000, Tiger Woods won three majors: The U.S. Open, the British Open, and the PGA Championship. Woods dominated the U.S. Open field at Pebble Beach, winning the tournament by 15 strokes. He took a one-stroke lead after the opening round, and built on it everyday. Woods finished at 12-under for the tournament, making him the first golfer in the history of the U.S. Open to finish at more than 10-under for the tournament. In July, Woods followed up his U.S. Open victory with an equally impressive win at the obstacle filled British Open at St. Andrews, Scotland. He won his first British Open by eight strokes over South African Ernie Els and Denmark's Thomas Bjorn. Woods took control of the tournament in the second round and never looked back. The 2000 PGA Championship proved significantly more competitive. Woods won a three-hole playoff against the little known Bob May at the Valhalla Golf Club in Louisville, Kentucky.

In 2001, Tiger Woods won the Masters by two strokes over David Duval, who won the British Open that summer, in a spirited battle. The victory at Augusta made Woods the first golfer in modern history to hold all four major championships simultaneously. Commentators referred to this as a "Tiger Slam." Woods has yet to achieve a true Grand Slam in one year, but he's young yet. The "Tiger Slam" remains one of the seminal accomplishments of his career. Woods won a total of five tournaments in 2001, including the Bay Hill Invitational and The Players Championship. At the age of 26, Woods already had 29 career tournament wins.

In 2002, Woods captured two more majors, the Masters and the U.S. Open. At Augusta, he held off South African Retief Goosen and "The Lefty," Phil Mickelson to capture the Green Jacket, making him the first golfer in more than a decade to repeat at the Masters. The golfing press portrayed Goosen and Mickelson as Woods's emerging rivals, though neither golfer has been able to consistently challenge Woods's hegemony on the PGA Tour. In 2001, they portrayed David Duval similarly after Duval battled Woods at the Masters and won the British Open. Duval's continuing struggles with vertigo prevented him from ever challenging Woods's dominance in the sport. In June, Woods held off Mickelson again, keeping him three strokes off the pace at Bethpage Black on Long Island, to capture the U.S. Open. Woods again won five tournaments in 2002 and earned nearly $7 million on tour.

Another apparent "slump" kept Woods from winning a major in 2003 or 2004, though he finished second and fourth in annual Tour earnings in those respective years. Some commentators blamed it on developments in Woods's personal life. Woods became romantically involved with a Swedish model named Elin Nordegren in late 2001. After two years of courtship, they were engaged in October 2003. The following October, they held an extravagant wedding in Barbados. The couple has had two children, a daughter named Sam Alexis (b. 2007) and a son named Charlie (b. 2009).

Tiger Woods's two year "slump" ended in 2005. The nearly 30-year-old golfer returned to the Tour with a noticeably more muscular physique for the 2005 season. Many commentators attribute Woods's continued success to his superior physical fitness. His well trained muscles continue to respond well to the conditions of a wide range of courses. Woods's strength and agility give him great control over his shots. Many of his rivals have taken up strength training to try to keep up with Woods, including Phil Mickelson. Tiger Woods won for the fourth time at Augusta in April 2005. The 69th Masters Tournament concluded after an exciting playoff between Woods and upstart Chris DiMarco. Woods put DiMarco away in the first sudden death playoff hole. Woods won his tenth major that July at St. Andrews. He held off local hero Colin Montgomerie by five strokes to win the British Open. Woods became the youngest player in the history of professional golf to win 10 majors.

A willingness to adapt his game to changing circumstances has characterized Woods's career up to this point. On several different occasions, Woods has altered his swing to correct bad habits that became evident in his game. He has shortened his stroke at times to improve accuracy on his short game. He engaged in extensive strength training to maintain his preeminence as a driver. He has shifted weight away from his plant foot to compensate for pain in his now-reconstructed left knee. Perceived shortcomings in his vision led Woods to undergo laser eye surgery to improve his line of sight on the links. Throughout his career, Woods has shown himself to be both an exemplary golfer as well as a student of the game. The continual fine-tuning of his game demonstrates his profound respect for a game which demanded unique precision from its participants.

> I've learned that success on the course was only part of what I wanted to achieve. In 1996, my father and I established the Tiger Woods Foundation to inspire dreams in America's youth because I believe in passing on the values I received from my parents and teachers.   —Tiger Woods

Personal tragedy struck Woods in 2006. His father Earl, who had long battled prostate cancer, succumbed to the disease in May. Woods took more than two months off from the Tour to grieve and console his family. After an initially shaky return, Woods returned to form, winning the final two majors of the year, the British Open and the PGA Championship. Woods battled Chris DiMarco to the finish for the second time in two years at a major, edging out the veteran golfer at the 2006 British Open at the Royal Liverpool Golf Club. Woods won by five strokes at the 2006 PGA Championship at the

Medinah Country Club near Chicago, Illinois. In his victory at Medinah, Woods displayed his characteristic ability to put away his opponents once he took the lead in a tournament, as he did on the tournament's opening day. The victories at the British Open and PGA Championship, combined with the golfer's ability to overcome personal tragedy, helped Woods earn his fourth selection as the Associated Press Athlete of the Year.

Woods dealt with serious injuries for the first time in his career in 2008. Following a poor showing at the Masters, Woods took time off from the Tour to undergo arthroscopic surgery on his ailing left knee. Many observers chalked up Woods's poor performance at the Masters to his inability to plant his feet properly when swinging with an injured knee. Woods returned for the 2008 U.S. Open, which was played at Torrey Pines, the Southern California course where he made his name as an amateur star at the age of eight. He hobbled around the course in pain all weekend, frequently wincing after tee shots and occasionally providing the viewers at home with some colorful language. Woods tied with little-known Rocco Mediate at 1-under after the final round on Sunday. Mediate battled Woods through an 18-hole playoff on Monday. The pair remained deadlocked after 18 holes. The 2008 U.S. Open was settled in sudden death fashion. Woods defeated Mediate on the sudden-death first hole to win the tournament. Following the victory, Woods announced that he would sit out the remainder of the 2008 golf season to continue rehabilitating his knee. In the lead up to the U.S. Open, Woods had reinjured his left leg, sustaining a stress fracture of his left tibia.

Tiger Woods entered his mid-thirties within reach of breaking golf's two most noteworthy records. His 14 major victories are four short of the mark set by Jack Nicklaus during his 37 years on the tour. Woods's 65 career tour victories are 17 short of the 82 career victories accomplished by Sam Snead (1912–2002) during his 30-year career. Tiger Woods is a mere 15 years into his professional career, and despite his stunning 2010 admission to having extramarital affairs stemming from what has been described as his "sexual addiction," and the loss of some of his leading sponsors, such as Gatorade and Accenture, Woods continues to be a barrier-breaker and icon who transcends his sport. He is an athletic iconoclast, eradicating notions of who can succeed on the PGA Tour and who has a place on the golf course. Woods's playing speaks for itself, but his activism on behalf of urban youth has received little public attention. Woods has invested a great deal of money in ensuring that students of color in U.S. cities have access to the same educational opportunities as their suburban peers. He has also sponsored the "In The City" Festival since its inception in 1997, an effort by Woods and the PGA to bring their game to underprivileged urban youth. On the golf course and in the community, Tiger Woods is an icon of black America, of white America, and of all America.

Clayton Trutor
Boston College

FURTHER READING

Callahan, Tom. *In Search of Tiger: A Journey through Golf with Tiger Woods.* New York: Three Rivers, 2004.

Londino, Lawrence. *Tiger Woods: A Biography.* Westport, CT: Greenwood Press, 2008.

Owen, David. *The Chosen One: Tiger Woods and the Dilemma of Greatness.* New York: Simon and Schuster, 2001.

Smiley, Bob. *Follow the Roar: Tailing Tiger Woods for All 604 Holes of His Most Spectacular Season.* New York: HarperCollins, 2008.

Carter G. Woodson
(1875–1950)

Recognized today as "The Father of Black History," prolific historian Carter Godwin Woodson was the driving force behind the early black history movement, and a leading black scholar-activist during the era of Jim Crow segregation. He founded the Association for the Study of Negro Life and History (ASNLH) in 1915, the *Journal of Negro History* (now *Journal of African American History*) in 1916, Associated Publishers, Inc. in 1921, and the *Negro History Bulletin* in 1937. He wrote numerous books, journal articles, newspaper columns, and book reviews; mentored generations of African American scholars and historians; consistently challenged mainstream black leadership strategies; and popularized black history by creating Negro History Week in 1926, which, 50 years later, became what we celebrate today as Black History Month. Between 1929 and 1933, Woodson established an expansive collection of archival materials and papers at the Library of Congress, Washington, DC.

His most famous and still widely read book is *The Mis-Education of the Negro* (1933), and since his death he has been memorialized and acknowledged in American popular culture in various ways. In 1958, he became "the third distinguished American" named to The *Ebony* Hall of Fame. On May 11, 1976, his former "office home" at 1538 Ninth Street Northwest, in Washington, DC was designated a National Historic Landmark. In 1984, the U.S. Postal Service issued a stamp of Woodson as a part of its Black Heritage Series. A decade later, the mayor of West Virginia, Robert Nelson, erected a life-size statue of Woodson on Hal Greer Boulevard in Huntington, West Virginia. Sampling from Woodson's *The Mis-Education of the Negro*, in 1998 Lauryn Hill released her Grammy Award winning album, *The Miseducation of Lauryn Hill*. And on December 19, 2003, the National Park Service was authorized to acquire The Carter G. Woodson Home to establish a National Historic Site, and since then has been working on restoring and renovating Woodson's Home that, in 2001, was placed on the National Trust for Historic Preservation's list of "America's 11 Most Endangered Places."

Woodson made monumental sacrifices for the cause of black history. As he testified to *Pittsburgh Courier* readers in "Carter G. Woodson Tells Reason Why He Never Married" (January 7, 1933, A2), he had to "take the vow of poverty" and made "every sacrifice" to maintain the ASALH. Beginning in the ASNLH's early years, Woodson routinely invested his salary back into his movement, and between 1938 and 1949, ASNLH records indicate that Woodson's debts surpassed his own personal income. Woodson wholeheartedly believed that black history was an essential element in the psychological and cultural struggle for African American self-knowledge and self-esteem, American educational reform, and the dismantling of widespread anti-black thought and behavior. In a 1926 essay, Woodson explained why the study of black history was so crucial. He proclaimed: "If a race has no history, it has no worth-while tradition, it becomes a negligible factor in the thought of the world, and its stands in danger of being exterminated" ("Negro History Week," *Journal of Negro History*, Volume 11, April 1926, 239).

The circumstances of Woodson's early years and upbringing clearly influenced later years, and perhaps help explain what his ASNLH co-workers often described as his cantankerous character and rough, intimidating exterior. The son of former slaves James Henry and Anne Eliza (Riddle) born during the unstable Reconstruction era in New Canton, Virginia, as a young man Woodson had to join the manual labor work force to help his family survive. He once told one of his protégés that he did not learn the fundamentals of reading, writing, and arithmetic until he was about 19 years old. Woodson was born in New Canton, Virginia, in Buckington County on December 19, 1875. Like many blacks of his time, he came from a large family, nine children in total, including two infants who died during a whooping-cough epidemic. Woodson's parents shared with him first-hand histories of life during slavery. For instance, his father, James Henry, told him how he had physically overpowered his master to take his freedom. Later in his life, Woodson commented that his parents' stories sparked his later interest in documenting the stories of ex-slaves.

In a rare 1932 autobiographical article, "And the Negro Loses His Soul," that appeared in the *Chicago Defender* and the *New York Age*, Woodson recounted how his literate mother and his father instilled "high morality," "a strong character," self-respect," and a "thirst for education" in their children. A year before Woodson's birth, his parents settled in New Canton, Virginia, buying a house and farm. Though landowners, the Woodson family's life was similar to the lives of many poor landowning blacks and sharecroppers. In the early 1930s, Woodson recalled that as a youth he had few articles of clothing, and often went to bed hungry. Like many black youth coming of age in the South during the immediate post-Reconstruction period, Woodson attended a rural school for only about four months out of the year. He, in part, learned how to read as a child by studying from old newspapers. Helping his impoverished yet proud family make ends meet, he regularly worked on the family farm until he was about 15. In the dawning of the 1890s, he hired himself out as a farm and manual laborer, and he drove a garbage truck in Buckingham County, Virginia.

In 1892, Woodson moved to Fayette County, West Virginia, to work in the coal mines. This was certainly hard and dangerous work. A piece of slate once fell on him, injuring his head. Woodson's years toiling in the coal mines left a deep impression on him. He later took great pride in his poor, working-class background, and knew from first-hand experiences the realities faced by the masses of black poor and working-class people. The years in the coal mines also inevitably reinforced Woodson's views of the value of hard work. Later, his ASNLH co-workers routinely commented on his herculean work ethic; he regularly worked 18 hours a day. While working in the coal mines, Woodson met a black Civil War veteran named Oliver Jones, who allowed a group of coal miners to use his home as an informal school and meeting place. Woodson read newspapers to his illiterate co-workers, as he had done and would later continue to do, for his father. Jones also had a valuable library of books containing classic works by pioneering amateur, self-trained black historians like George Washington Williams, J. T. Wilson, and W. J. Simmons. Woodson drew great inspiration from these scholars' works, especially Williams's two-volume *History of the Negro Race in America from 1619 to 1880* (1883) and *A History of Negro Troops in the War of the Rebellion, 1861–1865* (1888).

At the age of 20 in 1895, Woodson returned to Huntington, West Virginia, to live with his parents, attending Frederick Douglass High School from 1895 until 1896. In the fall of 1897, he then ventured to the abolitionist-founded Berea College in Kentucky. It took him about five years to receive a B.L. from Berea because he faced financial challenges and engaged in numerous black uplift activities. He left Berea in 1898, and until 1900, he worked as a teacher for a school in Winona, West Virginia, where he educated the children of black miners. Philosophically working-class to his core, he probably felt vindicated in educating black youth with whom he shared experiences. Between 1900 and 1903, he returned to his high school alma mater, Frederick Douglass High School, teaching history and serving as the principal. He finally received a BL degree from Berea on June 3, 1903.

From mid December 1903 until early February 1907, Woodson traveled abroad. For roughly five years under the auspices of the U.S. War Department, he went to the Philippines to teach classes in English, health, and agriculture, and to train Filipino teachers. He enjoyed this work very much, resigning due to sickness early in 1907. Woodson mentioned his experiences in the Philippines in *The Mis-Education of the Negro*, noting that the best way to educate the Filipinos was based upon their own history and culture. While in the Philippines, Woodson also mastered French and Spanish, a skill set upon which he would later draw when reading, collecting, and reviewing European scholarship on Africa. After leaving the Philippines, Woodson briefly traveled around the world to Africa, Asia, and Europe, spending roughly half of a year in Europe. He briefly attended the Sorbonne and studied European history, which helped widen his scope of knowledge and prepared him for the University of Chicago and Harvard University.

After returning from Europe, Woodson enrolled in the University of Chicago, and in the late summer of 1908 he received an MA degree in History, Romance Languages, and Literature. His MA thesis was on "The German Policy of France in the War of Austrian Succession." Woodson then enrolled in Harvard University as a doctoral student, and in 1909 he left Cambridge and settled down in the Washington, DC, area to teach first at Armstrong Manual Training School, and then French, Spanish, English, and History at the prestigious M Street High School. Woodson conducted research, completed his comprehensive examinations, and wrote his dissertation while working as a teacher full-time. Professors in Harvard's history department did not share Woodson's passion for black history. Albert Bushnell Hart—advisor to **W. E. B. Du Bois** and Woodson at Harvard—occasionally praised certain exceptional African Americans, but still wrote that African Americans were inferior. Nevertheless, Woodson finished his course work at Harvard in less than two years, and submitted the first draft of his dissertation in the spring of 1910. His committee, consisting of Hart, Edward Channing, and Charles Haskins, made many suggestions for revision, and by January 1911, Woodson finished the revised draft. After finally passing his American history comprehensive examination in April 1912, Woodson completed his PhD dissertation, "The Disruption of Virginia." Woodson's study could have been published, but he did not receive the necessary funding or support to do so.

Woodson became the second African American to earn a PhD in the United States (Harvard PhD Du Bois being the first to do so in 1895), and then committed his life to the cause of black history. Why did Woodson decide to devote his life to the study and promotion of black history? Woodson once recounted that his experiences at Harvard were pivotal in shaping his commitment to black history. At Harvard, Woodson directly challenged his professors' widespread beliefs that blacks had no history. When Woodson earned his PhD, American historians, including those at Harvard, embraced degrees of white supremacy. Between approximately 1890 and 1920, many leading U.S. historians were racists, promoted the notion of African American inferiority, and marginalized African Americans' contributions altogether. Woodson accepted the responsibility of overturning academic racism, producing revisionist and corrective historiography, and providing his African American readership with positive portrayals of the African American experience.

The later years of the Progressive era were vital years in Woodson's career as an historian and scholar-activist. In the spring of 1915, Woodson published his first monograph, *The Education of the Negro Prior to 1861*, a densely footnoted and positively reviewed monograph that explored the educational opportunities for African Americans during the antebellum era. While an active member of the Washington, DC, branch of the NAACP and a self-proclaimed radical, on September 9, 1915, Woodson co-founded the Association for the Study of Negro Life and History (ASNLH) in Chicago with George Cleveland Hall, James E. Stamps, and Alexander L. Jackson. The ASNLH, Woodson recounted in "Ten Years of Collecting and Publishing the Records of the Negro," "proclaimed as its purpose the collection of sociological and historical data on the Negro, the study of peoples of African blood, the publishing of books in this field, and the promotion of harmony between the races by acquainting the one with the other" (*Journal of Negro History*, Volume 10, October 1925, 598).

The ASNLH was much different than other professional historical associations of the Progressive era. Unlike the American Historical Association (AHA) or the Mississippi Valley Historical Association (MVHA), Woodson opened the doors of the ASNLH to lay historians, ministers, secondary and elementary school teachers, businessmen, and the African American community as a whole. Early on, the Association developed connections to the heart of black communities. Every year during Woodson's lifetime, the ASNLH meetings were held in black churches, community centers, colleges and universities, and high school auditoriums throughout the country. At every annual ASNLH meeting, schoolteachers of various levels and community activists presented papers, and in many cases even published these essays in the *Journal* alongside the research of leading black and white scholars. Under Woodson's guidance, the ASNLH also possessed a relatively progressive view of women's roles as black history promoters. Black female teachers, clubwomen, librarians, writers, and social activists played key roles in the ASNLH's day-to-day activities. They ran the *Negro History Bulletin* and various children's activities, and black women were elected to positions of power as exemplified in Mary McLeod Bethune being the Association's president from 1936 until 1952.

In 1916, without the consent of the other co-founders, Woodson launched the first issue of the *Journal of Negro History*, the first major scholarly and professional historical journal of the black American experience. While essays in the *Journal* addressed a wide range of issues pertaining to the histories of black American and African peoples, Woodson also used the *Journal* to summarize the ASNLH's annual meetings and activities, and to comment on the contemporary status of black America. In 1919, Woodson maintained that the *Journal* reached 4,000 people, that there were 1,648 subscribers, that 600 copies were sold at newsstands, and that 500 bound copies, including all four volumes in a single volume, were sold. While principal at Armstrong Manual Training High School, Woodson published his second major monograph, *A Century of Negro Migration* (1918). A substantial part of this study was aimed at dispelling the myths surrounding black migration during World War I. In the Association's early years, Woodson also began to popularize and democratize the study of black history. In 1919, for instance, he employed a full-time field agent to increase membership in the Association, appoint agents to sell books and subscriptions to the *Journal*, and organize black history clubs.

While Woodson was laying the foundations for the early black history movement, he was also active as a teacher of history. In 1918, Woodson became the principal of Armstrong Manual Training School in Washington, DC, where he advocated vocational and classical education, and inaugurated an adult education program. From 1919 until 1920, he served as the Dean of Howard University's School of Liberal Arts, introducing and teaching black history at Howard at both undergraduate and graduate levels. Woodson established rigorous graduate training in history at Howard as well. He was known among students for his seriousness and high expectations. Woodson did not share Howard's white dominated administration's visions, and left after one year. Many of his indictments of black colleges in *The Mis-Education of the Negro* (1933) stemmed from his experiences at Howard. From 1920 until 1922, he served as a Dean at West Virginia Collegiate Institute. In 1920, Woodson joined the Friends of Negro Freedom, a radical organization that stressed alleviating the economic problems facing black

America, founded by Chandler Owens and A. Philip Randolph. While he was a dean at Howard, he published his third major monograph, *The History of the Negro Church* (1921). In 1921, Woodson also wrote an unpublished manuscript, "The Case of the Negro," in which he challenged academic racism and Eurocentrism, indicted white America for its collective mistreatment of blacks, and critiqued black middle-class and elite leadership.

During the early 1920s, Woodson was very busy with many tasks: directing the ASNLH, editing a journal, and managing the Associated Publishers, Inc. that he founded in 1921 to provide black scholars with an outlet for publishing their scholarship. In 1922, Woodson published *The Negro in Our History*, a text-book written for students of black history at various levels, from secondary school students to college students. This text underwent 19 editions during Woodson's lifetime, and can be interpreted as one of Woodson's first major efforts to broaden his readership to include lay persons and the black youth. Despite the enduring popularity of *The Mis-Education of the Negro*, *The Negro in Our History* was Woodson's most popular book. By March 1941, Woodson noted that 40,000 copies of his text had been sold.

In 1922, Woodson decided to devote his life to the ASNLH. He resigned from his position at West Virginia Collegiate Institute, and moved to Washington, DC, where he purchased his home and the ASNLH's headquarters at 1538 Ninth Street Northwest. For the next 28 years, he devoted his life to maintaining the Association, to the scientific study of black America, to training younger black historians, to democratizing and popularizing the study of black history, and to an overall quest for equal rights and justice for his people.

In many respects, the 1920s were "golden years" for the Association. During this decade he received tens of thousands of dollars from the Carnegie Foundation, the Julius Rosenwald Foundation, and from three Rockefeller trusts. These funds allowed him to hire young black scholars. Throughout his career, Woodson mobilized a group of younger, professionally trained black historians who, despite their conflicts with him, worked with him for varying periods of time. Included in this group whom he sometimes called his "sons" or "boys," were Alrutheus A. Taylor, Charles H. Wesley, Luther Porter Jackson, Lorenzo Johnston Greene, Rayford W. Logan, William Sherman Savage, James Hugo Johnston, and John Hope Franklin. From 1922 until 1929, Woodson was prolific, publishing four articles in the *Journal of Negro History*, and many books including *Free Negro Owners of Slaves in the United States* (1924), *Free Negro Heads of Families in the United States in 1830* (1925), *The Mind of the Negro as Reflected in Letters Written during the Crisis, 1800–1860* (1926), *Negro Orators and Their Orations* (1926), *Negro Makers of* History (1928), *African Myths Together with Proverbs* (1928), and *The Negro as Businessman* (1929). In 1926, Woodson received the NAACP's Spingarn Medal, and by the mid-1920s, actively strove to open the Association's doors more widely to the black masses. By the early 1930s, after white philanthropists withdrew their support from the Association, Woodson relied upon black communities throughout the country to maintain the ASNLH's activities, and devoted a great deal of energy to writing more polemic newspaper columns. For instance, between 1931 and 1936, he wrote more than 100 essays in the *New York Age* and more than 30 articles in the *Chicago Defender*, which addressed a range of issues relating to the contemporary obstacles facing black America.

Exposing blacks to the "truth" about their history, Woodson's "mass education movement" took on many forms. Though a professional scientific historian to the core, Woodson published books aimed at attracting a wide readership—from elementary school students to university students—such as *The Negro in Our History* (1922), *Negro Makers of History* (1928), *African Myths Together with Proverbs* (1928), *The African Background Outlined* (1936), and *African Heroes and Heroines* (1939). The unfinished *Encyclopedia Africana* was also written in a very simple language. A high priority for him was reaching out to those reading and thinking at basic levels.

Woodson's most famous and perhaps most effective effort at attracting a mass following and popularizing the study of black history was through Negro History Week celebrations. In the second week of February 1926, in commemoration of Abraham Lincoln's and **Frederick Douglass**'s birthdays, Woodson inaugurated Negro History Week. With this celebration, Woodson sought to integrate the teaching of black history into secondary and high schools throughout the nation, and essentially popularize black history in black communities. During the celebrations there were accessible banquets, breakfasts, speeches, parades, exhibits, and lectures that were usually held in churches, black colleges and universities, and community centers. For this week, he stressed that speakers and organizers donate their time to the cause. By the 1940s, Negro History Week celebrations became increasingly popular. In November 1948, Woodson introduced Negro History Week Kits at $2.00 apiece, and by 1950 they were still affordable at $2.50 each. The Negro History Weeks of Woodson's times were significantly different than most Black History Month celebrations of the current era. Since the end of the Black Power era, Black History Month celebrations have been commercialized and watered-down. For Woodson, it was of the utmost importance for the people themselves, especially the children, to create their own unique, personalized celebrations. While Woodson offered many suggestions, he promoted black history active learning.

Woodson introduced black history to "ordinary" black people in other ways. Between the founding of the ASNLH (now the Association for the Study of African American Life and History (ASALH) and his death, Woodson and his entourage were among the most demanded lecturers in the black community nationwide, and since its inception the ASALH functioned as a "free reference bureau." In 1927, Woodson established the Association's Extension Division and the Home Study Department to expose more people to black history through public lectures and correspondence study. Another major form of extension work undertaken by Woodson was the founding of *The Negro History Bulletin* in 1937. Written in a simple language to help black teachers who had little or no knowledge about black history, the *Bulletin* was the vehicle by which schoolteachers, children, and other concerned citizens could discuss the black past and help Woodson take black history into the homes of the black masses. The magazine served as an advertising mechanism for the association's activities, especially for Negro History Week, and Woodson also used the *Bulletin* as an outlet for airing his political philosophy. Between 1941 and 1950, Woodson published approximately 57 essays in the *Bulletin*.

Woodson died suddenly from a heart attack on April 3, 1950. According to the *Pittsburgh Courier* (Washington Edition), Woodson died peacefully around noon in his bed. Woodson's will, drafted on November 30, 1934, bequeathed his "office home" and the vast majority of its contents to the ASALH. Woodson's sudden death shocked his co-workers and dealt a great blow to the Association. In his first "Report of the Director," published in the October 1950 volume of the *Journal of Negro History*, Rayford W. Logan surmised: "It would be impossible for any one to carry out the multitudinous tasks that Dr. Woodson had learned, through the years, to perform with efficiency and dispatch" (359). Though he was a late intellectual bloomer, Woodson contributed more than any other single individual to the professionalization, legitimization, and popularization of African American history. One of Woodson's protégés was indeed correct in declaring that black history and studies scholars since the Civil Rights Movement have stood "squarely on the shoulders of his work." Woodson's legacy is routinely re-invoked during February of each year when millions of Americans celebrate Black History Month, and black historians and scholars continue to debate the significance of this cultural celebration.

Pero Gaglo Dagbovie
Michigan State University

FURTHER READING

Dagbovie, Pero Gaglo. *The Early Black History Movement, Carter G. Woodson, and Lorenzo Johnston Greene*. Urbana: University of Illinois Press, 2007.

Goggin, Jacqueline. *Carter G. Woodson: A Life in Black History*. Baton Rouge: Louisiana State University Press, 1993.

Logan, Rayford W. "Carter G. Woodson: Mirror and Molder of His Times, 1875–1950." *Journal of Negro History* 58 (1973): 1–17.

Meier, August, and Elliott Rudwick. *Black History and the Historical Profession, 1915–1980*. Urbana: University of Illinois Press, 1986.

Scally, Sister Anthony. *Carter G. Woodson: A Bio-Bibliography*. Westport, CT: Greenwood Press, 1985.

Wesley, Charles H. "Carter G. Woodson—as a Scholar." *Journal of Negro History* 36 (1951): 12–24.

Woodson, Carter G. "My Recollections of Veterans of the Civil War." *Negro History Bulletin* 7 (February 1944): 103–4, 115–18.

Woodson, Carter G. *Negro History Bulletin*. Volume 13 (May 1950).

Library of Congress

Richard Wright
(1908–1960)

Richard Wright was born Richard Nathaniel Wright on September 4, 1908, on Rucker's Plantation in Roxie, Mississippi. Wright, an American novelist, is best known for his 1940 book, *Native Son*, which became the first best-selling novel by an African American writer and the first Book-of-the-Month Club selection by a black American. During his lifetime, Wright not only published five novels; but also wrote essays, poetry, and nonfiction, including his immensely successful 1945 autobiography, *Black Boy*. A number of Wright's works, several of which were considered too controversial for publication during his lifetime, were also published posthumously, including the second half of his autobiography, which relayed Wright's experiences with the Communist Party in Chicago during the 1930s. In addition to writing, Wright also traveled widely, especially in his later years, and was politically active throughout his life. A harsh critic of American racism, Wright devoted his life and his work to the pursuit of racial justice. However, the famed author was also criticized by many of his contemporaries for moving to France in 1947, where he became a permanent American expatriate and continued to travel and write until his untimely death in 1960.

The grandson of former slaves and the son of Nathaniel Wright, a sharecropper, and Ella Wilson, a school teacher, Wright had an unstable and difficult childhood. In 1911, Wright's family relocated to Memphis, Tennessee, where the young Wright and his brother, Leon, witnessed frequent arguments between their mother and father. In 1913, Wright's father abandoned the family for another woman, forcing Ella to take a job as a cook for a white family, and leave her children at home alone. Wright's mother soon became ill, and placed her sons in a Memphis orphanage for a brief period of time. In the spring of 1916, Ella withdrew her sons from the orphanage, and the family traveled to Elaine, Arkansas to stay with Wright's uncle and aunt, Silas and Maggie Hoskins. While Wright and his family spent a few enjoyable summer months with the Hoskins, their happiness came to an end when Wright's uncle was murdered by a white man, an experience that would haunt Wright and his writing for many years to come. At just eight years old, the young Richard was exposed to the reality of white terror for the first time. The family fled, and Wright moved around from place to place for several years. Around 1920, his mother suffered a stroke, and Wright was sent to live with his maternal grandparents in Jackson, Mississippi. Wright was deeply unhappy during this period in his childhood, as his grandparents were restrictive Seventh-day Adventists who thought fiction was the work of the devil and did not allow books in their house. Moreover, Wright resented his grandparents for attempting to force him to pray so that he might find God, leaving Richard with a lifelong resistance to religious solutions to everyday problems.

In 1924, at age 15, Wright published his first work of fiction, a short story entitled "The Voodoo of Hell's Half-Acre," in the *Southern Register*, a local black newspaper. The following year, Wright graduated from the ninth grade at Smith Robertson Junior High School, in Jackson, as the class valedictorian. However, controversy developed when the principal of the school attempted to persuade Wright to recite a speech that he had written for Wright to deliver. While Wright insisted that he wanted to write his own speech, the principal threatened that if Wright did not cooperate he might not graduate. Angrily, on graduation day Wright delivered the speech as expected, but was deeply upset at being forced to violate his principles.

Wright then began taking classes at Lanier High School, but soon dropped out to get a job and save up enough money to move to Memphis, which he did at age 17. While in Memphis, Wright began to read voraciously, and worked as a delivery boy for an optical company. In 1927, after two years in Memphis, Wright relocated once again, this time to Chicago. While Wright's decision to travel north was motivated by the oppressive and dangerous climate of the American South, the aspiring writer was surprised to learn of the racism and segregation that characterized Chicago. Wright persevered, however, and eventually secured employment as a postal clerk. However, after the Wall Street Crash of 1929 and the beginning of the Depression, Wright lost his job. For a period he found employment with the Negro Burial Society, but his employment there ended in 1931 and he was forced to go on relief. After several temporary jobs, Wright found work with the Federal Writers' Project. During his early years in the Windy City, Wright also developed a vibrant social life, occasionally attending parties on the South Side and engaging in frequent love affairs and sexual encounters with numerous women.

After some time, Wright began to devote himself more seriously to writing and politics. The author's first publication, a short story called "Superstition," appeared in *Abbott's Monthly* in April 1931. In 1932, Wright began attending meetings of the John Reed Club, an intellectual arm of the Communist Party. Wright formally joined the party in 1933, and wrote a number of radical poems for left-wing periodicals. By 1935, Wright was working with the Federal Negro Theater in Chicago. He also wrote some short stories and a novel—originally titled *Cesspool* but later released as *Lawd Today*—during this time, but they were not published until after his death. While in Chicago, Wright chaired the South Side Writers' Group, whose membership included Arna Bontemps and Margaret Walker. He briefly edited the communist magazine *Left Front*, until the publication was shut down in 1937. While he was deeply committed to the ideals of the Party, some Black Communists denounced Wright as a *bourgeois* intellectual and accused the writer of being overly assimilated into white society. In 1936, Wright had a falling out with the leading African American Communist, Buddy Nealson. His conflicts with the Party came to a head in 1936 when he was physically assaulted by former comrades as he tried to join them during the annual May Day march.

In 1937, Wright moved to New York City, where he helped start the short-lived publication, *New Challenge* magazine and renewed his communist connections. Wright also became the Harlem editor of the communist newspaper the *Daily Worker*, and wrote more than two hundred articles for the publication during his first year in New York. In addition, Wright worked on the WPA

Writers' Project guidebook to the city, *New York Panorama* (1938), and wrote the book's essay on Harlem. The author's move to Harlem facilitated the development of several important relationships for Wright; such as his friendship with fellow writer **Ralph Ellison**. Wright's first major literary success came in 1938, when the author's short story collection, *Uncle Tom's Children* (1938), won first prize for the *Story* magazine contest for best book-length manuscript. The book—which contained several stories about lynch violence in the American South—quickly gained national attention. By May of 1938, Wright had earned enough money from the sales of *Uncle Tom's Children* to move permenantly to Harlem, where he began writing *Native Son*. Wright also received a Guggenheim Fellowship to support his work on the book.

Published in 1940, the novel tells the story of Bigger Thomas, a 19-year-old Black teenager who lives in a Chicago ghetto. While things seem to be looking up for Bigger when he is offered a job working as a chauffer for the Daltons, a wealthy white family, his luck quickly changes when he is almost caught in the bedroom of his employers' teenage daughter. To mask his presence from the girl's blind mother, Bigger covers the young woman's face with a pillow, accidentally smothering her. The remainder of the story focuses on Bigger's attempt to cover up the crime, during which he brutally murders his own girlfriend, Bessie. In the end, Bigger is captured and sentenced to the electric chair, interestingly, for allegedly raping Mary, not for murdering her. While critics attacked the novel for its violent, brutish portrayal of Black masculinity, Wright defended his characterization of Bigger, arguing that the character represented the constraints white society placed on black Americans. Furthermore, Wright suggested that a racist America created Bigger and was thus responsible for his heinous actions. Despite some negative reactions to the book, *Native Son* became an instant bestseller. In fact, in some bookstores the stock sold out in within several hours; while overall the novel sold more than 200,000 copies in the first three weeks.

The aftermath of the publication of *Native Son* was a busy time for Wright. In the summer of 1940, Wright traveled to Chicago to conduct research for a folk history of blacks that he was working on with photographer Edwin Rosskam. He also visited the American Negro Exhibition with fellow black writers **Langston Hughes**, Arna Bontemps, and Claude McKay. In October 1941, the result of Wright's project with Rosskam, *Twelve Million Black Voices: A Folk History of the Negro in the United States*, was published to wide critical acclaim.

Earlier that year, Wright was rewarded for his success when he was chosen as the recipient of the National Association for the Advancement of Colored People's prestigious Spingarn Medal in January. In March, Wright's reputation continued to grow with the debut of a theatrical production of *Native Son*, directed by Orson Welles, on Broadway.

Dramatic changes were also occurring in Wright's personal life during this time. Although the writer had no romantic notions about marriage, now that he was approaching 30 and had begun to build a successful career, Wright felt that it was time to settle down. In 1938 and 1939, he proposed to numerous women, most of whom were associated with the Communist Party. After being rejected by two other women and discovering that a third potential marriage partner had syphilis, in 1939 he married Dhimah Rose Meadman, a Russian-Jewish ballet dancer. Several months after the marriage, Wright moved with his new bride, and her son and her mother, to Mexico for a few months. However, the union was strained from the beginning, with the pair (and Wright in particular) facing intense prejudice against their interracial union. Moreover, after their wedding Hughes discovered that his bride had likely lied about her age, and perhaps even the father of her son from a previous marriage. He returned to New York and divorced Dhimah in 1940. On his way back to New York, Wright stopped in Mississippi to visit his father, whom he had not seen in 25 years. However, as Wright would later admit in his autobiography, the reunion was unfulfilling, as the author realized that he and his father were nothing more than strangers to one another.

In 1941, Wright married fellow Communist Party member Ellen Poplar, a white woman with whom he had been in love—and had unsuccessfully proposed to—prior to his marriage to Dhimah. A year later, their first daughter, Julia, was born. Their second daughter, Rachel, would be born in Paris in 1949.

Shortly after his second marriage, in 1942, Wright quietly withdrew from the Communist Party, although throughout his life he continued to identify with their ideals. Wright's break with Party became public in 1944 with the publication of the article "I Tried to be a Communist" in *The Atlantic Monthly*. Despite Wright's estrangement from the party and his publication of anti-communist literature in his later years, up until the time of his death Wright was on the Hollywood blacklist and under investigation by the U.S. government. These hindrances, however, hardly interfered with the author's success.

In 1944, Wright also published a short novel, *The Man Who Lived Underground*. Like *Black Boy*, it considers the consequences of white racism and the plight of a young Black man who is forced to go into hiding after being accused by the police of a crime he did not commit. The novel also had strong anti-communist undertones. This particular publication later influenced Wright's dear friend and colleague Ralph Ellison, as he wrote his most famous book, *Invisible Man*.

Wright's next major publication was his autobiography, *Black Boy*, in 1945. Like *Native Son*, the book was well-received and became a best-seller and Book-of-the-Month Club selection. However, the book, which was denounced by the U.S. Senate as "obscene," was not published in its entirety due to the controversial nature of its second half, which deals with Wright's time in Chicago and his involvement with the Communist Party. It was not until 1977 that this second portion of the book was published under the title *American Hunger*. The first half of the book described Wright's early life, from his birth in Mississippi up until his move to Chicago, his clashes with his

Seventh-day Adventist family, his troubles with white employers, and the virulent examples of white racism and hatred that he witnessed as a youth growing up in the Southern United States.

Wright spent the summer of 1945 as an artist-in-residence at the Bread Loaf School for writers in Middlebury, Vermont. Shortly thereafter, he traveled with his family to Paris, where he met other writers and artists such as Gertrude Stein, André Gide, and Léopold Senghor. While he returned briefly to the United States, Wright decided that he and his family could no longer tolerate the racism they experienced, in particular because he and his wife were an interracial couple. In 1947, Wright permanently moved to France and settled in Paris, never to return to the United States again. After his move, Wright began to work on a film adaptation of *Native Son*, in which he played Bigger Thomas. At 40 years old and slightly overweight, portraying the novel's 19-year-old central character was a bit of a challenge for Wright. While the film was received favorably in Europe upon its release in 1951, the abridged version of it that played in the United States was unsuccessful.

Wright's next publication, in 1953, was an existentialist novel entitled *The Outsider*, which unfavorably depicts a Black man's involvement with the Communist Party in New York. While it was praised mostly in Europe, overall the novel received lukewarm reviews. *Savage Holiday*, Wright's only work that contains no Black characters, appeared in 1954. The twisted story of a white man who weds a prostitute and then brutally murders her, the novel was largely unsuccessful.

In 1947, Wright became a French citizen and traveled throughout Europe, Asia, and Africa. These experiences provided the basis for several of his nonfiction works, including the 1954 publication, *Black Power*, a commentary on the emerging nations of Africa. Meanwhile, Wright was under investigation by both the FBI and the CIA as a suspected communist, despite his break with the Party in 1944.

Throughout the 1950s, Wright continued to publish works such as *The Color Curtain: A Report on the Bandung Conference*, inspired by his visit to Indonesia in 1955, *White Man, Listen!*, a collection of his lectures given between 1950 and 1956, and *The Long Dream* (1958), the final novel Wright submitted for publication during his lifetime. While Wright drafted a sequel to his last novel entitled *Island of Hallucinations*, his agent responded to the work with overwhelmingly negative criticism. Thus, the novel was never published. In contrast to the warm reception of his earlier works, many critics were disappointed with Wright's publications in his later years, as they felt that his move to Europe alienated him from American Blacks and his emotional and physiological roots.

In June 1960, Wright recorded a series of radio interviews dealing primarily with his books and literary career. He also addressed race relations in the United States, and criticized American policy in Africa. In late September, Wright also did some promotional writing for Nicole Barclay, a Parisian record company executive, to finance his daughter Julia's move from London to Paris, to attend the Sorbonne. While he had enjoyed financial success and stability for most of his career, by the end of his life Wright was nearly penniless, largely as a result of his declining popularity in the United States. Wright's last major contribution to black American literature came in November 1960, when he delivered a lecture entitled "The Situation of the Black Artist and Intellectual in the United States," at the American Church in Paris. In his final years, Wright began to compose haikus. The author wrote almost four thousand of them before he died.

Near the end of his life, Wright grew restless in Paris and expressed a desire to move to London. However, in 1959, the author became ill with an attack of amoebic dysentery that he likely contracted during his international travels. Over the next year and a half, Wright grew increasingly ill, until he died suddenly in Paris in 1961 from an apparent heart attack. As Wright had requested, his body was cremated, and his ashes were mixed with the ashes of a copy of his most famous novel, *Black Boy*. While rumors suggest that Wright was murdered, a claim that his daughter Julia supports, there is no evidence to substantiate such allegations. After his death, Wright's wife Ellen published several of his works posthumously, including a collection of short stories entitled *Eight Men* (1961) and the previously unpublished novel *Lawd Today* (1963).

Today, Richard Wright is largely read and still considered one of the most successful and influential African American writers of the twentieth century. In 1991, the Library of America published a two-volume edition of Wright's work, including *Lawd Today, Uncle Tom's Children, Native Son*, "How 'Bigger' Was Born," *Black Boy (American Hunger)*, and *The Outsider* in their original "author's" versions, restoring cuts and various other changes made by editors and publishers.

Corie Hardy
Arizona State University

FURTHER READING

Fabre, Michel. *The Unfinished Quest of Richard Wright*. Chicago: University of Illinois Press, 1993.

Rowley, Hazel. *Richard Wright: The Life and Times*. New York: Henry Holt and Company, 2001.

Walker, Margaret. *Richard Wright: Daemonic Genius*. New York: Warner Books, 1988.

Wright, Richard. *American Hunger*. New York: Harper and Row, 1975.

Wright, Richard. *Black Boy*. New York: Harper Publishing, 1945.

Selected Bibliography

A. Philip Randolph Pullman Porter Museum. *A. Philip Randolph: Pullman Porter Museum.* http://www.aphiliprandolphmuseum.com/index.html.

Aasang, Nathan. *Florence Griffith Joyner: Dazzling Olympian.* Minneapolis: Lerner Publications, 1989.

Abdul-Jabbar, Kareem. *On the Shoulders of Giants: My Journey Through the Harlem Renaissance.* Boston: Simon and Shuster, 2007.

Adler, Bill. *The Cosby Wit: His Life and Humor.* New York: Carroll and Graf, 1986.

Aftab, Kaleem. *Spike Lee: That's My Story and I'm Sticking to It.* New York: W. W. Norton, 2005.

Alexander, Amy. *The Farrakhan Factor: African-American Writers on Leadership, Nationhood, and Minister Louis Farrakhan.* New York: Grove Press, 1998.

Ali, Muhammad, and Richard Durham. *The Greatest: My Own Story.* New York: Random House, 1975.

American Express Magic Johnson 2004 All Star Game Tribute. http://www.nba.com/allstar2004/magic_tribute/.

Anderson, Jervis. *A. Philip Randolph: A Biographical Portrait.* Berkeley: University of California Press, 1986.

Anderson, Jervis. *Bayard Rustin: Troubles I've Seen: A Biography.* New York: Harper-Collins, 1997.

Andrews, D. L. "The Facts of Michael Jordan's Blackness: Excavating a Floating Racial Signifier." *Sociology of Sport Journal* 13, no. 2 (1996): 125–58.

Andrews, D. L, ed. *Michael Jordan, Inc.: Corporate Sport, Media Culture and Late Modern America.* Albany: State University of New York, 2001.

Angelou, Maya. *The Collected Autobiographies of Maya Angelou.* New York: Modern Library Edition, 2004.

Angelou, Maya. *The Complete Collected Poems of Maya Angelou.* New York: Random House, 1994.

Angelou, Maya. *Letter to My Daughter.* New York: Random House, 2008.

Angelou, Maya. *Phenomenal Women.* New York: Random House, 2000.

Apollo Theater Webpage. www.apollotheater.org.

Aptheker, Herbert. *Nat Turner's Slave Rebellion: Including the 1831 "Confessions."* Mineola, NY: Dover Publications, 2006.

Ardell, Jean Hastings. "Baseball Annies, Jack Johnson, and Kenesaw Mountain Landis: How Groupies Influenced the Lengthy Ban on Blacks in Organized Baseball." *Nine*, Spring 2005, 103.

Armstrong, Louis. *My Life in New Orleans*. New York: Prentice-Hall, 1954.

Arnesen, Eric. *Brotherhoods of Color: Black Railroad Workers and the Struggle for Equality*. Cambridge, MA: Harvard University Press, 2002.

Asch, Christopher Myers. *The Senator and the Sharecropper: The Freedom Struggles of James O. Eastland and Fannie Lou Hamer*. New York: New Press, 2008.

Ashe, Arthur, and Neil Amdur. *Off the Court*. New York: New American Library, 1981.

Ashe, Arthur, and Frank Deford. *Arthur Ashe: Portrait in Motion*. New York: Carroll & Graf Publishers, 1993.

Ashe, Arthur, and Clifford George Gewecke, Jr. *Advantage Ashe*. New York: Coward-McCann Inc., 1967.

Ashe, Arthur, and Arnold Rampersad. *Days of Grace: A Memoir*. New York: Alfred A. Knopf, 1993.

Bak, Richard. *Joe Louis: The Great Black Hope*. New York: Da Capo, 1998.

Baker, Jean-Claude, and Chris Chase. *Josephine: The Hungry Heart*. New York: Random House, 1993.

Baker, William J. *Jesse Owens: An American Life*. New York: The Free Press, 1986.

Balaji, Murali. *The Professor and the Pupil: The Politics of W. E. B. Du Bois and Paul Robeson*. New York: Nation Books, 2007.

Baldwin, James. *Another Country*. New York: Dial Press, 1962.

Baldwin, James. *The Fire Next Time*. New York: Vintage International, 1993.

Baldwin, James. *Giovanni's Room; a Novel*. New York: Dial Press, 1956.

Baldwin, James. *Go Tell It on the Mountain*. New York: Delta Trade Paperbacks, 2000.

Banting, Erinn. *Halle Berry*. New York: Weigl Publishers, 2005.

Barkley, Charles. *I May Be Wrong but I Doubt It*. New York: Random House, 2003.

Barkley, Charles. *Outrageous!* New York: Random House, 1994.

Barkley, Charles. *Sir Charles: The Wit and Wisdom of Charles Barkley*. New York: Warner Books, 1994.

Barkley, Charles. *Who's Afraid of a Large Black Man?* New York: Penguin Press, 2005.

Barrow, Joe Louis, Jr., and Barbara Munder. *Joe Louis: 50 Years an American Hero*. New York: McGraw-Hill, 1988.

Bates, Beth Tompkins. *Pullman Porters and the Rise of Protest Politics in Black America, 1925–1945*. Chapel Hill: The University of North Carolina Press, 2001.

Bates, Gerri. *Alice Walker: A Critical Companion*. Westport, CT: Greenwood Press, 2005.

Bay, Mia. *To Tell the Truth Freely: The Life of Ida B. Wells*. New York: Hill and Wang, 2009.

Beard, Hilary, Venus Williams, and Serena Williams. *Venus and Serena: Serving from the Hip: 10 Rules for Living, Loving, and Winning*. Boston: Houghton Mifflin, 2005.

Beaulieu, Elizabeth Ann, ed. *The Toni Morrison Encyclopedia*. Westport, CT: Greenwood Press, 2003.

Bego, Mark. *Aretha Franklin: The Queen of Soul*. New York: Da Capo Press, 2001.

Belafonte, Harry. "Why I Married Julie." *Ebony*, July 1957, 90–95.

Berenson, Jann. *Will Power! A Biography of Will Smith*. New York: Spotlight Entertainment, 1997.

Berg, Herbert. *Elijah Muhammad and Islam*. New York: NYU Press, 2009.

Bernard, Emily, ed. *Remember Me to Harlem: The Letters of Langston Hughes and Carl Van Vechten*. New York: Vintage, 2002.

Berry, Venise T., and Carmen L. Manning-Miller. *Mediated Messages and African-American Culture: Contemporary Issues*. Thousand Oaks, CA: Sage Publications, 1996.

Bieze, Michael. *Booker T. Washington and the Art of Self-Representation*. New York: Peter Lang, 2008.

Bingham, Howard L., and Max Wallace. *Muhammad Ali's Greatest Fight: Cassius Clay vs. The United States of America*. New York: M. Evans and Company, 2000.

Biography. *The Harlem Globetrotters: America's Court Jesters*. A&E Television Networks, 2005.

Bird, Larry, Earvin Johnson, and Jackie MacMullan. *When the Game Was Ours*. Boston: Houghton Mifflin Harcourt, 2009.

Blackburn, Julia. *With Billie*. New York: Pantheon, 2005.

Blatt, Martin H., Thomas J. Brown, and Donald Yacovone. *Hope & Glory: Essays on the Legacy of the 54th Massachusetts Regiment*. Amherst: University of Massachusetts Press, 2001.

Blight, David W. *Frederick Douglass' Civil War: Keeping Faith in Jubilee*. Baton Rouge: Louisiana State University Press, 1989.

Bloom, Barry M. "Bonds Reflects on '01, Dad's Influence," October 5, 2005, MLB.com. http://barrybonds.mlb.com/NASApp/mlb/news/article.jsp?ymd=2005 1004&content_id=1237223&vkey=news_sf&fext=.jsp&c_id=sf (accessed August 1, 2006).

Bly, Nellie. *Oprah! Up Close and Down Home*. New York: Kensington, 1993.

Bogle, Donald. *Dorothy Dandridge: A Biography*. New York: Amistad Press, 1997.

Bontemps, Arna. *Free at Last: The Life of Frederick Douglass*. New York: Dodd, Mead, and Co., 1971.

Boskin, Joseph. *Sambo: The Rise & Demise of an American Jester*. Oxford: Oxford University Press, 1988.

Boyd, Herb. *Baldwin's Harlem: A Biography of James Baldwin*. New York: Atria Books, 2008.

Boyd, Valerie. *Wrapped in Rainbows: The Life of Zora Neale Hurston*. New York: Scribner, 2003.

Bradford, Sarah H. *Harriet Tubman: The Moses of Her People*. New York: Corinth. Books, Inc., 1961. Originally published 1886.

Bradford, Sarah H. *Scenes in the Life of Harriet Tubman*. New York: W. J. Moses, 1869.

Brawley, Benjamin. *History of Morehouse College, Written on the Authority of the Board of Trustees*. College Park, MD: McGrath, 1917.

Breitman, George. *The Last Years of Malcolm X*. New York: Pathfinder Press, 1976.

Brinkley, Douglas. *Rosa Parks*. New York: Penguin Lives, 2000.

Brode, Douglas. *Denzel Washington: His Films and Career*. Secaucus, NJ: Carol Publishing Group, 1997.

Brothers, Thomas. *Louis Armstrong in His Own Words*. New York: Oxford University Press, 1999.

Brundage, W. Fitzhugh, ed. *Booker T. Washington and Black Progress*. Gainesville: University of Florida Press, 2003.

Brunt, Stephen. *Facing Ali: 15 Fighters, 15 Stories*. New York: Lions Press, 2002.

Buckley, Annie. *Robert L. Johnson*. Ann Arbor, MI: Cherry Lake Publishing, 2008.

Buckley, Gail Lumet. *The Hornes: An American Family*. New York: Applause Books, 1986.

Bumiller, Elisabeth. *Condoleezza Rice: An American Life: A Biography*. New York: Random House, 2009.

Bunche, Ralph J. *The Political Status of the Negro in the Age of FDR*. Chicago: The University of Chicago Press, 1973.

Bundles, A'Lelia. *Madam C. J. Walker*. New York: Chelsea House Publishers, 1991.

Bundles, A'Lelia. *On Her Own Ground: The Life and Times of Madam C. J. Walker*. New York: Scribner, 2001.

Burchard, Peter. *One Gallant Rush: Robert Gould Shaw and His Brave Black Regiment*. New York: St. Martin's Press, 1965.

Burrell, Ian. "Hendrix Hits Top Note Again as Best Guitarist in History." *The Independent*, August 28, 2003.

Butley, Addie Louise Joyner. *The Distinctive Black College: Talladega, Tuskegee, and Morehouse*. Metuchen, NJ: Scarecrow Press, 1977.

Callahan, Tom. *In Search of Tiger: A Journey through Golf with Tiger Woods*. New York: Three Rivers, 2004.

Campbell, James. *Talking at the Gates: A Life of James Baldwin*. New York: Penguin Books, 1992.

Carmichael, Stokely. *Stokely Speaks: From Black Power to Pan-Africanism*. Chicago: Lawrence Hill, 2007.

Carmichael, Stokely, and Charles V. Hamilton. *Black Power: The Politics of Liberation*. New York: Vintage, 1967.

Carmichael, Stokely, and Michael Thelwell. *Ready for Revolution: The Life and Struggles of Stokely Carmichael*. New York: Scribner, 2003.

Carner, Gary. *The Miles Davis Companion: Four Decades of Commentary*. New York: Schirmer Books, 1996.

Caroll, Rebecca, ed. *Uncle Tom or New Negro?: African Americans Reflect on Booker T. Washington and Up from Slavery One Hundred Years Later*. New York: Harlem Moon, 2006.

Carter, Bob. "Ashe's Impact Reached Far Beyond the Court." *ESPN.com*. http://espn.go.com/classic/biography/s/Ashe_Arthur.html.

Carver, George Washington, and Gary R. Kremer. *George Washington Carver: In His Own Words*. Columbia, MO: University of Missouri Press, 1987.

Chang, Jeff. *Can't Stop, Won't Stop: A History of the Hip Hop Generation*. New York: Picador Press, 2005.

Childress, Boyd. "Arthur Ashe (1943–1993)." *Encyclopedia Virginia*. http://www.encyclopediavirginia.org/Ashe_Arthur_1943–1993.

Chisholm, Shirley. *The Good Fight*. New York: Harper & Row, 1973.

Chisholm, Shirley. *Unbought and Unbossed*. Boston: Houghton Mifflin, 1970.

Christgau, John. *Tricksters in the Madhouse: Lakers vs. Globetrotters, 1948*. Lincoln: University of Nebraska Press, 2004.

Clark, Glenn. *The Man Who Talks with the Flowers: The Life Story of Dr. George Washington Carver*. Austin, MN: Macalester Park Publishing, 2003.

Clarke, John Henrik, ed. *Malcolm X: The Man and His Times*. Trenton, NJ: Africa World Press, 1969.

Clarke, John Henrik, *William Styron's Nat Turner: Ten Black Writers Respond*. Westport, CT: Greenwood Press, 1987.

Cleaver, Kathleen, and George Katsiaficas, eds. *Liberation, Imagination, and the Black Panther Party: A New Look at the Panthers and Their Legacy*. New York: Routledge, 2001.

Clegg, Claude Andrew. *An Original Man: The Life and Times of Elijah Muhammad*. New York: St. Martin's Press, 1997.

Clinton, Catherine. *Harriet Tubman: The Road to Freedom*. Boston: Little, Brown and Company, 2004.

Coates, Ta-Nehisi. "Rice, Rice, Baby! My Big Fat Crush on Condoleezza." *Village Voice*, July 22, 2003. http://www.villagevoice.com/2003-07-22/news/rice-rice-baby/.

Collier, James Lincoln. *Duke Ellington*. New York: Oxford University Press, 1987.

Collins, Patricia Hill. *On Lynchings: Ida B. Wells-Barnett*. Amherst, NY: Humanity Books, 2002.

Colman, Penny. *Madame C. J. Walker: Building a Business Empire*. Brookfield, CT: Millbrook Press, 1994.

Cooper, Ralph. *Amateur Night at the Apollo: Ralph Cooper Presents Five Decades of Great Entertainment*. New York: HarperCollins, 1990.

Cornish, Dudley T. *The Sable Arm: Negro Troops in the Union Army, 1861–1865*. New York: Longmans, 1956.

Cosby, Bill. "Bill Cosby: Official website." http://www.billcosby.com/ Avery Ennis, LLC, 2007.

Cosby, Bill. *Come On People: On the Path from Victims to Victors*. Nashville, TN: Thomas Nelson, Inc., 2007.

Cosby, Bill. *Fatherhood*. Garden City, NY: Doubleday, 1986.

Cosby, Bill. *Love and Marriage*. New York: Doubleday, 1989.

Courtney-Clarke, Margaret. *Maya Angelou: The Poetry of Living*. New York: Clarkson Potter, 1999.

Cross, Charles R. *Room Full of Mirrors: A Biography of Jimi Hendrix*. New York: Hyperion Books, 2006.

Dagbovie, Pero Gaglo. *The Early Black History Movement, Carter G. Woodson, and Lorenzo Johnston Greene*. Urbana: University of Illinois Press, 2007.

Dagbovie, Pero Gaglo. "Exploring One Century of Historical Scholarship on Booker T. Washington." *Journal of African American History* 92 (Spring 2007): 239–64.

Dalfiume, Richard M. *Desegregation of the U.S. Armed Forces: Fighting on Two Fronts, 1939–1953*. Columbia: University of Missouri Press, 1969.

Dance, Stanley. *The World of Duke Ellington*. New York: Charles Scribner's Sons, 1970.

Dandridge, Dorothy, and Earl Conrad. *Everything and Nothing: The Dorothy Dandridge Tragedy*. New York: HarperCollins, 2000.

Davis, Angela Y. *The Angela Y. Davis Reader*. Blackwell Readers. Malden, MA: Blackwell, 1998.

Davis, Angela Y. *Angela Davis—an Autobiography*. New York: International Publishers, 1988.

Davis, Angela Y. *Are Prisons Obsolete?* New York: Seven Stories Press, 2003.

Davis, Angela Y. *Women, Race & Class*. New York: Vintage Books, 1983.

Davis, Gregory, and Lee Susman. *Dark Magus: The Jeckyll and Hyde Life of Miles Davis*. San Francisco: Backbeat Books, 2006.

Davis, Sammy, Jr., Burt Boyar, and Jane Boyar. *Sammy: An Autobiography*. New York: Farrar, Straus and Giroux, 2000.

Davis, Sharon. *Stevie Wonder: Rhythms of Wonder*. London: Anova Books, 2006.

Deardorff, Donald, II. "World Boxing Champion Jack Johnson, Contemptuous and Irritating, Taunted Whites." *St. Louis Journalism Review* 8, no. 3 (October 1995).

Dee, Kool Mo. *There's God on the Mic: The True 50 Greatest MCs*. New York: Thunder's Mouth Press, 2003.

Dent, Tom. *Southern Journey: A Return to the Civil Rights Movement*. Athens: University of Georgia Press, 2001.

Denton, Virginia Lantz. *Booker T. Washington and the Adult Education Movement*. Gainesville: University of Florida Press, 1993.

DeYoung, Karen. *Soldier: The Life of Colin Powell*. New York: Alfred A. Knopf, 2006.

Dobkin, Matt. *I Never Loved a Man the Way I Love You: Aretha Franklin, Respect, and the Making of a Soul Music Masterpiece*. New York: St. Martin's Press, 2004.

Donaldson, Madeline. *Venus and Serena Williams*. New York: First Avenue Editions, 2003.

D'Orio, Wayne. *Carol Moseley Braun*. Philadelphia: Chelsea House Publishers, 2004.

Douglass, Frederick. *Narrative of the Life of Frederick Douglass, an American Slave*. Boston: Bedford/St. Martins, 2002.

Drake, Dick. "Tommie Smith & Lee Evans Discuss Potential Olympic Boycott." *Track & Field News*, November 1967. http://www.trackandfieldnews.com/display _article.php? id=1605 (accessed August 5, 2009).

Dryden, Charles W. *A-Train: Memoirs of a Tuskegee Airman*. Tuscaloosa: University of Alabama Press, 1997.

Driven: Jay-Z. The Rise and Rise of Jay-Z, VH-1, 2003.

Du Bois, W. E. B. *The Autobiography of W. E. B. Du Bois: A Soliloquy on Viewing My Life from the Last Decade of Its First Century*. New York: International Publishers, 1968.

Du Bois, W. E. B. *Dusk of Dawn: An Essay toward an Autobiography of a Race Concept*. New York: Harcourt, Brace, and Co., 1940.

Du Bois, W. E. B. *The Souls of Black Folk*. New York: Library of America, 1903.

Dudziak, Mary L. *Cold War Civil Rights: Race and the Image of American Democracy*. Princeton, NJ: Princeton University Press, 2000.

Dudziak, Mary L. *Exporting American Dreams: Thurgood Marshall's African Journey*. Oxford: Oxford University Press, 2008.

Due, Tananarive. *The Black Rose: The Dramatic Story of Madam C. J. Walker, America's First Black Female Millionaire*. New York: One World, 2000.

Duke, Eric D. "Moseley Braun, Carol." In *Black Women in America*, edited by Darlene Clark Hine. New York: Oxford University Press, 2005.

Duncan, Russell, ed. *Blue-Eyed Child of Fortune: The Civil War Letters of Colonel Robert Gould Shaw*. Athens: University of Georgia, 1992.

Duncan, Russell. *Where Death and Glory Meet: Colonel Robert Gould Shaw and the 54th Massachusetts Infantry.* Athens: University of Georgia Press, 1999.

Dyson, Michael Eric. "Be Like Mike?: Michael Jordan and the Pedagogy of Desire." *Cultural Studies* 7, no. 1 (1993): 64–72.

Dyson, Michael Eric. *Holler if You Hear Me: Searching for Tupac Shakur.* New York: Basic Civitas, 2001.

Dyson, Michael Eric. *Is Bill Cosby Right?: Or Has the Black Middle Class Lost Its Mind?*
New York: Basic Civitas Books, 2005.

Dyson, Michael Eric. *Making Malcolm: The Myth and Meaning of Malcolm X.* New York, Oxford University Press, 1995.

Dyson, Michael Eric. *Mercy, Mercy Me: The Art, Loves, and Demons of Marvin Gaye.* New York: Civitas, 2004.

Early, Gerald, ed. *The Muhammad Ali Reader.* Hopewell, NJ: Ecco Press, 1998.

Early, Gerald. *One Nation under a Groove: Motown and American Culture.* Ann Arbor: University of Michigan Press, 2004.

Ebony Magazine Editors. *Ebony Special Tribute, Michael Jackson: In His Own Words and Notes from Those Who Loved Him.* Chicago: Johnson Publishers, 2009.

Edelman, Marian Wright. "Spelman College: A Safe Haven for Young Black Women." *Journal of Blacks in Higher Education* 27 (2000): 118–23.

Edgar, Robert R., ed. *An African American in South Africa: The Travel Notes of Ralph J. Bunche, 28 September 1937–1 January 1938.* Athens: Ohio University Press, 1992.

Editors of Life Magazine. *The American Journey of Barack Obama.* New York: Little, Brown and Company, 2008.

Edwards, Harry. *The Struggle That Must Be: An Autobiography.* New York: Macmillan, 1980.

Ellen Degeneres Show. "Michelle Obama Appearance," September 8, 2008. http://www.youtube.com/watch?v=ngqUSlVQfbY.

Ellington, Edward Kennedy. *Music Is My Mistress.* New York: Doubleday & Company, Inc., 1973.

Ellington, Mercer, with Stanley Dance. *Duke Ellington in Person: An Intimate Memoir.* Boston: Houghton Mifflin Company, 1978.

Elliot, Jeffrey M., ed. *Conversations with Maya Angelou.* Jackson and London: University Press of Mississippi, 1989.

Ellison, Ralph. *Invisible Man.* New York: Modern Library, 1992.

Ellison, Ralph. *Juneteenth: A Novel.* New York: Random House, 1999.

Emilio, Luis F. *A Brave Black Regiment: History of the 54th Regiment of Massachusetts Volunteer Infantry, 1863–1865.* Boston: Boston Book Co., 1891.

Erlewin, Michael. *All Music Guide to Jazz.* San Francisco: Backbeat Books, 1998.

Evans, Art. "Joe Louis as a Key Functionary: White Reactions toward a Black Champion." *Journal of Black Studies* 16, no. 1 (September 1985): 95–111.

Evanzz, Karl. *The Messenger: The Rise and Fall of Elijah Muhammad.* New York: Pantheon Books, 1999.

Fabre, Michel. *The Unfinished Quest of Richard Wright.* Chicago: University of Illinois Press, 1993.

Fade to Black. Dir. Patrick Paulson and Michael John Warren. DVD. Paramount, 2005.

Fainaru-Wada, Mark, and Lance Williams. *Games of Shadows: Barry Bonds, BALCO, and the Steroids Scandal That Rocked Professional Sports*. New York: Gotham, 2006.

Fainaru-Wada, Mark, and Lance Williams. "The Truth: Barry Bonds and Steroids." *Sports Illustrated*, March 13, 2006.

Fairclough, Adam. *To Redeem the Soul of America: The Southern Christian Leadership Conference and Martin Luther King, Jr.* Athens: University of Georgia Press, 2001.

Farrakhan, Louis. *A Torchlight for America*. Chicago: FCN Publishing, 1993.

Federal Bureau of Investigations. *Stokely Carmichael—the FBI Files*. Washington, DC: Federal Bureau of Investigations, 2009.

Federer, William J. *George Washington Carver*. New York: Amerisearch, 2002.

Fehrenbacher, Don E. *The Dred Scott Case: Its Significance in American Law and Politics*. New York: Oxford University Press, 1978.

Felix, Antonia. *Condi: The Condoleezza Rice Story*. New York: Newmarket Press, 2005.

Fidelman, Geoffrey Mark. *First Lady of Song: Ella Fitzgerald for the Record*. Seacaucus, NJ: Carol, 1994.

Finkelman, Paul. *Dred Scott v. Sandford: A Brief History with Documents*. Boston: Bedford Books, 1997.

Fishgall, Gary. *Gonna do Great Things: The Life of Sammy Davis, Jr.* New York: A Lisa Drew Book/Scribner, 2003.

Fitch, Suzanne Pullon, and Mandzuik, Roseann M. *Sojourner Truth as Orator: Wit, Story, and Song*. Westport, CT: Greenwood Press, 1997.

"Florence Griffith Joyner: The World's Fastest Woman." Estate of Florence Griffith Joyner. www.florencegriffithjoyner.com.

Fogelson, Genia. *Harry Belafonte: Singer and Actor*. Los Angeles: Melrose Square Publishing Company, 1991.

Foner, Philip S. *The Life and Writings of Frederick Douglass*. 5 vols. New York: International Publishers, 1950–1975.

Fowler, Virginia, ed. *Conversations with Nikki Giovanni*. Jackson: University of Mississippi Press, 1992.

Fox, Ted. *Showtime at the Apollo: The Story of Harlem's World Famous Theater*. Reprint, Rhinebeck, NY: Mill Road Enterprises, 2003.

Franklin, Aretha, and David Ritz. *Aretha: From These Roots*. New York: Villard, 1999.

Franklin, John Hope, and Alfred A. Moss. *From Slavery to Freedom: A History of African Americans*. 8th ed. New York: Alfred A. Knopf, 2000.

Freeman, Philip. *Running the Voodoo Down: The Electric Music of Miles Davis*. San Francisco: Backbeat Books, 2005.

French, Scot. *The Rebellious Slave: Nat Turner in American Memory*. Boston: Houghton Mifflin Harcourt, 2004.

Fritts, Ron, and Ken Vail. *Ella Fitzgerald: The Chick Webb Years and Beyond*. Lanham, MD: Scarecrow Press, 2003.

Gardell, Matthias. *In the Name of Elijah Muhammad: Louis Farrakhan and the Nation of Islam*. Durham, NC: Duke University Press, 1996.

Garrow, David. *Bearing the Cross: Martin Luther King, Jr., and the Southern Christian Leadership Conference*. New York: Harper Perennial, 2004.

Garvey, Amy Jacques, and Marcus Garvey. *The Philosophy and Opinions of Marcus Garvey: Africa for the Africans.* Dover, MA: The Majority Press, 1986.

Gates, Henry L., Jr. *Langston Hughes: Critical Perspectives Past and Present.* New York: Amistad Press, 1993.

Gates, Henry L., Jr. *Thirteen Ways of Looking at a Black Man.* New York: Vintage Books, 1997.

Gavin, James. *Stormy Weather: The Life of Lena Horne.* New York: Atria Books, 2009.

Gaye, Frankie. *Marvin Gaye, My Brother.* New York: Backbeat, 2003.

George Meany Memorial Archives of the National Labor College. *A. Philip Randolph Exhibit.* http://www.nlc.edu/archives/apr.html.

George, Nelson. *Where Did Our Love Go?: The Rise and Fall of the Motown Sound.* Urbana: University of Illinois Press, 2007.

Gerstle, Gary. *American Crucible: Race and Nation in the Twentieth Century.* Princeton, NJ: Princeton University Press, 2002.

Giddens, Gary. *Satchmo: The Genius of Louis Armstrong.* New York: Da Capo Press, 1988.

Giddings, Paula J. *Ida: A Sword among Lions: Ida B. Wells and the Campaign against Lynching.* New York: Amistad, 2008.

Gilbert, Olive. *Narrative of Sojourner Truth, a Northern Slave, Emancipated from Bodily Servitude by the State of New York, in 1828.* Boston: Printed for the Author, 1850.

Gilmore, Al-Tony. "Jack Johnson and White Women: The National Impact." *Journal of Negro History* 58, no. 1 (January 1973): 18–38.

Giovanni, Nikki. *The Collected Poetry of Nikki Giovanni, 1968–1998.* New York: William Morrow, 2003.

Giovanni, Nikki. *The Prosaic Soul of Nikki Giovanni.* New York: Perennial, 2003.

Giovanni, Nikki. *Rosa.* New York: Henry Holt and Company, 2005.

Gogerly, Liz. *Halle Berry.* Chicago: Raintree, 2005.

Goggin, Jacqueline. *Carter G. Woodson: A Life in Black History.* Baton Rouge: Louisiana State University Press, 1993.

Goldman, Peter. *The Death and Life of Malcolm X.* New York: Harper and Row, 1973.

Gonzalez, Doreen. *Alex Haley: Author of Roots.* Hillside, NJ: Enslow, 1994.

Goudsouzian, Aram. *Sidney Poitier: Man, Actor, Icon.* Chapel Hill: University of North Carolina Press, 2004.

Gourse, Leslie, ed. *The Billie Holiday Companion.* New York: Schirmer, 1997.

Gourse, Leslie. *The Ella Fitzgerald Companion.* New York: Schrimer, 1998.

Graham, Francis D., and Susan L. Poulson. "Spelman College: A Place All Their Own." In *Challenged by Coeducation: Women's Colleges since the 1960s,* edited by Susan L. Poulson and Leslie Miller-Bernal. Nashville: Vanderbilt University Press, 2006, 234–56.

Grant, Joanne. *Ella Baker: Freedom Bound.* New York: John Wiley & Sons, 1998.

Gray, Thomas R. *The Confessions of Nat Turner: The Leader of the Late Insurrection in Southampton, Virginia.* Whitefish, MT: Kessinger Publishing, 2004.

Gray, Todd. *Michael Jackson: Before He Was King.* New York: Chronicle Books, 2009.

Green, Ben. *Spinning the Globe: The Rise, Fall, and Return to Greatness of the Harlem Globetrotters*. New York: Amistad, 2005.

Greenberg, Kenneth S, ed. *The Confessions of Nat Turner and Related Documents*. New York: Bedford/St. Martin's, 1996.

Greenberg, Kenneth S. *Nat Turner: A Slave Rebellion in History and Memory*. New York: Oxford University Press, 2004.

Gutgold, Nichola D. "Carol Moseley Braun: 'A Fiscal Hawk and a Peace Dove.' " In *Paving the Way for Madam President*, 134–60. Lanham, MD: Lexington Book, 2006.

Guy, Jasmine. *Afeni Shakur: Evolution of a Revolutionary*. New York: Atria, 2004.

Guy-Sheftall, Beverly, and Jo Moore Stewart. *Spelman: A Centennial Celebration, 1881–1981*. Atlanta: Spelman College, 1981.

Halberstam, David. *Playing for Keeps: Michael Jordan and the World He Made*. New York: Random House, 1999.

Haley, Alex. *A Different Kind of Christmas*. New York: Doubleday, 1988.

Haley, Alex. *The Playboy Interviews*. New York: Ballantine, 1993.

Haley, Alex. *Roots: The Saga of an American Family*. New York: Doubleday, 1976.

Haley, Alex, and David Stevens. *Alex Haley's Queen: The Story of an American Family*. New York: Morrow, 1993.

Hamer, Fannie Lou. *To Praise Our Bridges*. Jackson, MS: KIPCO, 1967.

Hammond, Bryan, and Patrick O'Connor. *Josephine Baker*. London: Little, Brown and Company, 1988.

Hampton, Dream. "Hellraiser." *Source* 62 (1994): 80–82, 84–85, 88–89.

Hamrahi, Joe with Bill James. "Being Barry Bonds."*Baseball Digest*, May 29, 2006.

Haney, Lynn. *Naked at the Feast: A Biography of Josephine Baker*. London: Robson Books, 1995.

Harari, Oren. *The Leadership Secrets of Colin Powell*. New York: McGraw-Hill Companies, 2003.

Harris, Trudier, ed. *Selected Works of Ida B. Wells-Barnett*. New York: Oxford University Press, 1991.

Hartmann, Douglas. *Race, Culture, and the Revolt of the Black Athlete: The 1968 Olympic Protests and Their Aftermath*. Chicago: University of Chicago Press, 2003.

Haskins, James. *Lena Horne*. n.p.: Putnam Juvenile, 1983.

Hasse, John Edward. *Beyond Category: The Life and Genius of Duke Ellington*. New York: Simon & Schuster, 1993.

Haulman, Daniel L. *112 Victories: Aerial Victory Credits of the Tuskegee Airmen* (condensed version). Air Force Historical Research Agency, March 31, 2008, http://www.tuskegeeairmen.org/uploads/AerialVictories.pdf (accessed March 3, 2010).

Hauser, Thomas. *Muhammad Ali: His Life and Times*. New York: Simon and Schuster, 1991.

HBO Sports. *Arthur Ashe: Citizen of the World*. New York: HBO Home Video, 1994.

Heath, Thomas. "Johnson Readies His Next Gamble." *Washington Post*, February 16, 2009.

Hemenway, Robert E. *Zora Neale Hurston: A Literary Biography*. Urbana: University of Illinois Press, 1977.

Henderson, Joyce. *C. L. Dellums: International President of the Brotherhood of the Sleeping Car Porters and Civil Rights Leader*. Berkeley: The Regents of the University of California, 1973.

Henry, Charles P., ed. *Ralph Bunche: Selected Speeches and Writings*. Ann Arbor: University of Michigan Press, 1995.

Hentoff, Nat. *Jazz Country*. New York: HarperCollins, 1965.

Hine, Darlene Clark, ed. *Black Women in America*. Brooklyn: Carlson Publishing, 1993.

Hine, Darlene Clark. *Facts on File Encyclopedia of Black Women in America: Social Activism*. New York: Facts on File, Inc., 1997.

Hine, Darlene Clark, and Kathleen Thompson. *A Shining Thread of Hope: The History of Black Women in America*. New York: Broadway Books, 1999.

Hodgkinson, Mark. "Serena 'Shocked' by More Racist Abuse." *Telegraph.co.uk*, March 4, 2007. http://www.telegraph.co.uk/sport/main.jhtml?view=DETAILS&grid =A1YourView&xml=/sport/2007/03/28/sthodg28.xml (accessed, September 10, 2007).

Holloway, Jonathan Scott. *Confronting the Veil: Abram Harris Jr., E. Franklin Frazier, and Ralph Bunche, 1919–1941*. Chapel Hill: University of North Carolina Press, 2002.

Holway, John. *Blackball Stars: Negro League Pioneers*. Westport, CT: Meckler Publishing Company, 1988.

Holway, John. *Black Diamonds: Life in the Negro Leagues from the Men Who Lived It*. Westport, CT: Meckler Publishing Company, 1989.

Holway, John. *Voices from the Great Black Baseball Leagues*. New York: Da Capo Press, 1992.

Hooks, Bell, and Cornel West. *Breaking Bread: Insurgent Black Intellectual Life*. Boston: South End Press, 1991.

Hopper, Hedda. "Hattie Hates Nobody." *Chicago Sunday Tribune*, n.d., ca. 1947.

Horne, Lena. *Lena*. New York: Doubleday, 1965.

Horne, Lena. *The Rosie O'Donnell Show*, 1998, Parts 1 and 2.

Houck, Davis W., and David E. Dixon, eds. *Rhetoric, Religion, and the Civil Rights Movement, 1954–1965*. Waco, TX: Baylor University Press, 2006.

Houck, Davis W., and David E. Dixon. *Women and the Civil Rights Movement, 1954–1965*. Jackson: University Press of Mississippi, 2009.

Hoye, Jacob, and Karolyn Ali, eds. *Tupac: Resurrection 1971–1996*. New York: Atria, 2003.

Hughes, Langston. *The Big Sea*. New York: Alfred A. Knopf, 1940.

Hughes, Langston. *The Collected Poems of Langston Hughes*. New York: Knopf, 1994.

Hughes, Langston. *The Collected Works of Langston Hughes*. Columbia: University of Missouri Press, 2001.

Hughes, Langston. *I Wonder as I Wander*. New York: Rinehart, 1956.

Humez, Jean. *Harriet Tubman: The Life and the Life Stories*. Madison: University of Wisconsin Press, 2003.

Hurston, Zora Neale. *Dust Tracks on a Road*. New York: HarperCollins, 1996.

Ignatius, Idi. *Time President Obama: The Path to the White House*. New York: Time, 2008.

Ingham, Chris. *Billie Holiday*. London: Unanimous, 2000.

Inniss, Leslie B., and Joe R. Feagin. "The Cosby Show: The View from the Black Middle Class." *Journal of Black Studies* 25, no. 6 (July 1995): 692–711.

Jackson, Buzzy. *A Bad Woman Feeling Good: Blues and the Women Who Sing Them.* New York: Norton, 2005.

Jackson, Carlton. *Hattie: The Life of Hattie McDaniel.* Lanham, MD: Madison Books, 1990.

Jackson, David H. *Booker T. Washington and the Struggle against White Supremacy: The Southern Educational Tours, 1908–1912.* New York: Palgrave Macmillan, 2008.

Jackson, Lawrence Patrick. *Ralph Ellison: Emergence of Genius.* Athens: University of Georgia Press, 2007.

Jackson, Michael. *Moonwalk.* New York: Harmony, 2009.

James, Joy. "Ella Baker, 'Black Women's Work,' and Activist Intellectuals." *The Black Scholar* 24 (Fall 1994): 8–12.

"Jay-Z," Def Jam.com. http://www.islanddefjam.com/artist/bio.aspx?artistID=7304.

Jet Magazine, Chicago: November 1988.

Jefferson, Margo. *On Michael Jackson.* New York: Vintage, 2007.

Jimoh, A Yemisi. "Toni Morrison." *The Literary Encyclopedia*, October 25, 2002. http://www.litencyc.com/php/speople.php?rec=true&UID=3214.

Johnson, Earvin, and William Novak. *My Life.* New York: Random House, 1992.

Johnson, Jack. *Jack Johnson—in the Ring—and Out.* Chicago: National Sports Publishing Company, 1927.

Johnson, James Weldon. *Along This Way: The Autobiography of James Weldon Johnson.* New York: Da Capo Press, 2000.

Johnson, James Weldon. *The Autobiography of an Ex-Colored Man.* New York: Hill and Wang, 1960.

Johnson, James Weldon. *God's Trombones: Seven Negro Sermons in Verse.* Viking Compass Edition. New York: The Viking Press, 1969.

Johnson, Marilyn. "Oprah Winfrey: A Life in Books." *Life*, September 1997, 45–60.

Johnson, Robert L. *Current Biography* 55 (April 1994): 28.

Johnson, Wilfred. *Ella Fitzgerald: An Annotated Discography.* Jefferson, NC: McFarland, 2001.

Jones, Charles E., ed. *The Black Panther Party Reconsidered.* Baltimore: Black Classic Press, 1998.

Jones, Felecia Gilmore. "The Black Audience and Black Entertainment Television." PhD dissertation, University of Georgia, 1989.

Jones, Lisa, and Spike Lee. *Do the Right Thing.* New York: Fireside, 1989.

Jones, Quincy. *Q: The Autobiography of Quincy Jones.* New York: Harlem Moon, 2001.

Jones, Quincy, Maya Angelou, and Clint Eastwood. *The Complete Quincy Jones: My Journey & Passions.* New York: Insight Books, 2008.

Jordan, Barbara, and Shelby Hearon. *Barbara Jordan: A Self-Portrait.* Garden City, NY: Doubleday & Company, 1979.

Jordan, Michael, and David Halberstam. *Driven from Within.* New York: Atria, 2006.

Jordan, Michael, and W. Iooss. *Rare Air: Michael on Michael.* New York: HarperCollins, 1993.

Joseph, Peniel. *Waiting 'til the Midnight Hour: A Narrative History of Black Power in America.* New York: Henry Holt and Co., 2006.

Jules-Rosette, Bennetta. *Josephine Baker in Art and Life: The Icon and the Image.* Champaign: University of Illinois Press, 2007.

Kaplan, Carla, ed. *Zora Neale Hurston: A Life in Letters.* New York: Doubleday, 2002.

Kavanaugh, Lee Hill. *Quincy Jones: Musician, Composer, Producer.* Berkeley Heights, NJ: Enslow, 1998.

Kelley, Robin D. G., and Earl Lewis, eds. *To Make Our World Anew: A History of African Americans.* New York: Oxford University Press, 2000.

Keppel, Ben. *The Work of Democracy: Ralph Bunche, Kenneth B. Clark, Lorraine Hansberry, and the Cultural Politics of Race.* Cambridge, MA: Harvard University Press, 1995.

Kersten, Andrew E. *A. Philip Randolph: A Life in the Vanguard.* Lanham, MD: Rowan and Littlefield, 2006.

King, Martin Luther, Jr. *A Call to Conscience: Landmark Speeches of Martin Luther King, Jr.* Edited by Clayborne Carson et al. New York: Warner Books, 2002.

King, Norman. *Everybody Loves Oprah: Her Remarkable Life Story.* New York: William Morrow, 1987.

Kitwana, Bakari. *Why White Kids Love Hip Hop: Wangstas, Wiggers, Wannabes, and the New Reality of Race in America.* New York: Basic Civitas Books, 2005.

Kline, Johnny. *Never Lose: From Globetrotter to Addict to PhD: An Autobiography.* New York: Papa Joe's Book Company, 1996.

Knight, Athelia. "Track Star Griffith Joyner Dies at 38." *The Washington Post Company*, 1998. www.mmjp.or.jp/amlang.atc/di&legends/flojo/aboutflojo.htm (accessed October 28, 2006).

Kotz, Nick. *Judgment Days: Lyndon Johnson, Martin Luther King, Jr., and the Laws That Changed America.* New York: Houghton Mifflin, 2005.

Kramer, Edward, and John McDermott. *Hendrix: Setting the Record Straight.* New York: Grand Central Publishing, 1992.

Kunta Kinte–Alex Haley Foundation, Inc. Web site, www.kintehaley.org.

Kuska, Bob. *Hot Potato: How Washington and New York Gave Birth to Black Basketball and Changed America's Game Forever.* Charlottesville: University of Virginia Press, 2004.

Landan, Eline. *Colin Powell: Four Star General.* London: Franklin Watts, 1991.

Larson, Kate Clifford. *Bound for the Promised Land: Harriet Tubman, Portrait of an American Heroine.* New York: Ballantine Books, 2004.

Larson, Kate Clifford. "Tubman, Harriet Ross." In *Black Women in America*, edited by Darlene Clark Hine. Oxford: Oxford University Press, 2005.

Lauderdale, Pat. "Racism, Racialization and American Indian Sports." In *Native Americans in Sports*, edited by C. Richard King. New York: M. E. Sharpe, 2005, 248–52.

Lawrence, A. H. *Duke Ellington and His World.* New York: Routledge, 2001.

Lawrence, Sharon. *Jimi Hendrix: The Intimate Story of a Betrayed Musical Legend.* New York: Harper Paperbacks, 2006.

Lazenby, Roland. *The Show: The Inside Story of the Spectacular Los Angeles Lakers in the Words of Those Who Lived It.* New York: McGraw-Hill, 2005.

Leach, Laurie F. *Langston Hughes: A Biography.* Westport, CT: Greenwood Press, 2004.

Lee, Chana Kai. *For Freedom's Sake: The Life of Fannie Lou Hamer*. Athens: University of Georgia Press, 1999.

Lee, Spike. *She's Gotta Have It: Inside Guerilla Filmmaking*. New York: Fireside, 1987.

Lee, Spike.. *Uplift the Race: The Construction of School Daze*. New York: Fireside, 1988.

Lee, Spike, and Ralph Wiley. *By Any Means Necessary: The Trials and Tribulations of Making Malcolm X*. New York: Hyperion, 1992.

Lefever, Harry G. *Undaunted by the Fight: Spelman College and the Civil Rights Movement*. Macon: Georgia University Press, 2005.

Levy, Eugene D. *James Weldon Johnson, Black Leader, Black Voice*. Negro American Biographies and Autobiographies. Chicago: University of Chicago Press, 1973.

Lewis, David Levering. *W. E. B. Du Bois: Biography of a Race, 1868–1919*. New York: Henry Holt, 1993.

Lewis, David Levering. *W. E. B. Du Bois: The Fight for Equality and the American Century, 1919–1963*. New York: Henry Holt, 2000.

Lincoln, Eric C. *The Black Muslims in America*. Boston: Beacon Press, 1961.

"Little Sister, Big Hit: Williams Family Surprise-Serena Williams Wins the U.S. Open." *Sports Illustrated*, September 20, 1999.

Lodder, Steve. *Stevie Wonder: A Guide to the Classic Albums*. San Francisco: Backbeat Books, 2005.

Logan, Rayford W. "Carter G. Woodson: Mirror and Molder of His Times, 1875–1950." *Journal of Negro History* 58 (1973): 1–17.

Lois, George, ed. *Ali Rap: Muhammad Ali, the First Heavy Weight Champion of Rap*. New York: ESPN Books, 2006.

Lomax, Louis E. *When the Word Is Given; a Report on Elijah Muhammad, Malcolm X, and the Black Muslim World*. Cleveland: World Publishing, 1963.

Londino, Lawrence. *Tiger Woods: A Biography*. Westport, CT: Greenwood Press, 2008.

Louis, Joe. *My Life*. New York: Ecco, 1997.

Love, Dennis. *Blind Faith: The Miraculous Journey of Lula Hardaway, Stevie Wonder's Mother*. New York: Simon and Schuster, 2002.

Lowry, Beverly. *Her Dream of Dreams: The Rise and Triumph of Madam C. J. Walker*. New York: Alfred A. Knopf, 2003.

Lupton, Mary Jane. *Maya Angelou: A Critical Companion*. Westport, CT: Greenwood Press, 1998.

Lynch, Shola. *Chisholm '72: Unbought and Unbossed*. Realside Productions, 2004.

Mabee, Carleton, and Susan Mabee Newhouse. *Sojourner Truth: Slave, Prophet, Legend*. New York: New York University Press, 1993.

Mabry, Marcus. *Twice as Good: Condoleezza Rice and Her Path to Power*. Emmaus, PA: Modern Times, 2008.

MacAloon, John J. *This Great Symbol: Pierre de Coubertin and the Origins of the Modern Olympic Games*. Chicago: The University of Chicago Press, 1981.

Maese, Rick. "A Courageous Act of Defiance." *The Montreal Gazette*, August 20, 2004, C4+.

Magic Johnson Enterprises: http://magicjohnsonenterprises.com/.

Maltz, Earl. *Dred Scott and the Politics of Slavery*. Lawrence: University Press of Kansas, 2007.

Mandell, Richard D. *The Nazi Olympics.* Urbana: University of Illinois Press, 1987.

Mann, Peggy. *Ralph Bunche: UN Peacemaker.* New York: Coward, McCann and Geoghegan, Inc., 1975.

Margolick, David. *Beyond Glory: Joe Louis v. Max Schmeling, and a World on the Brink.* New York: Vintage, 2006.

Margolies-Mezvinskey, Marjorie, and Barbara Feinman. *A Woman's Place . . . The Freshman Women Who Changed the Face of Congress.* New York: Crown Publishers, 1994.

Marqusee, Mike. *Redemption Song: Muhammad Ali and the Spirit of the Sixties.* New York: Verso Books, 2004.

Marsh, Charles. *God's Long Summer: Stories of Faith and Civil Rights.* Princeton, NJ: Princeton University Press, 1999.

Martin, Reginald. "An Interview with Ishmael Reed." *Review of Contemporary Fiction* 4, no. 2 (Summer 1984): 176–87.

Martin, Reginald. *Ishmael Reed and the New Black Aesthetic Critics.* New York: St. Martin's, 1988.

Martin, Tony. *Literary Garveyism: Garvey, Black Arts and the Harlem Renaissance.* Dover, MA: The Majority Press, 1983.

Martin, Tony. *Marcus Garvey, Hero: A First Biography.* Dover, MA: The Majority Press, 1983.

Martin, Tony. *Message to the People: The Course of African Philosophy.* Dover, MA: The Majority Press, 1986.

Martin, Tony. *Race First: The Ideological and Organizational Struggles of Marcus Garvey and the Universal Negro Improvement Association.* Westport, CT: Greenwood Press, 1976.

Martin, Waldo E., Jr., *The Mind of Frederick Douglass.* Chapel Hill: University of North Carolina Press, 1984.

Massood, Paula. *The Spike Lee Reader.* Philadelphia: Temple University Press, 2008.

McCallum, Jack. "The Desire Is Not There." *Sports Illustrated* 79 (1993): 28–35.

McDonald, M. G. "Michael Jordan's Family Values: Marketing, Meaning and Post Reagan America." *Sociology of Sport Journal* 13 (1996): 344–65.

McDonald, M. G., and D. L. Andrews. "Michael Jordan: Corporate Sport and Postmodern Celebrityhood." In *Sport Stars: The Cultural Politics of Sporting Celebrity*, edited by D. L. Andrews and S. J. Jackson, 20–35. London: Routledge, 2001.

McFeely, William S. *Frederick Douglass.* New York: W. W. Norton, 1990.

McMurry, Linda O. *George Washington Carver: Scientist and Symbol.* New York: Oxford University Press, 1981.

Means, Howard. *Colin Powell: Soldier/Statesman Statesman/Soldier.* New York: Donald I. Fine, 1992.

Meier, August and Elliott Rudwick. *Black History and the Historical Profession, 1915–1980.* Urbana: University of Illinois Press, 1986.

Meldrum, Andrew. " 'Their Story Is My Story': Oprah Opens $40m School for South African Girls." *Guardian.co.uk*, January 3, 2007. http://www.guardian.co.uk/media/2007/jan/03/broadcasting.schoolsworldwide (accessed April 25, 2009).

Merritt, Raleigh H. *From Captivity to Fame or the Life of George Washington Carver.* Boston: Meador Publishing Co., 1929.

Miller, Keith D. *Voice of Deliverance: The Language of Martin Luther King, Jr., and Its Sources*. Athens: University of Georgia Press, 1998.

Miller, Matthew, ed. "The Celebrity 100." *Forbes.com*, June 11, 2008. http://www.forbes.com/2008/06/11/most-powerful-celebrities-lists-celebrities08-cx_mn_0611c_land.html (accessed April 1, 2009).

Mills, Kay. *This Little Light of Mine: The Life of Fannie Lou Hamer*. New York: Dutton, 1993.

Mitchell, Lisa. "More Than a Mammy." *Hollywood Studio Magazine*, April 1979.

Moore, Kenny. "Getup and Go: Florence Griffith Joyner's Dramatic Garb Made Her a Colorful Blur as She Smashed the World Record in the 100 Meters at the Olympic Trials." *Sports Illustrated*, July 25, 1998. http://Sportsillustrated.cnn.com/Olympics/features/joyner/flashback2.html (accessed October 14, 2006).

Moore, Kenny. "Go, Flo, Go: Florence Griffith Joyner Did Just That in Blazing to Victory in the 100 Meters." *Sports Illustrated*, October 3, 1988. http://Sportsillustrated.cnn.com/Olympics/features/joyner/flashback3.html (accessed October 14, 2006).

Mori, Aoi. *Toni Morrison and Womanist Discourse*. New York: Peter Lang, 1999.

Morris, Aldon D. *The Origins of the Civil Rights Movement: Black Communities Organizing for Change*. New York: The Free Press, 1984.

Morrison, Alec. "Arthur Ashe Chronology." *Sports Illustrated*. http://sportsillustrated.cnn.com/tennis/features/1997/arthurashe/biography1.html.

Morrison, Toni. *What Moves at the Margin: Selected Nonfiction*. Edited by Carolyn C. Denard. Jackson: University Press of Mississippi, 2008.

Morton, Brian. *Miles Davis*. London: Haus Publishing, 2005.

Motley, Mary Penick. *The Invisible Soldier: The Experience of the Black Soldier, World War II*. Detroit: Wayne State University Press, 1975.

Muhammad, Elijah. *A History of the Nation of Islam*. Phoenix: Secretarius Memps Publications, 2008.

Mundy, Liza. *Michelle: A Biography*. New York: Simon & Schuster, 2008.

Mungin, Lateef. "All-Male College Cracks Down on Cross-Dressing." *CNN.com*. http://www.cnn.com/2009/US/10/17/college.dress.code (accessed March 5, 2010).

Murray, Charles Shaar. *Crosstown Traffic: Jimi Hendrix and the Post-War Rock & Roll Revolution*. New York: St. Martin's Griffin, 1991.

Myler, Richard. *Ring of Hate: Joe Louis v. Max Schmeling: The Fight of the Century*. Baltimore: Arcade Press, 2006.

National Basketball Association. http://www.nba.com. NBA @ 50 interview. http://www.nba.com/history/players/magic_johnson_nba50_pt1.html and http://www.nba.com/history/players/magic_johnson_nba50_pt2.html.

The Negro History Bulletin. Volume 13, May 1950.

Newton, Huey P. *Revolutionary Suicide*. New York: Harcourt Brace Jovanovich, 1973; reprint, New York: Writers and Readers, 1995.

Newton, Huey P. *To Die for the People: The Writings of Huey P. Newton*. New York: Random House, 1972; reprint, New York: Writers and Readers, 1995.

Newton, Huey P. *War against the Panthers: A Study of Repression in America*. New York: Harlem River Press, 1996.

Newton, Huey P., and Erik Erikson. *In Search of Common Ground: Conversations with Erik H. Ericson and Huey P. Newton*. New York: Norton, 1973.

Nicholson, Stuart. *Billie Holiday*. Boston: Northeastern University Press, 1995.

Nicholson, Stuart. *Ella Fitzgerald: The Complete Biography*. New York: Routledge, 2004.

Nickson, Chris. *Denzel Washington*. New York: St. Martin's Paperbacks, 1996.

Noden, Merrell. "FloJo Lived Her Life in Fast-Forward." *Sports Illustrated*, September 22, 1998. http://Sportsillustrated.cnn.com/Olympics/features/joyner/flojo_noden .html (accessed October 14, 2006).

Norment, L. "Michael and Juanita Jordan Talk about Love, Marriage, and Life after Basketball." *Ebony* 47 (November 1991): 68–76.

Norrell, Robert J. *Up from History: The Life of Booker T. Washington*. Cambridge, MA: The Belknap Press, 2009.

Oates, Stephen B. *The Fires of Jubilee: Nat Turner's Fierce Rebellion*. New York: Harper Perennial, 1990.

Obama, Barack. *The Audacity of Hope: Thoughts on Reclaiming the American Dream*. New York: Crown Publishers, 2006.

Obama, Barack. *Change We Can Believe in: Barack Obama's Plan to Renew America's Promise*. New York: Three Rivers Press, 2008.

Obama, Barack. *Dreams from My Father: A Story of Race and Inheritance*. New York: Three Rivers Press, 2004.

Obama, Michelle. Democratic National Committee Speech. August 25, 2008. http:// www.youtube.com/watch?v=790hG6qBPx0.

O'Brien, Daniel. *Halle Berry*. London: Reynolds & Hearn, 2003.

The Official Sammy Davis Jr. Web site. Estate of Sammy Davis Jr. and The LaRoda Group. Sammy Davis Jr. http://www.sammydavis-jr.com/ (accessed June 11, 2009).

Olson, Lynne. *Freedom's Daughters: The Unsung Heroines of the Civil Rights Movement from 1830 to 1970*. New York: Touchstone Books, 2002.

"Oprah: 'Free Speech Rocks': Texas Cattlemen Lose Defamation Suit." *CNN.com*, February 26, 1998. http://www.cnn.com/US/9802/26/oprah.verdict/ (accessed April 15, 2009).

O'Sullivan, Christopher. *Colin Powell: American Power and Intervention from Vietnam to Iraq*. Lanham, MD: Rowman & Littlefield, 2009.

Osur, Alan M. *Blacks in the Army Air Forces during World War II: The Problem of Race Relations*. Washington, DC: Office of Air Force History, 1977.

Owen, David. *The Chosen One: Tiger Woods and the Dilemma of Greatness*. New York: Simon and Schuster, 2001.

Owens, Jesse, with Paul G. Neimark. *Blackthink: My Life as Black Man and White Man*. New York: William Morrow and Company, 1970.

Owens, Jesse, with Paul G. Neimark. *I Have Changed*. New York: William Morrow and Company, 1972.

Painter, Nell Irvin. *Sojourner Truth: A Life, a Symbol*. New York and London: W. W. Norton, 1996.

Parham, Sandra, ed. *Barbara C. Jordan: Selected Speeches*. Washington, DC: Howard University Press, 1999.

Parish, James Robert. *Denzel Washington: Actor*. New York: Ferguson, 2005.

Parks, Rosa, with Jim Haskins. *Rosa Parks: My Story*. New York: Scholastic, 1992.

"Party Crasher: Venus Williams Shakes Up Tennis." *Sports Illustrated*, September 15, 1997.

"Paul Robeson: Portraits of the Artist." *The Criterion Collection*, 2008. http://www.criterion.com/boxsets/443.

Pearlman, Jeff. *Love Me, Hate Me: Barry Bonds and the Making on an Anti-Hero.* New York: HarperCollins, 2006.

Pease, Andrew, and Paul R. Brewer. "The Oprah Factor: The Effects of a Celebrity Endorsement in a Presidential Primary Campaign." *International Journal of Press/Politics* 13, no. 4 (2008): 386–400.

Perry, Alex. "Oprah Scandal Rocks South Africa." *Time.com*, November 5, 2007. http://www.time.com/time/world/article/0,8599,1680715,00.html (accessed April 1, 2009).

Peterson, Robert W. *Only the Ball Was White.* New York: McGraw-Hill Publishing, 1984.

Pfeffer, Paula. *A. Philip Randolph, Pioneer of the Civil Rights Movement.* Baton Rouge: Louisiana State University Press, 1996.

Plant, Deborah G. *Zora Neale Hurston: A Biography of the Spirit.* Westport, CT: Praeger, 2007.

Podair, Jerald E. *Bayard Rustin: American Dreamer.* Lanham, MD: Rowman & Littlefield Publishers, 2009.

Poitier, Sidney. *Life beyond Measure: Letters to My Great-Granddaughter.* New York: HarperOne, 2008.

Poitier, Sidney. *The Measure of a Man: A Spiritual Autobiography.* New York: HarperSanFrancisco, 2000.

Posner, Gerald. *Motown: Money, Sex, and Power.* New York: Random House, 2002.

Powell, Colin. "General Colin Powell Speaks at the GOP National Convention." *Floor Speeches. PBS*, August 12, 1996. http://www.pbs.org/newshour/convention96/floor_ speeches/powell.html.

Powell, Colin, with Joseph Persico. *My American Journey.* New York: Random House, 1995.

Preston, Dickson J. *Young Frederick Douglass: The Maryland Years.* Baltimore: The Johns Hopkins University Press, 1985.

Pryor, Rain. *Jokes My Father Never Taught Me: Life, Love, and Loss with Richard Pryor.* New York: It Books, 2007.

Pryor, Richard. *The Richard Pryor Show, Vols. 1 & 2 Plus Bonus Disc.* Los Angeles: Image Entertainment, 2004.

Pryor, Richard, and Todd Gold. *Pryor Convictions, and Other Life Sentences.* New York: Pantheon Books, 1995.

Public Broadcasting Service. "People and Events: Dred Scott's Fight for Freedom, 1846–1857," 1999. http://www.pbs.org/wgbh/aia/part4/4p2932.html.

Pulley, Brett. *The Billion Dollar BET: Robert Johnson and the Inside Story of Black Entertainment Television.* Hoboken, NJ: John Wiley and Sons, 2004.

Quarles, Benjamin F. "A. Philip Randolph: Labor Leader at Large." In *Black Leaders of the Twentieth Century*, edited by John Hope Franklin and August Meier. Urbana: University of Illinois Press, 1982.

Quarles, Benjamin F. *Frederick Douglass.* Washington, DC: Associated Publishers, 1948.

Rampersad, Arnold. *Jackie Robinson: A Biography.* New York: Ballantine Books, 1998.

Rampersad, Arnold. *The Life of Langston Hughes: Volume I: 1902–1941, I, Too, Sing America*. New York and Oxford: Oxford University Press, 1986.

Rampersad, Arnold. *The Life of Langston Hughes: Volume II: 1914–1967, I Dream a World*. New York: Oxford University Press, 1988.

Rampersad, Arnold. *Ralph Ellison: A Biography*. New York: Alfred A. Knopf, 2007.

Ransby, Barbara. *Ella Baker and the Black Freedom Movement: A Radical Democratic Vision*. Chapel Hill: The University of North Carolina Press, 2003.

Redkey, Edwin S. *A Grand Army of Black Men: Letters from African-American Soldiers in the Union Army, 1861–1865*. London: Cambridge University Press, 1992.

Reed, Ishmael. *Chattanooga*. New York: Avon, 1972.

Reed, Ishmael. *Conjure*. New York: Avon, 1972.

Reed, Ishmael. *Flight to Canada*. New York, Avon, 1976.

Reed, Ishmael. *The FreeLance Pallbearers*. New York: Bantam, 1967.

Reed, Ishmael. *God Made Alaska for the Indians*. New York: Atheneum, 1982.

Reed, Ishmael. *Japanese by Spring*. New York: Atheneum, 1993.

Reed, Ishmael. *The Last Days of Louisiana Red*. New York: Avon, 1976.

Reed, Ishmael. *Mumbo Jumbo*. New York: Avon, 1972.

Reed, Ishmael. *Reckless Eyeballing*. New York: Atheneum, 1988.

Reed, Ishmael. *The Savage Wilds*. New York: Atheneum, 1990.

Reed, Ishmael. *Shrovetide in Old New Orleans*. New York: Avon, 1978.

Reed, Ishmael. *The Terrible Threes*. New York: Atheneum, 1990.

Reed, Ishmael. *The Terrible Twos*. New York: Atheneum, 1982.

Reed, Ishmael. "When State Magicians Fail." *Journal of Black Poetry*, Summer/Fall 1969, 17.

Reed, Ishmael. *Yellow Back Radio Broke Down*. New York: Bantam, 1969.

Reid, Mark. *Black Lenses, Black Voices: African American Film Now*. Lanham, MD: Rowman & Littlefield, 2005.

Remnick, David. *King of the World*. New York: Vintage Books, 1998.

Rennert, Richard, ed. *Female Leaders*. New York: Chelsea House Publishers, 1994.

Rhoden, William C. *Forty Million Dollar Slaves: The Rise, Fall and Redemption of the Black Athlete*. New York: Random House, 2006.

RichardPryor.com. "History." www.richardpryor.com/0/4113/0/1240 (accessed February 18, 2010).

Rieder, Jonathan. *The Word of the Lord Is upon Me: The Righteous Performance of Martin Luther King, Jr.* Cambridge, MA: Harvard University Press, 2008.

Riley, James A. *The Biographical Encyclopedia of the Negro Baseball Leagues*. New York: Carroll & Graf Publishers, Inc., 1994.

Ritz, David. *Divided Soul: The Life of Marvin Gaye*. New York: McGraw-Hill, 1985.

Ritz, David, and Ray Charles. *Brother Ray: Ray Charles' Own Story*. New York: Da Capo Press, 2004.

Rivlin, Benjamin, ed. *Ralph Bunche: The Man and His Times*. New York: Holmes and Meier, 1990.

RLJ Companies. RLJ Companies Management Team: Robert L. Johnson, Founder & Chairman. RLJ Companies Web site: www.rljcompanies.com/rljTeamRLJ.htm (accessed July 2009).

Robb, Brian J. *Will Smith: King of Cool*. New York: Plexus, 2002.

Robeson, Paul. *Here I Stand*. London: D. Dobson, 1958.

Robinson, Frazier "Slow," and Paul Bauer. *Catching Dreams: My Life in the Negro Baseball Leagues*. Syracuse, NY: Syracuse University Press, 1999.

Robinson, Jackie, and Alfred Duckett. *I Never Had It Made: An Autobiography of Jackie Jackie Robinson: A Biography*. New York: Harper Perennial, 2003.

Robinson, Jo Ann Gibson. *The Montgomery Bus Boycott and the Women Who Started It: The Memoir of Jo Ann Gibson Robinson*. Edited by David J. Garrow. Knoxville: The University of Tennessee Press, 1987.

Roby, Steven. *Black Gold: The Lost Archives of Jimi Hendrix*. New York: Billboard Books, 2002.

Rogers, Mary Beth. *Barbara Jordan: American Hero*. New York: Bantam Books, 1998.

Ronney, John. "Muhammad Ali: He Fought with His Fists and His Words." *U.S. News and World Reports*, August 20, 2001.

Rose, Phyllis. *Jazz Cleopatra: Josephine Baker in Her Time*. New York: Doubleday, 1989.

Rosenblatt, Dana, and Don Lemon. "White Valedictorian: A First for Historically Black Morehouse." *Black* in *American 2*. CNN.com. http://www.cnn.com/2008/US/05/16/ white.valedictorian/index.html (accessed March 5, 2010).

Ross, Pat. *Young and Female: Turning Points in the Lives of Eight American Women*. New York: Random House, 1972.

Rowley, Hazel. *Richard Wright: The Life and Times*. New York: Henry Holt and Company, 2001.

Royster, Jacqueline Jones, ed. *Southern Horrors and Other Writings: The Anti-Lynching Campaign of Ida B. Wells, 1892–1900*. Boston: Bedford Books, 1997.

Ruck, Rob. *Sandlot Seasons: Sport in Black Pittsburgh*. Urbana: University of Illinois Press, 1987.

Rurup, Reinhard. *1936 The Olympic Games and National Socialism*. 2nd ed. USZ, Wien: Institute F. Sportwissenschaften, 1996.

Rustin, Bayard. *Time on Two Crosses: The Collected Writings of Bayard Rustin*. San Francisco: Cleis Press, 2003.

Salamon, Julie. "The Courage to Rise Above Mammyness." *New York Times*, August 6, 2001.

Sandler, Stanley. *Segregated Skies: Black Combat Squadrons of World War II*. Washington, DC: Smithsonian Institution, 1992.

Sanello, Frank. *Halle Berry: A Stormy Life*. London: Virgin Books, 2003.

Scally, Sister Anthony. *Carter G. Woodson: A Bio-Bibliography*. Westport, CT: Greenwood Press, 1985.

Schafer, A. R. *Serena and Venus Williams*. Kentwood, LA: Edge Books, 2002.

Schechter, Patricia A. *Ida B. Wells-Barnett and American Reform, 1880–1930*. Chapel Hill: The University of North Carolina Press, 2001.

Schiffman, Jack. *Uptown: The Story of Harlem's Apollo Theatre*. New York: Cowles Book Company, Inc., 1971.

Schroeder, Alan, and Heather Lehr Wagner. *Josephine Baker: Entertainer*. New York: Chelsea House, 2006.

Schumacher, David. "Richard Pryor's Biggest Fight—Multiple Sclerosis." *Ebony*, September 1993. http://findarticles.com/p/articles/mi_m1077/is_n11_v48/ai_13230349/ (accessed February 20, 2010).

Schuman, Michael A. *Halle Berry: "Beauty is not Just Physical."* Berkeley Heights, NJ: Enslow, 2006.

Scott, Lawrence P., and Womack, William M., Sr. *Double V: The Civil Rights Struggle of the Tuskegee Airmen*. East Lansing: Michigan State University Press, 1994.

Seale, Bobby. *A Lonely Rage: The Autobiography of Bobby Seale*. New York: Times Books, 1978.

Seale, Bobby. *Seize the Time: The Story of the Black Panther Party and Huey P. Newton*. New York: Vintage, 1970.

Sears, Edward S. *Running through the Ages*. Jefferson, NC: McFarland & Company, 2001.

"Secretary of State Condoleezza Rice." U.S. State Department Web site. http://2001-2009 .state.gov/secretary/.

"Serena Williams—Awesome: The Next Target the French Open," *Sports Illustrated*, May 28, 2003.

Sernett, Milton C. *Harriet Tubman: Myth, Memory, and History*. Durham, NC: Duke University Press, 2007.

Sernett, Milton C, ed. "Section II: 'Slave Religion in the Antebellum South.'" In *African American Religious History: A Documentary Witness*. Durham, NC: Duke University Press, 2004.

Shadwick, Keith. *Jimi Hendrix, Musician*. Milwaukee, WI: Backbeat Books, 2003.

Shapiro, Harry, and Caesar Glebeek. *Jimi Hendrix: Electric Gypsy*. New York: St. Martin's Griffin, 1991.

Sharman, Jay, Mike Sear, David Houle, and Mannie Jackson, executive producers. *Harlem Globetrotters: The Team that Changed the World*. Burbank, CA: Warner Brothers, 2005.

Shaw, Arnold. *What Is the Secret Magic of Belafonte: An Unauthorized Biography*. New York: Pyramid Books, 1960.

Shaw, Stephanie J. *What a Woman Ought to Be and Do: Black Professional Women Workers during the Jim Crow Era*. Chicago: University of Chicago Press, 1996.

Sheridan, Earl. "Conservative Implications of the Irrelevance of Racism in Contemporary African American Cinema." *Journal of Black Studies* 37, no. 2 (November 2006): 177–92.

Sherman, Max, ed. *Barbara Jordan: Speaking the Truth with Eloquent Thunder*. Austin: University of Texas Press, 2007.

Shipp, E. R. "Rosa Parks, 92, Founding Symbol of Civil Rights Movement, Dies." *The New York Times*, October 25, 2005.

Shirley, David. *Alex Haley*. New York: Chelsea House, 1994.

Simmons, Russell. *Life and Def: Sex, Drugs, Money + God*. New York: Three Rivers Press, 2003.

Singh, Robert. *The Farrakhan Phenomenon: Race, Reaction, and the Paranoid Style in American Politics*. Washington, DC: Georgetown University Press, 1997.

Smiley, Bob. *Follow the Roar: Tailing Tiger Woods for all 604 Holes of His Most Spectacular Season*. New York: HarperCollins, 2008.

Smiley, Tavis. *Stand*. DVD. Smiley Group: Hay House, 2009.

Smith, Evelyn. *Alice Walker: A Life*. New York: W. W. Norton & Company, 2004.

Smith, Geoffrey Michael. "Tennis." *UCLA 1964–1965*. http://www.english.ucla.edu/ ucla1960s/6465/Smith3.htm.

Smith, Ronald L. *Cosby*. New York: St. Martin's Press, 1986.

Smith, Suzanne. *Dancing in the Street: Motown and the Cultural Politics of Detroit*. Cambridge, MA: Harvard University Press, 1999.

Smith, Tommie, with David Steele. *Silent Gesture: The Autobiography of Tommie Smith*. Philadelphia: Temple University Press, 2007.

Smith-Shomade, Beretta E. *Pimpin' Ain't Easy: Selling Black Entertainment Television*. New York: Routledge, 2008.

Smock, Raymond W. *Booker T. Washington in Perspective: Essays of Louis R. Harlan*. Jackson: University of Mississippi Press, 1988.

Stein, Karen F. *Reading, Learning, Teaching Toni Morrison (Confronting the Text, Confronting the World)*. New York: Peter Lang, 2009.

Steins, Richard. *Arthur Ashe: A Biography*. Westport, CT: Greenwood Press, 2005.

Steins, Richard. *Colin Powell: A Biography*. Westport, CT: Greenwood Press, 2003.

Stewart, Jeffrey C., ed. *Paul Robeson: Artist and Citizen*. New Brunswick, NJ: Rutgers University Press and the Paul Robeson Cultural Center, 1998.

Swick, David. "We Live in the Best of Times." *Shambhala Sun*, May 2007.

Szwed, John. *So What: The Life of Miles Davis*. New York: Simon and Schuster, 2002.

Tanenhaus, Sam. *Louis Armstrong*. Danbury, CT: Chelsea House Publishers, 1989.

Taraborrelli, J. Randy. *Michael Jackson: The Magic, the Madness, the Whole Story, 1958–2009*. New York: Hachette Book Group, 2009.

Taylor, Ula Yvette. *The Veiled Garvey: The Life and Times of Amy Jacques Garvey*. Chapel Hill and London: The University of North Carolina Press, 2002.

Taylor-Guthrie, Danille, ed. *Conversations with Toni Morrison*. Jackson: University Press of Mississippi, 1994.

Terrell, Mary Church. *A Colored Woman in a White World*. Foreword by Debra Newman Ham. Amherst, NY: Humanity Books, 2005. Originally published 1940.

Thomas, Ron. *They Cleared the Lane: The NBA's Black Pioneers*. Lincoln: University of Nebraska Press, 2002.

Titus, Frances W. *Narrative of Sojourner Truth; a Bondswoman of Olden Time, Emancipated by the New York Legislature in the Early Part of the Present Century; with a History of Her Labors and Correspondence, Drawn from Her "Book of Life."* Boston: The Author, 1875.

Trotter, Joe William, Earl Lewis, and Tera W. Hunter, eds. *The African American Urban Experience: Perspectives from the Colonial Period to the Present*. New York: Palgrave Macmillan, 2004.

Trudeau, Noah Andre. *Like Men of War: Black Troops in the Civil War, 1862–1865*. Boston: Little, Brown, and Co., 1998.

Tucker, Mark. *The Duke Ellington Reader*. New York: Oxford University Press, 1993.

Tucker, Mark. *Ellington: The Early Years*. Urbana and Chicago: University of Illinois Press, 1991.

Turner, Nat. *The Confessions of Nat Turner: The Leader of the Late Insurrection in Southampton, VA: Electronic Edition*. North Carolina Collection, University of North Carolina at Chapel Hill. http://docsouth.unc.edu/neh/turner/turner.html.

Turner, Steve. *Trouble Man: The Life and Death of Marvin Gaye*. New York: Ecco, 2000.

Tushnet, Mark. *Making Civil Rights Law: Thurgood Marshall and the Supreme Court, 1936–1961*. New York: Oxford University Press, 1994.

Tushnet, Mark. *Making Constitutional Law: Thurgood Marshall and the Supreme Court, 1961–1991*. New York: Oxford University Press, 1997.

Tushnet, Mark, ed. *Thurgood Marshall: His Speeches, Writings, Arguments, Opinions, and Reminiscences.* New York: Lawrence Hill Books, 2001.

Tuskegee Airmen, Inc. *Who Were the Tuskegee Airmen?* http://tuskegeeairmen.org (accessed March 1, 2010).

United Nations Resolution 1441. "Security Council Holds Iraq in 'Material Breach' of Disarmament Obligations, Offers Final Chance to Comply, Unanimously Adopting Resolution 1441." August 11, 2002. http://www.un.org/News/Press/docs/2002/SC7564.doc.htm.

Urquhart, Brian. *Ralph Bunche: An American Life.* New York: W. W. Norton and Company, 1993.

VanderVelde, Lea, and Sandhys Subramanian. "Mrs. Dred Scott." *Yale Law Journal* 106 (1997): 1033–1122.

The View. June 18, 2008. http://www.youtube.com/watch?v=59twO1fJwtQ.

Walker, Alice. *Anything We Love Can Be Saved.* New York: Ballantine, 1997.

Walker, Alice. *The Color Purple.* New York: Harcourt Brace Jovanovich, 2003.

Walker, Alice. *In Search of Our Mother's Gardens: Womanist Prose.* Fort Washington, PA: Harvest Books, 2003.

Walker, Alice. "In Search of Zora Neale Hurston." *Ms. Magazine,* March 1975, 74–89.

Walker, Alice. *Meridian.* Fort Washington, PA: Harvest Books, 2003.

Walker, Alice. *Once.* Fort Washington, PA: Harvest Books, 1976.

Walker, Alice. *The Third Life of Grange Copeland.* Fort Washington, PA: Harvest Books, 2003.

Walker, Alice. *We Are the Ones We Have Been Waiting For: Inner Light in a Time of Darkness.* New York: New Press, 2007.

Walker, Dennis. *Islam and the Search for African American Nationhood: Elijah Muhammad, Louis Farrakhan, and the Nation of Islam.* Atlanta: Clarity Press, 2005.

Walker, Margaret. *Richard Wright: Daemonic Genius.* New York: Warner Books, 1988.

Waller, Don. *The Motown Story.* New York: Scribner, 1985.

Walter, Ronald Anderson. *Oral History Interview with Nat D. Williams: Topic: Beale Street and the Fabulous World of Entertainment.* Memphis: Whitten Bros., 1976.

Ward, Geoffrey. *Unforgivable Blackness: The Rise and Fall of Jack Johnson.* New York: Afred A. Knof, 2004.

Washington, Denzel, and Daniel Paisner. *A Hand to Guide Me: Legends and Leaders Celebrate the People who Shaped Their Lives.* Des Moines, IA: Meredith Books, 2006.

Watkins, Mel. *On the Real Side: Laughing, Lying, and Signifying: The Underground Tradition of African-American Humor That Transformed American Culture, from Slavery to Richard Pryor.* New York: Simon and Schuster, 1994.

Watson, Yolanda L., and Sheila T. Gregory. *Daring to Educate: The Legacy of the Early Spelman College Presidents.* Sterling, VA: Stylus Publishing, 2005.

Watts, Jill. *Hattie McDaniel: Black Ambition, White Hollywood.* New York: HarperCollins, 2005.

Weinraub, Bernard. "Turning the Tables of Race Relations." *New York Times,* February 6, 1995, C11.

Wellman, Sam. *George Washington Carver: Inventor and Naturalist.* New York: Barbour Publishing, 1998.

Wells-Barnett, Ida B. *Crusade for Justice: The Autobiography of Ida B. Wells.* Chicago: University of Chicago Press, 1970.

Werner, Craig. *Higher Ground: Stevie Wonder, Aretha Franklin, Curtis Mayfield, and the Rise and Fall of American Soul.* New York: Crown Publishers, 2004.

Wesley, Charles H. "Carter G. Woodson—as a Scholar." *Journal of Negro History* 36 (1951): 12–24.

West, Cornel. *Hope on a Tightrope: Words & Wisdom.* Carlsbad, CA: Smiley Books, 2008.

West, Cornel. "On Obama Not Going to Memphis." *Huffington Post.* April 4, 2008. http://www.huffingtonpost.com/cornel-west/on-obama-not-going-to-mem_b_95179 .html (accessed August 14, 2009).

West, Cornel. *Prophesy Deliverance!: An Afro-American Revolutionary Christianity.* Louisville, KY: Westminster John Knox Press, 2002.

West, Cornel. *Race Matters.* New York: Vintage Books, 1994.

Whitaker, Matthew C., ed. *African American Icons of Sport: Triumph, Courage, and Excellence.* Westport, CT: Greenwood, 2008.

White, Deborah Gray. *Too Heavy a Load: Black Women in Defense of Themselves, 1894–1994.* New York: W. W. Norton, 1999.

White, John. *Billie Holiday, Her Life & Times.* New York: Universe Books, 1987.

Wiley, Ralph, and Spike Lee. *Best Seat in The House: A Basketball Memoir.* New York: Crown, 1997.

Williams, John A., and Dennis A. Williams. *If I Stop, I'll Die: The Comedy and Tragedy of Richard Pryor.* New York: Da Capo Press, 2005.

Williams, Juan. *Thurgood Marshall: American Revolutionary.* New York: Times Books/Random House, 1998.

Williams, Venus. "Wimbledon Has Sent Me a Message: I'm Only a Second-Class Champion." *New York Times*, June 26, 2006.

Wilson Mbajeke, Carolyn. *The Future of Historically Black Colleges and Universities: Ten Presidents Speak Out.* Jefferson, NC: McFarland, 2006.

Wolfenstein, Eugene Victor. *The Victims of Democracy: Malcolm X and the Black Revolution.* New York, Guilford Press: 1993.

Wood, Ean. *The Josephine Baker Story.* London: Sanctuary, 2000.

Woodson, Carter G. "My Recollections of Veterans of the Civil War." *The Negro History Bulletin* 7 (February 1944): 103–4, 115–18.

Wooten, Sara McIntosh. *Denzel Washington: Academy Award-Winning Actor.* Berkeley Heights, NJ: Enslow Publishers, 2003.

Wright, Lewis E., Jr. "Elijah Muhammad's Political Thought on God and Authority: A Quest for Authenticity and Freedom." *Journal of Religious Thought* 51, no. 2 (Winter–Spring 1994–1995): 47–75.

Wright, Richard. *American Hunger.* New York: Harper and Row, 1975.

Wright, Richard. *Black Boy.* New York: Harper Publishing, 1945.

Wyman, Carroll. *Ella Fitzgerald: Jazz Singer Supreme.* New York: Franklin Watts, 1998.

X, Malcolm. *Malcolm X Speaks.* New York: Grove Press, 1965.

X, Malcolm, and Alex Haley. *The Autobiography of Malcolm X: As Told to Alex Haley.* New York: Ballantine Books, 1987.

Young, Al. "I'd Rather Play a Maid Than Be One." *New York Times*, October 15, 1989.

YouTube, 1988 Olympic Trials 100m, "Flo Jo" World Record and Interview. www.youtube.com/watch?v=dAvBonP6JDw (accessed October 24, 2006).

Zeigler, Ronny. "Hattie McDaniel: '(I'd) ... Rather Play a Maid.' " *N.Y. Amsterdam News*, April 28, 1979.

Zirin, Dave. "The Living Legacy of Mexico City: An Interview with John Carlos." *Counterpunch*. November 1/2, 2003. http://www.counterpunch.org/zirin 11012003.html (accessed August 5, 2009).

Zirin, Dave. *What's My Name, Fool? Sports and Resistance in the United States*. Chicago: Haymarket Books, 2005.

About the Editor and Contributors

VOLUME EDITOR

MATTHEW C. WHITAKER is Associate Professor of History and Director of the Center for the Study of Race and Democracy at Arizona State University-Tempe. He is also an affiliate faculty in African and African American Studies and the School of Social Transformation at ASU. He specializes in American history, African American history, the African Diaspora, civil and human rights, sports history, popular culture, and the American West. Whitaker is the co-editor, with Jeremy I. Levitt, of *Hurricane Katrina: America's Unnatural Disaster* (University of Nebraska Press), editor of *African American Icons of Sport* (Greenwood), and author of *Race Work: The Rise of Civil Rights in the Urban West* (University of Nebraska Press). He is also the author of the forthcoming *Over Jordan: A History of Modern Black America* (Harlan Davidson), and *Facing the Rising Sun: A History of African Americans in Arizona* (University of Oklahoma Press).

CONTRIBUTORS

REBECCA BAIRD is a PhD candidate in history in the School of Historical, Philosophical, and Religious Studies at Arizona State University. Her research interests include twentieth century U.S. history and gender history.

JASON BELL earned a BA degree in history at California State University at San Marcos, and an MA degree in history at Arizona State University with an emphasis in public history. He is an archivist with experience working in state, national, and corporate archives. He is currently under contract with Toyota Motor Sales, USA, Inc. where he is responsible for preserving, maintaining, and making accessible the company's historic assets in the United States.

ADAM P. BOYD is a BA in History at Arizona State University-Tempe, and is currently completing a JD at the University of California-Los Angeles. His interests include the intersection of race, class, gender in sports, and the American legal process. He has written on professional baseball, and possesses a keen interest in the history and life of hip-hop.

GERRY BUTLER earned a BA in History from the University of Washington. Although his interests are broad, he specializes in Military History. In addition to being a Technical Support Analyst who works with healthcare software for Lynx Medical Systems in Bellevue, Washington, he is an independent history author. He is particularly interested in African American history, and contributed 18 vignettes to internationally known www.blackpast.org.

MONICA L. BUTLER is a Professor of History at Seminole State College of Florida. She specializes in modern Indigenous and African American history, with an emphasis on gender and political representation in popular culture. She is a graduate of Arizona State University, where she earned her PhD in history and is developing her work regarding Indigenous activism in the television industry.

JAMES R. COATES is Associate Professor of Education at the University of Wisconsin-Green Bay, where he has also served as a diversity liaison to the UW-Green Bay Athletic Department. He specializes in American sports history, African American sports history, coaching, African American history, culture, and multicultural education.

WILLIAM JELANI COBB is Professor of History at Rutgers University and he specialized in post-Civil War African American history, 20th century American politics, and the history of the Cold War. He is a recipient of fellowships from the Fulbright and Ford Foundations, and he is the author of the award winning *The Substance of Hope: Barack Obama and the Paradox of Progress* and *To The Break of Dawn: A Freestyle on the Hip Hop Aesthetic.* His articles and essays have appeared in *The Atlantic, The Washington Post, Essence, Vibe, Emerge, The Progressive,* and *Ebony.* He has also been a featured commentator on National Public Radio, CNN, Al-Jazeera, CBS News, and a number of other national broadcast outlets.

BRIAN S. COLLIER is Assistant Professor of History at Grand Valley State University in Allendale, Michigan. He is completing a book entitled *Steve Gachupin: Native American Runner and King of the Mountain.* He specializes in Indigenous history, the history of education, and the intersection of race, class, gender, and religion in American history.

PERO GAGLO DAGBOVIE is Associate Professor of History at Michigan State University. He specializes in American history, and African American history and life. His articles include "Black Women, Carter G. Woodson, and the Association for the Study of Negro Life and History, 1915–1950" (*Journal of African American History*), and his books include *The Early Black History Movement, Carter G. Woodson, and Lorenzo Johnston Greene* (2007) and *African American History Reconsidered* (2010).

THOMAS J. DAVIS teaches history and law at Arizona State University, Tempe. He is the author of *Race Relations in the United States, 1940–1960* (Greenwood), *Race Relations in America: A Reference Guide with Primary Documents* (Greenwood), *A Rumor of Revolt: "Great Negro Plot" in Colonial New York* (University of Massachusetts Press), which the Gustavus Myers Center for the Study of Bigotry and Human Rights in North America prized as one of the outstanding books of 1985 on race relations. He is also author of numerous articles on race and law, and co-author of *African in the Americas: History of the Black Diaspora* (The Blackburn Press).

MEGAN FALATER is a PhD student in the Department of History at the University of Wisconsin-Madison. She also works as a freelance copyeditor editorial consultant. She has presented a number of papers, and participated in various panels and round table discussions at critical religious symposia and professional historical conferences in the United States. Her research interests emphasize race, gender, and religion in the United States.

ELYSSA FORD earned her PhD in American history from Arizona State University-Tempe, where her dissertation examined women and race in the American rodeo. She is active in the field of public history, and holds a certificate in Museum Studies. She has put this expertise to use at institutions like the Arizona Jewish Historical Society and the National Cowgirl Museum and Hall of Fame. Ford was a Fulbright scholar in Romania in 2009–2010, where she taught in American Studies programs.

R. MARK HALL is assistant professor of rhetoric, composition, and literacy studies at the University of North Carolina at Charlotte. He teaches writing, directs the Writing Resources Center, and writes about composition, literacy, and writing center theory and practice. His essay "The 'Oprahfication' of Literacy: Reading *Oprah's Book Club*" appears in *College English*. His chapter "Oprah's Book Selections: Teleliterature for The Oprah Winfrey Show" is included in *The Oprah Affect: Critical Essays on Oprah's Book Club*, edited by Cecilia Konchar Farr and Jamie Harker.

CORIE HARDY is a PhD student in the Department of Women and Gender Studies at Arizona State University-Tempe. Her research interests include representations of interracial relationships in popular culture, film studies, masculinity studies, critical race theory, and the intersections of race, class, and gender in American popular culture. In 2007, Hardy graduated summa cum laude with a BA in Women's Studies and English from Old Dominion University in Norfolk, VA. Following graduation, she embarked on a study abroad trip to Capetown, South Africa, where she completed a poetry project based on interviews with South African women regarding their experiences of apartheid. Hardy currently serves as Chair of Programming of ASU's Gender Studies Graduate Student Association. She is also a member of the National Women's Studies Association.

MEAGHAN E. HEISINGER is a PhD student in the Public History Program within the School of Historical, Philosophical, and Religious Studies at Arizona State University-Tempe. She specializes in North American Indigenous history, museum studies, and the representations of ethnicity, race, and cultural identity in public cultural institutions. Heisinger, a graduate of Union College in Schenectady, New York, works as a contract archivist at the Heard Museum Library in Phoenix, Arizona, and authors National Register Nominations and Cultural Landscape Inventories for the National Park Service, Southwestern Region.

MORGAN HOODENPYLE is a PhD student in the Department of History at Arizona State University-Tempe, where she studies twentieth century performance history. She is particularly interested in the construction of gender and sexuality in popular culture, and hopes to focus her dissertation on female nudity in Broadway musical theater of the American interwar period. She is an avid community volunteer, including working with the Center for Community Solutions in San Diego, where she was trained as a Rape Crisis and Domestic Violence Victim Advocate.

LASANA O. HOTEP is a graduatestudent in the School of Historical, Philosophical, and Religious Studies at Arizona State University. He is also the lead consultant of Hotep Consultants, and a student affairs staff member at Arizona State University in Tempe, Arizona. Hotep also serves as a faculty member of the Student African-American Brotherhood (SAAB). He has contributed essays and chapters to a number of publications, including *African American Men in College* (Jossey-Bass), *The State of Black Arizona* (Arizona State University), *Be a Father to Your Child: Real Talk from Black Men of the Hip Hop Generation* (Soft Skull), and *The Black Male Handbook: A Blueprint for Life* (Atria).

BENJAMIN HRUSKA is a PhD in Public History at Arizona State University. His interests include U.S. Navy servicemen in World War II. He has served as a public history consultant for the Department of Defense in Washington, DC, and the Administrator of the Block Island Historical Society on Block Island, Rhode Island. During his tenure at this institution, Hruska was awarded the Regional Tourism Award from Governor Donald Carcieri and the State of Rhode Island. He earned an MA in Public History from Wichita State University, and a BA in History from Pittsburg State University in 2000.

VICTORIA L. JACKSON is a PhD student in the Department of History at Arizona State University-Tempe. She specializes in Indigenous history, African American history, the history of education, and the intersections of race, class, and gender in U.S. history. Her forthcoming dissertation is entitled "Indigenous Education in the Age of Jim Crow: Complicating the Black/White Binary." Jackson, a summa cum laude history graduate of the University of North Carolina, is also an accomplished athlete who distinguished herself as a championship runner on the nationally-ranked Arizona State University Cross Country and Track and Field teams, and a rising star among professional long distance runners worldwide.

BLAKE JONES is a PhD student in the School of Historical, Philosophical, and Religious Studies at Arizona State University. He specializes in American foreign relations, global history, and the intersections of religion and politics in American history. His forthcoming dissertation is entitled "Jimmy Carter and the Age of Global Religious Counterrevolution," an examination of how Carter, as the nation's first openly "born again" president, dealt with the rise of the Christian Right in the United States, the emergence of Islamic fundamentalism in the Middle East and Central Asia, and the conservative Catholic response to liberation theology in Central America.

KENDRA KENNEDY is earned PhD student in the Department of History at the University of Utah. She specializes in early American history, slavery, African American history, and the intersection of race, class, and gender in early American history.

LAUREN L. KIENTZ is a Post Doctoral Fellow in the Department of History at the University of Kentucky. She earned a PhD in the Department of History at Michigan State University. Her specialties include African American Intellectual History and Black Internationalism. Her forthcoming dissertation is entitled "Untrammeled Thinking: The Promise and Peril of the Second Amenia Conference, 1920–1940." Kientz, a summa cum laude history graduate of Arizona State University, earned the Founders Dissertation Fellowship Award from the Western Association of Women Historians for 2006, the Milton Muedler Graduate Student Fellowship in 2009, and the Michigan State University Dissertation Completion Fellowship for 2010. She is also on the board of advisers for the U.S. Intellectual History Blog and Conference.

JOHNATHAN KOEFOED is a PhD student in the Department of History at Boston University, where he holds a Dean's Fellowship and teaches courses on American History. His research focuses on American intellectual and religious history generally, and transatlantic Romanticism specifically. Jonathan holds an MA in Historical Theology from Saint Louis University, and a BA in Philosophy and in History—summa cum laude—from Arizona State University and its Barrett Honors College.

PAT LAUDERDALE is Professor of Justice and Social Inquiry and Adjunct Professor of Law at Arizona State University-Tempe. He specializes in the comparative sociology of law—political trials, diversity and deviance, terrorism, world systems, global inequity, social movements, protest, dispute negotiation, Indigenous Jurisprudence, and justice theory. He is the author, co-author, and editor of a number of books, including *Terrorism: A New Testament* (Sage), *Globalization and Post-Apartheid South Africa* (de Sitter Publications), *A Political Analysis of Deviance, New Edition* (de Sitter Publications), *Terror and Crisis in the Horn of Africa: Autopsy of Democracy, Human Rights, and Freedom* (Ashgate), and *Terrorism: A New Testament* (de Sitter Publications, 2005), with Annamarie Oliverio.

JEREMY I. LEVITT is Associate Dean for International Programs and Distinguished Professor of International Law at Florida A&M University. He is a public international lawyer and political scientist with expertise in the law of the use of force, human rights law, African politics, democratization, and state dynamics and regional collective security. Levitt is the author or editor of four books and numerous law review articles. Prior to entering law teaching, he served as Special Assistant to the Managing Director for Global Human and Social Development at the World Bank Group. He was recently appointed as senior member of the International Technical Assistance Committee (ITAC) of the Truth and Reconciliation Commission (TRC) of Liberia by the United Nations High Commissioner for Human Rights and the President of the Republic of Liberia, Ellen Johnson-Sirleaf, Africa's first democratically elected female head of state.

REGINALD MARTIN is Professor of Composition and past Coordinator of African American Literature Programs at the University of Memphis. His publications include *Erotique Noire* (1991), *Dark Eros* (1997) and the blues novel *Everybody Knows What Time It Is* (2001). His forthcoming book is *Blues Eroticism* from Thundersmouth Press. He is also an accomplished musician and blues guitar player.

MARY G. McDONALD is Associate Professor of Kinesiology and Health at Miami University in Oxford, Ohio. She is also an affiliate faculty in Women's

Studies at Miami, and a former Assistant Basketball Coach at Xavier University in Cincinnati, Ohio and Indian University in Bloomington, Indiana. Her published work includes articles on gender and racial politics in sports, third wave feminism, and the intersections of gender, race, class, and sexuality in sport and American culture. She is the editor, with S. Birrell, of *Reading Sport: Critical Essays on Power and Representation* (Northwestern University Press).

JOAN MARIE MILLER is a PhD student in the Department of History at Arizona State University-Tempe. She studies twentieth century American history, with an emphasis on foreign relations, the conflict in Vietnam, and human rights. Miller graduated with honors from The College of Wooster and received an M.Div. from Yale University. She is an ordained minister in the Presbyterian Church (U.S.A.).

KEITH MILLER is an Associate Professor in the *Department of English* at Arizona State University. His research focuses on the rhetoric and songs of the Civil Rights Movement. He is the author of *Voice of Deliverance: The Language of Martin Luther King, Jr., and Its Sources*, and his essays on Martin Luther King, Jr., Malcolm X, Jackie Robinson, Frederick Douglass, C. L. Franklin, and Fannie Lou Hamer have appeared in many scholarly collections and leading journals. Miller's co-edited books include *Selected Essays of Jim W. Corder* (with James Baumlin), *Beyond PostProcess and Postmodernism* (with Theresa Enos), and *New Bones: Contemporary Black Writers in America* (with Kevin Everod Quashie and Joyce Lausch). His forthcoming book is *Martin Luther King's Biblical Epic: His Final and Greatest Speech*.

MICHAEL MITCHELL is an Associate Professor of Political Science at Arizona State University-Tempe. He earned a BA in political science from Fordham University and an MA and PhD in Political Science from Indiana University. The author of book chapters and articles on race and ethnicity, he has contributed articles to *Comparative Politics, Afro-Diaspora, Centennial Review, Social Forces* and *Law and Society Review*. Professor Mitchell's teaching and research focuses on democratization in Latin America and the politics of ethnic minorities.

STEPHANIE A. L. MOLHOLT is Assistant Professor of History at the Community College of Baltimore County, Maryland. She specializes in U.S. history, Indigenous history, and the intersection of race, gender, class, and nation in American history.

CRYSTAL MARIE MOTEN is a PhD student in the Department of History at the University of Wisconsin-Madison. Her research interests include twentieth-century African American women's activism, migration, and politics.

CATHERINE O'DONNELL earned a PhD in American history from the University of Michigan. She was an NEH postdoctoral fellow at the Omohundro Institute of Early American History and Culture at the College of William and Mary, before joining the faculty at Arizona State University-Tempe. Her work to date explores culture, politics and literature in the early republic. She is the author of *Men of Letters in the Early Republic: Creating Forums of Citizenship, 1790–1812* (University of North Carolina Press, 2008), as well as articles appearing in the *Journal of the Early Republic and Early American Literature*. She is currently working on a study of Elizabeth Seton, John Carroll, and the development of Catholicism in the young American nation.

MOLLY PATTERSON is an Assistant Professor of Middle Eastern and Islamic History at the University of Wisconsin, Whitewater. She is currently working on a book about the early development of Muslim culture in East Africa. Ms. Patterson's research interests include Arabian Gulf History, Islam in East Africa, and Islamic identity formation.

MICHAEL PERRY is Assistant Professor of English at Rockford College. He specializes in the life and works of Toni Morrison and the works of other black authors, literary criticism, and popular culture. He has also contributed to a collection from SUNY University Press that explores the broad culture of Oprah's Book Club.

JOHN ROSINBUM is a PhD student in the School of Historical, Philosophical, and Religious Studies at Arizona State University-Tempe. He specializes in migration history, borderlands history, refugees, and religious activism. He earned a BA in History and BA in Secondary Education from the University of Portland. His forthcoming dissertation on the Sanctuary Movement will be a comparative study of the networks created by and for Central Americans in Toronto, Ontario and Tucson/Phoenix, Arizona during the 1980s.

HERBERT G. RUFFIN II is an Assistant Professor of African American Studies at Syracuse University. He earned a PhD in American history from Claremont Graduate University. He has published several articles, book reviews, and many online academic publications which focus on the Black West, African Diaspora, and Ethnic Studies. Ruffin also worked as an intern, fellow, and contractor for the Smithsonian Institution in the Center for Folklife and Cultural Heritage, and Program in African American Culture (PAAC) at the National Museum of American History from 1997 to 2002.

CALVIN SCHERMERHORN is an Assistant Professor of history at Arizona State University-Tempe. His research focuses on African American families in slavery in the nineteenth-century South and their responses to the slave trade and forced migration, including the republication of a major slave narrative,

Rambles of a Runaway from Southern Slavery, by Henry Goings, with Mike Plunkett and Edward Gaynor. He is a graduate of the University of Virginia, Harvard Divinity School, and St. Mary's College of Maryland. His teaching includes nineteenth-century U.S. history, the modern Atlantic world, and the African roots of American history.

JILL S. SCHIEFELBEIN is Online Programs Manager in the School of Sustainability and Faculty Associate in the Hugh Downs School of Human Communication at Arizona State University-Temple. She specializes in business and organizational communication, with foci in computer-mediated communication, multimedia writing and technical communication, strategic and crisis communication, and communication technology. Schiefelbein is the co-author of *Business and Professional Communication in the Global Workplace* (Cengage, 2010) and is the owner of Impromptu Guru, a speech and public relations consulting company.

BROOKS D. SIMPSON is Distinguished Foundation Professor of History, in the School of Historical, Philosophical, and Religious Studies at Arizona State University-Tempe. Simpson's primary area of expertise is nineteenth century American political and military history, especially the Civil War and Reconstruction Eras, and the American presidency. He is interested in sports history, and the intersections of race, class and gender in American history. His books include studies of Ulysses S. Grant, Henry Adams, and Reconstruction policy and politics, as well as several documentary editions and shorter works. His publications include: *Let Us Have Peace: Ulysses S. Grant and the Politics of War and Reconstruction* (University of North Carolina Press); *Ulysses S. Grant: Triumph Over Adversity, 1822–1865* (Houghton Mifflin); and *The Reconstruction Presidents* (University Press of Kansas).

MAUREEN MARGARET SMITH is a Professor in the Department of Kinesiology and Health Science at California State University-Sacramento. Raised in Norwich, New York, Smith earned her Bachelor of Science and Master of Science degrees in Physical Education from Ithaca College. At Ohio State University, Smith completed a Master of Arts degree in Black Studies and her Doctor of Philosophy in Cultural Studies of Sport. She has written widely on gender, masculinity, race, and religion and sports, and is the author of "Muhammad Speaks and Muhammad Ali: Intersections of the Nation of Islam and Sport in the 1960s," in *With God on Their Side: Sport in the Service of Religion*, edited by Tara Magdalinski and Tim Chandler (London: Routledge).

DONALD F. TIBBS is Associate Professor of Law at Drexel University. Tibbs received his JD from the University of Pittsburgh School of Law, and his PhD from Arizona State University. Tibbs's research interests include Civil Rights/ Black Power Legal History; Law and Liberation; Critical Race Theory; Race and Punishment; and the 4th Amendment. His publications have appeared in the *Southern California Interdisciplinary Law Journal*, the *Seattle Journal for Social Justice*; the *African American National Biography* (Oxford University Press 2008), and the *Encyclopedia of the Supreme Court*. His forthcoming book is *Black Power, Prison Power: Legal Consciousness and the Prisoner Union Movement*.

CLAYTON TRUTOR is a PhD student in the Department of History at Boston College. He specializes in U.S. Cultural and Intellectual History. He earned a BA and MA degrees in history at the University of Vermont, and was inducted into Phi Beta Kappa. Trutor is the editor of *American Polymath*, an online culture and current events journal.

JACKI HEDLUND TYLER is an MA candidate in history in the Schools of Historical, Philosophical, and Religious Studies at Arizona State University. Her research interests include antebellum politics, enslavement and freedom, black citizenship, and foreign relations and diplomacy.

COVEY L. WHITAKER earned a BA in English literature and an MA in English as a Second Language at Arizona State University. A retired educator, Whitaker taught at the elementary and secondary levels for more than 35 years. Now an independent author, Whitaker's publications include the forthcoming *Jambalaya and Canolis*, a children's book that examines early childhood and the bi-racial familial experience of her African American and Italian American grandchildren.

BRADLEY T. WILES is a PhD student in American history in the School of Historical, Philosophical, and Religious Studies at Arizona State University. His dissertation focuses on the development of social science research in the twentieth century, with particular attention to its impact on museum exhibitions and other public settings. He earned his Master of Arts in Public History from Arizona State University in 2008.

KATHERINE SCHAAP WILLIAMS is a PhD student in English literature at University of Pennsylvania. She specializes in Renaissance literature and disability studies, with a specific focus on performances of disability, gender, and race on the early modern English stage.

Index

Guevara, Ernesto "Che," 647
Guggenheim Fellowship, 410
"A Guide to Healthy Living for African
  Americans," 527
Guinea, 154–56, 362
Guy, Joe, 391
Guy-Sheftall, Beverly, 842

Haiti, 246–47
Hale v. Kentucky, 577
Haley, Alex, **345–53**; awards, 351–52;
  Baldwin, James and, 349; biographical
  sketches, 349–50; childhood and
  education, 346–47; Coast Guard,
  347–49; Davis, Miles and, 350; legacy
  of, 352–53; letter writing, 348; Malcolm
  X and, 349–50; National Book Award
  and, 352; personal life, 348, 351;
  television appearances, 352; works of or
  about: *The Autobiography of Malcolm
  X*, 87, 346, 350, 352–53; *A Different
  Kind of Christmas*, 352; "The Harlem
  Nobody Knows," 349; "Mr.
  Muhammad Speaks," 349; *Queen*, 352;
  *Queen: The Story of an American
  Family* (miniseries), 105; *Roots: The
  Saga of an American Family*, 346,
  351–52
Haley, Simon Alexander, 346–47
Hall, Arsenio, 452, 528
Hall, Charles B., 890
"Hallelujah I Love You So" (Charles), 171
Hallelujah: The Welcome Table
  (Angelou), 20
Hall of Fame for Great Americans, 167
Hallowell, Edward N., 296
Hallowell, Norwood Penrose, 293
Halls of Fame: baseball, 780; basketball, 84,
  90, 510; boxing, 10; college football, 769
Hallyday, Johnny, 381
Hamer, Fannie Lou, **355–63**; activism,
  358–59; arrest and beating, 360–61;
  childhood, 356–57; Council of
  Federated Organizations (COFO) and,
  360; economic justice issues in Civil
  Rights Movement, 362–63; Freedom
  Farm Corporation, 363; health, 363;
  involuntary sterilization, 357;
  Mississippi Freedom Democratic Party
  (MFDP) and, 361–62, 791; Mississippi
  Freedom Labor Union (MFLU) and,
  363; nonviolence and, 360; personal life,

357; registering to vote, 358–60;
  retribution for activism, 359–60;
  Student Nonviolent Coordinating
  Committee (SNCC) and, 358, 360;
  testimony at Democratic National
  Convention, 361–62; trip to Guinea,
  362; work as a sharecropper, 356–58
Hamer, Perry "Pap," 357
Hamilton, Alexander, 796
Hamilton, Charles, 152
Hammarskjold, Dag, 144
Hammond, John, 313, 389–90
Hampton, Lionel, 492
Hampton Normal and Agricultural
  Institute, 923
Hancock, 834
Hancock, Herbie, 495
Handbook for Revolutionary Warfare
  (Nkrumah), 154
Hanks, Tom, 937–38
Hansberry, Lorraine, 79, 701–2
Hansberry, William Leo, 149
Harbel, 100
Harden, Lillian, 37
Hardenbergh, Charles, 858
Hardenbergh, Johannes, 858
A Hard Road to Glory (Ashe), 49
Hardy, Charles, 892
Hardy, Juanita, 700
Harlem: Apollo Theater, 24; Baldwin,
  James in, 74–77; Belafonte, Harry in, 94;
  Ellington, Duke in, 262–63; Ellison,
  Ralph in, 275–76; Fitzgerald, Ella in,
  303; Garvey, Marcus in, 323–24; Haley,
  Alex and, 349; Hughes, Langston in,
  412; Hurston, Zora Neale in, 419; riots
  of 1943, 699; Wright, Richard in, 1022
Harlem (Ellington), 267
Harlem Globetrotters, **365–75**; vs. College
  All-Stars, 371; College All-Star tour,
  373; Cosby, Bill and, 370; discrimination, 372; early barnstorming years,
  368–69; financial dealings, 369; during
  the Great Depression, 368–69; vs. the
  Harlem Rens, 370–71; international
  tours, 373; Jackson, Mannie and, 374; vs.
  Minnesota Lakers, 372–73; as a minstrel
  show, 370; National Basketball
  Association (NBA) and, 373–74; origins
  of, 366; Owens, Jesse and, 372, 373;
  promotion of, 369–70; racist claims
  about, 370; Saperstein, Abe and,